Buchenwald
Concentration Camp
1937–1945

Buchenwald Concentration Camp 1937–1945

A Guide to the
Permanent Historical Exhibition

Edited by the
Gedenkstätte Buchenwald

Compiled by
Harry Stein

WALLSTEIN VERLAG

Bibliografische Information Der Deutschen Bibliothek

Die Deutsche Bibliothek lists this publication in the
Deutsche Nationalbibliografie; detailed bibliographic data
is available in the Internet at http://dnb.ddb.de.

© Wallstein Verlag 2004
German-English translation: Judith Rosenthal, Frankfurt a.M.
English lecturer: Katherin Machalek
Vom Verlag gesetzt aus der Adobe Garamond und der Frutiger Light
Umschlag: Basta Werbeagentur, Alexandra Ritterbach
Lithos: Basta Werbeagentur, Tuna Çiner
Druck: Hubert & Co, Göttingen

ISBN 3-89244-695-4

Table of Contents

Death and Survival, 1944-45

Epilogue

Appendices

Volkhard Knigge

Instead of a Foreword: The Case History of an Exhibition

The present permanent exhibition on the Nazi camp in Buchenwald was opened in the former camp depot on April 11, 1995, the fiftieth anniversary of the liberation of Buchenwald Concentration Camp. Counting the tour of the grounds that took place on April 16, 1945 by order of General Patton, the commander of the Third U.S. Army, it is the seventh exhibition to be presented on the grounds of the former camp. Just five days after liberation, over 1,000 citizens of Weimar, primarily members of the NSDAP, were compelled to view the camp virtually in its original state; many of its completely debilitated inmates were still present, many were still dying. The second exhibition was set up in 1951/52, in a wing of the gate building, by former German Communist inmates. For the most part, these men had been prominent members of the Illegal International Camp Committee formed in 1942/43, organised after the war in the Buchenwald Committee of the Vereinigung der Verfolgten des Nazi-Regimes (VVN) in East Berlin. Then, on the occasion of August 18, 1954 – the tenth anniversary of the murder of Ernst Thälmann, the last KPD chairman of the Weimar Republic – a new, larger exhibition was opened in the building of the so-called "inmates' canteen" at the top of the muster ground. By that time, the majority of those who had initiated the 1951/52 exhibition had already fallen victim to Stalinist purges within the SED. Ernst Busse, a former camp senior, a capo in the inmates' infirmary and one of three KPD party leaders in the camp, had been arrested by Soviet authorities and ultimately deported to Vorkuta. The same fate had befallen the former Camp Senior One Erich Reschke, a member of the KPD since 1922. Walter Bartel, likewise a KPD party leader and chairman of the Illegal International Camp Committee, had been the driving force behind the commemoration of Buchenwald in the GDR and in Communist circles until 1953, when he was removed from all of his offices and placed under intermittent house arrest.[1] The Museum für Deutsche Geschichte in East Berlin had taken over the preparations for the exhibition, at whose inauguration the three men no longer played a role, their photos and those of other former inmates having been removed from the display. It was not until late 1955, in some cases even later, that these persons were implicitly rehabilitated. Ernst Busse had already died in Vorkuta. One could regard it a self-evident act of justice that pictures of Stalin later disappeared from the exhibition as well: a memo made in 1958 on a picture showing Stalin "drawing up the plan of action for Stalingrad with his comrades-in-arms" reads "Better left out!"[2]

The 1954 exhibition was the first intended for permanent display, and every effort was made to create the impression that it was borne by a wide, even international, consensus. Yet there was criticism, traces of which can still be found today: in a letter dated July 27, 1957, for example, a French visitor objected to the political instrumentalisation of the concentration camp history. "The camp speaks for itself; it is 'presumptuous' to want to 'control' its voice, and I am certain that many of the dead, if they returned, would protest." "Of course we 'control' our voice. There are even more *living* who do *not* protest!" noted Anna Dorothea Miethe on the margin of the letter, thus disposing of the objections.[3]

The exhibition was indeed politically controlled. The politburo of the SED had the ultimate say on the content of this presentation and those that followed. The committee expressed its approval of the exhibition plans by stating: "We hereby sanction the establishment of a permanent exhibition in the former canteen of the Buchenwald camp, an exhibition which shows the patriotic character of the antifascist resistance struggle carried out by Ernst Thälmann and other heroes of the resistance, as well as documents and illustrative material on the crimes of fascism and its successors."[4] With regard to Germany, the "patriotic character of the antifascist resistance" meant that the struggle had been conducted for the sake of a new and better Germany, realised in the shape of the German Democratic

Republic. The reference to Ernst Thälmann served to point out that the history of Buchenwald Concentration Camp was to be written first and foremost as part of the history of the KPD and German Communist resistance. In accordance with the Dimitrovian theory of fascism, the fascist crimes were to be understood as the crimes committed by crisis-ridden capitalism, particularly the "monopoly lords" and financial capital. Seen in that light, the identities of fascism's "successors" were obvious: Western Germany and the U.S.A.

This presentation was modified for the inauguration of the National Buchenwald Memorial in 1958 – if only with regard to certain details: even the Soviets had found fault with its narrow focus on the GDR and its "overly strong emphasis on the past."[5] Though perhaps not consciously, the Secretary General of the Soviet Peace Committee Kotov had stumbled over the fact that the exhibition was intended to veil the KPD's share of responsibility for the political triumph of Nazism. After all, until 1935 the KPD had regarded its prime enemy to be the "socio-fascist" SPD and not the NSDAP.[6] The exhibition therefore took recourse to the era before the end of World War I as a means of presenting "the antifascist defensive action" as a persevering, efficient and finally successful struggle.

In the early 1960s the exhibition was expanded and moved to the former camp disinfection station. In 1944 a group of Communist inmates had secretly held a memorial service for Ernst Thälmann in the cellar of the building, leading to its exemption from the large-scale demolition measures carried out in the camp in 1952-1954. In 1985, the GDR's final and most modern Buchenwald display was opened in the neighbouring former depot, which had likewise escaped wreckage due to its function as a granary from the early 1950s on. The new presentation once again reflected the above-sketched commemoration programme. Now, however, the historians involved in the preparation had voiced criticism of this insistence on the old concept. They referred especially to the marginalisation of the victims of racial persecution, i.e. to the systematic underexposure of the genocide of the European Jews and the Sinti and Romani. Particularly if one took a closer look, the theory of the total loss of moral control within the process of capitalist exploitation did not suffice to explain these horrendous crimes. On the other hand, closer investigation would have shaken the very foundations of the Communist outlook on fascism – and with it the self-legitimisation of the GDR. Thus it is not surprising that this criticism of the SED image of history was hardly reflected in the actual exhibition. Still, for the very first time, there was mention of the fact that the inmate population of the concentration camp had included "Zigeuner" (gypsies).

The history of Buchenwald Concentration Camp was already being recorded in written and pictorial form even before the camp's liberation. Inmates such as the Dutchman Henri Pieck and the Frenchmen Paul Goyard and Boris Taslitzky secretly managed to produce drawings. A very small group including the Germans Ernst Thape and Karl Barthel succeeded in keeping more or less detailed journals, which survived and were later published.[7] The writer Ernst Wiechert wrote his Buchenwald memoirs as early as 1939, following his release from the camp; they were published after World War II under the title *Der Totenwald*.[8] The first edition of Eugen Kogon's epochal work *Der SS-Staat. Das System der deutschen Konzentrationslager* appeared in 1946.[9] An international bibliography on the history of Buchenwald Concentration Camp would comprise more than a thousand titles.

The number of photos taken in the camp following its liberation – particularly by press photographers of the American army – is endless. The reports, film coverage and press photos produced directly after liberation had a lasting influence on the entire western world's perception of Nazi crimes and the realities of the concentration camps, for Buchenwald was the first such camp to be reached by a Western Allied army and immediately documented: Buchenwald, located in the heart of the German Reich. The wave of shock that arose from Buchenwald is tangible in an excerpt from the memoirs of Dwight D. Eisenhower, the supreme commander of the Allied forces and later American president. The passage refers to his visit to the Buchenwald sub-camp Ohrdruf, located near the town of Gotha, on April 12, 1945. "I have never felt able to describe my emotional reactions when I first came face to face with indisputable evidence of Nazi brutality and ruthless disregard of every shred of decency. ... I have never at any other time experienced an equal sense of shock. ... As soon as I returned to Patton's headquarters that evening I sent communications to both Washington and London, urging the two governments to send instantly to Germany a random group of newspaper editors and representative groups from the national legislatures. I felt that the evidence should be immediately placed before the American and British publics in a fashion that would leave no room for cynical doubt."[10]

By the time the Cold War had commenced, and all the more so after the founding of the two German states, the historiography of Buchenwald took a divided course as well: an (SED) Communist, hegemonialised form of commemoration on the one hand and, in the West, a variety of forms with little in common besides their independence from the Eastern German approach. In the first years of post-war Western Germany, the memory of the camp was kept potentially alive by the Buchenwald Trials the Americans conducted in Dachau. In the 1950s, a cloak of silence was drawn around the Nazi crimes; their perpetrators, even heavily incriminated war criminals, were granted amnesty and reintegrated into society. Within this context, the remembrance of the scenes and personnel of Nazi crime became vague and generalised, was associated at best with an extremely limited clique of virtually abnormal offenders, identical with the very highest-ranking protagonists of the NS system or "the SS," which had the status of a group of demons entirely isolated from German society.[11] Concepts for a new political beginning, such as that submitted by the former Buchenwald inmate and Social Democrat Hermann Brill,[12] fell into oblivion if they had ever been acknowledged in the first place. Intensive research on the history of Buchenwald Concentration Camp never got underway. Beginning in the 1970s, a large number of Eastern German publications appeared under licence in Western Germany, but aside from those, Eugen Kogon's *SS-Staat* remained the most important source of information with regard to the history of the camp.

Despite the fact that the former Communist inmates around Walter Bartel had become grist for the Stalinist mill, they ultimately dominated the image formed in the GDR of Buchenwald Concentration Camp. A concept was drawn up for the publication of a three-volume work on the history of the camp, also intended to focus on the achievements of the political – particularly the Communist – inmates in the establishment of the new Germany in the Soviet Occupied Zone / GDR. Volume I appeared in 1949.[13] Its first edition, however, was changed before it had even come off the printing press, an incident quite symptomatic of the practises of GDR memory formation. The name of Josef Jenniges, who had co-edited the book along with Walter Bartel and Stefan Heymann, was deleted because he, a member of the Eastern German CDU and former non-Communist political inmate of Buchenwald, had escaped to Western Germany. All who refused to bow to the political criteria laid down for the memory of Buchenwald were excluded from the formulation of this memory. This principle also applied, for example, to Hermann Brill and Eugen Kogon, who were debarred from the Buchenwald Committee. Kogon's *SS-Staat* was banned in the GDR, just as the memoirs of the young Jewish inmate Rolf Weinstock had been.[14] What is more, Communist accounts were revised, one example being the above-mentioned memoirs of Karl Barthel, which were based upon journal entries. Originally published under the title *Welt ohne Erbarmen* (world without mercy), they later appeared as *Rot färbt sich der Morgen* (red is the morning).[15]

In view of these circumstances, only roughly sketched above, the new, post-reunification conception of the permanent exhibition on the history of Buchenwald Concentration Camp could neither pick up the thread of non-Communist – to put it pointedly: Western – formations of memory, nor could the GDR exhibition of 1985 simply be revised, much less continued in the same vein. On the contrary, the camp history had to be thoroughly researched and newly shaped on the basis of the insights thus gained. It is a matter of course – or should be – that no historical statement has a legitimate claim to validity unless it is founded on specialised research. In this particular case, the fact that research was to form the core of the new conception also represented a clear rejection of "findings" oriented towards pre-established political concerns or any other kind of group interests. Yet the insistent focus on research also signified that the new conception was not simply out to topple a (GDR) monument with whatever was available in the way of (Western German) Federal Republican forces, although a considerable number of voices called for such an act.

From a practical point of view, research meant three things: All available archival material was to be investigated and analysed, including material that had gone unused in the GDR era, for example archives located in North America and Israel. Secondly, reports by former inmates – those whose memories had been rejected for political reasons as well as those who had never had the opportunity to articulate their memories in the first place – had to be gathered and integrated into the analysis and the presentation. And finally, the grounds of the former camp had to be newly investigated and made accessible as a testimony to the events and an original monument of the era. As alluded to above, the camp had survived almost in its entirety until the first half of the 1950s, when it was dismantled and razed. The preservation as well as the demolition had been carried out in the spirit of "triumph through death and combat." This concept, intended to authenticate the historically necessary triumph of Communism, resulted in the disappearance of the camp buildings, as they were regarded as an expression of impotence and imprisonment. What is more, however, entire zones – such as the grounds of the so-called "Little Camp," which had served among other things as the destination for death marches from Auschwitz in 1945 – had been eliminated from the memorial and left to be obscured by natural overgrowth because their histories could not be smoothly integrated into the GDR view of the past. In this context, research meant the actual uncovering of remains and historical traces, their protection and their explanation; in other words, they were to undergo processing by the methods of archaeology.

The fronts which had been formed within the politically pre-formed memories of Buchenwald were now to be overcome, the actual circumstances – to the extent that they were at all reconstructible – to be elucidated. Would research suffice? Let us consider an example: the events surrounding the liberation of the concentration camp were already controversial soon after April 11, 1945. According to the Communist point of view, an independent act of self-liberation had been achieved on the part of the inmates. It was even claimed that the troops of the Third U.S. Army did not reach the camp until April 13. Other survivors recalled the arrival of American tanks and the flight of the SS at around noon on April 11. For decades, the issue of 'liberation by American troops' versus 'self-liberation under the leadership of the armed Communist resistance' was a symbol of political self-conception and political affiliation. The terms became so charged with political meaning that to speak of self-liberation meant to profess one's loyalty to the GDR and its view of history. In keeping with this perspective, to speak of liberation meant to conduct oneself in an anti-Communist manner, intentionally and groundlessly. On the other hand, the use of the term 'liberation' could also mean to contest the validity of the GDR view, both factually *and* politically. It is not difficult to imagine the battles fought over 'liberation' as opposed to 'self-liberation' – although (with reference to Harry Kuhn, a member of the illegal KPD leadership and the International Camp Committee) the minutes of the first legal meeting of the KPD party activists, held on the morning of April 12, 1945, stated that "the strategy of the German inmates to delay, and not to rise up, [had] proved right." This document accordingly makes no mention of self-liberation, but rather of "the liberation of twenty-one thousand inmates by the Allied troops in collaboration with the antifascist inmate cadres."[16] In this way, account was taken of the fact that the SS guard units had fled from the approaching American tanks, while the camp resistance had opened the almost entirely unguarded camp, set up a means of protecting it, cleared the surrounding area of scattered members of the SS and the Wehrmacht and, what is more, prevented chaos from breaking out among the liberated inmates. At the same time, the roundabout language used in the minutes are an indication of how difficult it was for the German Communist inmates to accept that the camp had been liberated by the wrong force, so to speak – by the American as opposed to the Red Army.

In the light of the much more precise knowledge gained through research, it became clear that no mono-perspectival approach could do justice to the history of Buchenwald Concentration Camp. For one thing, the camp had undergone several changes of function in the period from 1937 to 1945, leading to its representing different things to different inmates, depending upon when the latter were committed to the camp. Furthermore, there were a number of various special zones whose conditions differed greatly from those of the main camp in many respects. The same is true of the 136 sub-camps which the Buchenwald imperium eventually comprised. And finally, a circumstance of equal significance is that, in Buchenwald, inmates of a wide range of nationalities, cultures, political and religious affiliations were crowded together for better or for worse and, what is more, they also differed greatly with regard to the reasons for their persecution and imprisonment: the combat of political opponents, socio-racist and racial exclusion, sometimes the mere intention of "recruiting" slave labour for SS factories and the armament industry meshed with one another and influenced the fates of the inmates in different ways. "There were many different Buchenwalds," said Pierre Durand, the chairman of the International Committee of Buchenwald, Dora and Sub-Camps, summarising these circumstances at a meeting of the former concentration camp inmates' advisory board.[17]

Against this background, and in consideration of the fact that Buchenwald Concentration Camp was set up in the heart of Germany as a district of the city of Weimar, the exhibition is not structured according to a single, central, necessarily selective narrative thread, but adheres to a multi-perspectival leitmotif: "A Crime in the Heart of Germany." In the manner of a court exhibit, it presents evidence of the crimes and attempts to elucidate them within the context of each respective stage of the camp's history. Under each main theme there are myriad cross-references between original objects, historical photos, drawings by inmates, documents and biographies of the victims and the perpetrators. At the places of transition between one chapter of the exhibition and the next, the respective aspects are summarised in short texts. At the same time, the visitor is required to participate actively and independently, with the help of the material on view, in his/her visualisation of the history of Buchenwald Concentration Camp. Memory is not something that can – or indeed should – be carried out vicariously. In the place of active involvement, visitors to the GDR exhibition were to identify with a pre-established view of history, then to be released into the "Promised Land." The "roots of fascism" were considered eradicated, thanks to the abolishment of the "private ownership of production means" and the establishment of the "supremacy of the labourers and farmers." The fascist threat was present only in the West. Today's visitor receives no such low-cost guarantees, relieving him/her of all self-responsibility. No such guarantees can be made. That which was possible once can happen again, entirely, partially or similarly, as is shown not only by world history but also by the history of post-World-War-II Europe. Freedom, constitutionality, tolerance, inter-human solidarity, the decisive negation of anti-Semitism, racism and enmity toward those defined as strangers and, finally, human rights are dependent on the practical realisation of political and individual responsibility. Otherwise they would not exist. If this exhibition has a function above and beyond the preservation of knowledge about the German crimes committed in the middle of the twentieth century, then it lies in this conclusion, which must be continuously refilled with new content and new life.

1 Cf.: Lutz Niethammer (ed.), *Der "gesäuberte" Antifaschismus. Die SED und die roten Kapos von Buchenwald*, Berlin, 1994.

2 Archiv Deutsches Historisches Museum, MfDG, Abteilung Gedenkstätten, o.S.

3 Archiv Deutsches Historisches Museum, MfDG, Abteilung Gedenkstätten, o.S.

4 Archiv Deutsches Historisches Museum, MfDG, Abteilung Gedenkstätten, o.S.

5 Archiv Deutsches Historisches Museum, MfDG, Abteilung Gedenkstätten, o.S.

6 Cf.: Siegfried Bahne, *Die KPD und das Ende von Weimar. Das Scheitern einer Politik 1932-1935*, Frankfurt/M, New York, 1976.

7 Karl Barthel, *Die Welt ohne Erbarmen*, Rudolstadt, 1946. Manfred Overesch, "Ernst Thapes Buchenwalder Tagebuch von 1945: Dokumentation," in: *Vierteljahreshefte für Zeitgeschichte*, No. 4 / 1981, pp. 632-672.

8 Ernst Wiechert, *Der Totenwald*, Zürich, 1946.

9 Eugen Kogon, *Der SS-Staat. Das System der Deutschen Konzentrationslager*, München, 1946.

10 Dwight D. Eisenhower, *Crusade in Europe*, Baltimore: Johns Hopkins University Press, 1997, p. 408-9.

11 Cf.: Norbert Frei, *Vergangenheitspolitik. Die Anfänge der Bundesrepublik und die NS-Vergangenheit*, München, 1996. Wilfried Loth, Bernd-A. Rusinek (eds.): *Verwandlungspolitik. NS-Eliten in der westdeutschen Nachkriegsgesellschaft*, Frankfurt/M, New York, 1998.

12 On April 13, 1945, in the "cinema barrack" of the concentration camp, Hermann Brill had presented the "Manifesto of the Democratic Socialists," which was published in 1946 in his book *Gegen den Strom*. Hermann Brill, *Gegen den Strom*, reprint of the original 1946 edition, with a commemorative article by Eugen Kogon, Erfurt, 1995.

13 Walter Bartel, Stefan Heymann, Josef Jenniges (eds.), *Das Konzentrationslager Buchenwald. Band I. Bericht des Internationalen Lagerkomitees*, Weimar, 1949.

14 Rolf Weinstock, *Das wahre Gesicht Hitler-Deutschlands: Häftling Nr. 59.000 erzählt das Schicksal der 10.000 Juden aus Baden, der Pfalz und aus dem Saargebiet in den Höllen von Dachau, Gurs, Drancy, Auschwitz, Jawischowitz, Buchenwald*, Singen, 1948.

15 Karl Barthel had been elected to the Reichstag in January 1933 as the youngest member of the KPD parliamentary group. His personal notes, which he had managed to smuggle out of the camp, were published in 1946 under the title *Die Welt ohne Erbarmen* and soon censored. In 1959 they reappeared, extensively revised to conform to the verdict of certain Communist victory, under the title *Rot färbt sich der Morgen*. Karl Barthel, *Rot färbt sich der Morgen*, Rudolstadt, 1959.

16 Thüringisches Hauptstaatsarchiv Weimar, BW 45.

17 Pierre Durand at the meeting of the inmates' advisory board on Dec. 1, 1998.

"… in the midst of the German people."

"… for we were alive – living underground in countries under German occupation, in Germany itself, working in the factories or imprisoned in the dungeons and camps – in the decisive years we were living right in the midst of the German people."

Jean Améry

The Assumption of Power

Nazism emerged during a period of economic decline, exploding mass unemployment and social and political eruptions triggered by a world-wide economic crisis. By inciting fear of Communism and responding to the longing for stability and community, the new ideology profited from the antagonism between the various political orientations within the Weimar Republic. Nazism's initial political success was attained by means of aggressive polemics against democracy and the Treaty of Versailles, which was generally considered a "Treaty of Disgrace" as it had placed the responsibility for the war on Germany and forced its surrender of territories with German populations to neighbouring countries. The Nazis thus gained favour not only with a large majority of their voters, but also with various nationalist associations and parties, the churches and prominent representatives of private enterprise.

The opponents of National Socialism failed to agree on a defence strategy for the Republic. When Hitler seized power in 1933, he could thus count on the open approval or at least passive acceptance of a large proportion of the German population. Among his most enthusiastic supporters were young middle-class people from rural areas who identified with the Nazi projections of economic upswing and strength. The large majority of Germans welcomed the steps Hitler took to revise the Treaty of Versailles as well as the threats and shows of power with which he attained those revisions. The economic and social measures undertaken by the regime beginning in 1936-37 to guarantee bread and work for all were also met with approval – despite widespread discontent and a state

Illustration 1: Regional-level party convention of the Thuringian NSDAP, Nov. 4-6, 1938. The population of Weimar welcomes Hitler.
Source: Stadtarchiv Weimar, F/5

of affairs that remained deplorable. Aside from a large number of small-time climbers, those to profit from economic activity based primarily on war preparations were the big industrialists, for whom Hitler's supremacy guaranteed high returns and new possibilities for expansion.

Illustrations 2-3: On March 16, 1933, on the way to a council meeting, Ernst Riegraf – a respected SPD municipal councillor of Heilbronn – is attacked and beaten by three members of the NSDAP; a passive crowd watches. Photo caption: *"… and gets a good licking."*
Source: Heilbronner Stimme

Hitler's power machine was founded on the NSDAP (National Socialist German Workers' Party), its subdivisions and associations, ministerial bureaucracy, the Wehrmacht and economic organisations. He met with approval when he promised to create order "with a heavy hand" and "a firm sweep." Terror was an instrument of his regime from the very start. The Reichstag fire provided the occasion for an initial wave of arrests legitimised by the emergency decree which the President of the Reich issued on February 28, 1933 "for the protection of the people and the Reich," an act essentially serving the securement of

power. Throughout Germany, over 150 provisional concentrations camps, SA torture facilities and special penitentiary departments for preventive custody were set up in the year 1933 alone, allowing for the imprisonment of some eighty thousand Nazi adversaries, primarily members of the outlawed labour parties and unions. These were the persons who had carried out the first decisive organised resistance against the new regime. The Communist Party, subjected to the most brutal persecution from the very beginning, often fell victim to the new system.

The Persecution of the Jewish Population

The approximately 600,000 Jews living in Germany were excluded from the "Volksgemeinschaft" (national community) from the outset, due to the fact that "race" was propagated by the Nazis as the basic foundation of society. What is more, as Theodor W. Adorno later observed, the Jews were regarded by the Nazis to be the "counter-race, the negative principle as such". The "solu-

tion to the Jewish question" thus became a yardstick for the ability of the NSDAP – as a rigorously anti-Semitic party – to assert its totalitarian claim. Its propaganda of hatred was the culmination of the conspiracy and race theories belonging to a form of nationalist anti-Semitism that had taken hold as a political current in Germany and Austria at the beginning of the twentieth century, marking a new chapter in the long history of Christian-influenced anti-Judaism, now with a clear element of racism.

Illustration 4: With the aid of civilians, the SA sets up anti-Semitic signs on the access roads to Weimar, Aug. 7, 1935. Photo caption: "German mother! Continue to hold your shielding hand over your child! Protect your child from the Jew!" *Source: Stadtarchiv Nürnberg*

17

Once the Nazis had seized power, anti-Semitism spread in Germany without meeting any appreciable resistance, taking on an increasingly aggressive form within the context of everyday life. It began with open provocations against Jews and led to a controlled boycott of Jewish-owned shops and businesses on April 1, 1933. In September 1935 the **Nuremberg Laws** used racist criteria to define who was a Jew and created the term "Mischling" ("half-breed") to identify a group of persons also subjected to discrimination and persecution. According to one of the laws, no Jew could be a citizen of the Reich. Once the Nuremberg Laws had been promulgated, the policy of expulsion was supported by a wide consensus within the Nazi state.

The forms and means of persecution changed as time went on, reflecting the state of domestic stability as well as the Reich's foreign policy situation. By the end of 1937 Jews had been expelled from the civil service, their participation in public life being increasingly limited in the process. In 1938, the forced annexation of Austria was accompanied by open terror and additional repressive anti-Jewish measures, first in Austria, soon thereafter in Germany. With the aid of terrorist means, Jews were now systematically and entirely excluded from all business activity. The demolition of shops and homes, the destruction of synagogues and the brutal physical abuse carried out during and after the pogrom night of November 9, 1938 was intended to force the Jews to flee. Many of them lacked the means even to take this way out.

Illustration 5: Burning synagogue on Börneplatz, Frankfurt a. M., during the pogrom of Nov. 10, 1938
Source: Stadtarchiv Frankfurt a. M.

The "Advanced Community" and its Enemies

The Nazi regime strove from the start to penetrate and subjugate every area of the society – work, leisure time, education, social welfare and every aspect of cultural life. This was achieved by forcing the institutions of society and politics to adopt Nazi ideology (replacing personnel where necessary), promising social improvements and registering a large proportion of the German population for future active military service. Even before Hitler's August 1936 memorandum on the "Four-Year Plan," the Nazi regime was preparing for **mobilisation**. From 1935 on, most employed persons had to be in possession of a "workers' pass" intended to place every member of the labour force at the disposal of the Nazi state and allow his or her involuntary engagement for labour allocation at any time. By inundating modern mass culture with Nazi propaganda, the regime successfully spread a vision of society in which the "natural simplicity of the German people" would unite with energy, strength and assertiveness. A racially founded principle of performance was propagated in all areas of the economy and all professions, finding practical realisation in professional contests and production competitions.

The will to perform was regarded as evidence of hereditary "racial value." Persons who found no place in the "**Leistungsgemeinschaft**" (**advanced community**) were accordingly considered "racially inferior." The first victims of this socio-politically founded racism were the men and women forcibly sterilised on the basis of the law "for the prevention of genetically ill offspring" in 1933. The regime viewed handicapped persons living in sanatoriums as nothing more than an encumbrance. Once they had been deprived of their right to live, most of them were murdered within the framework of the Nazi Euthanasia Programme after the war began.

In order to uphold the idea of the "people's community," an internal enemy had to be created. Due to the fact that this community remained an illusion in social and political everyday life – apart from

Illustration 6: Lapel button for May 1, 1934
Catalogue 2/2
Photo: N. T. Salmon

staged events such as "pot-luck Sundays" and mass demonstrations – it was compelled to define itself to a large extent in contrast to those groups who were expelled by the NS state as "**community enemies**." In the war mobilisation phase, persecution expanded to affect those who evaded "labour allocation" or lived on the margins of the National Socialist society. They were referred to as "asocials," "professional criminals" and "national vermin." Their unexplained disappearance, never to return, served as a means of disciplining the rest of the population and was part and parcel of normalcy and order in Nazi society.

Beginning in 1935 the detective police made increasing use of "**preventive police detention**" as a means of committing "previously convicted habitual offenders" to concentration camps. A concept of "preventive crime suppression" developed from this practise, with the aim of "cleansing" society in a manner compatible with racist ideology. A societal concept based on blood lineage, hereditary transmission and race validated the expulsion of "asocials" and "professional criminals" and the persecution of homosexuals as acts of "racial hygiene." Entire groups were considered "asocial" and "racially inferior" by virtue of their lifestyle, and were committed to the concentration camps. There, within the structure of the camp system, they were to be "re-educated", in other words: decimated. In February 1937, even before the establishment of the Reich detective police authority, Himmler ordered the "committal of approximately 2,000 professional and habitual criminals or dangerous sexual criminals to preventive police detention." A number of the persons arrested during the campaign that was carried out a month later were among the first inmates of Buchenwald Concentration Camp. An ordinance issued by the Reich ministry of the interior on December 14, 1937 expanded this measure to apply in general to persons who "endanger the public through their asocial behaviour." This provided the grounds for mass arrests leading to the committal of thousands of persons to Buchenwald Concentration Camp in 1938.

The Persecution of the Sinti and Romani

In an ordinance dated December 8, 1938, Himmler called for "the settlement of the gypsy question" with a strategy "derived from the intrinsic nature of this race." He thus confirmed the theoretical background for the persecution of the gypsies, which was already well under way in the form of bans from professional/vocational practise as well as social and political discrimination and isolation. From the mid 1930s on, a large number of cities and communities in Germany forced the Sinti and Romani members of the population – referred to derogatorily as "Zigeuner" ("gypsies") – to lead miserable lives in "detention camps", many of which were fenced in and guarded. Reduced to the status of study objects for "racial research," they were required to register with the Reich health authority's "Eugenic Research Department," founded in 1936, and classified according to racist criteria. It was against this background

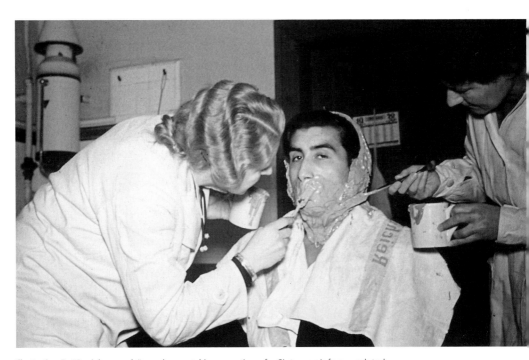

Illustration 7: "Racial research" employees taking a casting of a Sinto man's face, undated
Source: Bundesarchiv, Koblenz

that, under the pretext of "preventive crime suppression" by the detective police, their deportation to the concentration camps began in 1938.

The Concentration Camp System

The first concentration camp was established in early March 1933 upon the initiative of the Thuringian government under Nazi Gauleiter Fritz Sauckel in the village of Nohra a few kilometres to the west of Weimar. Also in March 1933, the SS established a permanent concentration camp in Dachau, a town near Munich. The majority of camps set up throughout Germany in this period existed for only a short time, their facilities being for the most part temporary and their functions and future uses still unclear. "Preventive custody" in concentration camps was initially substantiated by the officially decreed state of emergency which was, in actuality, indefinite. Once the preventive custody ordinance had been issued by the Reich Ministry of the Interior on April 12, 1934, any person who "represents / has represented an *immediate* threat to public safety and order through his/her behaviour, especially through subversive activities" could still be imprisoned without a court sentence. In the early years, the regime made no secret of the existence of the concentration camps; there was written and photographic coverage of them in the press.

In the context of the power struggles within the NSDAP, the SS had proved itself under its Reich Leader Heinrich Himmler to be Hitler's loyal Praetorian guard. It now saw the control of the camps as the perfect opportunity to achieve distinction. In 1934 the department of **Concentration Camp Inspection** was founded as the central camp authority. The department head, Concentration Camp Inspector Theodor Eicke, worked systematically on setting up the concentration camps from 1935 on.

By the second half of the 1930s, the illegal structures of labourers' resistance had been seriously disrupted, if not completely eradicated, throughout most of Germany. Yet even after the imprisonment of active political opponents and the far-reaching incapacitation of domestic resistance in

Illustration 8: Inmates in Colditz Concentration Camp, 1934
Source: Buchenwaldarchiv

21

the mid 1930s, Hitler had no intention of giving up the instrument provided by "preventive custody" and closing the concentration camps. On the contrary, the Gestapo's radius of action was further expanded.

The **Gestapo** (secret state police) had emerged in 1933 from the political intelligence department of the Prussian police. Under the secret state police office (Gestapa), which bore the status of a regional police authority, it grew into a special secret police apparatus with executive powers. This structure was then adopted in the other German states. Essentially the Gestapo was an ideologically oriented police force that strove to exercise unrestricted authority over the population. Its primary aim was to classify every form of unconventional behaviour – regardless of any and all legal provisions – as hostile to the central authority, the Nazi party or the nation, and to take action against it. Jehovah's Witnesses, oppositional clergymen, pacifists and persons who vented their dissatisfaction publicly could all be arrested as political enemies and committed to concentration camps.

Following his appointment as "Reich Leader of the SS and Chief of the German Police" in June 1936, Himmler collaborated with Reinhard Heydrich, the Chief of the Security Service (SD) of the Reich Leader of the SS, to unite the police with the SS. With Hitler's approval, they carried out this process largely independently of the state and its administration. The complete reorganisation of the police apparatus led to the establishment of the Regular (rural and municipal) Police under Kurt Daluege and the Security Police (Gestapo and detective police) under Reinhard Heydrich. The Secret State Police Office became the main headquarters for the regional Gestapo authorities, whose personnel was expanded considerably. During this phase, a power apparatus gradually took shape alongside the traditional governmental institutions, a system which was not required to make allowances for justice or the law in the fulfilment of domestic functions. At its core was the SS, and its harshest weapon was a new type of concentration camp. The

structures of the detective police were changed to correspond to those of the state police.

Himmler envisioned a **"theatre of war"** in **"Inner Germany,"** where SS units would take over the role of mobile special domestic troops. These included the units detached to the concentration camps and bearing the characteristic name **"SS Totenkopf** (literally: "Death's-Head") Squadrons" from late March 1936 on. These developments led in 1936 and 1937 to the dissolution of the smaller concentration camps and the construction of larger, more permanent camps modelled on Dachau Concentration Camp. In 1936 the SS opened Sachsenhausen Concentration Camp to replace the former Oranienburg Camp near Berlin. The construction of Buchenwald Concentration Camp began one year later. The Dachau camp was expanded.

On November 8, 1937, in an address to his Gruppenführer (major generals), Himmler elaborated on the size of the existing concentration camps:

"I am of the conviction – and it is good to voice this conviction – that in the case of war, even they would not suffice. Rather, I am of the opinion that a large proportion of the political and criminal prisoners … will have to be kept in the camps for many years of their lives, at least until they have become accustomed to order, not to the extent that they will have become orderly human beings in our view, but to the extent that their will is broken. There will be very many whom we will never be able to set free …"

On January 25, 1938 a **revision of the regulations governing preventive custody** was issued, to remain in effect until the fall of the regime. There it was stated: "As a means of warding off all subversive endeavours, preventive custody can be ordered as a coercive measure of the Secret State Police against persons who threaten the existence and security of the people and the state through their behaviour." The Secret State Police Office thus obtained sole control over "preventive custody," which was to be enforced exclusively in state concentration camps. "Preventive custody" and "preventive police detention" – originally not designed as substitutes for judicial punishment – could now be used to penalise persons for nonconformist behaviour, homosexuality, etc., and isolate entire groups of individuals in concentration camps on grounds of being "asocial." **New concentration camps** were still being established in 1938 and 1939 – Mauthausen for Austria, Flossenbürg for Southeast Germany, and a women's camp near Fürstenberg (Ravensbrück). In late September 1939, immediately following the invasion of Poland, Himmler ordered the fusion of the Security Police (Gestapo and detective police) and the SD in what was called the Reich Department of Security.

During the war, the concentration camps would become the harshest instrument of the German occupiers for asserting a "**new national order**" in the territories under German control. The concentration camps were closely associated with other camps and detention facilities which served the purposes of internment and imprisonment throughout occupied Europe. The SS attached great importance to the recognisable identity of the camp type under its administration. In early May 1940, the chief of the Security Police and the SD therefore issued an order to the effect that *"only the camps subject to the jurisdiction of the Inspec-*

Illustration 9: Labour allocation form from Sachsenburg Concentration Camp, 1936
Source: Buchenwaldarchiv

Illustration 10: Inmates in Lichtenburg Concentration Camp, 1934
Source: Buchenwaldarchiv

tor of the Concentration Camps, such as Dachau, Sachsenhausen, Buchenwald, Flossenbürg, Mauthausen and the women's concentration camp Ravensbrück" be allowed to bear the designation of concentration camp.

The difference between these and other camps would become quite tangible for the persons committed to the death mills. They lost everything which had previously characterised their personality and their outward appearance; they were shorn, numbered, divided into groups and marked with cloth triangles of different colours. In an endless cycle of hunger, beating, murder and forced labour, camp imprisonment was intended to eradicate any form of individuality and leave compliant, broken labour slaves in its place.

During the first years of the war, the number of concentration camp inmates increased rapidly – from 25,000 at the start of the war to approximately 60,000 in early 1942. New camps were set up in the East, in Stutthof near Danzig (September 1939), in Auschwitz (June 1940) and in Groß-Rosen (August 1940), and a sub-camp of the Sachsenhausen camp near Hamburg was converted into Neuengamme Concentration Camp in 1940. In late 1941, in specially erected **extermination factories** concealed behind camp facades in Chełmno, Bełzec, Sobibór, Treblinka, Majdanek and Auschwitz, the SS began murdering all Jews living on German and German-occupied territory in gas chambers – and later the Sinti and Romani as well.

Buchenwald Concentration Camp was established and developed as one of the main camps in this system: by early 1945 it was the largest concentration camp still in existence. All of the system's functional expansions found concrete realisation here. Buchenwald was the camp for the isolation of "community enemies" and for the repression of resistance in Germany and the occupied countries. Furthermore, with its altogether 136 sub-camps, it was part of the SS's vast forced labour imperium. Like the other concentration camps, it was not a phenomenon on the margins of Nazi society, but part and parcel of the Nazi concept of society and "normal" everyday life. During the war there were camps throughout Germany. As pointed out by Jean Améry, a survivor of Auschwitz and Buchenwald, the majority of the inmates and forced labour convicts lived and worked in cities, armament factories and mines – in the midst of the German people.

The Establishment and Administration of Buchenwald Concentration Camp

Establishment

"It was a city of its own, built solely by the labour of the inmates. It was pure slave labour; there were neither motors nor horses to pull the wagons. There were villas alongside immense garages, barracks and streets; there were barracks, detention cells, a central kitchen, laundries, bath facilities – modernly equipped but without water. There were production workshops, a sawmill, pig-breeding facilities, a vegetable garden, a brickyard, quarries, a riding school, a zoo, dog breeding facilities for bloodhounds, an infirmary, a general records department, a depot and a wood yard, hairdressers, guard and command towers, music bands, a sculptors' workshop and a woodcarving shop."

Julius Freund

The Site

In early November 1933, several months after the dissolution of Nohra Concentration Camp near Weimar, the Thuringian Ministry of the Interior had a new concentration camp constructed in the town of **Bad Sulza** to the east of Weimar. It consisted of a single building with an inner courtyard and accommodated some 250 inmates. On April 1, 1936 it was turned over to the SS. At the same point in time, the Reich Finance Ministry suspended payment of all subsidies to the Lands for the maintenance of camps and inmates and commenced with the remuneration of the existing SS guard units – with the exception of those at the concentration camps of Kislau (Baden), Kuhberg (Württemberg) and Bad Sulza. The Bad Sulza Concentration Camp, in which 130 to 160 inmates were still in custody in 1936-37, was thus earmarked for closure.

On May 20, 1936, the Inspector of the Concentration Camps and Chief of the SS "Totenkopf" Squadrons Theodor Eicke met with Reichsstatthalter Fritz Sauckel of Thuringia, who was interested in the continued existence and expansion of the camp. They agreed to move the Prussian concentration camp in **Lichtenburg** Castle near Prettin and "Elbe", the Second SS Totenkopf Battalion stationed there, to Thu-

ringia. On June 3, 1936, Eicke conveyed Heinrich Himmler's approval of these plans to Sauckel. Sauckel was now required to obtain Hitler's signature and take charge of financing the "new construction of a modern c. camp" for three thousand inmates and one SS barrack. Eicke pointed out in this connection "that a Thuringian c. camp was an absolute imperative, not only in the A case [outbreak of war – author] but also for reasons of national security, due to the fact that, in the case of war, the Land of Thuringia – the heart of Germany – will be particularly strongly exposed to subversive elements."

Naturally, Eicke knew that Thuringia – a former Nazi "Trutzgau" (military defence district) – was no centre of resistance. In reality, this assertion was an attempt to convey the fact that the SS was not interested in the structural alteration of the relatively small Bad Sulza Concentration Camp merely for the Thuringian region, but was planning a prototypical new construction that would take into account the goals and dynamics of the SS. Like Sachsenhausen Concentration Camp near Berlin, the Thuringian camp was to represent a **new type of concentration camp** which – after the example of the camp in Dachau – would optimally combine the organisational, political and economic interests of the SS in a single complex.

Illustration 11: Theodor Eicke, Concentration Camp Inspector, to the Thuringian Ministry of the Interior re the new construction of a concentration camp in Thuringia, Oct. 27, 1936.
Source: Thüringisches Hauptstaatsarchiv, Weimar

Illustration 12:
Hellmuth Gommlich
(1891-1945), 1937
Source: Thüringisches Hauptstaatsarchiv, Weimar

Four months passed before the Thuringian State Ministry commissioned the chief of the police department of the Thuringian Ministry of the Interior, **Hellmuth Gommlich**, to search for a site for the future camp. Thus the planning process was taken over by an SD official who had the reputation of being ruthless and determined. Gommlich had won Sauckel's confidence through the zeal he had exhibited in his function as the chief investigator for the expropriation of the Jewish arms firm Simson & Co. in Suhl. His career is symptomatic of the fusion of the police, the SS and the SD. It began in 1924 when, as a discharged first lieutenant of the navy, he trained as a police superintendent. In 1926, at his appointment as detective inspector of the Land criminal investigation bureau in Weimar, he swore to uphold and defend the republic. Just one year after his transfer to Zella-Mehlis (Thuringia) as a police councillor he clandestinely joined the NSDAP and the SS and worked for the SD. His membership, which he did not reveal until 1933, paved his way from then on. During the proceedings against the Simson Firm he gained admission into the circle of close confidantes of Himmler, Sauckel and Göring. Clearly motivated by anti-Semitic sentiment, his enthusiasm for prosecution earned him special promotion to senior executive officer and chief of the police department of the Thuringian Ministry of the Interior in 1935.

On October 27, 1936, Eicke wrote with unveiled impatience about plans for a camp intended for three to six thousand inmates and requiring an area of at least sixty hectares. On November 16, 1936 he joined the Thuringian authorities in an inspection of the grounds of the state-owned farm Magdala; this proposal was later rejected. At the end of January 1937, Hitler approved the expansion of Bad Sulza Concentration Camp which Sauckel had applied for. But it was not until a conference took place in the central SS office in Berlin on April 23, 1937 – attended by Eicke, Gommlich and other representatives of the SS executive, the Reich Ministry of Finance and the State Police Bureau – that the preparations were pushed forward. At the suggestion of

Eicke, Gommlich now set out in search of a forest area of seventy-five hectares near Weimar with the criterion that there be ample clay or loam deposits in the vicinity. Gommlich hastily called a meeting for April 26, 1937 at the Thuringian Ministry of the Interior, inviting representatives of the Reich Agriculture Bureau. The Land Geological Bureau of Jena submitted maps of the Ettersberg near Weimar, thus introducing the state forest on the north slope of the mountain as a possible site for a camp. A limestone quarry to the west of Jena and the Fahnersche Höhen near Erfurt, where loam deposits were also to be found, were likewise discussed. A letter written by Gommlich to Eicke on April 29, 1937 formed the prelude for the decision in favour of the Ettersberg. From this letter it can be inferred that certain parties had already announced their interest in the labour that would be provided by the concentration camp inmates. Gommlich wrote:

Illustration 13: View of the Ettersberg from the periphery of Weimar, 1933
In the foreground are tents which have been set up for a mammoth event with Adolf Hitler, who stopped here on November 1, 1933 whilst on a speaking tour. Here he spoke about Germany's withdrawal from the League of Nations.
Source: Brochure "Kampf und Sieg in Thüringen," Weimar, 1934

"The Farmers' Association of the Land of Thuringia has informed me of its receipt of a letter from the Reich Agricultural Bureau according to which preventive custody inmates are to be made available for agricultural labour within the framework of the four-year plan. At a joint meeting, the Farmers' Association submitted a declaration to me to the effect that the establishment of a camp at the site I have proposed meets with their fullest approval. The association urgently requests the realisation of the plan as quickly as possible. Aside from the fact that minable loam deposits are to be found in the vicinity of the camp, the site is also advantageous due to the fact that the main turnip fields – some five thousand ha – located quite nearby to the northwest and west can be reached easily from the site."

On May 5, 1937 Eicke endorsed the choice of sites and announced that an inspection would soon take place. With the deforestation of the north slope of the Ettersberg two months later, the construction of the camp – now intended for eight thousand inmates – got under way. Hellmuth Gommlich, who was promoted to the rank of SS Obersturmführer following the inauguration of the camp, oversaw the building process as a special representative of Himmler, and for three years he was in charge of all formalities concerning the camp.

The site chosen for the camp – the primarily wooded limestone ridge of the **Ettersberg** (elev.: 478 m) north of Weimar – had belonged to the hunting grounds of the dukes of Saxony-Weimar from the sixteenth to the nineteenth centuries. The Ettersburg hunting lodge dated 1706/12 was located at its northern edge. At the end of the eighteenth century it had been used by Duchess Anna Amalia as a summer residence, serving the writers and artists of the Weimar court as a meeting place and retreat. It was furthermore the site of an amateur theatre in which plays by the young Johann Wolfgang von Goethe and others were performed. In the second half of the nineteenth century, Grand Duke Carl Alexander had had the park facilities redesigned. Particularly following the erection in 1900 of the forty-three-metre-high Bismarck Tower with a restaurant for excursionists on the south slope, the Ettersberg had become popular among the citizens of Weimar as a destination for day-trips.

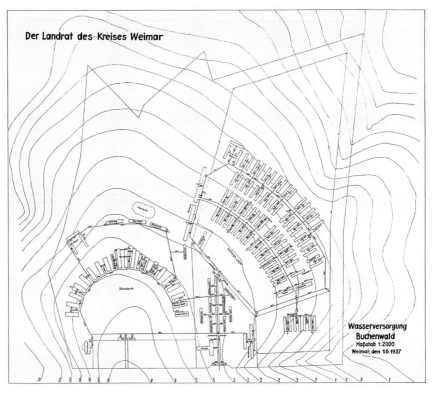

Illustration 14: Design for a concentration camp in the rural district of Weimar, June 1, 1937
This design, produced six weeks before construction began, was realised only with regard to the SS area. The location of the inmates' camp on a slope had not yet been taken into consideration, and the arrangement of the barracks on this plan is modelled on the Sachsenhausen Concentration Camp.
Source: Sammlung Gedenkstätte Buchenwald, Weimar

A District of Weimar

Even the earliest plans for the construction project provide evidence that the functions envisioned by the SS for the new facility far exceeded the immediate task of building a concentration camp. They provided for all the features of a military garrison, including civilian quarters for the personnel and their families. The commencement of the project was thus virtually the foundation of a new community, and when Buchenwald was incorporated into Weimar in 1938, the latter gained an **SS suburb** – albeit eight km from city limits – whose population of SS and inmates nearly equalled its own in number by the end of the war. The solidly built SS accommodations were constructed to last at least fifty years, an estimation later confirmed by the duration of the contracts

concluded for the supply of power. The camp's incorporation into the regional road network got under way in 1938.

Weimar was the capital of the Free State and NSDAP region of Thuringia. As the city of Goethe and Schiller, it bore permanent significance for the cultural self-image of the German bourgeoisie. A town of civil servants and the middle class, it thrived in the awareness of this heritage and for decades its gates had remained closed to the turbulence of modern society. As the venue of the constituent national assembly, it gave the Weimar Republic its name. This circumstance and the conviction that, by virtue of its past glory, Weimar would always remain the centre of German culture gave the city a magical attraction for the opponents of the Weimar Republic quite early on. Weimar was already the site of NSDAP

28

parades and party conventions in the 1920s; it was the place where the Hitler Youth received its name and it served as an arena for warlike consecrations of the Nazi flag.

The first government posts to be held by members of the NSDAP were in the capital of Thuringia, including the office of the minister-president from August 1932 on. As the heart of the "NSDAP-Trutzgau Thüringen," Weimar became a basis of the Nazi movement towards Berlin; more than half of its citizens voted for Hitler in 1933. As the concentration camp was being constructed in Buchenwald, monumental party edifices were going up in the Weimar city centre. The city was thus ideologically prepared for the establishment of the "**K. L. Ettersberg**."

The only objections to be raised in connection with the camp were those concerning its name. The Weimar chapter of the "**NS cultural community**" protested against "K.L. Ettersberg" because until that time the name Ettersberg had been exclusively associated with a commemorative site of the Weimar classical period. The "NS cultural community" had emerged in 1934 from the fusion of the Deutsche Bühne e.V. (a theatre association which had undergone forced orientation towards Nazi ideology) and the nationalist Nazi "Combat League for German Culture." It was not an NSDAP organisation but a Nazi association whose members included well-known personalities among Weimar's cultural elite. Despite the fact that the "cultural community" was dissolved in favour of the NS association "Kraft durch Freude" (strength through joy) in June 1937 (i.e. a few weeks before the inauguration of the camp), Himmler responded to the objection by ordering the renaming of the camp. In a letter of July 28, 1937, Camp Commander Karl Koch informed Senior Executive Officer Gommlich of the camp's new name: "**K. L. Buchenwald, Post Weimar**." The Buchenwald inmate Eugen Kogon later wrote:

"The choice of the site was symbolic in a higher sense: Weimar, the national centre of German culture, formerly the city of the German classical writers who had given German emo-

tion and intellect their highest expression, and Buchenwald, a raw piece of land on which the new German emotion was to flower. Together, a sentimentally cultivated museum culture and the unscrupulous, brutal will for power thus created the typical new connection Weimar-Buchenwald."

The business people and tradesmen soon overcame their initial reserve and a wide range of contacts developed between the city and the camp. They resulted from Weimar's role as the seat of the Land administration, the NSDAP regional administration and the Reichsstatthalter. The officials of the Thuringian Ministry of the Interior carried out the preparations for the camp, the Secret State Police, the police head-

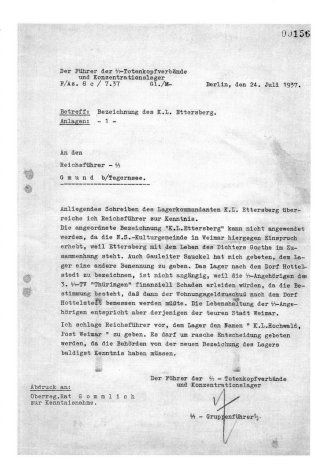

Illustration 15: Theodor Eicke, Inspector of the Concentration Camps, to Heinrich Himmler concerning the name of the concentration camp, July 24, 1937
Source: Thüringisches Hauptstaatsarchiv, Weimar

quarters and the court of the Land made their prisons available for transit detention, the prosecuting attorneys of the Land handled the execution cases until 1939, and the clemency pleas submitted by the inmates' families initially crossed the desk of Fritz Sauckel.

The **municipal administration** was also involved with the camp even before the incorporation of Buchenwald in late 1937. Between 1937 and 1940 some 2,000 inmates' corpses were cremated in the facilities of Weimar's main cemetery. During the same period, the municipal cemetery bureau was in charge of shipping the urns to the families of the deceased. From the outset, both the city and the concentration camp thus evaded the regulations requiring the consent of family members before cremating the remains of the deceased person. The camp commander provided this consent in place of the respective family. The agree-

ment on these proceedings had been reached before the first inmate died. The respective Chief Burgomaster's order states:

"As concerns the letter of 7/29/1937 I hereby consent to the petition of the concentration camp commander to carry out the cremation of the corpses in question for a lump-sum fee of 20 RM.
I request that the camp command headquarters be informed of this and be instructed that the certificate required according to Article Three, Item Two of the Reich law governing cremation be submitted at the time of the transport of the corpse. For the sake of simplicity I am enclosing a number of forms.
Item One of the form is to be completed by the command headquarters of the concentration camp,
Item Two by the respective registrar,
Item Four by the police authority of the place of death.

Illustration 16: Photo caption: "Picture XII. Re: view of concentration camp in Ettersberg. The photograph shows the arrival of the first preventive custody inmates in the concentration camp at the Ettersberg. Photo taken on the morning of July 15, 1937." This photo is part of a series produced between July and November 1937 by the State Detective Police, Weimar Detective Police Headquarters, in order to document the construction of the camp. Fifty-two original photos from this series are in the collection of the Buchenwald Memorial.
Source: Sammlung Gedenkstätte Buchenwald, Weimar

For the purposes of burial, officials of the concentration camp may collect the remains upon submission of a receipt to the cemetery custodian."

Many circumstances testify to the close relationship between Buchenwald and Weimar. In 1942, the municipal department of works made a futile attempt to obtain a share in the camp's electricity supply. The German National Theatre of Weimar held several performances for the SS in Buchenwald. In the final phase of the camp's history, following the air raids of 1944-45, several inmates' detachments cleared rubble on behalf of the city. There is ample evidence of the public presence of the Totenkopf SS in the town and at political parades. Yet the **inmates' presence in Weimar** is also sufficiently documented, whether upon their arrival at the main railway station and further transport to the concentration camp or in the many small labour detachments, including the one assigned to the city's largest industrial operation: from 1942 on, a Buchenwald sub-camp was located at the Fritz-Sauckel-Werk of the Wilhelm-Gustloff-NS-Industriestiftung. The camp's territory did not end at the crossing gate on the Ettersberg, but – even before the entire camp system had merged with war society – in the middle of the city.

The First Expansion Phase

The government of Thuringia had originally provided 46 ha of state forest on the Ettersberg for the establishment of the new concentration camp. This area was increased to 104 ha by means of the enforced sale of forests belonging to the Ettersberg communities of Hottelstedt and Ottstedt a.B., private land and over three ha of forest owned by the Hottelstedt parish. The undeveloped terrain, expanded by additional purchases to 190 ha in the following years, was almost entirely wooded, more than fifty percent of it by high forest that could be processed as construction timber.

The SS built the first barracks on the north side of the mountain even before the first inmates arrived. Late on the morning of July 15, 1937 the first 149 inmate craftsmen arrived on lorries from Sachsenhausen Concentration Camp. This marked the inauguration of the "Konzentrationslager Ettersberg," which the SS filled with inmates from the dissolved concentration camps of Sachsenburg (near Chemnitz) and Lichtenburg in the weeks that followed. Helmut Thiermann describes his arrival as follows:

"On SS transports of 7/27/1937, 108 inmates were moved from Sachsenburg Concentration Camp to a destination unknown to us. The transport was carried out with the highest degree of surveillance. The lorries were covered with tarps and it was only through the noises on the roads and the ventilation flaps in the tarps that we could guess more than witness the course of the journey. Because of the fact that speaking was not allowed among the inmates, we communicated by means of sign language. When we drove into a densely wooded area (on the far side of Weimar), we knew that we were at our destination. ...
Once we had been counted and turned over to the new camp administration we were taken to our accommodations. They consisted of a crude wooden barrack constructed of pre-fabricated parts and surrounded by a barbed-wire fence. On the first night we shared the barrack with the SS and already the next day we moved to the actual camp, Block 7. Following our arrival, we received red cloth triangles and two long canvas strips with numbers which we had to sew to our jackets and trousers in precisely designated places. I received Number 318. From now on we were mere numbers and nameless beings.
We were awakened before daybreak. Following roll call and division into labour detachments we went – closely guarded – to the actual inmates' camp. We completed the construction of a partially built barrack, Block 7, and moved into this block the same day."

The construction began in a great hurry and, as the forest superintendent later asserted, "... without the responsible finance ministry or the Ettersburg Forestry Office having been informed in any way." The SS directed the camp construction project. The first construction phase, which lasted into the second year of the war, comprised

Illustration 17: Photo caption: "Picture 19. Re: View of concentration camp in Ettersberg. The photo-graph shows preventive custody inmates carrying out surveying and excavation work for the construction of new barracks. Photo taken on July 23, 1937."
Source: Sammlung Gedenkstätte Buchenwald, Weimar

Illustration 18: Photo caption: "Re: View of c.c. in Ettersberg. Picture 22. The picture shows the view from the provisional left-hand m.g. [machine gun] tower. The first barrack of the third ring is under construction. (Photo taken on Aug. 4, 37)"
Source: Sammlung Gedenkstätte Buchenwald, Weimar

the basic structure of the SS area and the "preventive custody camp" and was carried out under the direction of SS Construction Chief Robert Riedl, who had been the "camp architect" of Sachsenhausen Concentration Camp (1936-37). Driven merci-lessly by the SS, the inmates cleared the forest, laid sewage and power lines and built roads and paths. They often worked from the break of day until well past sundown. The material for the paths and foundations was obtained from the nearby quarry, the inmates often transporting it to its prescribed destinations with their bare hands.

It was in this manner that the stretch of road connecting the camp to Weimar – referred to by the inmates as "**Blutstraße**" (Blood Road) – was also paved. This was a concrete road of over five kilometres in length which the SS had camp inmates construct between mid 1938 and late autumn 1939 to replace the old route leading from the Weimar-Ramsla state road to the camp, where it ended at the intersection with "Caracho Path." The planning and re-alisation of this construction project was carried out by a private motorway construction company which had a labour detachment of two hundred inmates at its disposal. Jews who had been transported to the Ettersberg in June 1938 lugged the stones for the sub-base from the quarry to the construction site. The number of casu-

Illustration 19: Photo caption: "Re: view of c. camp Buchenwald. Picture 46. The photograph shows the entrance building to the inmates' camp during construction. Photo taken on Nov. 10, 1937."
Source: Sammlung Gedenkstätte Buchenwald, Weimar

alties was high and gave the road its epithet. In the years that followed, thousands of inmates were driven down this road, frequently arriving at the camp dripping with blood.

The building construction was also carried out entirely by inmates. In the midst of the **SS garrison**, which already occupied a central position in the plans, were sixteen so-called "Hundertschaftsgebäude," (buildings for one company each), the barracks of the SS Totenkopf Regiment Three "Thuringia." The garrison also comprised casinos, armouries, a troop hospital, shooting ranges and drilling grounds, multiple-vehicle garages and two petrol stations. For the members of the SS and their families, two housing developments were built nearby, containing single and multiple dwellings in the regional style. There was a falcon yard in the old German style and an indoor riding arena. Due to its capacity for accommodating more than an entire regiment, Buchenwald served during the war as one of the major Armed SS bases for the training of SS division replacements. The camp further encompassed a central construction management office of the Armed SS as well as a central depot for building materials. In the spring of 1945, the final seat of the Armed SS's head operations office was housed in the barracks.

Illustration 20: Signpost at the intersection between the SS garrison and the concentration camp, 1943
Source: Musée de la Résistance et de la Déportation, Besançon (SS Photo Album: "Buchenwald Jahresende 1943")

Illustration 21: SS company barracks, 1943
Source: Musée de la Résistance et de la Déportation, Besançon (SS Photo Album: "Buchenwald Jahresende 1943")

Illustration 22: SS Officers' Colony I, 1943
Source: Musée de la Résistance et de la Déportation, Besançon (SS Photo Album: "Buchenwald Jahresende 1943")

Illustration 23: The buildings of the camp command and adjutancy, 1943
Source: Musée de la Résistance et de la Déportation, Besançon (SS Photo Album: "Buchenwald Jahresende 1943")

The overall layout clearly separated the SS residential and training areas from the inmates' camp. The **command headquarters** was located to the left and right of the "Caracho Path" that led to the "preventive custody camp" entrance. It consisted of buildings, some of them wooden barracks, housing the offices of the camp commander, the adjutancy and the Gestapo, as well as facilities for the troop staff. For the most part, these buildings were occupied only during the daytime. Apart from the commander's offices, none of these facilities were furnished to serve representational purposes. A particularly striking feature was the zoo which Commander Koch had constructed next to the camp fence for the amusement of the SS. The straight path of some three hundred metres in length leading from the main camp entrance (guard station and post office) through the command headquarters to the gate of the inmates' camp was dubbed "**Carachoweg**" by the SS (Caracho Path – from the Spanish "carajo," a colloquialism for breakneck speed). Newly arriving inmates were often driven down this path and into the camp at a run, and brutally beaten or attacked by dogs along the way.

In the two wings of the gate building were the offices of Department III of the command headquarters and the dreaded cells of the "Bunker" (detention cell building). Above the gate, in cast-iron letters, was the inscription "Jedem das Seine" – "to each his own." Along the path leading to it, there were signposts depicting various scenes such as committal to the camp. Inmates working in the wood-carving workshop had been compelled to produce these scenes in the traditional regional style.

The inscription "**Jedem das Seine**" originated in early 1938 with the approval of the concentration camp inspection authority. On the order of Camp Commander Karl Koch it was positioned so that it could be read from inside – when standing on the muster ground, the inmates were constantly confronted with it. It was an old saying which the SS had chosen as a motto for the concentration camp, now newly interpreted in keeping with NS ideology as the right of the "Herrenmenschen" (members of the "master race") to practise discrimination, even to the extent of destroying entire groups of the population. At the same time, they took recourse to the traditions of Prussian nobility, perverting a slogan of the Prussian kings. In its Latin version, the saying is two thousand years old and rooted in a dictum of classical antiquity and the Roman legal maxim "suum cuique." The latter was inscribed on the highest decoration that could be awarded by the Prussian royal dynasty from 1701 on, the Order of the Black Eagle, and its bearers were admitted to the Prussian hereditary nobility.

Beyond the camp gate, the so-called preventive custody camp was located, built on terraces on the north slope of the Ettersberg. The highest elevation within the camp is 445 metres above sea level, the lowest 375. This incline had an important function for the overall layout of the camp. In order to achieve optimal surveillance with the smallest possible amount of personnel, the three entrances to the camp – the west, main and east gates – were located along the highest elevation line of the "pre-

Illustration 24: Camp fence at Watchtower 18, 1939
Source: Sammlung Gedenkstätte Buchenwald, Weimar

ventive custody camp." From the wooden platform above the main gate, one could survey the entire camp. Beginning in the spring of 1938, the camp was surrounded by a barbed-wire fence three kilometres long and over three metres high, connecting the twenty-two solidly built watchtowers and the main gate building. All the way around the camp, the fence was electrified at 380

volts; no human being could survive the attempt to climb over it.

Along the inside of the fence there was a security strip, i.e. a strip of sand comprising a system of trip wires and chevaux-de-frise.

Illustration 25: View from a western watchtower over the barrack roofs towards the east, 1945
Source: Sammlung Gedenkstätte Buchenwald, Weimar

Anyone who entered this "neutral zone" would be shot. The SS protected themselves from touching the fence by means of a clearance wire on the outside, along the guard path. Guards patrolled along this path, forming the "little sentry line" whose counterpart – the "big sentry line" – surrounded the inmates' working areas by day.

The camp itself consisted of nine densely staggered rows of barracks which were numbered from west to east: during the first year of the camp's existence the SS had had six rows of one-storey prefabricated wooden barracks built. Then, in 1938-39, fifteen massive two-storey accommodation barracks were built in the lower three rows, forming the outermost edge of the barrack area for the time being. To the northwest was an infirmary which had not been built according to any specific long-term plans. The barrack camp integrated a grid-like network of access paths which originated at the muster ground, an area of some twenty thousand square metres.

In 1940 the crematorium was built to the east of the muster ground. In the winter of 1939-40, this corner had been the site of a makeshift tent camp in which hundreds of Viennese Jews and Poles had perished

Illustration 26: Buildings of the Deutsche Ausrüstungswerke (DAW), 1943
Source: Musée de la Résistance et de la Déportation, Besançon (SS Photo Album: "Buchenwald Jahresende 1943")

miserably. From there towards the north and down the slope was a row that formed the eastern edge of the camp and consisted of the storage barracks, the kitchen, the potato cellar, the laundry and the depot as well as clothing and equipment storage buildings, which towered over the rest of the facilities, and finally the vegetable garden and greenhouses. In 1942 the SS had workshop barracks built on the muster ground next to the crematorium. Originally carbines were assembled here for the Gustloff-Werk in Weimar; later the structures housed a locksmith's shop. In 1938 the western end of the muster ground served as the site of a temporary kitchen, then as a special camp for the Jews committed after the pogroms of late 1938, and finally accommodated a solidly built **inmates' canteen**. The SS had this facility built for the sale of wares which had been purchased cheaply or produced in the camp, as a means of siphoning off the little money the inmates' families were permitted to transfer to the camp administration for their rela-

tives in the camp. From 1943 on, the SS occasionally awarded canteen coupons as bonuses for high labour performance in the arms factories.

For the SS, the concentration camps were also a source of income. Although in the early years the construction activities monopolised nearly the entire labour force, inmate labour in camp production plants had already been conceived of during the planning stage as a means of profit. In 1938, when the limestone quarried near the camp proved unsuitable for the construction of NSDAP party buildings in Weimar, the SS company **Deutsche Erd- und Steinwerke GmbH (DESt)** had inmates set up a brickyard in the nearby community of Berlstedt.

Whereas the camp and its subsidiary facilities remained the property of the German Reich, the SS purchased the camp plants in the autumn of 1940 and founded a branch of the arms factory **Deutsche Ausrüstungswerke GmbH (DAW)**. The camp commander soon took on the additional role of works manager. This operation initially occupied five hundred inmates on average, later as many as fourteen hundred, and manufactured an assortment of wooden and light-metal products oriented primarily towards the wartime requirements of the Armed SS.

With the addition of the Deutsche Ausrüstungswerke in 1940, the functional tripartition of the camp complex had been established: SS area, the "preventive custody camp" and the production plants.

The SS Totenkopf Squadrons

In 1937-38 the SS had two barracked squadrons under its control: SS Totenkopf units large enough to be defined as full regiments at the concentration camps Dachau, Buchenwald and Sachsenhausen, and the SS Disposal Troops. For the **SS Totenkopf Regiment Three "Thüringen,"** which formed the "guard block" of Buchenwald Concentration Camp from the autumn of 1937 until September 1, 1939, duty in the camp was part of training. Until 1939, service was carried out on the basis of voluntary registration and commitment for four or twelve years. The officers of the SS Totenkopf Regiments viewed themselves as representing the elite of the SS, and the selection of new recruits was made according to rigourous standards during the initial stages. However these were relaxed once the war had begun. Originally, members were obliged to own German citizenship and a certificate of one hundred years of "pure-bloodedness," and had to be at least 1.72 m tall, young and healthy. The average age of the majority of the men was therefore considerably below the full legal age of twenty-one. Between June 23 and July 8, 1938, 25 inmates were shot dead whilst attempting to escape in Buchenwald, Dachau and Sachsenhausen. Among the SS executioners, four were 16 years of age, six were 17, eight were 18 and five were 19.

The hard drill to which they subjected themselves was intended to fulfil two fundamental purposes in addition to basic military training: firstly, it was to strengthen the consciousness of being a member of an elite corps and the feeling of "racial"

superiority. To enforce these ideals, all non-official interaction with inmates was strictly prohibited and punished. Secondly, the members of the SS were to be taught to act violently and cold-bloodedly towards their "inferiors," who were to be combated in the call of political duty. The command headquarters order of October 1, 1940, for example, reads as follows:

"9. Behaviour towards inmates:
The SS man is to exhibit pride and dignity and to express through his soldierly example that he is an upholder of the Third Reich.
The use of the familiar form "Du" is tantamount to fraternisation. It is degrading for a Totenkopf bearer to be made a messenger of any kind by a state enemy serving a sentence. These persons are not affected by words, but by deeds. An SS man who is not willing to impose these constraints upon himself for the purposes of his self-education should leave the camp. The SS escort guard is forbidden to conduct non-official communication with the prisoners."

Their heroic self-image as "**political soldiers**" stood in sharp contrast to the banal military routines, the boorish demagoguery, the comradeship and the cruelties that constituted their everyday lives. Anti-Semitism played a leading role. The training agenda included lectures on this subject. In October 1940, for example, by order of the commander, the NS propaganda film "Jud Süss," was to be viewed by the Buchenwald guard units "as a collective."

Shortly before the war began, the SS members designated to serve as "**police reinforcements**" were called to the concentration camps, thus providing "K.L. Verstärkung" (concentration camp reinforcement). The SS Totenkopf Regiment "Thüringen" (later part of the Armed SS division "Totenkopf") joined the Wehrmacht (German armed forces) in the invasion of Poland and was already subjecting the civilian population to severe brutality in the first days of the war. In its place, the guard battalion raised from the concentration camp reinforcement took charge of the entire surveillance of the camp on September 1, 1939. Because of the fact that men under

Illustration 27:
The SS Totenkopf
Regiment
"Thüringen" in
Weimar (Karls-
platz) on the day
of the Thuringian
NSDAP party
convention,
Nov. 7, 1938
Source: Der
Führer in Weimar,
1925-1938,
Weimar, 1938

Mit brausendem Beifall empfangen, marschiert die ϟϟ schneidig vorüber

Illustration 28:
SS belt buckle, 1938
Object found on
Buchenwald firing
range. Inscription:
"Meine Ehre
heißt Treue"
(my honour is
called loyalty)
Catalogue 2/22
Photo: N. T. Salmon

thirty could not be recruited for concentration camp service during the war, the age structure of the guard units underwent a distinct change. During the war years, men from the guard units and command staff were pulled from camp service to reinforce the front units of the Armed SS, which meant that all able-bodied younger men were called away. After the war began, they were replaced mainly by General SS members over thirty years of age, some even over forty. From 1942 on, seriously war-disabled SS men were also sent to the guard units with increasing frequency. When they were too disabled even to carry out guard duty, they were given administrative positions.

As the war continued, the guard units were also increasingly reinforced with Ukrainian and Latvian auxiliary units as well as SS volunteers from the German minorities in Hungary and Romania. The fluctuation within the concentration camp units was nevertheless so great that in the final year of the war Himmler ruled that service in the camps was to be regarded as

SS strength at Buchenwald Concentration Camp			
	January 1938	December 1938	End of July 1944	January 15, 1945
SS command headquarters	115	142	338	?
Guards	1,262	2,176	2,654 SS 2,735 air force	6,297 (incl. 1,530 in parent camp) 532 female warders
Inmates	2,633	11,028	66,609	110,560 (men and women)
Overall number of guards in all concentration camps	5,371	9,172	?	39,842

"front service." Dogs trained to attack inmates played an increasing role in the surveillance of the camps. Due to the growing number of sub-camps, the SS could no longer meet the demand for guard units with its own reserves. In July 1944, 2,735 members of the air force were therefore transferred to the Buchenwald guard battalion, integrated into the SS and charged with the surveillance of the sub-camps. In some cases, commanders of the guard battalion rose further up in the SS hierarchy and two of them – Otto Förschner and Richard Baer – even eventually become concentration camp commanders.

The Everyday Life of the Command Staff Members

Whereas the composition of the guard units underwent frequent change, the SS members with positions on the command staff settled in for a more permanent stay. Many married and had children or moved their already existing families to the vicinity of the camp. During the first two years of the camp's existence the registrar's office, which opened in Buchenwald in 1939, performed forty-eight SS marriage ceremonies and registered twelve births. In keeping with their ranks, the members of the command staff lived in two housing developments, of which the one directly adjoining the camp – SS Colony I – was reserved for officers. The families, most of them with several children, led a secure life in which inmates were constantly present as construction workers and servants. All personal contact was, however, strictly prohibited. Commander Koch repeatedly admonished his subordinates to educate their wives in the SS way of life and avoid all familiarity with "enemies of the state." The following excerpts from his orders illustrate the manner in which Koch intervened in the private sphere of his subordinates:

Command Order No. 64, Oct. 12, 1938, signed Koch
"4. A number of you apparently still do not comprehend the purpose of the Sunday communal meal. The point is not only to make donations to the meal collections but also to practise fellowship with the entire German nation by participating in the communal meal on the appointed days. Outsiders who are incapable of doing so have no business belonging to the Security Echelon and should stuff their fat bellies somewhere else. It goes without saying that the kitchens of the command staff are to prepare communal dishes only on these Sundays. I will either investigate the content of the pots of my married staff members myself or send an agent to do so."

Command Order No. 149 a, Apr. 13, 1940, signed Koch
"3. Re: Clan evening
Be advised that another clan evening will be carried out on May 1, 1940 at 7:55 p.m. All married command staff members are ordered to attend with their wives."

Command Order No. 85, Mar. 20, 1939, signed Koch
"1. Declarations of withdrawal from church membership
The final declarations of withdrawal from church membership have not yet been submitted by the SS members of the Bu. Con. Cmp. command staff listed below: …
The declarations are to be submitted to the staff Scharführer immediately; final deadline: Apr. 3, 1939."

Command Order No. 103, July 1, 1939, signed Koch
"This morning in the Klein-Obringen Colony I ascertained that the children of SS members associate with enemies of the state and possibly still lend them assistance. I expect all SS men to educate their wives in the SS way of life and this atrocious state of affairs, which appears hardly conceivable for an SS man, to be corrected immediately."

Most members of the staff made a clear distinction between their private lives and their concentration camp service, and the worst tormentors led a petit-bourgeois family life just a few kilometres from the camp. As observed by Buchenwald inmate Eugen Kogon in this connection: "Within the SS order, honour, loyalty and a clean family life by no means precluded every form of meanness, treachery and sexual dissipation in relationships to others, and even to classes regarded as lower in rank."

The **family of Camp Commander** Koch distinguished itself from the other SS families only inasmuch as Ilse Koch actively participated in the activities and affairs of her husband and did not limit her role as the partner of a camp commander to the domestic realm. Having completed her school education, **Ilse Koch**, formerly Köhler (1906-1967), had worked as a saleswoman and typist until 1933. In 1932 she joined the NSDAP. Her acquaintance with Karl Koch began in 1934 and led to their marriage and move to Buchenwald in 1937. In 1938, in "Haus Buchenwald" (as the commander's mansion was called), her first child was born. She gave birth to her second a year later and her third in 1940. The Kochs raised their children in the immediate vicinity of the camp; on Sundays they went for a walk in the SS zoo directly adjacent to the camp fence.

Ilse Koch took an active part in her husband's rapid advancement within the SS, which was characterised by ruthlessness, brutality and a pronounced desire to dominate and was closely tied with the development of the concentration camp system. In order to finance his extravagant household, Karl Koch uninhibitedly enriched himself with the property of the inmates and misappropriated a portion of the funds intended for the camp. The reputation for extreme cruelty which he gained as camp commander was also associated with his wife. She is known to have appeared at the SS men's places of work and incited them to beat inmates or report them for punishment. The inmates referred to her as the witch or beast of Buchenwald. Following the war she was compelled to take a share of the responsibility for the crimes which had been committed by her husband, who was shot to death at the end of the war.

Illustration 29: Commander Karl Koch and his wife, 1938
Source: Sammlung Gedenkstätte Buchenwald, Weimar

Illustration 30: Commander Koch and his son at the zoo, near the camp fence, 1941. Photo caption: "At the zoo with Daddy" The photo was in the Koch family album. *Source: National Archives and Record Administration, Washington D.C.*

Administration

"Everything in Buchenwald is administered, classified, registered, inventoried and initialled: the inmates' money, the number of articles manufactured in the factories, the number of working hours and leisure time, the living and the dead, the cost of operating the crematorium, the homosexuals and the gypsies, the watches and the hair of the new arrivals, the professional qualifications and studies of the deportees, the purchases of beer and machorka in the canteen, even the 'visits' to the brothel. Bureaucratic order prevailed within the SS realm."

Jorge Semprun

Dept. I: The Camp Command Headquarters

Buchenwald had two camp commanders: SS Standartenführer Karl Koch (July 1937 to December 1941) and SS Oberführer Hermann Pister (January 1942 to April 1945). They were appointed by the central Concentration Camp Inspection. Both commanders came from the lower classes of society, had received an ordinary school education, served in the First World War as soldiers and joined the SS before 1933. The fact that their reigns nevertheless differed distinctly can be attributed in part to the differences between their characters and their careers within the SS, and in part to the change in framework conditions brought about by the adjustment of the concentration camps to meet the requirements of labour allocation. The latter made a commander of the Karl-Koch type dispensable and promoted the bureaucrat Pister.

Karl Otto Koch was born on August 2, 1897 in Darmstadt. He attended Mittelschule and completed a commercial apprenticeship. Having volunteered for wartime service in 1914, he served on the western front from 1916 on and was later taken prisoner by the English. During the period of the Weimar Republic he worked as a commercial manager, an authorised signatory and insurance agent and became unemployed in 1932. He had joined the NSDAP and the SS a year earlier. His SS career began in 1932 with his transfer to the

Illustration 31: Heinrich Himmler in Buchenwald, 1938. Fourth from left: Heinrich Himmler, Reich Leader of the SS. Second from left: Karl Koch, camp commander, 1937-1941
Source: American Jewish Joint Distribution Committee, New York / USHMM

Illustration 32:
Commander's
Office Order No. 46,
May 7, 1938
Source: Thüringisches Hauptstaatsarchiv, Weimar

Kommandantur
aus Konz.-Lag. Buchenwald

Weimar-Buchenwald, den 7.Mai 1938.

114

Kommandantur-Befehl-Nr. 46.

1.) Ab Montag, den 9.Mai 1938, beginnt die Neueinteilung des Dienstes wie folgt:

a) Häftlinge: W e c k e n : 4,15 Uhr
Mittagspause: 12.oo - 12.3o Uhr
Bettruhe : 21.3o Uhr.

Ab Montag, den 9.Mai 1938 beginnt der Arbeitsdienst um 6.oo Uhr, d.h. die Arbeitskommandos beginnen auf ihren Arbeitsstellen innerhalb des Lagerbereiches pünktlich 6.oo Uhr. Arbeitsschluss auf den Arbeitsstellen und Abrücken von dort um 16.oo Uhr.

b) Kommandanturstab:

Der Dienst für die Abteilungen I, II und IV beginnt ab 9.5.38 um 7.oo Uhr und endet um 16.3o Uhr. Das gemeinsame Abendessen für die Kommandanturangehörigen findet dann um 17.oo Uhr statt. Sonnabends beginnt der Dienst um 7.oo Uhr und endet um 12.oo Uhr. Wecken des Kommandanturstabes mit Ausnahme der Abtlg.III ist auf 5.3o Uhr festgesetzt. Den Dienst der Abtlg.III regelt der 1.Schutzhaftlagerführer nach der Arbeitszeit der Häftlinge selbständig und meldet mir hierüber.

c) Wachblock:

Mit Rücksicht auf die Neueinteilung der Arbeitszeit muss ab 9.5.38 die Aufstellung der Postenkette um 5.3o Uhr beendet und der Begleitpostenzug um die gleiche Zeit am Eingang des Schutzhaftlagers stehen.

2) Ab 9.5.38 übernimmt SS-Obersturmführer W e d e l l den Frühsport des Kommandanturstabes K.L.Buchenwald. Antreten um 5.35 Uhr auf der Lagerstrasse im Sportanzug. Daran teilzunehmen haben alle Kommandanturangehörigen mit Ausnahme der Abtlg.III. Eine Befreiung hiervon ist nur mit Genehmigung des Adjutanten, SS-Obersturmführer Hüttig, möglich.

Durch die neue Diensteinteilung ist die Möglichkeit geschaffen, dass an den zu erwartenden schönen Tagen die SS-Männer abends noch einige Stunden der Ruhe für sich haben.

3.) Sonntagsdienst für die Abteilungen I,II und IV:

Sonnabend nach Dienstschluss bis Montag früh zum Dienst ist abwechseln ein diensttuender Stabsangehöriger einzusetzen für jede Abteilung, der für diese Zeit im Lager zu verbleiben hat. Der Diensttuende der Ab.IV ist im Besitz der Schlüssel für das Verpflegungsmagazin und die Kommandanturkammer, der Diensttuende der Abt.I hat den Schlüssel zur Waffenkammer und zu den Munitionsbunkern. Die Diensthabenden sind an den Abt.-Leiter zu melden.

4.) Der primitiven Wäscherei ist es verboten, Wäsche von SS-Angehörigen des Kommandanturstabes zu waschen. Ausserdem ist es verboten, sich von Häftlingen Wäsche waschen oder bügeln zu lassen. Für Instandhaltung von Wäsche und Bekleidung hat der Betreffende selbst aufzukommen. Wenn die Wäscherei fertig ist, kann die Wäsche gegen Bezahlung dort gewaschen werden und zwar nur von unverheirateten Kommandanturangehörigen.

5.) Ich weise nochmals darauf hin, dass die Mittagspause eine halbe Stunde beträgt und zwar von 12.oo - 12.3o Uhr, in allen Abteilungen. In der Zwischenzeit möchte ich niemanden in der Kantine oder in den Stuben sehen.

6.) Ich habe nicht gewusst, dass es erst einer Erinnerung in einem Kommandanturbefehl bedarf, um den SS-Angehörigen klar zu machen, dass beim Betreten des Unterführerheims die Mütze vom Kopf zu nehmen ist.

Thirty-Fifth SS Regiment Kassel. In September 1933 he was commissioned to raise the SS Special Detachment Saxony. A year later he took command of Sachsenburg Concentration Camp. After that – again for brief periods – he was the officer in charge of the Esterwegen Concentration Camp guard unit, officer in charge of the preventive custody camp at Lichtenburg Concentration Camp and adjutant at Dachau Concentration Camp. His career as a notorious concentration camp commander began at Columbia Concentration Camp (1935). In 1936 he was the commander of the Esterwegen and then the Sachsenhausen Concentration Camps. Within the space of a few years he advanced to SS Standartenführer (September 1937) which corresponded to the military rank of colonel. From the time he took office in Buchenwald, Koch was reputed to be the most brutal camp commander of all. The fact that he had overseen the camp construction process protected him from having to answer to charges of corruption made in 1941 and led to his transfer to Lublin. There, along with several of the thugs and killers who had made up his Buchenwald command staff, he established the Majdanek concentration and extermination camp. Himmler later abandoned him and he was prosecuted by an SS court standing as an example for all other corrupt concentration camp commanders. In early April 1945 he was shot by the SS in Buchenwald.

Hermann Pister was born on February 21, 1885, the son of a financial secretary in Lübeck. He joined the Imperial Navy at the age of sixteen and served there with various interruptions until the end of World War I. Not until 1918 did he begin an apprenticeship as an automobile mechanic, then went on to become an automobile salesman and manager. He joined the NSDAP and the SS Motor Echelon in 1931. His career within the SS was relatively inconspicuous, consisting of higher-ranking positions in SS Motor Regiment Nineteen (1933), SS Motor Regiment One (1936) and the motor pool of Himmler, the Reich Leader of the SS (1937). In 1939 he was promoted to commander in charge of the "supervision and management of educational camps in the West" (western fortification ring construction labourers belonging to the Organisation Todt), and later to commander of Hinzert Special SS Camp, which was under the control of the Inspector of the Concentration Camps. "Once he had proven himself there," states a report written by Concentration Camp Inspector Richard Glücks, "on Jan. 19, 1942 he was given the Buchenwald Camp, whose previous commander had made a complete mess of it. With great energy, never-ebbing diligence and through his own example he turned Buchenwald into a model camp." From the point of view of the SS command, this meant above all that Buchenwald ran smoothly as a commercial concentration camp operation. By the end of the war Pister was an SS Oberführer, which corresponded to a military rank between

Illustration 34: Desk set of Hermann Pister, camp commander from 1942 to 1945
Carving by Bruno Apitz, German political inmate, 1937-1945
Catalogue 2/31
Photo: N. T. Salmon

colonel and general. He was arrested in 1945 and sentenced to death by an American military tribunal in Dachau in 1947. His death on September 28, 1948 in the Landsberg am Lech penal institution was caused by acute myocardial paralysis.

From his office in the **command headquarters**, the camp commander controlled the concentration camp, the "guard block" and the SS officers in charge of the various departments, while also wielding sole authority over virtually all of the internal affairs of the camp. Even after Concentration Camp Inspection had been incorporated into the SS Department of Economic Administration in 1942, the commander still bore the primary responsibility for the conditions within the camp. From the point of view of the SS Department of Economic Administration he was also answerable "for the greatest possible productivity of the commercial operations" and for all framework conditions related to the labour carried out by the inmates. Concentration Camp Inspection only occasionally called commander conferences in Oranienburg, and commanders' staff meetings took place even less frequently (usually on rare special occasions).

With the aid of **Department I (the adjutant's office)**, the commander supervised all official correspondence, requests made by the inmates' families, and the camp penal system. Koch had altogether five successive adjutants: Hartwig Block (1937), Johannes Wellershaus (1937), Hans Hüttig (1938-39), Hermann Hackmann (1939-40) and Heinz Büngeler (1941-42); after Büngeler's transfer to another location, Pister had only one: Hans Schmidt. Following his departure from Buchenwald, Koch's last adjutant Heinz Büngeler requested his release from concentration camp duty. He was killed in the Soviet Union in 1943 as a member of the Armed SS.

Of all of Koch's adjutants, Hermann Hackmann in particular, had the reputation of being a corrupt and dangerous SS man, who obeyed his commander devotedly. Born the son of a bricklayers' foreman in Osnabrück in 1913, Hackmann was one of the younger SS officers. In 1933, at the age of twenty, he had completed his qualifying examination as a bricklayer and joined the SS. He entered concentration camp duty in the guard unit of Esterwegen Concentration Camp one year later. He became the officer in charge of the general records department at Buchenwald Concentration Camp in 1937, and Koch appointed him adjutant and personal confidante in 1939. Hackmann quickly advanced to the rank of SS officer and was involved in the misappropriation of funds as well as in numerous killings both in Buchenwald and, later, elsewhere. In 1941 he was transferred to the Political Department of Concentration Camp Inspection (Oranienburg), and later to Lublin-Majdanek Concentration Camp where he was first officer in charge of the preventive custody camp under Koch. Together, he and Koch were condemned by a special SS court in 1944 on charges of "continued theft" of Reich property. He received a double death sentence and expulsion from the SS. In the 1947 Buchenwald Trial, Konrad Morgen, who had served as the investigation officer of the special SS court, said of Hackmann:

"He had climbed to a high position within an unusually short period of time. This was only possible because he was favoured by Koch in an unusual manner. Hackmann is one of the persons who belonged to the small circle of criminals around Koch.
... What I want to express is that for Hackmann – in view of his profit to the detriment of the inmates and also in view of the fact that his criminal offences were based on the execution of orders by Koch – it must have been easy to recognise the criminal nature of his actions. ... Hackmann was a servile toy of Koch's."

Among the inmates he was known as "Johnny," a name which alluded to his arrogant, unpredictable nature. Bruno Heilig recalls:

"'... Johnny, be especially careful of him...'" whispers Lewit and continues walking. ... The Obersturmführer abuses us in Bavarian with a strongly alcoholised voice, Johnny with the growling tone of the Prussian lieutenant. Johnny is conspicuously well-groomed and elegant. Now we would finally find out what a concentration camp is, they say. The cosiness and slovenliness of Dachau is over. 'You birds,' that's what they call us. Johnny starts every sentence with 'You birds.' ... The roll call is attended by Oberkommandant Standartenführer Koch, Officer in Charge of the Camp Rödl and Johnny, who acts as Koch's adjutant. ... We are divided into labour detachments. All labour detachments march past the gate in rows of five. There a block officer stands with Camp Senior Richter and

Illustration 35:
Hermann
Hackmann with
SS Unterführer,
ca. 1939
Adjutant, 1939-
1941
*Source: Thürin-
gisches Haupt-
staatsarchiv,
Weimar*

the inspectors. The gangs of workers are counted.

Johnny pushes his way through the detachments, dealing out blows and insults. He is as nimble as a cat and always turns up whenever you have just seen him disappearing in the opposite direction. How cruelly this maidenly boy can strike, how disgustingly he can insult ..."

The adjutant was the chief of the **staff company** which comprised the SS block and detachment officers (i.e. the barrack and labour detachment supervisors with the rank of SS Unterführer or sergeant). They formed the permanent SS troop in the camp, were present in the barracks and labour detachments on a daily basis, dealt out beatings and wreaked havoc almost entirely without constraint, harassed the block seniors and inmate capos (labour detachment foremen) and thus exerted a major influence on the everyday lives of the

Illustration 36: SS Unterführer in Buchenwald, ca. 1939
Source: Thüringisches Hauptstaatsarchiv, Weimar

inmates. New members for the raiding squads for camp and block controls and execution squads were recruited from their ranks. "Kommando 99," the squad which killed some eight thousand members of the Red Army by shooting them in the back of the neck, also consisted of members of the staff company. Under Commander Koch, ruthless and corrupt block and labour detachment officers had promotion opportunities and nothing to fear when they abused inmates or "**shot** [them] **to death during an attempt to escape**." This was one of the favourite methods of killing at Buchenwald. In 1947, investigators of the U.S. military tribunal in Dachau questioned Gustav Heigel, a former labour detachment officer, on this subject:

"How often did you see inmates being chased through the sentry line while at work in the quarry?"
"One day I saw it happen three times. ... then I had to go up and report to Adjutant Obersturmführer Schmidt by telephone. As soon as someone went through the sentry line, it had to be reported to the adjutant immediately. Then the commission came out."
"What did you report to the adjutant?"
"'One inmate ran through at post no. so-and-so and was shot by the guard at that post.' Then the adjutant and several sergeants came driving out on motorcycles. ..."

"Did you also report to Adjutant Schmidt that this inmate wasn't trying to escape but was chased through the sentry line?"
"They all knew that."
"Who?"
"The adjutant and the commander and all the rest of them must have known that. Once I saw an inmate run through voluntarily. But otherwise they were always chased through."

The adjutancy was housed in a wooden barrack next to the commander's building. In addition to a **photo lab**, a **motor transport pool**, an **armoury** and an **I.D. office** it comprised the following sub-departments:

I a (**General Records Department**; German: "Schreibstube"): The orderlies processed the official incoming mail received by the Buchenwald Postal Agency and had it delivered by runners, who were usually inmates. It also processed the official correspondence from the departments, which crossed the desk of the camp commander. The postal agency with the official designation Weimar-Buchenwald had been established as a branch of the Weimar Post Office on Dec. 6, 1937. On Oct. 1, 1938 the Weimar Post Office occupied offices in one of the two entrance buildings to the command headquarters area. Correspondence from inmates to addresses outside the camp was censored. The censorship office was subordinate to the preventive custody camp management (Department III).

Teletype office and radio station: Housed in the adjutant's barrack, these offices facilitated fast, direct contact between the camp commander and superior SS offices as well as other camps.

Legal department: The legal department was a branch of the court of the Senior SS and Police Commander in Kassel, who was represented in the camp by the adjutant. The SS had its own system of jurisdiction which was independent of the national system from 1939 on. Among other things it investigated cases of assistance provided to inmates or escapees and "shooting executions during escape attempts."

Detention cell building (referred to as the Bunker): This was an ill-famed site of torture and murder, particularly under Koch and the chief jailor Martin Sommer.

Here, by order of the camp commander, inmates and in some cases SS men who had fallen out of favour were arbitrarily killed by beating, poisoning or lethal injections.

Crematorium: In place of the family members, the commander released the inmates' bodies for cremation, both formally, by signing the necessary documents for the Weimar Municipal Crematorium (until 1940), as well as by actually transporting the corpses.

Registry office: On April 1, 1939, the Special Registry Office "Weimar II" was opened in Buchenwald. Here, with the aid of a municipal registry official, the private affairs of the SS members were processed and certificates issued for deaths taking place in the camp. A copy of the death records was delivered to the Weimar Registry Office annually. Once mass executions got under way in the autumn of 1941, the SS had only a percentage of the deaths formally processed, and from 1943 on the deaths of Russians, Poles and Jews were generally no longer reported to the registry office.

Dept. II: Political Department

The branch of the Gestapo located in the camp was called the Political Department. In the manner of a police records department, its staff recorded all of the inmates' personal data upon their committal to the camp and kept inmate files which were submitted to the camp commander or the Gestapo offices in charge of the committals upon request. It was the task of the Political Department officials to interrogate and torture inmates on their arrival. Very little reliable information is available concerning the composition of the department's staff during the first phase of the camp history. From 1942 on it was headed by Detective Secretary Walter Serno, who was both a

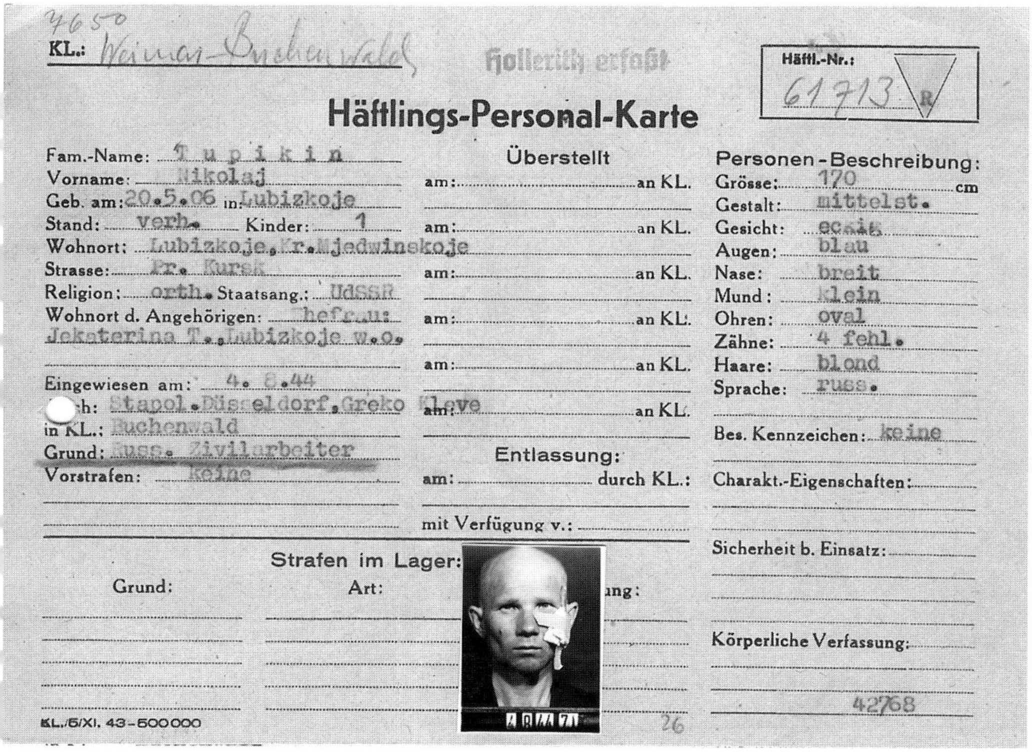

4650
KL.: Weimar-Buchenwald
Hollerith erfaßt
Häftl.-Nr.: 61713 R

Häftlings-Personal-Karte

Fam.-Name: Tupikin
Vorname: Nikolaj
Geb. am: 20.5.06 in: Lubizkoje
Stand: verh. Kinder: 1
Wohnort: Lubizkoje, Kr. Mjedwinskoje
Strasse: Pr. Kursk
Religion: orth. Staatsang.: UdSSR
Wohnort d. Angehörigen: Ehefrau: Jekaterina T., Lubizkoje w.o.
Eingewiesen am: 4. 8.44
durch: Stapol. Düsseldorf, Greko Kleve
in KL.: Buchenwald
Grund: Russ. Zivilarbeiter
Vorstrafen: keine

Überstellt
am: an KL.
am: an KL.
am: an KL.
am: an KL.
am: an KL.
am: an KL.

Entlassung:
am: durch KL.:
mit Verfügung v.:

Personen-Beschreibung:
Grösse: 170 cm
Gestalt: mittelst.
Gesicht: eckig
Augen: blau
Nase: breit
Mund: klein
Ohren: oval
Zähne: 4 fehl.
Haare: blond
Sprache: russ.
Bes. Kennzeichen: keine
Charakt.-Eigenschaften:
Sicherheit b. Einsatz:
Körperliche Verfassung:
42768

Strafen im Lager:
Grund: Art: Bemerkung:

KL./5/XI. 43-500000
26

Illustration 37: Inmate's personal record card
Source: Buchenwaldarchiv, Weimar

member of the SD and an official in the Weimar branch of the Gestapo. He also oversaw the detective police department which was a sub-office of the Political Department.

Until 1942, the SS carried out the "**admission**" procedures personally, subjecting the new arrivals to blows, kicks and verbal abuse and humiliating them in every manner imaginable while questioning them on their personal data. During the early years, inmates who provided inaccurate information during the admission procedure were severely punished. It was not until the number of inmates began to increase rapidly that the circumstances for new arrivals began to improve: the Gestapo now delegated the registration of personal data to an inmate labour detachment which had previously carried out office work. From 1939 until the air raid of 1944, photos were made of the inmates upon arrival. Gerhard Harig recalls his period of occupation as an inmate orderly in the Political Department:

"In Nov. 1942 we were still given orders in a harsh peremptory tone often characterised by loud yelling; upon entering and leaving the large office room we were expected to obey the salutation regulations to a T. The inmates brought to the Political Department for questioning or admission were subjected to a much harsher tone. They were often compelled to stand in the corridor unnecessarily for hours, sometimes for days on end, and were yelled at if they so much as leaned on the wall. Hauptscharführer Pfaff and later Rotten, and still later Unterscharführer Harwarth were particularly merciless until the end, never following our proposals to take the inmates back to camp if the officers didn't have time to process them, and have them called back later. A lot of beating also accompanied the admission of new arrivals, particularly until the spring of 1943 when the active SS men were called to combat duty and replaced by reservists. But in the treatment of inmates the reservists had already adopted the style of the active SS, beating and kicking them to the same extent. Those of the new arrivals who had [not] signed their arrest warrant at the police station because they were being falsely charged had a particularly

bad time of it. They were led into a small interrogation room. The other inmates were dismissed and within a very short time all had signed. We often had to take the inmates to the infirmary because they were bleeding from their noses, mouths and ears. The arrivals were often slapped and kicked on account of their records of conduct or the crimes and statements of which they had been accused and which were documented in their records. They were often threatened with death and reminded of the crematorium. Those committed on grounds of having insulted the SS or the Führer were subjected to especial brutality. What is more, every member of the SS had his 'favourites.'...

Deathly ill inmates were frequently committed by the police as new arrivals. Neither the police nor the transport officers showed the least consideration for these people's conditions, being solely concerned with getting rid of them before they died because a death caused additional work and inconvenience."

The **release** of inmates was also processed by the Political Department. The persons discharged had to pledge not to undertake any action against the NS state, to report anti-Nazi activities and above all to reveal nothing about the camp. Occasionally they were forced to agree in writing to collaborate with the Gestapo.

The Political Department also carried out the functions of the Gestapo within the camp – particularly the prosecution of political activities among the inmates – and were aided in this task by a network of informers. When inmates escaped, the Political Department ordered the police to undertake search measures. Searches and the interrogations that followed the recapture of escapees accounted for a considerable proportion of the department's activities, particularly in 1944-45, when at times over seven hundred inmates were registered as being at large. Following interrogation and unspeakable torture in the detention cell building, the recaptured escapees were frequently hanged in the cellar of the crematorium.

The death registry department recorded the deaths and entered them into the files. The files of released or deceased inmates were archived. A major proportion of the files were destroyed in the fires brought about by the air raid of August 24, 1944. Afterwards, as many as eighty-five inmates at a time worked day and night shifts to reconstruct these files.

Dept. III: Preventive Custody Camp Management

Department III dictated the inmates' daily routine and forced them to absolute submission to the **camp regulations** as well as the commander's orders. There was no set of camp regulations tailored specifically to Buchenwald Concentration Camp. During preliminary investigations for the Buchenwald Trial in Dachau in 1947, Max Schobert, the first officer in charge of the preventive custody camp in Buchenwald from 1942 to 1945, addressed this topic as follows:

"The camp regulations, which governed the surveillance system, the life of the inmates, punishment for disciplinary offences and the relationship between the inmates and the surveillance units, were originally designed by Eicke for Dachau Concentration Camp and later adopted by the other concentration camps as well. When the concentration camps were placed under Pohl's command as Bureau D in 1942 he made only one change in the camp regulations, namely new rules concerning the increased labour allocation of the inmates."

Every day began and ended with the counting of the inmates on the muster ground, a procedure for which the entire camp generally had to report and which lasted hours, the ultimate purpose being to draw up the daily "strength report." The "first officer in charge of the preventive custody camp," the most powerful SS man after the camp commander, ruled over the camp. He appointed the inmate functionaries, ordered "block inspections" and played a central role in dictating the extent of the terror carried out on an everyday basis.

As was also the case in other camps, the SS recruited personnel from among the inmates. These functionaries had to enforce the daily routine and the camp regime on

the SS' behalf. A considerable proportion of the administration and supply-related tasks were also delegated to inmates. A class of **inmate functionaries** thus developed, divisible into three groups with regard to their status and responsibility: inmate functionaries with the authority to issue orders and impose penalties (camp seniors, block seniors, capos, inspectors), those in the offices, depots and storerooms, kitchens and the infirmary, and those with special duties (camp craftsmen, runners, barbers, trusties).

Until the end of January 1939, Jews were excluded from all functions. The later appointment of Jewish block seniors was the result of purely practical considerations on the part of the SS. Other inmate categories such as Sinti and Romani, homosexuals and the majority of the "asocials" were also excluded from important functions.

The **officers in charge of the preventive custody camp** at Buchenwald are described as being unpredictable, crude, brutal characters, some of them also notorious drinkers. Four of them – Jakob Weiseborn, Arthur Rödl, Hermann Florstedt and Hans Hüttig – later took on commanders' positions in other concentration camps.

Jakob Weiseborn (1892-1939) came to Buchenwald with Karl Koch from the command headquarters of Sachsenhausen

Number of inmates in internal camp service, 1938/1941		
	12/31/1938	12/31/1941
Camp seniors	3	3
Block seniors	40	45
Barrack room duty/ purchasers/barbers	259	325
Medical orderlies and trusties (inmates fulfilling ancillary services)	32	75
Inmates' kitchen	47	78
General records department	25	17
Labour administration	2	5
Depots for equipment/ inmates' clothing/ inmates' belongings	20	149
Laundry		83

Concentration Camp. He was considered brutal and mean and, as Richard Seifert recalls, "often punched inmates in the face or kicked them in the belly with his boot." His concentration camp career had already begun in 1934 in the guard unit of Dachau Concentration Camp. Having been frequently transferred, in one case on account of a drinking bout, Buchenwald formed the basis of his rapid climb to commander of camp construction at Flossenbürg Concentration Camp (1938). For reasons never clarified, he died suddenly in January 1939. His successor **Arthur Rödl (1898-?)** was one of the "old fighters" by virtue of his early membership in the NSDAP and the SS and his position as officer in charge of the "Political Alert" in Munich (1933). Despite his repeatedly confirmed limited intelligence, he was promoted to Obersturmbannfüh-

Illustration 38: Instruction issued by the officer in charge of the preventive custody camp, Arthur Rödl, Oct. 9, 1937
Source: Thüringisches Hauptstaatsarchiv, Weimar

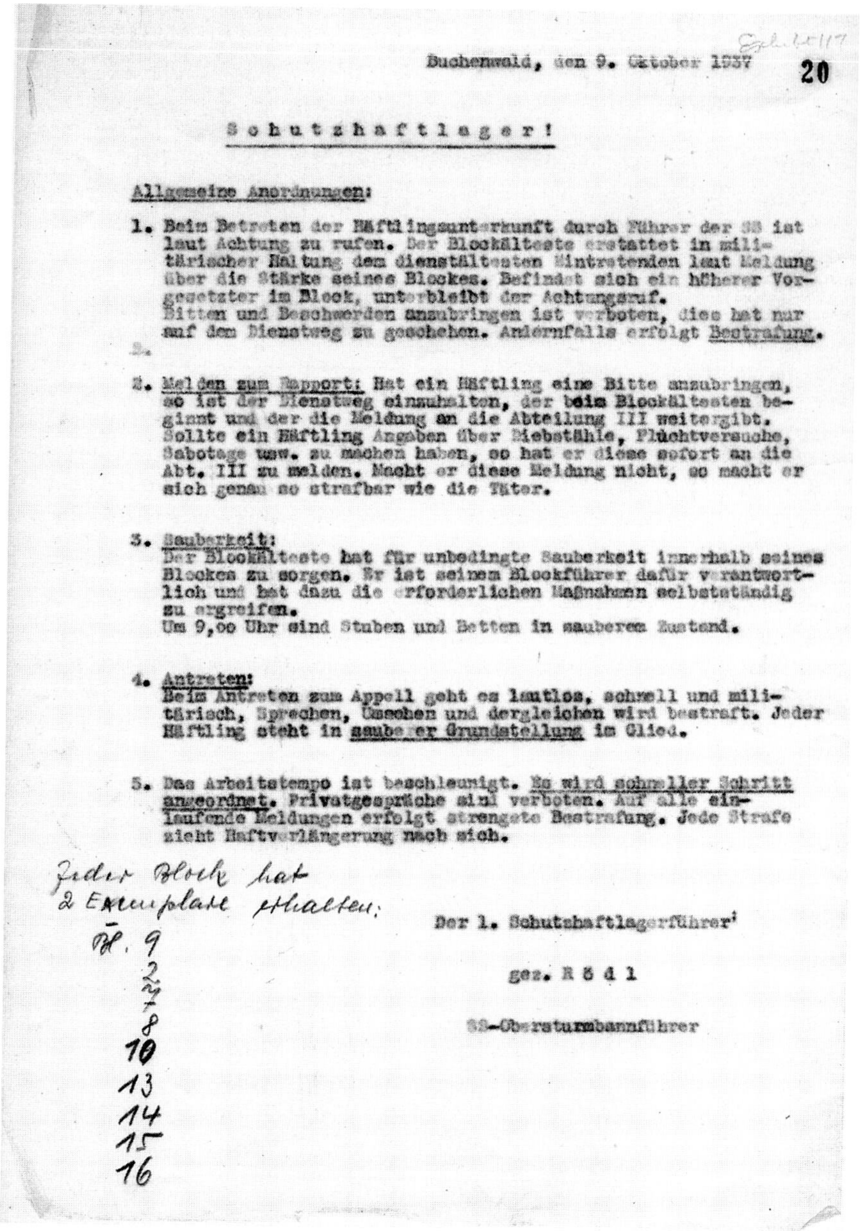

Buchenwald, den 9. Oktober 1937 **20**

S c h u t z h a f t l a g e r !

Allgemeine Anordnungen:

1. Beim Betreten der Häftlingsunterkunft durch Führer der SS ist laut Achtung zu rufen. Der Blockälteste erstattet in militärischer Haltung dem dienstältesten Eintretenden laut Meldung über die Stärke seines Blockes. Befindet sich ein höherer Vorgesetzter im Block, unterbleibt der Achtungsruf.
Bitten und Beschwerden anzubringen ist verboten, dies hat nur auf dem Dienstweg zu geschehen. Andernfalls erfolgt Bestrafung.

2. Melden zum Rapport: Hat ein Häftling eine Bitte anzubringen, so ist der Dienstweg einzuhalten, der beim Blockältesten beginnt und der die Meldung an die Abteilung III weitergibt. Sollte ein Häftling Angaben über Diebstähle, Fluchtversuche, Sabotage usw. zu machen haben, so hat er diese sofort an die Abt. III zu melden. Macht er diese Meldung nicht, so macht er sich genau so strafbar wie die Täter.

3. Sauberkeit:
Der Blockälteste hat für unbedingte Sauberkeit innerhalb seines Blockes zu sorgen. Er ist seinem Blockführer dafür verantwortlich und hat dazu die erforderlichen Maßnahmen selbstständig zu ergreifen.
Um 9,oo Uhr sind Stuben und Betten in sauberem Zustand.

4. Antreten:
Beim Antreten zum Appell geht es lautlos, schnell und militärisch, Sprechen, Umsehen und dergleichen wird bestraft. Jeder Häftling steht in sauberer Grundstellung im Glied.

5. Das Arbeitstempo ist beschleunigt. Es wird schneller Schritt angeordnet. Privatgespräche sind verboten. Auf alle einlaufende Meldungen erfolgt strengste Bestrafung. Jede Strafe zieht Haftverlängerung nach sich.

Jeder Block hat
2 Exemplare erhalten:
Nr. 9
2
7
8
10
13
14
15
16

Der 1. Schutzhaftlagerführer
gez. R ö d l
SS-Obersturmbannführer

rer, approximately equivalent to a lieutenant colonel in the military, the highest SS rank ever attained by a first officer in charge of the preventive custody camp in Buchenwald. Following his transfer in 1940, Rödl was the commander of Groß-Rosen Concentration Camp near Breslau (1941-42). He is last known to have served in the Armed SS; at the end of the war he disappeared.

Hermann Florstedt (1895-?) also belonged to the clique surrounding Karl Koch. Having broken off his vocational training in order to serve in World War I, he had eked out a living doing odd jobs for many years, finally running a taxi business in Eisleben. He had frequently made himself conspicuous by participating in drunken brawls. He joined the NSDAP and the SS in 1931 and was chairman of the Eisleben municipal council in 1933. He had already fulfilled various functions within the SS when he began his concentration camp career as the officer in charge of the Buchenwald guard block in 1939. In 1940 he was temporarily transferred to the position of first officer in charge of the preventive custody camp at Sachsenhausen Concentration Camp, but then Koch brought him back to Buchenwald to fill the same position in 1940-41. Here he had the reputation of being unpredictable and violent. He reintroduced the singing of the "Judenlied" (Jew Song) and had the habit of showing off the Jewish inmates to his guests by making them parade on the muster ground and sing this song for hours.

The "**Judenlied**," which was to be sung exclusively by Jewish inmates, had been composed by an inmate in 1938. From August 1939 on, along with the Esterwegen Camp Song and the Buchenwald Song, it was one of the three songs officially allowed by the SS. It consists of five verses containing one self-accusation after another and anti-Semitic clichés: "All we did was profiteer, profiteer and lie," "Now our crooked broker hands must do their first real work," "We are … generally known by our ugly faces," "We frauds of the nation long dreaded what has become reality overnight," "Now our crooked Jew noses are mourning," etc. "The German" who has

Illustration 39: Max Schobert (1904-1948), 1934 First officer in charge of the preventive custody camp, 1942-1945 *Source: Bundesarchiv, Berlin*

seen through the Jews and exposed them, and "put them safely behind barbed wire" is also extolled. The physician Dr. Paul Heller of Prague, a Jewish survivor of the camps at Buchenwald and Auschwitz, later recalled a day on which Jewish inmates had to stand until midnight, singing the Jew Song for four hours on end. SS men went through the ranks and checked to make sure the song was being sung correctly:

"One of the most horrible cruelties for me was the emotional torture of having to sing after roll call; particularly the Jews had to sing, sometimes for hours, for the amusement of the commander."

In 1942 Florstedt followed Koch to Lublin, and was his successor there as the commander of Majdanek Concentration Camp from November 1942 until 1943. Along with Koch he was condemned by the special SS court. In April 1945 he escaped from the Weimar Prison and went into hiding.

Hans Hüttig (1894-?), referred to by the inmates as "Soldaten-Maxe," was thus the only one of the officers in charge of the Buchenwald preventive custody camp with an unbroken career as a commander to the very end. From Buchenwald he went on to become an SS officer on the staff of Flossenbürg Concentration Camp, officer in

Illustration 40: Hans Hüttig in the camp, 1938; in 1938 Hüttig was the Adjutant, in 1939 he was made second officer in charge of the preventive custody camp.
Source: Sammlung Gedenkstätte Buchenwald, Weimar

charge of the Sachsenhausen preventive custody camp and commander of Natzweiler Concentration Camp in Alsace (1942) and of the Hertogenbosch-Vught camp in the occupied Netherlands (1944). In an interview with the historian Tom Segev, he looked back on his period as adjutant and second officer in charge of the Buchenwald preventive custody camp (1938-39) as the most precarious stage of his SS career:

"When I served in Africa I saw many abominable conditions. I was wounded and taken prisoner of war. Buchenwald was nevertheless a shock for me. On the other hand I did not arrive there unprepared; after all, I had gone through all those years in the guard unit. I survived everything. Sachsenhausen, Flossenbürg, none of those places caused me difficulties any longer. They all came after Buchenwald."

Felix Rausch described Hüttig in connection with the special camp set up by the SS alongside the muster ground in 1939:

"Now and then, Hauptsturmführer Hüttig made sure there was popular entertainment. He had the 'Bock' – a structure for adminis-

tering floggings – brought into the Little Camp, then showed up himself with a number of block officers and arbitrarily had twenty-five blows administered to every tenth inmate. In one case, an inmate wanted to take the flogging in the place of his brother who had drawn the lot: Hauptsturmführer Hüttig showed his appreciation by having both brothers flogged."

The **SS officer in charge of the general records department** was subordinate to the officer in charge of the preventive custody camp and responsible for the daily strength report, the assignment of the block officers' duties and the execution of punishments. It was to him that the **general records department** (established in July 1937) was accountable. In December 1938, 25 inmates served on the records department labour detachment; by June 1944 the number had risen to 75. The inmate clerks kept three card indexes: the inmates' personal card index, the number card index and the records department card index containing data on the barrack, labour detachment and profession of each inmate. From approximately 1939 to 1941, they also kept a "labour card index" arranged according to profession. They drew up the daily "**revision report**" (i.e. the report on deaths, discharges and the overall number of inmates within the cycle beginning and ending at midnight) and the daily "**strength report**" (i.e. the change in the overall number of inmates in the camp and within the individual inmate groups from one morning roll call to the next) as well as various lists (e.g. the list of inmate functionaries and the "light labourer list"), statistics (e.g. the monthly age statistics) and the preventive custody camp report. The location of each individual inmate at each respective time of day was recorded in the "number books".

Dept. III E: Labour Allocation

The so-called labour allocation of the inmates was an essential element of the concentration camp system. From the point of view of the SS, it implied four primary aspects which varied in importance during the various stages of the system's development:

1. In the regime of terror, labour played a major role. It was a means of ensuring the purpose of concentration camp custody, i.e. it directly served the deformation of the personality, the mental and physical destruction of the inmate.

2. The costs of camp custody were to be covered by inmate labour – not least of all due to the fact that it took a load off the civilian labour force in connection with the construction and expansion of the camps.

3. The camps represented a labour force potential that could be profitably exploited for SS enterprises or rented to private enterprises to the economic advantage of the state.

4. During the war, the flagrant shortage of labour in the arms industry of the German Reich opened up new areas of economic activity for the SS.

Before the war began, an average of about ninety percent of the inmates – the proportion varying slightly depending on the season and fluctuations in the numbers of incoming inmates – worked on the construction of the camp. Under the supervision of the officer in charge of the preventive custody camp, the assignment of labour and the raising of the "detachments" were overseen by the SS officer in charge of labour allocation and members of the command staff bearing the rank of sergeant. With the aid of **"labour duty forms"** they inspected the strengths of the labour detachments as they marched in and out. The so-called **"claim voucher"** – a form on which the number of hours worked and the corresponding fees were entered – was used to invoice the private companies and public agencies for which the inmates were made to work from a very early phase on. Under Camp Commander Koch, inmate labour was a favourite means of terror, which could be controlled by way of the extreme differences between the labour detachments. In the early years, their productivity was a matter of secondary importance. The SS economised in every way possible, particularly with regard to working equipment.

Once the first construction phase had been concluded, the SS began to focus primarily on possible means of economically exploiting inmate labour. For reasons of security, however, the inmates were initially kept inside or near the camps. This development paved the way for new means of inmate exploitation throughout the concentration camp system. In 1941 the SS Department of Economic Management /

Illustration 41: Albert Schwartz (1905), 1944
Officer in charge of labour allocation, 1942-1945
Source: Bundesarchiv, Berlin

Illustration 42: Instruction issued by Albert Schwartz, Jan. 20, 1945
Source: Thüringisches Hauptstaatsarchiv, Weimar

Construction therefore assigned the officer in charge of the preventive custody camp a special agent for the administration of inmate labour: the preventive custody camp officer "E" (for "Einsatz": allocation). Following the incorporation of Concentration Camp Inspection into the SS Department of Economic Administration in 1942, **Department III E** (labour allocation) was established and initially overseen in Buchenwald by labour service officer Philipp Grimm, who was succeeded by Albert Schwartz.

Philipp Grimm (1909-?), who had been transferred to Buchenwald as an "economic management officer" by Office I/5 of the SS Department of Economic Management / Construction, was initially confronted with Camp Commander Koch's general mistrust towards and rejection of all centralised control. Grimm had worked in the SS administration in a professional capacity since 1937. To the ambitious bureaucrat, Buchenwald meant the beginning of a career as a labour allocation officer, which he continued in the concentration camps of Sachsenhausen, Płaszow/Krakow and Neuengamme. As SS Obersturmführer, corresponding to the rank of first lieutenant, he worked for the SS Department of Economic Administration in 1943-44. In Buchenwald he introduced the category of "unproductive Jews" into his calculations as early as 1940, strongly advocating their transferral, along with all handicapped inmates, to other locations. In a "progress report" made by Grimm to the SS Department of Economic Management / Construction on Feb. 19, 1941, it is stated:

"Disabled inmates: In K.Z. Buchenwald there are presently approx. 500 completely disabled inmates and cripples. It is of urgent necessity that they be transferred to Dachau, as here they merely represent a colossal burden."

And on June 20, 1941:

"Disabled inmates:
With reference to the progress report of Feb. 19, 1941, I once again request that this matter be treated as urgent and the transfer to K.L. Dachau arranged. In the meantime, the

Illustration 43: Philipp Grimm (1909), 1934 Preventive custody camp officer "E"/ Officer in charge of labour allocation, 1941/42
Source: Bundesarchiv, Berlin

number has risen considerably. It is of urgent necessity to undertake an exchange because of the fact that very high strengths appear in all reports and only a certain percentage can actually be allocated and invoiced accordingly. For the same reason, the possibility should also be considered of putting all Jews into one camp, where this business could be properly taken care of, e.g. Mauthausen."

In July 1941 the SS began gassing handicapped inmates to death in the Sonnenstein extermination facility.

The labour allocation officer was in charge of the inmate detachment for **labour administration** which had been established in the construction office in early 1938 at the instigation of the SS construction manager. Until 1941, this detachment was responsible primarily for the registration and ad valorem offsetting of inmate labour. Once the war began, it also drew up the "Weekly Labour Allocation Surveys": monthly reports and claim vouchers. The detachment consisted of 3 inmates in 1938 and 5 in 1941. Beginning in 1941, the labour administration function was carried out under the supervision of Preventive Custody Camp Officer E / Labour Allocation

Officer and moved to its own premises adjoining those of the general records department. From 1942/43 on, the labour administration office consisted of five departments: 1. Compensation Department (compensation for inmate labour / surveys of labour allocation); 2. Card Index Department (professional card index, labour allocation card index); 3. Transport Department (organisation of transports to Buchenwald's sub-camps and other camps, drawn up for approval by the labour allocation officer); 4. Labour Allocation Department (bookkeeping on labour detachments in Buchenwald); 5. Quarantine Records Office (recording of professional qualifications of new arrivals). Seventeen inmates made up the staff of the labour administration detachment in mid 1944; by year-end the number had risen to over seventy.

Dept. IV: Administration

Department IV, headed by administration officers Mohr (1937), Karl Weichseldorfer (1937-1942) and Otto Barnewald (1942-1945), was in charge of supplying the SS

Übersicht
über die
Unterhaltskosten für Häftlinge in den Konz.-Lagern

Die Kosten für Bekleidung, Unterkunft und Verpflegung betragen pro Kopf und Tag:

a) für weibl. Häftlinge RM. 1.22
b) für männl. Häftlinge RM. 1.34

Diese Beträge wurden wie folgt errechnet:

a) Bekleidung

Die Kosten für männl. Bekleidung wurden auf Grund des Ausstattungs-Solls v.18.1.44 (unter Berücksichtigung der Tragezeiten) einschl. Reinigung und Instandsetzungsmaterialien errechnet. Somit stellen sich die Kosten für männl. Häftlinge an Bekleidung deren Instandhaltung und Reinigung jährlich auf RM. 142.35 = pro Kopf u. Tag RM. -.39

Die Kosten für weibl. Bekleidung wurden auf Grund des Ausstattungs-Solls v. 19.1.44 (unter Berücksichtigung der Tragezeiten) einschl. Reinigung und Instandsetzungsmaterialien errechnet. Somit stellen sich die Kosten für weibl. Häftlinge an Bekleidung deren Instandhaltung und Reinigung jährlich auf RM. 96.34 = pro Tag u. Kopf RM. -.27

b) Unterkunft

Die Kosten für die Unterbringung wurden unter Anlehnung an die H.Dv. 32o/2, Seite 12, Nr.56 errechnet. Demnach betragen die Kosten für die Unterbringung pro Häftling und Tag Rpf. 3o

Diese Summe setzt sich wie folgt zusammen:

a) für Lager- u. Unterkunftsgerät und deren Ersatzbeschaffung Rpf. 5
b) für Bewirtschaftungskosten (Beheizung, Beleuchtung, Reinigung, Be- u. Entwässerung usw.) Rpf. 15
c) für Raumgebühr (Gebäudemiete) Rpf. 1o

zusammen: Rpf. 3o

c) Verpflegung

Auf Grund der Rückfragen bei den Konz.-Lagern stellt sich die Verpflegung einschl. Schwerarbeiterzulage pro Häftling und Tag auf Rpf. 65

Illustration 44: Survey of maintenance costs for concentration camp inmates, 1944
Source: Thüringisches Hauptstaatsarchiv, Weimar

garrison and the concentration camp with food, water, power, fuel, clothing and equipment and for the interior furnishings of the barracks and the barracks. It also oversaw the kitchens and storage facilities in the SS area and the camp. The administration department thus had a major influence on the conditions that prevailed within the camp. Its activities were charac-

terised by flagrant supply shortages, which were to a considerable extent the result of intentional neglect. Particularly during the period in which Karl Koch was camp commander, but also later, the administration department was involved in the misappropriation of funds and inmates' property and large-scale trafficking in foodstuffs.

Illustration 45:
Otto Barnewald
(1896-1973),
1934
Officer in charge
of administration,
1942-1945
*Source: Bundes-
archiv, Berlin*

Illustration 46: Stamp: "Der Leiter der Verwaltung des Konzentrationslagers Buchenwald" (Chief of Administration of Buchenwald Concentration Camp (Rabe Company, Weimar)
Catalogue 2/42
Photo: N. T. Salmon

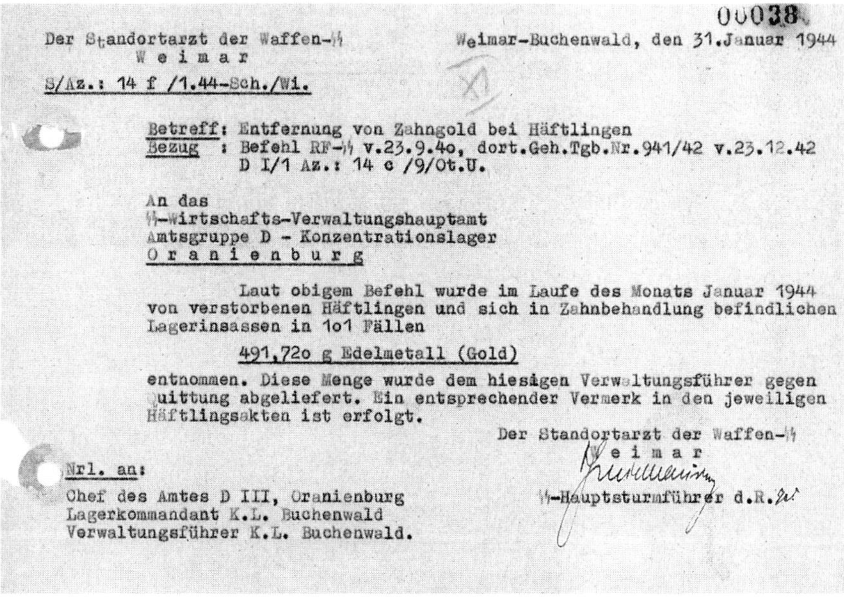

Illustration 47:
Record concerning
collection of
inmates'
gold fillings,
Jan. 31, 1944
*Source: Thürin-
gisches Haupt-
staatsarchiv,
Weimar*

Der Standortarzt der Waffen-ϟϟ
W e i m a r
S/Az.: 14 f /1.44-Sch./Wi.

Weimar-Buchenwald, den 31.Januar 1944

00038

Betreff: Entfernung von Zahngold bei Häftlingen
Bezug : Befehl RF-ϟϟ v.23.9.4o, dort.Geh.Tgb.Nr.941/42 v.23.12.42
D I/1 Az.: 14 c /9/Ot.U.

An das
ϟϟ-Wirtschafts-Verwaltungshauptamt
Amtsgruppe D - Konzentrationslager
O r a n i e n b u r g

Laut obigem Befehl wurde im Laufe des Monats Januar 1944 von verstorbenen Häftlingen und sich in Zahnbehandlung befindlichen Lagerinsassen in 1o1 Fällen

491,72o g Edelmetall (Gold)

entnommen. Diese Menge wurde dem hiesigen Verwaltungsführer gegen Quittung abgeliefert. Ein entsprechender Vermerk in den jeweiligen Häftlingsakten ist erfolgt.

Der Standortarzt der Waffen-ϟϟ
W e i m a r

Nrl. an:
Chef des Amtes D III, Oranienburg
Lagerkommandant K.L. Buchenwald
Verwaltungsführer K.L. Buchenwald.

ϟϟ-Hauptsturmführer d.R.

From 1940 on, Department IV was also responsible for handling the gold fillings and teeth that were extracted from the mouths of corpses in the pathological facilities in compliance with a decree issued by Himmler in September 1940. In September 1943 the SS Department of Economic Administration informed all commanders that the return of dental gold to the families of the deceased was prohibited and that "any and all requests made by family members to the concentration camps" were to be rejected. According to statements made by Otto Barnewald, the dentist delivered approximately 180 grams of dental gold to him per month; he collected it and turned it over to Office D IV (concentration camp administration) twice a year, on April 1 and October 1. These transactions were overseen by the Reich Audit Office. In March 1944, for example, Buchenwald Concentration Camp turned in 383 grams of gold, in April 1944 504 grams.

Dept. V: Camp Physician

"In this camp there are only healthy people or dead people" is a remark ascribed to Camp Commander Koch. It is not only characteristic of the way in which the inmates were treated, but also of the status originally held by Department V within the command system. Under Karl Koch there was accordingly strong fluctuation in the offices of the camp and troop physicians, the SS medical orderlies, SS dentists and SS camp pharmacists who were responsible for the health of the SS members and the inmates as well as for the general hygienic conditions.

The inmates' infirmary was established during the months following the camp's opening as an outpatient facility for the treatment of simple illnesses. Its subsequent expansion to an infirmary with inpatient barracks and operating rooms was not carried out due to any concern for the health of the inmates, but rather as a result of the endeavours of the SS to avoid dependency on the hospitals of Weimar and the Jena University. In his monthly report of June 8, 1938, the SS garrison physician wrote:

"Further efforts are being made to attain the means of treating as many inmates as possible in the infirmary without having to transfer them to an external hospital. The clinical treatment of inmates in the Weimar Municipal Hospital, where there is a lockable cell with two beds in it, is carried out only in certain kinds of cases.

… In the month in question, four outpatient sterilisations were carried out in the Weimar Municipal Hospital. In the operating room of the inmates' infirmary, two castrations were carried out. The new operation room in the inmates' infirmary fulfils the requirements for sterile surgery. Applications for castration and emasculation are constantly being submitted and processed. The entire body of inmates is being processed alphabetically with regard to sterilisation and emasculation applications."

On the basis of the Law for the Prevention of Hereditarily Diseased Offspring (1933), the SS physicians pushed for legal rulings providing for the forced sterilisation of inmates, particularly in the pre-war years, and carried out the respective operations themselves, as confirmed by the excerpt above.

In the early years, due to epidemics and the arrival of new inmates in batches, the expansion of the **infirmary** was stepped up, its efficiency always dependent on the degree of commitment demonstrated by the inmate orderlies who were confronted with a state of medical emergency on a daily basis. Even after the Koch period, inmates with medical licences were prohibited from practising in the inmates' infirmary. The inmate nurses, who were also required to carry out minor operations, were thus without exception medical autodidacts.

The SS garrison physician was responsible for the general supervision of the hygienic conditions and health care, and in cases of death he assumed the functions of a public health officer. The final garrison physician at Buchenwald (1943-1945), SS Hauptsturmführer Dr. Gerhard Schiedlausky, was also in charge of the health-care and hygiene conditions of the entire subcamp system. Particularly the area of hygiene was constantly neglected, so that in

Illustration 48:
Waldemar Hoven
(1903-1948),
during the
1946 trial in
Nuremberg
Camp, troop
and garrison
physician, 1939-
1943 and 1945
Source:
Yad Vashem,
Jerusalem

autumn of 1943. He participated in medical experiments, the killing of sick persons and selections for extermination; he allowed himself to be corrupted by Commander Koch and bribed by inmates. In the autumn of 1943 he was arrested by the SS within the framework of the corruption suit against Koch, but the proceedings were suspended by the SS in March 1945, whereupon Hoven resumed his position as camp physician at Buchenwald. The inmate nurse Ferdinand Römhild later reported:

"When Dr. Hoven was of the opinion that a prisoner could not be saved under the prevailing conditions he took him into an operating room of the hospital and killed him by means of phenol injections. … The number of prisoners who were killed by him in the operation room is so great that it is impossible for me to provide an even remotely precise estimation."

effect the camp was never once free of epidemic diseases. The first typhus epidemic broke out as a result of overcrowding in late 1938, leading to an entire camp quarantine which lasted for weeks. A year later, when the camp was once again overcrowded, a dysentery epidemic claimed many casualties among the inmates.

Of all the garrison and camp physicians, SS Hauptsturmführer **Waldemar Hoven** was at Buchenwald the longest. The fact that two inmates wrote the dissertation leading to the attainment of his medical doctorate shortly before his arrest in 1943 is characteristic of his career. Born in Freiburg in 1903, he went to Sweden at the age of sixteen to work as a farm hand and then to the U.S. For a brief period he worked as an extra in Hollywood, then for several years in the sanatorium run by his parents. From 1930 to 1933 he lived in Paris and earned his livelihood by working odd jobs. He joined the SS in November 1933, passed his secondary school-leaving examination in 1935 and took up the study of medicine at the University of Freiburg shortly thereafter. Before his conscription in October 1939 he took an emergency medical examination, on the basis of which he began working as the camp physician at Buchenwald. He remained there until the

Not only Hoven but nearly all the other SS camp physicians were involved in crimes against the inmates. **Dr. Werner Kirchert**, for example, (camp and garrison physician in 1937-38) introduced an ingenious "intelligence test;" if an inmate failed the test Kirchert applied to the hereditary health court for his sterilisation on grounds of "inborn mental deficiency." He also blackmailed homosexuals into applying for "voluntary" emasculation. Following the assassination of Ambassadorial Secretary vom Rath in Paris in 1938, Kirchert prohibited the treatment of Jewish inmates in the infirmary and even had seriously ill persons discharged. In 1940, Kirchert became the Chief Physician of Concentration Camp Inspection and in 1943 Chief Physician in the Reich Department of Security. **Dr. Erwin Ding** (camp physician in 1938-39) initiated the epidemic typhus experiments carried out in Buchenwald beginning in 1942. He was the director of the Department of Epidemic Typhus and Virus Research established in Buchenwald in 1943 as a branch of the Hygiene Institute of the Armed SS. **Dr. Erich Wagner** (camp physician in 1939-1941) used injections to kill the victims of a contagious eye disease which broke out among the Romani inmates in

Illustration 49: Heinrich Himmler inspects the medical service of an SS division, presumably the "Totenkopf" division, Meiningen, Mar. 4, 1940
l. to r.: Heinrich Himmler (Reich Leader of the SS), Karl Genzken (chief concentration camp physician,
1937-1939, from April 1940 chief of the medical department of the Armed SS), Karl Wolff (SS group
leader, chief of the personal staff of the Reich Leader of the SS), v. Egelstein, Dr. Erwin Ding, Dr. Werner
Kirchert.
Source: J. M. Suard, Paris

the winter of 1939-40. The removal, tanning and processing of tattooed skin from
the corpses of inmates was undertaken
upon the initiation of **Dr. Hans Müller**
(camp physician in 1941-42), who later became the SS garrison physician at Ober-
salzberg. This practise took on such pro-
portions that, after Müller's departure in
1942, Garrison Physician Hoven was compelled to prohibit the further manufacture
of "gift articles" in the pathological facilities. The inmate capo who worked in the
pathology department, Gustav Wegerer, reported on these circumstances:

*"It was Müller who ordered the removal of
tattoos from the bodies of deceased inmates,
the tanning of the skin and the production of
lampshades from this skin. When he gave this
order he cited a central order from Berlin. Repeatedly, hundreds of pieces of tattooed skin
were tanned using a wide variety of methods
and delivered to the chief of Office D III of
the economic and administration apparatus
in Berlin, Obersturmführer Lolling. ... I was
required to pass on Müller's order to Stöckel
and Werner Bach to manufacture pocket
knife cases and other articles from this tanned
skin."*

The inmates gave **Dr. Hanns Eisele** (troop
and camp physician in 1941), who was particularly ruthless towards the Jews, the epi-
thets "Spritzendoktor" (injection doctor)
and "Weißer Tod" (white death). SS Sanitätsdienstgrad Friedrich Wilhelm, a medical orderly under Eisele, later remarked:
"Eisele was a Jew-hater." Within the few
short months of his employment as camp
physician at Buchenwald, the killing of tuberculosis patients by means of injections –
a method with which the name Eisele
became connected – was commenced in
compliance with a centrally issued order.

Everyday Life in the Camp: 1937-1942/43

The Inmates

"In reality, a concentration camp was a world – full of contradictions and abysses, with a hierarchy that, although it fluctuated, was nevertheless precisely determinable at every instant, a hierarchy in which each had his rank. ... The feeble ones were condemned to remain at the bottom forever and wait helplessly until they were ground down to nothingness and there was no other place for them but the crematorium. On the other hand, almost everyone who could fight did fight – for a better position, for a bit of food, for a better bed, for a less badly torn blanket, for a piece of soap, for a whole shirt. It was every man for himself ... because what one person managed to get, the other had less of, and fighting could only make the common cake smaller, but never bigger."

Benedikt Kautsky

Committal and Division into Categories

In July and August of 1937, the SS transferred nearly all of the inmates from Lichtenburg, Sachsenburg and Bad Sulza Concentration Camps to the newly established Buchenwald Concentration Camp. Due to the fact that all three of these camps were disbanded within the same period, several of the transports were laid over at Sachsenhausen for a few days or weeks. The committal of new inmates by regional Gestapo and detective police bureaus also got under way in early August. This accounted for an increase in the number of inmates to 2,561 by the end of 1937. On September 20, 1937, in response to a request, the Gestapo provided the governor of Thuringia with **committal guidelines** assigning certain inmate categories to each of the three existing concentration camps:

"a) to Sachsenhausen: the preventive custody inmates from the eastern, northern and centrally located regions,
b) to Buchenwald: the preventive custody prisoners from the western and north-western regions of the Reich as well as from Saxony, Thuringia, Hesse and the northern section of Bavaria, approximately north of the Würzburg-Bamberg-Bayreuth line,
c) to Dachau: the preventive custody prisoners from the southern German state police bureaus."

In the early years, inmates from the Gestapo prisons in these regions and the Prussian province of Upper Silesia arrived at the camp either singly or in small groups. It was the **police operation "Arbeitsscheu Reich"** ("work-shy, Reich") that was responsible for the first rapid increase in the number of inmates: the number of camp inmates tripled during the first half of 1938. Like the campaign of March 1937 during which the detective police arrested unemployed persons with police records, the new operation was one component in the concept of the comprehensive "racial cleansing" of which the detective police regarded itself the instrument. The mass arrests of "inferiors" was also used to justify the further expansion of the concentration camp system, while at the same time providing the SS with the labour force required for this expansion. The raids, having been carefully pre-planned, were carried out abruptly in several locations at once. In collaboration with the employment offices, lists had been drawn up on the basis of which thousands were taken into preventive police detention and committed to the camps. As would also be the case with later "operations," these arrests were intended to affect the mood within the population or groups thereof. A comparison of the camp's composition before and after the operation provides an indication of its consequences for the circumstances within the camp. In March 1938 there were 2,728 inmates at

Stärke am:	Polit.	Berufs-verbr.	Emi-granten	Aussie-Häftlge.	Bibel-forsch.	Homo-sexuelle	Arbeits-scheue R. / G.		Rasse-Schänd.	Besserungs-Häftlinge Abg. I / Abt. II			Gesamt-stärke	Davon: Kranke Revier / krankenhaus		Arrest	Flügel-haft	Ur-laub	nicht in Arbeit	in Arbeit
Spalte	1.	2	3	4	5	6	7	8	9	10	11	12	13	14	15	16	17	18	19	20
a 30.8.	1834	1045	9	62	439	14	4379		6	1			2	7791	166		10	4	1		7610
b Zugang	77	9	–	7	19	1	33		3	–	–	–		149	115		15	1	–		
c Abgang	14	118	–	4	2	–	174		–	–	–	–		312	127		8	4	–		
d 16.9.	1897	936	9	65	456	15	4238		9	1			2	7628	154		17	1	1		7456
Davon sind Juden 30.8.	15	3					849		5					872							
Zugang	1	–					3		3					7							
Abgang	–	–					124		–					124							
16.9.	16	3					728		8					755							
Davon sind nicht Arier 30.8.	255				31		2							288							
Zugang	12				1		–							13							
Abgang	3				–		–							3							
16.9.	264				32		2							298							

Auf der Rückseite (oder? kurz) müssen namentlich erläutert werden:
1) *Spalten 10, 11, 12, 15, 16, 17, 18*
2) *Alle Häftlinge, die im öffentlichen Leben besonders bekannt sind,*
   rot unterstreichen.
3) *Sonstige besondere Vorkommnisse.*

Im Schutzhaftlager K.L.Bu. können 1o ooo Häftlinge unter-
gebracht werden.

Der SS-Schutzhaftlagerführer

[signature]

SS Obersturmbannführer

[signature]

St.-

Illustration 50: Two-week report by the SS command of Buchenwald Concentration Camp, Aug. 30, 1938 – Sept. 16, 1938
Source: Thüringisches Hauptstaatsarchiv, Weimar

Buchenwald, 1,689 of whom had been committed by the Gestapo as "preventive custody inmates." Of the altogether 7,723 inmates counted on July 1, 1938 (i.e. after the "operation"), 4,582 were "work-shy" and 1,064 were "professional" or "habitual" offenders.

In the period that followed, police operations repeatedly led to sharp rises in the numbers of inmates. The most rapid increase took place as a consequence of the pogroms of 1938, when the Gestapo arrested 26,000 Jews and deported them to the Sachsenhausen, Buchenwald and Dachau concentration camps. During the war, such operations along with similar forms of mass arrest were carried out in most of the German-occupied countries, primarily as a means of political persecution. A few days after the outbreak of the war, the Gestapo carried out a police operation in Germany for the arrest of potential political opponents. Following abrupt operations carried out in Vienna in 1939, during the invasion of Poland and following the occupation of the Netherlands, thousands of persons who had been arrested by the security police were committed to the camp.

Until 1942, there were seldom large transports from other camps. The camp system was still in the process of development and Buchenwald provided inmate construction detachments for the camps at Flossenbürg, Neuengamme, Mauthausen and Lublin-Majdanek. The largest transports came from Dachau Concentration Camp near Munich, which was temporarily evacuated in 1938 and 1939. In September 1938, the SS transferred nearly 2,400 Jewish inmates from Dachau to Buchenwald; at the outbreak of war over 2,000 inmates of various nationalities followed. In July 1941, the first large transports designated for "labour allocation" – 2,000 inmates – also came from Dachau.

The inmates came from all strata of society and had practised a wide range of occupations in civilian life. Statistics taken in

September 1940 indicate over two hundred different professions among the inmates. Labourers and salaried employees accounted for the largest proportion, but there were also many tradesmen and 261 farmers. At this particular point in time there were also 356 civil servants, 175 teachers, 29 students, 161 Jewish, Catholic and Protestant clergymen, 84 musicians, 3 opera singers, 1 dance teacher, 6 architects, 45 engineers, 27 technicians, 9 former judges, 66 persons from other legal professions, 32 doctors, 2 psychologists, 12 dentists, 2 veterinarians, 29 editors, 1 translator, 1 publisher, 14 writers, 33 former officers, 27 variety artists and actors, 1 biologist, 9 chemists, 1 physicist and 4 painters.

In the camp, background and profession carried as little weight as former merits. It was above all the camp badge, a mark to be worn by all, which determined an inmate's position and immediate circumstances in the camp. It was a triangular, coloured patch, sewn to the front left side of the uniform top and to the right trouser leg. The division of the inmates into categories was carried out by the Political Department, each category having been assigned its own badge colour. Only Jewish inmates had to wear a second, yellow triangle underneath the triangle representing their category. The two triangles were sewn together in such a way that they formed a Star of David. The following badges were used in Buchenwald:

Triangle	Additional mark	Inmate group
red		political inmate
	red stripe	recidivous political inmate
	yellow triangle	political inmate of Jewish origin
	letter	foreign political inmate (initial letter of native country)
	letter K	political "K" inmate (war offence)
	number on badge	political "Aktion" inmate (1939)
	black dot (all groups)	delinquent company
green		preventive police detention inmate (BV criminals)
	yellow triangle	preventive police detention inmate of Jewish origin
	letter S	security detention inmate (SV) beginning in 1942
	letter K	preventive police detention "K" inmate (war offence)
black		"work-shy" (ASR)
	yellow triangle	"work-shy" of Jewish origin
	letter A	labour discipline inmate (beg. 1941)
purple		"Bible researcher" (Jehovah's Witness)
	purple stripe	recidivous "Bible researcher"
	yellow triangle	"Bible researcher" of Jewish origin
	letter	foreign "Bible researcher" (initial letter of native country)
blue		emigrant
	yellow triangle	emigrant of Jewish origin
pink		homosexual
	yellow triangle	homosexual of Jewish origin
yellow	black triangular contour	"race defiler" of Jewish origin

Illustration 51:
Depot, 1943
*Source: Musée
de la Résistance et
de la Déportation,
Besançon (SS
Album: "Buchen-
wald Jahresende
1943")*

Illustration 52: Depot tag
Found in northern section of camp. These tags were attached to the duffle bags in which the inmates' personal belongings were stored.
Catalogue 3/1
Photo: N. T. Salmon

The gradation by means of badges implied a camp order which changed with the introduction of each new inmate group, particularly in the early phase. Until April 1938, for example, the political inmates and Jehovah's Witnesses were subjected to the worst conditions. Their circumstances improved when the arrest of the so-called work-shy (black triangle) commenced, a category defined "racially inferior" by the SS. Beginning in mid June 1938, when over

a thousand Jews were committed to the camp, the work-shy no longer occupied the lowest rung of the hierarchy. Like the Sinti, Romani and homosexuals, however, they still enjoyed no privileges and had little chance of establishing themselves in inmate functions. Walter Poller recalls his committal to the camp in 1938:

"We enter the inmate clothing depot. Large quantities of uniforms, underwear, boots, etc. are piled up on the shelves. Inmates who look relatively healthy and clean work here. Nearly all of them wear the red triangle. The first thing they do is sort us, the new arrivals. Here the politicals, who will have the red triangle, there the work-shy and asocials for the black triangle, the Bible researchers for the purple, the criminals for the green, the homosexuals for the pink. The Jews receive a second, yellow badge which they are to cross with their coloured one to form a Star of David.
Nearly every inmate behind the issue counter asks me what colour I have. A 'black' is standing next to me. The clothing he gets is obviously worse than what I get. At the boot issue counter I first get a pair of worn-out slippers. As the inmate is handing them to me he asks: 'Political?' and when I answer in the affirmative he goes and fetches me a better pair of boots. Only we politicals are asked whether we have brought a wool sweater or jacket with

us. Those who haven't, receive an article of that kind; all of the other inmate categories do not."

Political Inmates

The spectrum of political prisoners was as wide as the scope of discretion employed by the Gestapo for the imposition of preventive custody. In effect, they were not required to limit this scope as long as the persons or offences they were proceeding against could be defined as "hostile to the state or nation." Political custody might be the consequence of investigation, denunciation or a charge brought by an NSDAP functionary, frequently directed against a rival or unpopular neighbour. If there was a prospect of legal conviction, the SS turned the arrestee over to the court. If the sanctions which the court could apply were insufficient, it imposed "preventive custody," as is illustrated by the example of the locksmith **Wilhelm Bludau**. In a beer hall in Düsseldorf, Bludau had boasted of his role as leader of the bread riots of 1923 and was reported to the police by NSDAP members who had witnessed the scene. Having served a six-week prison sentence inflicted by the municipal court, he was arrested again by the Gestapo and committed to Lichtenburg Concentration Camp. On

August 7, 1937 he was transferred from there to Buchenwald. Following each of the subsequent reports made on his conduct – at first quarterly, later at longer intervals – his release was refused. As a capo at the postal agency he accepted bribes for smuggling letters, leading to his placement in a delinquent company. In July 1941 he was included on a list for transport to the Sonnenstein extermination facility.

Other political prisoners remained in custody for only a short time, their detention serving as a means of exerting pressure on certain groups of the population. In May 1938, for example, the Gestapo broke up a public demonstration against the introduction of a state-run school and for the retention of the Catholic denominational school in Goldenstedt (Oldenburg) by arresting the alleged spokesmen. In June 1938, two of them – Johann Herbrügge and Johannes Meyer – were committed to Buchenwald, ten to Sachsenhausen Concentration Camp. They were released two months later and kept under regular police surveillance until March 1939. The well-known writer Ernst Wiechert was also arrested in May 1938 on grounds of "subversive remarks" and taken to Buchenwald in early July. Following his release at the end of August 1938 he wrote a report on his experiences – entitled *Totenwald* (death forest) – which he hid until the end of the war.

Illustration 53: Wilhelm Bludau (1896-1941), photo from the Gestapo personal file, 1936
Source: Nordrhein-Westfälisches Hauptstaatsarchiv, Düsseldorf, RW 58-1620

Illustration 54:
Warrant for
preventive custody
arrest of Franz
Plath, 1937
*Source: Buchen-
waldarchiv, Weimar*

```
Buchenwald-archiv
Sign. 52 11-122                                         3 1. AUG 1937  405
                                                                        14

      Geheime Staatspolizei              Dresden, am   18.August 1937.
      Staatspolizeileitstelle Dresden
      Aktenz.: I 4 - 1100/34


                    Schutzhaftbefehl.
                    ------------------


         Der - Die -   Klavierstimmer
  405/14         P l a t h , Franz Paul,
                 .............................................
                 geb. am .7.9.79...... in ...Delitzsch...
                 wohnh. in  Leipzig-Mockau, Contardweg 7o
                 z.Zt. in ..der Straf- und Sicherungsanstalt Waldheim


         ist auf Grund von § 1 der Verordnung des Reichspräsidenten
         zum Schutze von Volk und Staat vom 28.2.1933 in Schutzhaft
         zu nehmen.

         Begründung:    Dringender Verdacht staatsfeindlicher
                        Betätigung.


                                        Buchenwald
         Er ist dem Schutzhaftlager Sachsenburg zuzuführen.
         Er - Sie - ist dem - im - Polizei - Amtsgerichtsgefängnis
         in                     zuzuführen. - zu verwahren -.

         Eine Beschwerde gegen diesen Schutzhaftbefehl ist nicht
         zulässig.

                                     Im Auftrag:
                                   gez. Jedamzik,
                 Herrn                Reg.-Rat.
                 Franz Plath
                 z.Zt.Straf-u.Sicherungs-           Ausgefertigt:
                 anstalt Waldheim              Dresden, am 19. Aug. 1937
```

There were also **Protestant and Catholic clergymen** among the inmates. As in the case of the Protestant pastor Paul Schneider, the SS did everything in their power to humiliate these men and crush their will to resist – which had brought about their arrest – within the shortest time possible. Schneider's death during this process was not intended. The Gestapo would prob-ably have preferred to release him as a broken man to serve as a deterrent to others, but he was tortured to death on account of his refusal to yield. Among the small number of Catholic clergymen in the camp was Leonhard Steinwender, a Catholic priest from Austria, who later reported that there were two other Catholic clergymen in Buchenwald when he was committed, one of them a curate from the diocese of Paderborn. A former dean from Prüm in the Eifel region is also known to have been committed to Buchenwald with his companion for having refused to salute to Hermann Göring. At the camp he was forced to stand for hours on the muster ground and salute to an SS cap.

Most of the political inmates were in the camp simply because they had little or no connection to the NS regime. In other words, conscious, organised opponents did not make up a majority. There were a large number of **long-term political prisoners**, or persons who had been in custody since 1933. Often by the time they had finished serving one prison sentence for alleged "preparation for high treason," the next "preventive" detention sentence had already been applied for. The fifty-eight-year-old blind piano tuner Franz Plath, for example, was arrested by the Central Gestapo Office of Dresden upon his release from prison, where he had served a sentence of three years and two months, and taken to Buchenwald in early September 1937. He was forced to remain there until June 1939. Before his arrest in May

1934 he had allowed his flat in Leipzig to be used as an illegal printing shop and courier station.

The functionaries of left-wing political parties and labour unions of the Weimar Republic underwent particularly rigorous treatment in the form of systematic registration in card indexes and strict surveillance. Once in concentration camp custody, they had little to no prospect of ever being released. Among their ranks were former members of the Reichstag and various Landtage (national and Land parliaments), and particularly former local and regional functionaries and members of the Communist Party of Germany (KPD), the Social Democratic Party of Germany (SPD) and the labour unions. Members of small parties and left-wing opposition groups, including the International Socialist Combat Alliance (ISK) and the KPD (Opposition), as well as left-wing socialists such as Werner Scholem were also to be found among the political prisoners.

By 1942, the following former members of the German Reichstag (M.d.R.) had been committed to Buchenwald by the Gestapo:

Karl Barthel (1907-1974)	M.d.R. 1932/33 (KPD), Buchenwald 1937-1945, intermittently camp and block senior
Fritz Benedum (1902-1965)	M.d.R. 1932/33 (KPD), Buchenwald 1939-40
Max Benkwitz (1889-1974)	M.d.R. 1924 (KPD), Buchenwald 1939-1945
Ernst Brandt (1896-1956)	M.d.R. 1932/33 (KPD), Buchenwald 1939-1943
Ernst Busse (1897-1952)	M.d.R. 1932/33 (KPD), Buchenwald 1937-1945, camp senior and capo
Ottomar Geschke (1882-1957)	M.d.R. 1924-32 (KPD), Buchenwald 1937-1940
Ernst Grube (1890-1945)	M.d.R. 1930-33 (KPD), Buchenwald 1937-1939, joinery capo, died in Bergen-Belsen Concentration Camp in 1945
Ernst Heilmann (1881-1940)	M.d.R. 1928-33 (SPD), Buchenwald from 1938; killed in 1940
Max Herm (1899-1982)	M.d.R. 1932/33 (KPD), Buchenwald 1937-1939
Anton Krzikalla (1887-1944)	M.d.R. 1930/31 (KPD), Buchenwald 1938/39, died in Sachsenhausen Concentration Camp
Dr. Richard Merton (1881-1960)	M.d.R. 1932/33 (DVP), Buchenwald following anti-Jewish pogroms of November 1938
Dr. Carl Mierendorff (1897-1943)	M.d.R. 1930-33 (SPD), Buchenwald 1937, killed during air raid on Leipzig

Dr. Theodor Neubauer (1890-1945)   M.d.R. 1924-33 (KPD), Buchenwald 1937-1939, decapitated in Brandenburg-Goerden Prison

Werner Scholem (1895-1940)   M.d.R. 1924-28, left-wing socialist, Buchenwald 1938-1940, shot to death

Paul Schreck (1892-1948)   M.d.R. 1928-32 (KPD), Buchenwald 1939-1945

Walter Stoecker (1891-1939)   M.d.R. 1920-32 (KPD), Buchenwald 1937-1939, died of typhus

Arthur Ullrich (1894-1969)   M.d.R. 1933 (KPD), Buchenwald 1938-1945

Paul Voigt (1876-1944)   M.d.R. 1930-32 (SPD), Buchenwald 1937-1939, killed by Gestapo in 1944

The former members of the Reichstag Ernst Heilmann, Carl Mierendorff, Theodor Neubauer, Werner Scholem, Walter Stoecker, Ernst Grube, Ottomar Geschke and Max Herm had been held in "preventive custody" since the spring of 1933 without trials or legal court sentences. Their prestige and above all the solidarity of their fellow prisoners afforded them a certain amount of protection, but the SS always had their eye on Ernst Heilmann and Werner Scholem because of their Jewish heritage. Ernst Heilmann, who had been the leader of the SPD parliamentary group in the Prussian Landtag, was subjected to extreme torments. On April 3, 1940 he was killed in the "Bunker" of Buchenwald by means of an injection. The proportion of political prisoners of Jewish heritage was particularly large in the pre-war period; like Ernst Heilmann, they were brought to the camp in September 1938 on transports from Dachau.

The Communists accounted for the largest share of members of political parties of the Weimar Republic. There were five to ten times as many Communists as Social Democrats in the camp, a ratio that corresponds roughly to that of the arrests made by the Gestapo. In 1936, for example, 11,687 Communists and 1,374 Social Democrats were arrested in Germany. From the outset, the Communists used their superiority in number to assume a dominant position among the political prisoners. Their unconditional belief in a Communist future provided them with a certain degree of stability and created a basis on which they were able to carry on their pol-

Illustration 55: Ernst Heilmann (1881-1940), before 1933
Source: Sammlung Gedenkstätte Buchenwald, Weimar

itical activities within the camp, where they organised themselves illegally as a party, trained their members and gained new followers. With Stalinist zeal, they also carried on the struggle against their opponents within the political left wing and among the "deviationists." As the Communist in-

Illustration 56:
Walter Bartel's
certificate of
exclusion from
military service,
1940
This certificate was
issued during
custody in
Buchenwald.
The photo was
taken in the camp
photography
department. From
1943 on, Walter
Bartel was the
head of the illegal
International Camp
Committee.
Source: Buchen-
waldarchiv, Weimar

mate functionaries gained power, the threat faced by persons who held other opinions grew.

In 1938/39, the majority of committals to Buchenwald Concentration Camp were related to the war preparations; concentration camp custody was also applied as a means of disciplining conscripts and soldiers. On April 20, 1938, for instance, the Hamburg Gestapo committed twenty-

one "draft evaders" as political prisoners. Beginning in May 1938 there was a small inmate group in Buchenwald designated "**special Wehrmacht detachment**." It consisted of "difficult cases" from the delinquent units (special detachments) of the Wehrmacht: men who had been committed to concentration camps as a means of increasing their penalties. Given the generalised label of "psychopaths," they had been assigned to delinquent units on account of disciplinary offences, theft, "renitence" or homosexuality, as well as – in isolated cases – for being convinced pacifists or Jehovah's Witnesses.

In as early as 1936, the Gestapo had set up card indexes intended to serve as the basis for arrest operations in case of **war mobilisation**. The so-called **Card Index A** registered persons regarded as potential political enemies of the state who were to be committed to the concentration camps either before the outbreak of war (i.e. preventively), after this event, or in critical situations. Criteria for inclusion in the card index were the public voicing of political sentiment, membership in a political party or fulfilment of a party function during the period of the Weimar Republic. "**Case A**" ensued with the outbreak of war and led within the framework of the "A-Aktion" to the mass arrest of former members of the KPD, the SPD, the labour unions and the Centre Party. Hundreds of the arrestees were committed to Buchenwald, above all Communists and Social Democrats but also, for example, Werner Hilpert, who had been a functionary in the Centre Party in Saxony until 1933. Political inmates from Austria and the Sudeten areas came after the outbreak of war on two transports from Dachau.

Following the German population's rather subdued response to the outbreak of war, the popularity of the regime rose quickly after the first military successes. There was nevertheless resistance and a minority which refused to accept the circumstances, although every form of opposition represented an enormous risk. During the war, many resistance activities were heard before special courts or the People's Court.

Many of the political inmates committed when the war began were assigned to the new category of persons "**unworthy for armed service**" whose number rose to over 700. The term was derived from national defence legislation which excluded persons with prison sentences of over nine months from armed service on grounds of "unworthiness." The "Aktion inmates" classified as unworthy for armed service remained recognisable to the SS because they were required to sew their inmate number across their triangular badge instead of beneath it, as was otherwise the practise.

In 1941, thirty-three "**Red Spaniards**" were brought from internment camps in Southern France to Buchenwald. These were Germans who had fought in the Spanish Civil War in the International Brigades alongside the republican troops and had subsequently been interned in France. Only one of them remained in Buchenwald; the others were soon sent on to another camp.

Red badges were also worn by former members of the NSDAP as well as legionnaires who had returned to Germany and been arrested, as long as they had not been previously convicted for criminal offences. If the Gestapo regarded the judicial penalty for "treachery" to be too mild or suspected a repetition of the offence would occur, they placed outsiders, discontent persons and "grumblers" who could not or did not adjust to the conditions of the "people's community" into "preventive custody." Until 1942, approximately one in seven political inmates was considered "recidivous" because he had repeatedly been committed to concentration camps on account of anti-Nazi activities. That meant limitations to his postal correspondence, at least three months in a delinquent company and no opportunity for release. "**Recidivous Politicals**" wore a red stripe above their triangles.

Percentage of political inmates					
Date	7/1/1938	8/30/1939	2/28/1940	7/31/1941	5/31/1942
Number	1,621	1,652	3,793	3,300	2,885
Total inmates	7,723	5,382	10,323	8,582	7,601
Percentage	21	31	37	39	38

69

Illustration 57:
Letter form
for Jehovah's
Witnesses ("Bible
researchers"), 1941
The message
written on the
back was to consist
of no more than
twenty-five words.
*Source: Buchen-
waldarchiv, Weimar*

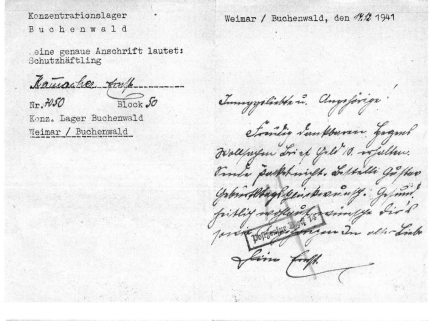

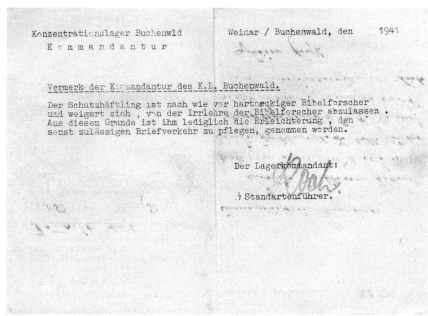

Jehovah's Witnesses

For reasons of religious conviction, the followers of the "International Society of Serious Bible Researchers" (Jehovah's Witnesses) refused the allegiance the regime demanded and conscientiously objected to military service. In many cases, despite the prohibition, they continued advertising for their religious community and circulating its publications. Beginning in 1935, these activities led in an increasing number of cases to committal to concentration camps. Here they had to wear the purple triangle. Already represented among the very first inmates, the number of "Bible researchers"

Illustration 58:
The jacket of the "Bible researcher" Paul Hirschberger, bearing the recidivous inmates' identification mark. Paul Hirschberger was committed to Lichtenburg Concentration Camp in 1937 and was an inmate of Buchenwald Concentration Camp from 1937 to 1945.
Catalogue 3/1
Photo: N. T. Salmon

in Buchenwald reached its peak on December 16, 1938 with 477 persons and from 1940 on averaged 250-300. Their custody usually began with three to nine months in a delinquent company. Only in exceptional cases did Jehovah's Witnesses consider abjuring their faith, a step which could bring about their quick release from the camp. Nearly all of them endured the tribulations to which the SS subjected the "Bible researchers" particularly in the early years. The following is an excerpt from a report, written after liberation, on the sufferings of the "Bible researchers":

"*The delinquent company was set up in August 1937; it would not be disbanded until the year 1944. All Bible researchers, with the exception of a few skilled workers, were put into*

this company. On September 6, 1938 the Bible researchers were offered the opportunity of buying their freedom by signing an agreement to recognise the state and desist from practising their faith. With the exception of a few cases, this offer by the camp commander was refused. Now the abuse and the pressure began in earnest, to wear us down. From the beginning of March until December 1938 we were prohibited from conducting postal correspondence and making purchases. After this ban was over we were permitted to write only one letter of twenty-five words to our families per month.

On Easter Sunday 1939 a further attempt was made by the officer in charge of the general records department to persuade us to acknowledge the state and the Führer. Nicknames such as 'Himmelskomiker' [comedians of heaven] and 'Bibelwürmer' [Bible worms] were the order of the day. He had no success whatsoever."

BV Inmates

Buchenwald Concentration Camp was planned and constructed during a phase of reorganisation of the police apparatus and the concentration camp system, a circumstance that had a major influence on the composition of the inmates' community, particularly in the years 1937 to 1939. One fifth of the persons committed in the early years – until the end of 1941 – were the victims of racist cleansing strategies who were straitjacketed in categories such as "professional criminals," "asocials" and "work-shy." Buchenwald's first inmates were brought from Sachsenhausen Concentration Camp and the dissolved concentration camps of Lichtenburg and Sachsenburg in the summer of 1937; half of this group were so-called "professional criminals" (referred to as BV for "Berufsverbrecher" [professional criminals] or "befristete Vorbeugehaft" [short-term preventive detention]). More specifically, these were persons with multiple criminal offence records, whom the detective police had taken into custody "preventively," often directly after they had completed their prison sentences.

From the very beginning, the "greens" – as the BV inmates were called on account of the colour of their badge – were dominated by violent criminals, whose cliques influenced the atmosphere in the camp, particularly in the years 1937-38. Names such as Hubert Richter and Otto Osterloh often come up in Buchenwald memoirs in connection with blackmail, brutal physical abuse at workplaces and in the barracks, as well as the first public execution in Bu-

chenwald, carried out by BVs on behalf of the SS. Between October 1938 and April 1939 the SS had a large proportion of them transferred to the new camps at Mauthausen and Flossenbürg, where they worked in construction detachments; others were killed or released. Their number did not increase again until mid 1941. They never regained their status of the early years, however, except for a brief interval in 1941/42 when the SS camp command appointed a BV inmate – Josef Ohles – as camp senior. In view of the overall increase in the number of inmates, the proportion of BV inmates decreased steadily, finally levelling off at approximately two percent.

ASR Inmates

The abbreviation "ASR" stood for "Arbeitsscheu Reich" (work-shy, Reich). In early 1938 the Gestapo began planning an "operation" by the same name, which they carried out between April and June. On January 26, 1938 Himmler had ordered preparations to be undertaken for the arrest of all able-bodied men "who have ascertainably refused two offers of employment without justification or have begun employment but quit it again after a brief time for no valid reason." Such persons were regarded "asocial." In a manner already practised to some extent on the Land level, beggars, vagabonds and alcoholics were to be forced to perform labour in the concentration camps. An entire group of the population was thus committed to the concentration camps.

With this "operation" – this "comprehensive and abrupt action" – Buchenwald Concentration Camp received altogether 4,000 new forced labour convicts for the construction of the camp, the first arriving

Percentage of inmates designated "work-shy"					
Date	7/1/1938	8/30/1939	2/28/1940	7/31/1941	5/31/1942
Number	4,582	2,873	2,899	1,469	781
Total inmates	7.723	5,382	10,323	8,582	7,601
Percentage	59	53	28	17	10

in the last week of April 1938. In the International Camp Committee report, the situation is described as follows:

"Until the arrival of the Jews in masses, the 'blacks' were the whipping boys. Only very few of them managed to break out of the excavation detachments and get better work. The large majority always worked in excavation detachments and the quarry."

The report further implies that the radius of "Operation Work-Shy, Reich" expanded in a second wave of arrests, referred to as the "Juni-Aktion" (June operation). Among the 2,378 men arriving in Buchenwald between June 14 and 19, 1938, 1,256 were Jews. There was thus a direct connection between the "June Operation" – the first mass arrest of Jews in Germany and Austria – and the intensification of anti-Jewish expulsion policies in that year. At the same time, the operation served as a pretext for the committal of hundreds of Sinti and Romani to the concentration camps. After 1938 no further "operation" was carried out on this scale. The number of "ASR inmates" decreased steadily and played an insignificant role in the later years, by which time the circumstances within the camp had changed radically.

Homosexuals

For decades, homosexuality had been a standard offence whose perpetrators had been criminally prosecuted according to Articles 175 or 176. The Nazis, who had declared "hereditary-disease-free procreation" to be the goal of human sexuality, regarded homosexuality not merely as a violation of the norm but as a fundamental threat to the biologically standardised "people's community." Within the SS, it was thus considered a crime worthy of death and homosexuals were persecuted with the utmost brutality. Speaking to a group of SS Gruppenführer on February 18, 1937, Himmler elaborated on the subject:

"We have to be clear about the fact that if we continue to have this vice in Germany without a means of combating it, then that will be the end of Germany, the end of the Germanic world. Things are unfortunately no longer as easy for us as they were for our ancestors. In their day, there were only isolated cases of this abnormal species. Homosexuals, who were called Urning, were drowned in the swamp. … This was not punishment, but merely the extermination of abnormal life. It had to be removed, just as we get rid of nettles, throw them onto a heap and burn them. It was not a feeling of revenge, the person in question simply had to be gotten rid of."

The sharpening of Article 175 in 1935 led to an increasing number of arrests and sentences. The homosexuals to be committed to concentration camps were above all those with multiple previous convictions or those arrested for intercourse with minors. Always insignificant in number, their presence in the camp community was sporadic; they were isolated outcasts who spent most of their period of detention in delinquent units.

Homosexuals in Buchenwald Concentration Camp							
Year-end	1937	1938	1939	1940	1941	1942	1943	1944
Number	1	30	43	11	51	75	169	189

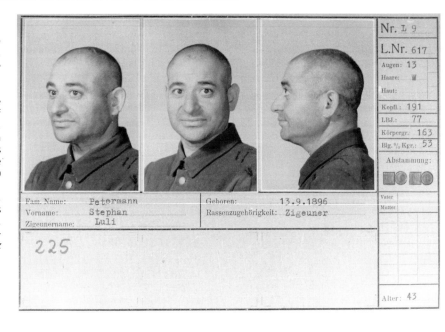

Illustration 59: "Racial research" file card, 1939 The photograph was taken in the camp in 1939. On July 14, 1941, within the framework of Operation 14 f 13, Stephan Petermann was taken to the Sonnenstein (Pirna) "euthanasia" killing facility, where he was gassed to death. *Source: Bundesarchiv, Koblenz*

Sinti and Romani

Isolated Sinti were already among the "preventive custody inmates" on the first transports of 1937. Hundreds of them were brought to Buchenwald in conjunction with the mass arrests of June 1938 and assigned to the "ASR inmate" category. Many of them were broken by the strains of the daily drill and forced labour. Soon after their committal in June 1938 they were subjected to public flogging and other

Illustration 60: Otto Schmidt (1918-1942), late 1930s The photo was taken by the detective police. *Source: Landeshauptarchiv Magdeburg*

abuses in groups. Extant index cards provide evidence of the fact that the Gestapo provided the "Eugenic Research Department" of the Reich Board of Health with access to Buchenwald in order to expand its "Gypsy Card Index."

A count made in the spring of 1939 indicates that just over 100 Sinti and Romani lived in the camp at that time. Immediately following the outbreak of war in 1939, the SS transferred 600 Romani from Dachau Concentration Camp to Buchenwald. Before the war the detective police had already arrested them in Burgenland, where they had lived for generations. This mass arrest, officially designated a "preventive measure for the combat of the gypsy plague," virtually led to the annihilation of the entire group. One in three of them died in Buchenwald in the winter of 1939/40. In 1940 the SS began deporting the remaining Sinti and Romani to Mauthausen Concentration Camp, where they were destroyed through labour in the quarries.

Following the last Mauthausen transports of 1941, only very few Sinti and Romani were left in Buchenwald. One of them, the Sinto Otto Schmidt of Magdeburg, had already been placed in "preventive police detention" on account of his heritage at the age of twenty. He survived the torments of the construction years and evaded the transports to Mauthausen. In the summer of 1942, Camp Physician Hoven selected him for a series of epidemic typhus experiments, the first to be carried out in Experimentation Block 46. Otto Schmidt was among the "controls," i.e. he was infected with epidemic typhus so that the "normal course" of the disease could be studied. By the end of the experiment,

which lasted from October 15 to November 20, 1942, four inmates had died in the "control." Otto Schmidt was killed immediately upon conclusion of the experiment. According to the later testimony of inmate nurse Gustav Steigerwald: "The control group consisted of 20 inmates, of whom 17 were killed in the infirmary by Dr. Hoven by means of injection." Otto Schmidt never saw his daughter, who was born shortly after his arrest. Along with his life

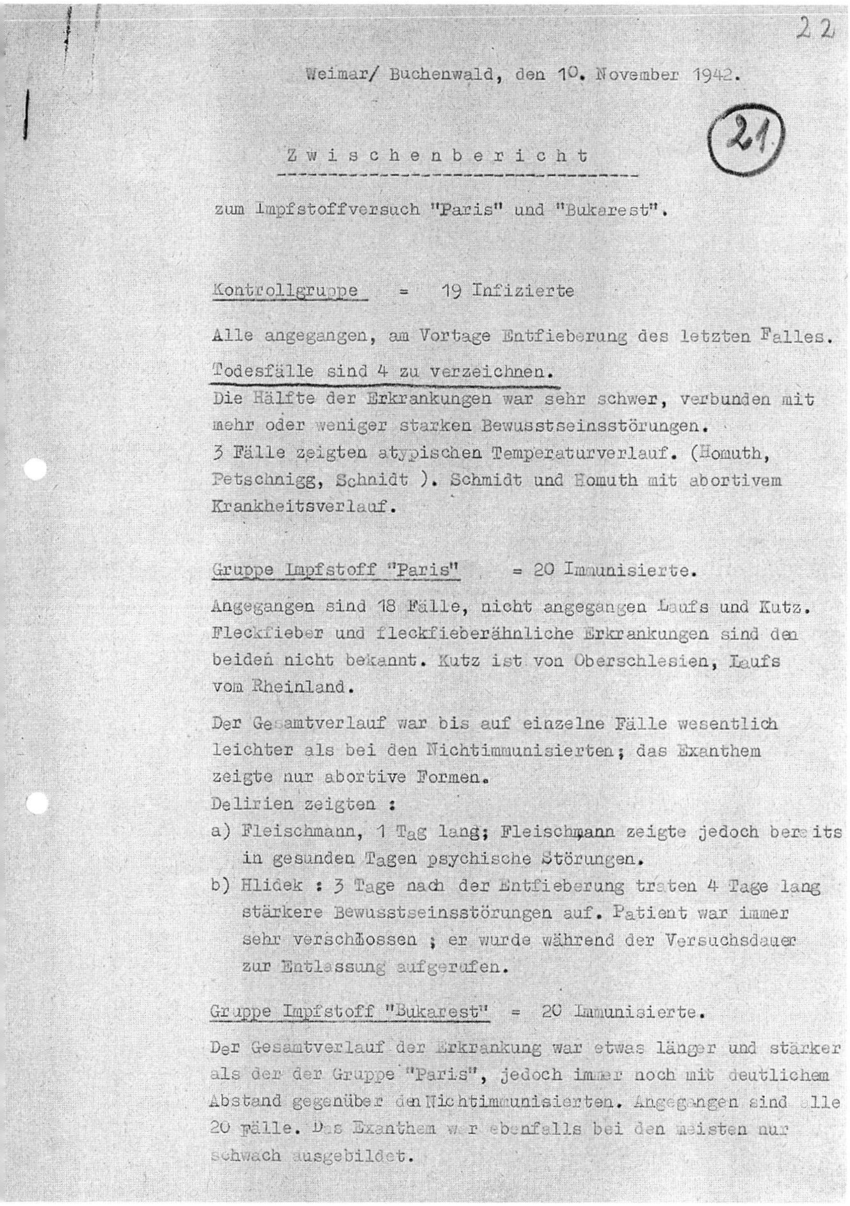

2 2

Weimar/ Buchenwald, den 1⁰. November 1942.

Z w i s c h e n b e r i c h t
----

zum Impfstoffversuch "Paris" und "Bukarest".

Kontrollgruppe   =   19 Infizierte

Alle angegangen, am Vortage Entfieberung des letzten Falles.
Todesfälle sind 4 zu verzeichnen.
Die Hälfte der Erkrankungen war sehr schwer, verbunden mit
mehr oder weniger starken Bewusstseinsstörungen.
3 Fälle zeigten atypischen Temperaturverlauf. (Homuth,
Petschnigg, Schmidt). Schmidt und Homuth mit abortivem
Krankheitsverlauf.

Gruppe Impfstoff "Paris"   = 20 Immunisierte.

Angegangen sind 18 Fälle, nicht angegangen Laufs und Kutz.
Fleckfieber und fleckfieberähnliche Erkrankungen sind den
beiden nicht bekannt. Kutz ist von Oberschlesien, Laufs
vom Rheinland.

Der Gesamtverlauf war bis auf einzelne Fälle wesentlich
leichter als bei den Nichtimmunisierten; das Exanthem
zeigte nur abortive Formen.
Delirien zeigten :
a) Fleischmann, 1 Tag lang; Fleischmann zeigte jedoch bereits
   in gesunden Tagen psychische Störungen.
b) Hlidek : 3 Tage nach der Entfieberung traten 4 Tage lang
   stärkere Bewusstseinsstörungen auf. Patient war immer
   sehr verschlossen ; er wurde während der Versuchsdauer
   zur Entlassung aufgerufen.

Gruppe Impfstoff "Bukarest"   = 20 Immunisierte.

Der Gesamtverlauf der Erkrankung war etwas länger und stärker
als der der Gruppe "Paris", jedoch immer noch mit deutlichem
Abstand gegenüber den Nichtimmunisierten. Angegangen sind alle
20 Fälle. Das Exanthem war ebenfalls bei den meisten nur
schwach ausgebildet.

Illustration 61:
Interim report of the epidemic typhus experimental station at Buchenwald Concentration Camp, Nov. 10, 1942
Otto Schmidt "with abortive [radically worsening] course of illness." *Source: Thüringisches Hauptstaatsarchiv, Weimar*

companion Erna Lauenburger (the character "Unku" in the children's book *Ede und Unku* by Grete Weiskopf), the little girl died in Auschwitz in 1943.

Alfred Hönemann, the block senior of the "Gypsy Block" – the barrack of the Sinti and Romani – recalls:

"In the winter of 1939/40 many of the gypsies suffered frostbite on their feet, hands and ears. In the sub-camps they were often exposed to the weather, and the flimsy inmates' uniforms offered them little protection. They went to the inmates' infirmary frequently; there they had to take alternating hot and cold baths and many underwent amputations of their legs and other limbs. The emaciated inmates could not find the strength to keep their bodies in motion. I remember well how we carried several inmates to the infirmary after every evening roll call. The demand there was so high that the majority did not get a bed. The gypsies were given the floor of the washroom and the toilet room to lie on. There they lay until the following morning. They did not survive the night and those who were still alive were sent to the hereafter with Epiran [He meant Evipan. – Author] injections administered by the 'angel of destruction' Dr. Hans [sic] Eisele, SS Hauptscharführer Wilhelm or Dr. Wagner. At Buchenwald there was a period in which no gypsy dared go to the infirmary for treatment. Once the little twelve-year-old, black-headed gypsy boy Alex Karoly, who worked for me in barrack room duty, came to me and asked me: 'Block Senior, none of my comrades will go to the infirmary anymore because no-one ever comes back from it. I think we gypsies will all have to die in Buchenwald.'"

Jewish Inmates

From early 1937 until the spring of 1938 the Gestapo committed inmates of Jewish heritage exclusively to Dachau Concentration Camp. Most of them had been arrested for political reasons. So-called "Mischlinge" ("half-breeds"), for example the lawyer Dr. Hans Litten (who had been brought to Buchenwald from Lichtenburg Concentration Camp in 1937 as a political inmate),

were transferred to Dachau by the SS in the autumn of the same year. Litten, who had already brought animosity upon himself by acting as a lawyer for NS opponents before 1933, died in Dachau in 1938 under mysterious circumstances.

In 1938 the NS regime began to apply terror to accelerate the economic elimination and **expulsion** of the Jewish population. During that year, the mass committal of German and Austrian Jews to Buchenwald began and reached its peak. Between April and December 1938 the detective police and the Gestapo committed 13,687 Jews. Because of the fact that arrest often served the exclusive purpose of forcing the person to relinquish his property and emigrate, release from the camp was often possible upon presentation of an exit visa. In 1938 alone, 10,012 Jews were released from the camp under this condition. Of the approximately 17,000 Jews committed between 1937 and the end of 1941, over 11,600 were released. Although they were usually not long in custody, the Jewish inmates suffered the highest proportion of deaths.

Following the first arrests made at the end of April 1938 within the context of "Operation Work-Shy, Reich," the SS of Buchenwald introduced the inmate category "Jews" as a sub-group of all other categories. The first Jews committed at this point in time as well as the 1,256 Jewish "ASR inmates" of the "June Operation" became the favourite target of SS terror. "They are extending the working time indefinitely; the sadistic tormenting of the Jews exceeds everything we have seen until now," recalls Moritz Zahnwetzer. The 2,395 Austrian and German Jews who arrived from Dachau Concentration Camp in the last week of September 1938 were the next to become acquainted with this terror. The majority of them were Austrian and German political inmates. But the transports also brought 113 "race defilers," 51 so-called emigrants and 26 so-called expulsion inmates.

The category of "**race defilers**" consisted of Jews who had violated the prohibition against sexual relations with non-Jewish women which had gone into effect with the Nuremberg Laws. Usually they had already been penalised for this offence with prison sentences before their committal to a concentration camp. Life companionships and relationships were sometimes criminalised even when they had existed long before the Nuremberg Laws went into effect, as in the case of the arrest and sentencing of **Ferdinand (Faybusch) Itzkewitsch**. Itzkewitsch had already lived with his companion in a marriage-like relationship for over a decade; they had a son who was twelve years old when the Nuremberg Laws went into effect. A victim of denunciation, he was convicted in 1936 of "race defilement" by the First Great Criminal Division of the Hildesheim Regional Court. After he had served his sentence, the Gestapo arrested him in November 1938 and took him to Buchenwald where, like all inmates of the "race defiler" category, he was immediately assigned to a delinquent company, where he stayed until his murder in the Sonnenstein (Pirna) extermination facility.

In 1938, the "**emigrants**" were an inmates' group consisting primarily of Jews who had been sent back or extradited to Germany. They were considered a risk to political security. As in the case of the primarily non-Jewish "**expulsion inmates**," the placement of the "emigrants" in concentration camp custody was intended to force the inmates to leave the country as quickly as possible.

The Jews were the only group to be concentrated by the SS camp command in separate living and working areas, and to be subjected to particularly cruel harassments, collective punishment and the heaviest forced labour. The Jews were also the first to be affected when the living conditions in the camp worsened radically due to overcrowding. The SS often purposely brought about states of emergency in the Jewish barracks. The SS doctors furthermore frequently banned the Jews from medical treatment or, in 1938/39, transferred them to a "Judenrevier" (Jews' infirmary) which was primitive in every respect.

The "**Judenrevier**" was established in December 1938 when the SS moved the in-patient medical treatment for Jews from the inmates' infirmary to Barrack 2 adjoining the muster ground. This facility officially employed four inmate nurses and

Illustration 62: Faybusch Itzkewitsch (1891-1941), mid 1930s
Source: Buchenwaldarchiv, Weimar

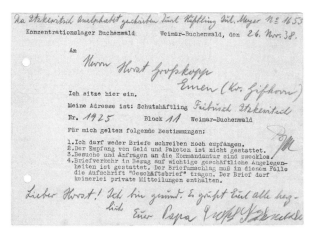

Illustration 63: First letter written by Faybusch Itzkewitsch from the camp, Nov. 26, 1938
Source: Buchenwaldarchiv, Weimar

Illustration 64:
Document
concerning
transport of urn,
Aug. 20, 1941
*Source: Buchen-
waldarchiv, Weimar*

four to six Jewish inmates as corpse bearers. In the first inmates' infirmary quarterly report of 1939 it is described as a block "in which exclusively Jews receive inpatient treatment." Stefan Heymann reports:

"Naturally, less medication was allotted to the Jews' infirmary than was otherwise the case in the normal infirmary. The situation was especially unpleasant for the Jewish comrades who required operations and were brought to the Jews' infirmary in all weathers to have them performed. Many contracted pneumonia and other illnesses in this manner. Except in the initial phase, the care of the patients was left exclusively to Jewish nurses and Jewish inmate doctors. Whereas no inmate doctors were permitted to work in the main infirmary, Jewish inmate doctors were employed in the Jews' infirmary for the simple reason that SS doctors naturally did not attend to Jews."

In 1939, after it had been in existence for about half a year, the "Jews' infirmary" was closed down. Block 2 remained the "invalid ward" of the inmates' infirmary.

Under Camp Commander Koch, open hatred of Jews was advantageous to the advancement of one's career within the SS, and there were many block and labour detachment officers who attracted attention to themselves by abusing Jews. Even in the otherwise rather laconic punitive reports, there were frequent references to "Mistjuden" (shitty Jews), "Saujuden" (Jewish pigs) and "Stinkjuden" (stinking Jews). One of the SS's favourite harassments was "shit-bearing," the transport of vats full of excrement from the latrines and the sewage plant to the garden. Inmates of the "4711" labour detachment (named after the eau de cologne), to which particularly Jewish intellectuals and artists were assigned,

Percentage of Jewish inmates					
Date	7/1/1938	8/30/1939	7/31/1940	7/31/1941	5/31/1942
Number	1,272	750	1,355	1,463	831
Total inmates	7,723	5,382	7,270	8,582	7,601
Percentage	16	14	19	17	11

scooped out the latrines with jam buckets and even with their bare hands.

In November 1938, following the pogroms carried out in Germany and Austria, the camp temporarily accommodated some 13,000 Jewish inmates. Many of them were released by mid 1939. For the others, the camp was a death trap once war had broken out. The same was true for the 1,035 stateless Jews from Vienna and hundreds of Polish, Dutch, German and Czech Jews committed to the camp during the initial years of the war. Only 114 Jews were released between 1940 and 1942. In 1942 the SS killed about one third of the remaining Jews in the "euthanasia" extermination facility in Bernburg and deported the majority of the others to Auschwitz.

Illustration 65: Jura Soyfer (1912-1939)
Source: Dokumentationsarchiv des Österreichischen Widerstandes, Vienna

Austrians

The first foreign inmates to be demonstratively classified as "Reich Germans" were the Austrians in the Dachau transports of September 1938. These persons of primarily Jewish origin had been systematically arrested during the weeks following the occupation of Austria. There were many eminent artists, politics, writers, scholars, scientists and members of the Jewish community of Vienna among them – for example the writer Jura Soyfer, the two well-known actors / cabaret artistes Paul Morgan and Fritz Grünbaum and the social democratic politician and publicist Benedikt Kautsky. The talented young **Jura Soyfer** died in Buchenwald. Julius Freund, another Austrian, recalls:

"His main task was to wrap up the dead in blankets and, with the help of other inmates, carry them to the camp gate on a stretcher… The dead human cargo was then crammed into longitudinal wooden crates, covered with sawdust, the cover fastened down with a simple hook and everything loaded onto a lorry for transport to the Weimar crematorium. … But one day something happened – something that was unfortunately to be expected as a result of this work, during which Soyfer touched the corpses with his bare hands. He became infected with a disease that for him would be fatal. Exhibiting all the signs of typhus, he collapsed

Illustration 66: Paul Morgan (1886-1938)
Source: Dokumentationsarchiv des Österreichischen Widerstandes, Vienna

among his dead and had to be put to bed with a high fever. Cruel vagary of fate! The very same hour, lying on his sickbed, he was informed that he was to be released from the camp to follow his parents, who had emigrated to the U.S.A."

Bruno Heilig reports on the death of **Paul Morgan**:

"In Block 16, a block officer found food in the beds. The block is ordered to carry out a pack drill. It is raining; a bitter wind is blowing. A

79

man steps out of the back row, removes his cap and walks unsteadily toward the block officer supervising the pack drill. 'I am ill – I have a fever…'… The block officer chases him back. The block drills until the whistle sounds. Paul Morgan is carried back on a stretcher. In a state of agony, he is taken to the infirmary. The camp command permits his colleagues Leopoldi and Grünbaum to carry the dead Morgan from the infirmary to the gate."

In early October 1938 the inmates from the municipal police prisons of Vienna arrived at Buchenwald, among them a number of former high-ranking government officials. The Dachau transports of a year later, at the outbreak of war, also contained many Austrians. In the course of the year 1939, the number of Austrians decreased substantially due to releases and deaths. After the war had begun, the last large transport from Vienna containing stateless Jews arrived at the camp; most of their number died within a short period of time.

In 1938-39 the Austrians played a decisive role in determining the intellectual atmosphere among the political inmates. The artists among them became active dur-

Buchenwald Song

Wenn der Tag erwacht, eh' die Sonne lacht,	*[When the day awakens, ere the sun smiles,*
die Kolonnen ziehn zu des Tages Mühn	*The gangs march out to the day's toils*
hinein in den grauenden Morgen.	*Into the breaking dawn.*
Und der Wald ist schwarz und der Himmel rot,	*And the forest is black and the heavens red,*
und wir tragen im Brotsack ein Stückchen Brot	*In our sacks we carry a piece of bread*
und im Herzen, im Herzen die Sorgen.	*And in our hearts, in our hearts – sorrow.*
O Buchenwald, ich kann dich nicht vergessen,	*O Buchenwald, I cannot forget you,*
weil du mein Schicksal bist.	*For you are my fate.*
Wer dich verließ, der kann es erst ermessen,	*He who has left you, he alone can measure*
wie wundervoll die Freiheit ist!	*How wonderful freedom is!*
O Buchenwald, wir jammern nicht und klagen,	*O Buchenwald, we do not whine and wail,*
und was auch unser Schicksal sei,	*And whatever our fate,*
wir wollen trotzdem ja zum Leben sagen,	*We will say yes to life,*
denn einmal kommt der Tag: dann sind wir frei!	*For the day will come when we are free!*
Und das Blut ist heiß und das Mädel fern,	*And my blood is hot and my sweetheart far away,*
und der Wind singt leis, und ich hab' sie so gern,	*And the wind sings softly, and I love her so.*
wenn treu sie, ja, treu sie nur bliebe!	*If only, yes, if only she stays true!*
Und die Steine sind hart, aber fest unser Tritt,	*And the stones are hard, but our stride is firm,*
und wir tragen die Picken und Spaten mit	*And we carry our picks and spades*
und im Herzen, im Herzen die Liebe.	*And in our hearts, in our hearts – love.*
O Buchenwald, ich kann…	*O Buchenwald, I cannot forget you …*
Und die Nacht ist kurz, und der Tag ist so lang,	*And the night is short and the day so long,*
doch ein Lied erklingt, das die Heimat sang:	*Yet a song rings out that was sung at home:*
wir lassen den Mut uns nicht rauben!	*We won't be robbed of our courage!*
Halte Schritt, Kamerad, und verlier nicht den Mut,	*Keep in step, comrade, and don't lose heart*
denn wir tragen den Willen zum Leben im Blut	*For in our blood we carry the will to live*
und im Herzen, im Herzen den Glauben.	*And in our hearts, in our hearts – faith.*
O Buchenwald, ich kann…	*O Buchenwald, I cannot forget you …]*

Text: Fritz Löhner-Beda, Melody: Hermann Leopoldi

ing idle hours. Jewish doctors from Vienna illegally trained the inmate medical orderlies, and the authors of the **"Buchenwald Song"** – the writer Dr. Fritz Löhner-Beda and the composer Hermann Leopoldi – were also Austrians. The song was written and composed in December 1938 and came to be sung officially when the labour gangs marched out of the camp. Its text instilled courage in many inmates.

Polish Inmates

The percentage of foreign inmates in Buchenwald rose sharply after the outbreak of war, then remained relatively constant until 1941. More than half of the altogether 4,514 Poles deported to Buchenwald by the end of 1941 were arrested immediately following occupation in September 1939. The committal of the first Poles at the end of that month occasioned their introduction as an inmate category in the camp records.

The approximately 2,100 Poles who arrived on the transports of October 15/16, 1939, came exclusively from areas which had belonged to Germany until the 1919 Treaty of Versailles – Poznán, West Prussia – and from the industrial area of Upper Silesia. Many of them died during the first months; others were transported to Mauthausen Concentration Camp in early March 1940. The 474 Poles, among them 35 clergymen, who arrived on August 16, 1940 from the notorious reception camp Fort VII in Poznán had been arrested in the newly formed "Reichsgau" (Reich region) Wartheland. Not until August 22, 1940 did the SS bring the first transport of 622 Poles from the so-called "Generalgouvernement" to the camp. Many Poles were also arrested by the Gestapo in Germany for breach of employment contract or re-

sistance against / violation of the regulations issued for Polish forced labourers in Germany. The Gestapo brought a certain percentage of them to the camp solely for the purpose of killing them.

Dutch Inmates

In 1940, German troops invaded and occupied the Netherlands. On July 21/22, 1940 the commander of the Security Police and the SD for the occupied Dutch territories committed the first 232 **Dutch hostages** to Buchenwald. This number included 14 women, who were transferred to Ravensbrück Concentration Camp. By October 1940, a further 124 Dutchmen had joined them. The group consisted primarily of government officials who had been arrested in retaliation for the internment of Germans in Dutch-occupied India and deported to a concentration camp as a deterrent. Despite privileged conditions such as separate accommodations, permission to receive packages and exemption from work, lives were lost within this group as well. Its survivors stayed in Buchenwald until mid November 1941.

On October 22, 1940 the Reich Commissioner for the Netherlands, Arthur Seyss-Inquart, issued the first drastic anti-Jewish ordinance, which in many respects resembled the Nuremberg race laws with regard to content. Encouraged by the ruthless manner in which the German occupying power proceeded, mobs of NSB (Nationaal-Socialische Beweging) supporters invaded the Jewish residential districts of Amsterdam on February 9, 1941. Within the context of a defensive measure, a member of the regular police was killed. In retaliation, the Senior SS and Police Commander, SS Brigadeführer Rauter, had 400

Percentage of Poles*				
Date	2/28/1940	7/31/1940	7/31/1941	5/31/1942
Number	1,446	643	1,752	1,065
Total inmates	10,323	7,270	8,582	7,601
Percentage	14	9	20	14
				*not including Polish Jews

81

Illustration 67:
Arrest of Jewish
residents in
Amsterdam,
Feb. 22, 1941
"Penal round-up" to
counter the
resistance of
Amsterdam Jews.
Following the
transport of the
arrestees to
Buchenwald
Concentration
Camp, tens of
thousands of Dutch
people participated
in a general strike.
*Source: Rijksinstituut
voor Oorlogs-
documentatie,
Amsterdam*

Jewish men between the ages of twenty and thirty-five arrested. The public announcement of their deportation to a German concentration camp brought about a wave of strikes in which tens of thousands of Dutch people in many parts of the country participated, particularly in the vicinity of Amsterdam.

Of the 400 **Dutch Jews** arrested, 389 arrived in Buchenwald on February 28, 1941. They were assigned to Barracks 16 and 17. Three days later the SS put them to hard labour in load-bearing and construction labour detachments. Despite their initially healthy constitutions – among the deportees there was a group of dock and port workers – physical deterioration soon set in as a result of nutrition shock, cold and dampness. Pneumonia and diarrhoea occurred frequently. Gustav Herzog, the Jewish block senior, recalls:

"Because the Dutch Jews were labourers, the political inmates sought to protect them, and their liquidation was progressing too slowly in the eyes of the camp command. The camp physician at that time, the notorious injection doctor Eisele, therefore ordered that no Dutch Jews be admitted to the infirmary. Those already in the infirmary were either put out onto the street or, in cases of serious illness, killed by poisonous injections. Outpatient treatment was severely prohibited.

These measures led to altogether intolerable conditions in the two blocks housing the Dutch Jews, 16 and 17. All of the Dutchmen were supposed to go to work – no mercy was shown – but there were persons among them whose legs and arms were covered with festering wounds or half decayed. During block inspections they were hidden at the greatest peril; doctors among the inmates obtained several instruments with the active help of political

Illustration 68: Photo, taken by an SS photo correspondent, which appeared in the magazine *Das Schwarze Korps*, June 26, 1941
This picture, part of a series, shows the Jews from Amsterdam after their arrival in Mauthausen. The original text accompanying the series: *"Lucratively related. The pictures in this series are neither the result of many years of collecting nor photographs from the wax and freak cabinet, nor are they pictures saved from the cleansing of the German nation of Jewish criminals that took place several years ago. These pictures show exclusively former Dutch 'labour leaders' who – on grounds of considerable crimes – are now literally to be lucratively exploited, this time through involuntary labour. Not too long ago, they will have had quite a different picture of their "business future".*
Source: Sammlung Gedenkstätte Buchenwald, Weimar

inmates of the main infirmary, and operated in the nighttime hours, adhering to the strictest precautionary measures and often with the most rudimentary means. In the most serious cases, help could not be provided with the means available, and the smell of festering, decaying wounds soon became unbearable."

The SS camp administration supplied no footwear appropriate for work in stone and mud, and foot diseases were rampant. *"Our feet got sore and swollen, and every step was anguish and nearly everyone had to seek medical treatment,"* recalls Meyer Nebig. *"One day the infirmary was closed to the Dutch Jews. All such Jews already in the in-firmary were thrown out; new arrivals were not admitted."* In May the SS transferred the entire group to Mauthausen Concentration Camp, where none of them would survive.

"Protectorate Inmates"

Following the occupation of Czechoslovakia and the establishment of the "Protectorate of Bohemia-Moravia," some 700 Czech officials, scientists, clergymen and politicians were arrested and brought to Buchenwald in late September 1939 with the transports from Dachau. They were re-

Illustration 70: Cardboard Gestapo tag for the transport of Bohumir Hendrych to Buchenwald (attached to clothing), 1939
Catalogue 3/1
Source: Buchenwaldarchiv, Weimar

Illustration 69: Bohumir Hendrych (1894)
Czech political inmate, 1939-1945, one of the 756 so-called protectorate inmates committed after the outbreak of war in 1939.
Source: Buchenwaldarchiv, Weimar

Illustration 71:
Postcard sent to his daughter from Buchenwald
Catalogue 3/1
Source: Buchenwaldarchiv, Weimar

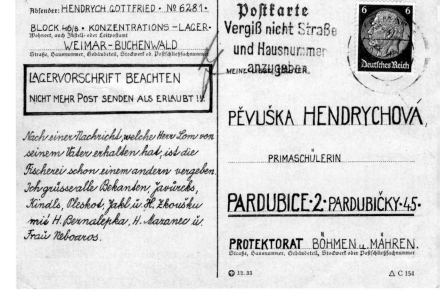

ferred to as "protectorate inmates." While the Jews in this group were from the beginning subjected to the conditions under which all Jewish inmates lived in the camp, the non-Jews enjoyed a special status for a time. They were not required to work, their heads were not shorn and they had a number of other privileges. With the January 1940 prohibition against the receipt of packages, the SS began reducing these privileges until, by 1942, they had been completely abolished.

Prisoners of War

The prisoners of war turned over to the SS by the Wehrmacht had a special status among the foreign inmates. Their committal had been carried out in connection with the implementation of measures to repress resistance in the prisoner-of-war camps, the supply of manpower and intentions of extermination. On April 18, 1940 the Kassel Gestapo transferred 56 Polish military clergymen from the officers' POW camp in Rothenburg-Fulda to Buchenwald. They lost their status as prisoners of war upon entering the camp. In early July 1942, 51 of them were taken to Dachau Concentration Camp by order of the Reich Department of Security.

In 1941 the SS demanded manpower in the form of thousands of Soviet prisoners of war, turned over by the Wehrmacht in the autumn of 1941. Two thousand of them came to Buchenwald from POW camp Stalag X D (Wietzendorf / Hamburg military district) on October 18. They were in such a miserable condition that over 600 of them died within a year as a result of exhaustion and disease. The SS surrounded the wooden Barracks 1, 7 and 13 of the westernmost row of barracks with barbed wire, thus establishing a self-contained prisoner-of-war camp. A BV inmate was selected as POW camp senior. Administratively, the prisoners of war were still under the control of the Wehrmacht POW system. Beginning in 1942 they were forced to perform the heaviest labour tasks.

Illustration 72: Alexander Makeev (1920-1942), during harvest (far right), 1939. A. Makeev died in Buchenwald on Jan. 1, 1942.
Catalogue 3/37
Loan from Iranda Efimovna Makeeva, Grodno

Illustration 73: Alexander Makeev's student ID, 1938
Catalogue 3/37
Loan from Iranda Efimovna Makeeva, Grodno

Life in the barracks

"I take a closer look at one of the 'black barracks.' In the stuffy dayroom the inmates are crowded in even more tightly than in our stone block. I observe that communal life proceeds there with less discipline. … The sleeping accommodations in the black barracks consist merely of wooden plank beds with bare sacks of straw on them; a wool blanket lies rolled up at the foot end. Three or four inmates are compelled to lie on two straw sacks, whereas in my block, the political block, everyone at least has his own bed."

Walter Poller

The Inmates' Social Circumstances

To the extent that it was determined by the SS, daily life in the camp was completely unpredictable for most inmates: the struggle to survive was just as much a part of the concentration camp concept as the hierarchy designed by the SS. According to this hierarchy, the Jewish inmates had the least chance of survival and all groups labelled "inferior" were demoted from the outset. If the term 'camp society' can be used at all in view of these circumstances, then in the sense of a forced society of ever-widening social extremes. At its apex was the inmate functionary and at its base the so-called "Muselmann": camp jargon for inmates who had lost the last remnants of their will to survive and entered the transitional stage between life and death.

The majority of inmates lived in rudimentary **wooden barracks** 53 metres long, slightly over 8 metres wide and 2.65 metres high, so-called "blocks" which were as poorly isolated against cold and heat as they were inadequately ventilated. The entrance was at the middle of the barrack, as were the toilets and washing facilities which, due to the constant water shortage, hardly had a function until 1939. To the right and left were the "wings," A and B. Each wing had a dayroom of 64 m² and a sleeping room of 96 m² and was intended for 85 persons. The furnishings included narrow, usually triple-decker metal beds in the sleeping room as well as lockers, tables and benches in the dayroom.

At the end of 1937 the camp consisted of eighteen of these blocks; in the years that followed, thousands of human beings were jammed into between twenty-five and twenty-eight wooden barracks. From approximately mid 1938 on, the **classification of the blocks** essentially corresponded to the various inmate categories. There were the blocks of the political inmates, the BV inmates and the ASR inmates, the block of the Jehovah's Witnesses, the blocks of the Dutch hostages and of the "protectorate inmates." In the initial years, the SS continually reassigned the blocks to different categories. Only the Jewish inmates were completely isolated in their own "Jewish blocks," always wooden barracks of the type described above.

The first five two-storey **stone blocks** were occupied in August 1938 by non-Jewish political inmates. Each of the stone blocks, of which ten more were built before the outbreak of war, had four wings and was intended for a total of at least 340 inmates. They offered a certain amount of protection from the harsh and changeable weather on the north slope of the Ettersberg.

In the early years, phases of catastrophic **overcrowding** alternated with periods of tolerable inmate strength in rapid succession. In the summer of 1938 the camp was so overcrowded that some 500 Jewish inmates arrested within the framework of "Operation Work-Shy, Reich" were jammed into a sheep stall on the northern edge of the camp. The arrival of Jewish inmates from Dachau Concentration Camp in the autumn of the same year caused the number of occupants in the Jewish barracks to double temporarily to 300 persons each. In

Illustration 74: Henri Pieck: "The Interior of a Barrack in the Big Camp," charcoal drawing, 1943/1945
Source: Henri Pieck: Buchenwald. Reproduktionen nach seinen Zeichnungen aus dem Konzentrationslager, Berlin, Potsdam, 1949. Sammlung Gedenkstätte Buchenwald, Weimar

these situations, many inmates slept on the floor of the dayroom. The special camps set up after the anti-Jewish pogroms of 1938 and following the outbreak of war consisted merely of wooden sheds or tents.

Irrespective of the actual circumstances, the camp command boasted to Concentration Camp Inspection of greater and greater admission capacities, particularly in 1938. In mid June 1938, a supplement to the preventive custody camp report stated that "the K. L. Bu. normally holds 6,000 inmates; in view of the special circumstances: 7,500 inmates." Two weeks later, a similar supplement claimed that "10,000 inmates can be accommodated by the preventive custody camp K. L. Bu.," and on November 28, 1938: "20,000 inmates can be accommodated in the Buchenwald Preventive Custody Camp." Buchenwald, the concentration camp with the most humiliating living conditions and least number of accommodations, recorded 20,122 admissions in the year 1938 – by far the sharpest inmate population increase of the three existing concentration camps.

Each of the periods of overcrowding brought about by the SS had an immediate effect on the provisioning of the inmates, the hygienic conditions and the terror which prevailed particularly in the emergency accommodations. While the average **daily ration** consisted of no more than some 350-500 grams of bread, a litre of thin

87

Illustration 75:
Camp street
between stone
barracks, 1943
*Source: Musée de
la Résistance et de
la Déportation,
Besançon
(SS Photo Album:
"Buchenwald
Jahresende 1943")*

soup and a bit of margarine, sausage or cheese, the SS often reduced it to half that amount in the emergency quarters. From 1940 on, the provision of the inmates with staple foods was based on standard guidelines established by the Reich Minister of Food and Agriculture or the corresponding offices of the SS Department of Economic Management / Construction and the SS Department of Economic Administration and passed on to the camp commanders in writing. The actual rations only seldom corresponded to these guidelines, however, and most of the inmates suffered continual **starvation**. Even in the pre-war period, during the first of the famines provoked by the SS in late 1937, Commander Koch demanded the tightening of mail censorship so that the word hunger would not reach the outside. Richard Seifert recalls:

"An inmate's daily ration consisted of cabbage soup and approx. four to five hundred gr [ams] of bread with a spoonful of jam flung onto it. There was no way this little bit of food could suffice for a person doing heavy labour. I myself would have been able to devour one to two kilos of bread in a few minutes. Many comrades controlled themselves and put a bit of bread on the shelf where their food bowl was kept. But many ate all of their bread the

same evening – so hungry they could not resist the temptation. One morning, just after we were woken, a comrade called out: 'My bread is gone!' In other words, there was a thief among us. This happened repeatedly in the days that followed. Who was it? But one night, with the aid of a trick, the culprit was caught. He got quite a thrashing from his fellow inmates and the block officer (SS) found out about it. Everyone now avoided the inmate (thief) and he was transferred to another block. He could count on a delinquent company and the quarry. ...

One evening, shortly after roll call, the camp siren suddenly sounded – alarm! What had happened? There was an inmate in the strip (cheval-de-frise) along the electr.[ically] charged fence.

The SS guard in the nearest watchtower shot him – he aimed poorly – the inmate couldn't die – he died only after several shots had been fired – the alarm was over. This inmate was the bread thief from our block."

Care packages from the inmates' families were prohibited throughout the entire initial period. Inmates could have thirty Reichsmark, sometimes more, transferred to them monthly; the inmates' funds office managed this money and permitted withdrawals for canteen purchases. Initially the

88

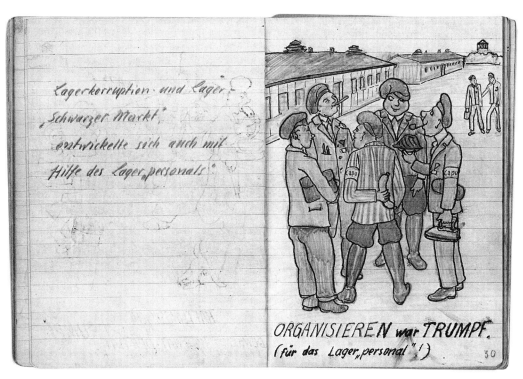

Illustration 76: Kurt Dittmar: "Organising was Trump,"watercolour, 1945
From the notebook "Wir und die anderen." By Kurt Dittmar, political inmate in Buchenwald, 1939-1942, produced after his liberation from Dachau in 1945.
Source: Buchenwaldarchiv, Weimar

"block purchasers" collected the **money** and made purchases in the SS canteen; in January 1942 an inmates' canteen was also opened in the camp. Money played a major role in social relations during the camp construction years. Particularly after the committal of inmates from the middle classes of society in the autumn of 1938, it was used to bribe the capos and block seniors for better sleeping and working places. Inmates who regularly received money from the outside and were thus in a position to make "donations" to the SS or to inmate functionaries could buy themselves protection and integration in a group. The constant shortage of provisions resulted in the development of an illegal barter system in which the products purchased in the inmates' canteen – cigarettes, clothing, shoes, etc. – continually changed hands.

In mid 1938, during one of the earlier phases of overcrowding, there were already inmates who, in their desperation, ate refuse or stole bread from others. According to the report written by the International Camp Committee in 1945:

"It was in this phase that the term "Tonnenadler" [rubbish bin eagles] was coined. Those were inmates who, driven by hunger and lack of restraint, plundered rubbish crates and dumps. In the interest of the entire camp, measures had to be taken against these demoralised inmates. In that period bread theft also became more frequent, and a very rigorous camp judiciary developed as a preventive measure."

Like other terms in the camp jargon, "**Tonnenadler**" and "**Lagerjustiz**" (camp judiciary) described everyday community life with words which did not exist or possessed entirely different meanings outside the camp. "Lagerjustiz" (also called "Feme" [vehmic justice]) referred to the unwritten laws of the camp, usually enforced in an ar-

89

bitrary and brutal manner, depending on the general degree of privation at a given time. Bread thieves, alleged informers, corrupt or brutal inmate functionaries and "Tonnenadler" were excluded, beaten, even lynched. Such proceedings, which arose from the circumstances, required no moral justification in the camp. In connection with Buchenwald, Benedikt Kautsky speaks of the *"development of a veritable judicial*

organisation, which performed its functions quite in the manner of a medieval Vehmic-court. Its centre was in the infirmary and it was controlled by the Communist stratum which ruled the camp. It arose within the context of a struggle against the greens, who constantly attempted to regain the position of power which had been wrested from them in early 1939."

Other camp jargon terms were:

4711	(perfume brand)	latrine cleaner labour detachment
Abgang	departure	inmate deleted from the camp records: dead persons, those transferred elsewhere or released
abhängen	to unhitch	to exclude a person from a group
abkochen	to boil down	to obtain things illegally by taking clever advantage of a situation; to obtain extra food
abspritzen	to shoot down	to kill by means of injection
Achtzehn!	eighteen!	call warning of approach of a capo or SS guard
Alm	mountain pasture	TB isolation ward; place of murder
Buchenwalder Ananas	Buchenwald pineapple	Turnip cooked in turnip leaves
Erdkunde	geography	term for crawling across the muster ground on one's belly
Grüner	green	inmate with a green badge
Himmelfahrts-kommando	suicide mission	deportation with fatal outcome
Kretiner	cretin	mentally disturbed and physically deteriorated inmate
Lampenbauer	lamp builder	someone who accidentally or intentionally talks about something that is supposed to be kept secret
Latrinen-Parolen	latrine slogans	implausible rumours
Muselmann	zombie	inmate who has given up his will to live
organisieren	organise	to obtain important articles on the camp black market or by means of theft
Prominenz	celebrities	better-dressed and better-provided-for camp functionaries
Roter	red	inmate with a red badge
Schwarzer	black	inmate classified as "work-shy"
singende Pferde	singing horses	gang of Jewish inmates forced to sing while hauling heavily laden wagons
singender Wald	singing forest	forest to the north of the barracks where "tree-hanging" took place
über den Rost gehen	to cross the grate	to be taken to the crematorium, to die
umlegen	to lay down	to kill
Vogel suchen	to search for a bird	SS expression for the search for an inmate who has escaped or is absent from roll call
Wikingersalat	Viking salad	salad of boiled turnips and carrots with whale oil mayonnaise
Zaunkönig	wren (lit.: "fence king")	one who commits suicide on electric barbed-wire fence
Zinker	–	traitor, spy
Zugang	new admission	newly committed inmate

105	Radinger, Eduard	10,-	6483	Burstyn, Josef	✓	10,-
589	Lieser, Arthur	10,-	6471	Reismann, Edmund	✓	10,-
1066	Kautsky, Benedikt	10,-	6468	Schwarz, Robert	✓	10,-
1273	Kornitzer, Berthold	10,-	6892	Lustig, Alfred	✓	10,-
2272	Taussig, Emil	15,-	6975	Herschmann, Otto	✓	10,-
2280	Bondy, Josef	15,-	7044	Filgut, Max	✓	10,-
2721	Tysson, Chaim	10,-	7125	Herschmann, Franz	✓	10,-
3117	Lindenbaum, Jakob	10,-	7182	Denemark, Jankel	✓	10,-
3265	Uhrmacher, Salomon	10,-	7192	Heller, Heinrich	✓	10,-
3536	Majerowicz, Hermann	10,-	7222	Igelberg, Simon	✓	10,-
3603	Klapholz, Salomon	10,-	7305	Katz, Juda	✓	10,-
3699	Klahr, Felix	10,-	7628	Klement, Paul	✓	15,-
3762	Stiel, Joachim	10,-	7646	Schorr, Emil	✓	10,-
4699	Taussig, Leopold	10,-	7700	Moravec, Wolf	✓	10,-
6142	Adel, Fritz	10,-	7743	Tischler, Moses	✓	10,-
6200	Taussig, Richard	10,-	7785	Sternbach, Maier	✓	10,-
		170,-				335,-

Illustration 77: Money collection in Block 22, Feb. 11, 1941
It has not been established whether the money was donated voluntarily or whether this was one of the frequent compulsory collections through which the SS extorted money, primarily from Jewish inmates, under various pretexts. The occupants of Block 22 were Jewish.
Source: Thüringisches Hauptstaatsarchiv, Weimar

The first **inmates' clothing** in Buchenwald consisted of old, worn-out police uniforms. The blue-and-grey or blue-and-white striped uniform, supplemented in the wintertime with a striped coat, was introduced in 1938; after a few years there were no longer enough of these uniforms to go around. Due to the changeable, often harsh climate on the northern slope of the Ettersberg and the lack of warm clothing, inmates frequently contracted pneumonia, particularly in winter. In the winter of 1938/39 there were also numerous cases of frostbite on hands and feet. In the December 1938 inmates' infirmary report, there is mention of "a particularly sharp rise in frostbite" and an increase in the number of amputations. In the entire history of the camp there was never any uniform supply of footwear, and frostbite on the feet occurred regularly in the winter months. Not until September 1941 did Concentration Camp Inspection permit the receipt of private packages with warm underwear for the coming winter.

The **water supply** was subject to shortages throughout the camp's history. This problem was constant during the first two years of camp construction, and personal hygiene during this phase was considerably restricted or entirely impossible. Skin diseases of every kind, for example scabies, were the result. In May 1938 Camp Commander Koch fixed the daily water ration at four buckets per barrack. Until 1939, the toilets which had been installed in the barracks thus remained unused for the most part, and the inmates were compelled to relieve themselves in open latrines between the barracks.

Water was not only scarce but, for many years, potable only when boiled. According

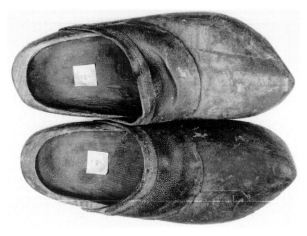

Illustration 78: Dutch-style wooden shoes, so-called "Holländer" Manufactured in the inmates' carpentry shop. These were worn by more than half of the inmates and often caused inflammation of the feet.
Catalogue 3/5
Photo: N. T. Salmon

inmate nurses surrounding the infirmary capo, a locksmith by the name of Walter Krämer. Krämer taught himself medical skills and carried out operations. The fact that he had treated the camp commander for syphilis and therefore had knowledge of the latter's condition is certain to have been why Koch had him and the deputy capo of the infirmary shot in 1941.

In 1941 the infirmary became an extermination facility, and older inmates or those classified as "inferior" avoided going there in order to escape the danger of "Abspritzen," as murder by injection was called. The records of illnesses treated thus contain little mention of general or minor afflictions, but primarily list the serious injuries, frostbite, extreme deficiency diseases and epidemics that were direct consequences of heavy labour, occupational accidents and the hygienic conditions.

Primitive living conditions, excessively hard labour and terror claimed the first lives in August 1937. On August 14, 1937, one week after his arrival from Lichtenburg Concentration Camp, the twenty-three-year-old labourer Hermann Kempek of Altona hanged himself. On August 16, the forty-year-old mason Richard Groschke of Tilsit, who had been on the first transport of July 15, was "shot while attempting to escape;" the labourer Artur Klötzner, twenty-eight years of age, died of peritonitis. A day later the SS shot the typographer Friedrich Bogdahn of Königsberg. The first citizen of Weimar to die in Buchenwald was the sixty-year-old butcher Richard Kohlmann. He had been placed in preventive custody by the Gestapo in 1936 and, after having served time in the Bad Sulza and Lichtenburg Concentration Camps, brought to Buchenwald on July 31, 1937. There he died of pneumonia on August 22. The forty-two-year-old Heinrich Klein died on September 5, 1937, having been shot by the SS the day before; he was the first inmate to die in a Weimar hospital. On grounds of "refusal to work" and resistance he had already received twenty-five lashes on the "Bock" in August. In the pre-war period, Buchenwald had the highest mortality rate of all concentration camps.

to an SS inspection report of December 1938, each inmate received a quarter litre of drinking water per day. Already in the weeks following the opening of the camp, the poor quality of the water led to the first diarrhoea epidemic, a "Buchenwald disease" which occurred particularly in the emergency accommodations. Until the very end, new arrivals regularly suffered from this ailment. At the turn of the year 1938/39, the shortage of water led to a **typhus epidemic** which spread to the villages north of the Ettersberg. The SS officially registered twelve inmate casualties, but had not reported the epidemic or undertaken quarantine measures until weeks after its outbreak. In 1939 a **dysentery epidemic** broke out, and the camp was under quarantine for several weeks.

Many illnesses were treated as outpatient cases – if at all – because **ill or injured persons** were justifiably in constant fear of reprisals. The camp medical records thus provide only a very rough indication of the state of the inmates' health, for it comprises only the illnesses treated and the deaths. As a rule, only those who were visibly ill were admitted to the infirmary. Because of the fact that the SS doctors acted primarily as jailors and otherwise pursued their own interests, medical care was contingent on the

Illustration 79: Inmates' infirmary, 1945
Source: Sammlung Gedenkstätte Buchenwald, Weimar

All who died in Buchenwald Concentration Camp were cremated. Between August 1937 and mid 1940, the **cremations** were carried out in the Weimar Municipal Crematorium, from mid 1940 on in the camp crematorium. Only very few cases are known of the families of the deceased obtaining the release of the mortal remains before cremation in order to bury them; one such case was that of the Protestant minister Paul Schneider in the summer of 1939. Particularly in situations where public knowledge of the death might have caused unrest, emphasis was placed on adherence to a formal legal framework. Leonhard Steinwender recalls:

"Only in exceptional cases were corpses laid out and commemorated with flowers for propaganda purposes. Otherwise, the dead inmate "crossed the grate," as it was termed in camp jargon. Every inmate was cremated, and this principle also applied to clergymen, despite an urgent petition from Cardinal Bertram of Breslau."

Daily Routine in the "Camp under Construction"

The inmate's day began with being woken, generally an hour before sunrise. Once dressed, the inmates marched in blocks to morning roll call to the sounds of the camp brass band, and directly from there to their workplaces, where most of them performed hard labour outdoors until late afternoon.

The **camp brass band** was founded in 1938 as a labour detachment and was directly subordinate to the camp commander. It initially comprised 10-12 musicians, including several Sinti, Jehovah's Witnesses and a Czech inmate. In February 1941 it was expanded and furnished with new instruments. Beginning in the spring of 1942, it was led by the Czech Vlastimil Louda. From the winter of 1942 until the camp's liberation, the band consisted of a nearly constant constellation of 32 inmates. In the end its members numbered 38, primarily Czechs and Slovaks. The band had to play while the inmates were falling into line on the muster ground, as the labour gangs marched out of the camp to their workplaces and during the execution of punishments. It also played for the prisoners at camp and block concerts.

The actual working time of most of the inmates averaged ten to eleven hours per day, interrupted only by a short break at noon. On their return, the inmates lugged stones and tree trunks to the camp and then lined up immediately for the evening **count**. In the initial years, the latter procedure often lasted hours, even well into the

night if there were inmates missing. During the entire ordeal the inmates had to stand in rows, tear their caps from their heads on command, sing marching songs or watch the cruel execution of punishment on the "Bock." Then they marched to the barracks, where little time remained for the warm meal (which was served in the evening), the distribution of mail and the food for the following day, and attendance to personal matters. At about eight or nine o'clock p.m. the final whistle was blown and the quiet hours commenced.

In the early years of Buchenwald Concentration Camp, the SS used **forced labour** primarily as a means of torture. The efficiency and purpose of work were of secondary importance. The camp commander during this phase – Karl Koch – was one of the most extreme supporters of this option. The consequences of labour suffered by each inmate fundamentally depended on the type of work allocated and the personalities of the SS labour detachment officers, the capos and the foremen. With regard to these criteria, the conditions of the construction period were particularly unfavourable. The heaviest detachments – quarry, hauling, excavation

Illustration 80: Camp brass band, 1940 (SS photo)
Source: Sammlung Gedenkstätte Buchenwald, Weimar

Illustration 81:
Inmate gang in
Gaberndorf, a
village outside
Weimar, 1939
*Source: Rolf Lange,
Gaberndorf*

94

Illustration 82: Inmates in the quarry immediately after the opening of the camp in 1937. Photo caption: "Re. view of c. camp Buchenwald. Picture 35. The photograph shows Quarry II of the c. camp. Photo taken on Sept. 7, 1937."
Source: Sammlung Gedenkstätte Buchenwald, Weimar

and road-building – were also the largest. For a long time they were supervised above all by criminal capos and foremen. Like camp life in general, the performance of labour was subject to a command structure which demanded blind obedience and rendered any demonstration of personal initiative a life-threatening act.

Under these circumstances, all inmates with **indoor workplaces** – in workshops, in the Deutsche Ausrüstungswerke and in so-called indoor detachments such as the kitchen, the laundry, the storage facilities, offices and the infirmary – or those carrying out services for the SS were considered privileged. It was seldom vocational qualification which determined this privilege, but much more frequently membership in a certain group and the duration of one's custody in the camp.

Until 1941, the majority of the inmates worked at the various construction sites, in road-building detachments or in the quarry. Not only the execution of the entire above- and below-ground construction but also the transport of building material al-

most completely **without the aid of machinery** was all part of the system. Hauling detachments of 500 inmates lugging stones and wood were nothing out of the ordinary in 1938. Human wagon teams, called the "singing horses," hauled crude wagons laden with hundredweights of stone into the camp or to the road-building sites. The lack of basic working aids corresponded to the complete lack of appropriate working clothes and other **protection against occupational hazards**. On the contrary, the conditions were frequently set up in such a way that injuries would necessarily occur and if they didn't, or if inmates attempted to avoid the dangers, brutal abuse by the SS, the capos and the foremen took their place.

The slave-driver system permitted no **rest** except the short break at midday. Labour detachment officers, capos and foremen alike often reported inmates for laziness or loitering, but were just as likely to beat or even kill them directly at the place of work. Although the number of **occupational accidents** was accordingly large, in-

Illustration 83: The construction of the road through the command area to the main gate building (Caracho Path), spring 1938 (SS photo)
Source: Sammlung Gedenkstätte Buchenwald, Weimar

juries were often treated merely as outpatient cases or not at all. Contusions, crush injuries, fractures and the loss of limbs were daily occurrences. In the first quarter of 1939 – a period which cannot even be considered representative because some of the projects had been interrupted due to the weather – there were sixteen serious fractures, one inmate burned his face and both hands with boiling tar and another suffered a wide tear in the cornea of his left eye. In the winter months frostbite on hands and feet was a major problem, caused by the lack of gloves and proper footwear. A series of "occupational accidents" resulting in death were nothing other than murder. On July 15, 1938, for example, on the road to the quarry, the SS chased the Jewish inmate Horst Loewenberg from Berlin under a moving lorry. Exhaustion, illness and death constituted the fate of the inmates who stayed in heavy labour detachments for longer periods of time. The Czech Jaroslav Bartl recalls:

"My first occupation in the quarry was working on the 'Lore.' The 'Loren' were iron dump cars which we loaded with stones until they were nearly overflowing; then 16 inmates would pull such a car up the steep slope. This was tremendous drudgery, the tracks were laid on crushed stone and we had crude wooden shoes on our feet. At the top the 'Lore' was dumped and we took it back downhill at a run. There were often leg fractures and head injuries. The foremen particularly enjoyed accompanying the loaded dump cars up the hill, beating the inmates on their heads and backs with sticks.

Within half an hour we had to pull the dump car five hundred metres up the slope, then run back with it five hundred metres, holding the heavy car to keep it from rolling down uncontrolled. When the car jumped the track, and that happened quite frequently, all hell broke out. The next wagon often just rolled right through a group of inmates, causing serious injuries. Often inmates whose legs had been run over by a dump car had to be carried away – such an inmate was done for. He was taken to the infirmary and never seen in the camp again. In the infirmary an SS doctor gave him a fatal injection – after all, what use was a legless inmate in the concentration camp?"

The **length of the working day** was determined above all by the seasonally changing rhythm of darkness and light. Six hours on average were allotted to sleeping, the roll calls went on for hours, free time was

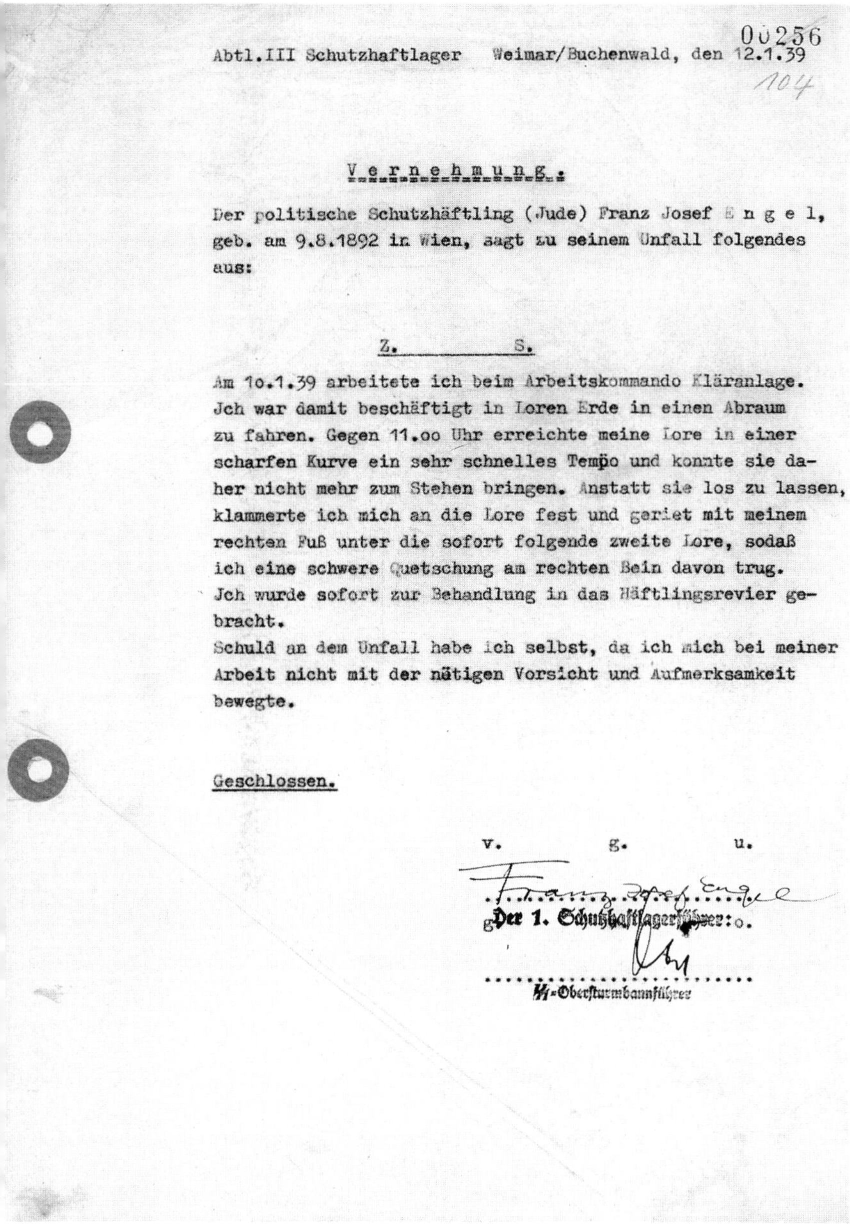

Abtl.III Schutzhaftlager   Weimar/Buchenwald, den 12.1.39

00256

104

V e r n e h m u n g :

Der politische Schutzhäftling (Jude) Franz Josef E n g e l,
geb. am 9.8.1892 in Wien, sagt zu seinem Unfall folgendes
aus:

Z.   S.

Am 10.1.39 arbeitete ich beim Arbeitskommando Kläranlage.
Jch war damit beschäftigt in Loren Erde in einen Abraum
zu fahren. Gegen 11.oo Uhr erreichte meine Lore in einer
scharfen Kurve ein sehr schnelles Tempo und konnte sie da-
her nicht mehr zum Stehen bringen. Anstatt sie los zu lassen,
klammerte ich mich an die Lore fest und geriet mit meinem
rechten Fuß unter die sofort folgende zweite Lore, sodaß
ich eine schwere Quetschung am rechten Bein davon trug.
Jch wurde sofort zur Behandlung in das Häftlingsrevier gebracht.
Schuld an dem Unfall habe ich selbst, da ich mich bei meiner
Arbeit nicht mit der nötigen Vorsicht und Aufmerksamkeit
bewegte.

Geschlossen.

v.   g.   u.

Franz Josef Engel

Der 1. Schutzhaftlagerführer:

H-Obersturmbannführer

Illustration 84: Statement following the interrogation of Franz Josef Engel by the officer in charge of the preventive custody camp, Rödl, on dump car accident, Jan. 12, 1939 *Source: Thüringisches Hauptstaatsarchiv, Weimar*

extremely limited. Thus the majority of the inmates' time – an average of eleven hours per day – was spent doing forced labour. In the construction phase, certain work gangs or sometimes the entire inmate population had to work in the camp after evening roll call until dusk. In summer that meant a working day of fourteen to sixteen hours. Sunday was the only free day, but half of it was also often spent doing work in the camp.

Whereas heavy forced labour dominated the days and lives of the inmates, **free time** played a very minor role in the daily routine, although it was of major importance for the maintenance of physical strength. Like time in the camp in general, the amount of free time was also controlled by

Illustration 85:
Inmates' library,
1943
*Source: Musée de
la Résistance et de
la Déportation,
Besançon
(SS Photo Album:
"Buchenwald
Jahresende 1943")*

the SS. Whether or not the breaks actually provided recuperation depended on the number of occupants in the barrack and the interpersonal atmosphere. In overcrowded barracks where the dayroom was used as a sleeping room, it was impossible to rest. Benedikt Kautsky recalls:

"The ability to live and move around in the block was primarily dependent on the number of occupants. Life is unbearable even in the best and cleanest block if it is jammed with human beings. The few hours of free time are poisoned with noise and bickering over space for eating, reading and playing games."

There were barracks in which the serving of food was carried out according to a strict routine, in which there was a system for who would have a place at the table when, and screaming and hitting fights over places in the food distribution line or at the table remained an exception. In these barracks it was possible to use Sundays and the few free hours during the week to read a book from the inmates' library, hold a conversation or enjoy performances by the artists who were present in the camp.

The **inmates' library** was opened in early 1938 and located until the end in Barrack 5, which also housed the general records department and the labour administration office. Three thousand books were initially acquired from donations made by the inmates. Some of the books were sent by inmates' families. The first library capo was the political inmate Walter Husemann. For a time, the bookbinding labour detachment was part of the library system. The inmates were required to have a library card to use this facility, a privilege to which the Little Camp inmates had no access. In April 1945 the library had a stock of 13,811 volumes.

In May 1941 the SS had a large storage barrack moved from the SS area to the camp and a "**cinema barrack**" set up in it. Until 1943, Ufa films were shown there regularly; the inmates were charged a fee for admission. In addition to film showings, the SS also allowed the barrack to be used for sports events, theatre performances and concerts organised by the inmates. Later the SS also executed floggings in the "cinema barrack." Beginning in January 1945 it was used for the distribution of rations in the Little Camp and as mass accommodation.

It was possible to go on visits or temporary leave from the camp only in a very small number of special cases exclusively

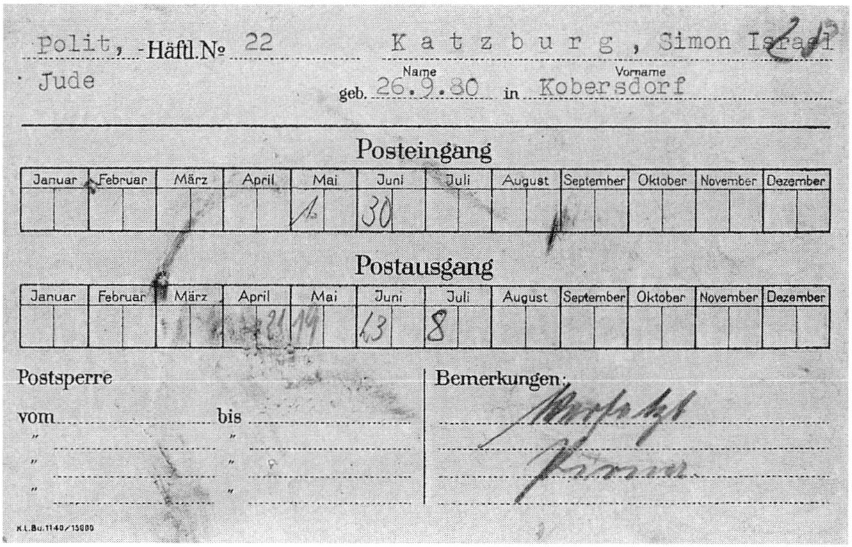

Polit, -Häftl.Nº 22	Katzburg, Simon Israel
Jude	geb. 26.9.80 in Kobersdorf

Posteingang

Januar	Februar	März	April	Mai	Juni	Juli	August	September	Oktober	November	Dezember
				1	30						

Postausgang

Januar	Februar	März	April	Mai	Juni	Juli	August	September	Oktober	November	Dezember
				14	13	8					

Postsperre

vom .... bis ....

Bemerkungen:

K.L.Bu.1140/13080

Illustration 86:
Card documenting the incoming and outgoing mail of Simon Katzburg, 1941
Handwritten memo: "versetzt Pirna" (transfer Pirna). On July 15, 1941, the Jewish inmate Simon Katzburg was taken to the Sonnenstein (Pirna) "euthanasia" killing facility and gassed to death.
Source: Buchenwaldarchiv, Weimar

involving privileged inmates. For this reason, **mail correspondence** with relatives was extremely important for the inmates' morale. According to camp regulations, each inmate was allowed to write a maximum of two letters per month; they had to be written on a printed form and were censored. After the outbreak of war, the amount was reduced to one letter and one card. For the "recidivous," the "Bible researchers" and inmates in the delinquent units there were further limitations, changing the length of the letter to a few lines and the frequency to once every three months. Only a few privileged inmates – the Dutch hostages, for example – were permitted to receive packages from their families during the initial phase of the camp's existence.

The Inmates' Administration

From the time the camp went into operation there were inmate functionaries, appointed by the SS. Unconditional obedience was demanded of them in the form of active participation in the enforcement of the camp regime, the surveillance of other inmates, the organisation of forced labour and later the selections. To the extent that they had no support among the inmates, they remained dependent on the SS. Dismissal from office frequently meant death, as is seen in the examples of the camp seniors Hubert Richter and Josef Ohles. The camp functionaries thus usually found themselves walking on a tightrope between the inmates and the SS. In a statutory declaration made by Benedikt Kautsky in 1951, he recalls:

"For the inmates who participated in the administration of the camp there were constantly a number of problems which were quite difficult to solve because they had to take and carry out orders from the SS. The camp thus regarded them so to speak as the 'extended arm' of the SS. On the other hand, the SS frequently didn't take time to check the detailed execution of their orders, particularly in view of the sharp rise in the number of inmates beginning in 1938. The inmates in the administration thus had the opportunity of alleviating the brutality of many orders if they did not choose to further intensify them.
The leaders within the inmate self-administration thus had access to an abundance of power – so much power that it would amaze anyone who had no opportunity of observing the internal workings of a German concentration camp. And with it came all of the temp-

Illustration 87: Walter Krämer (1892-1941)
Inmate capo of the inmates' infirmary, 1938-1941. Shot to death in Goslar Sub-Camp.
Source: Sammlung Gedenkstätte Buchenwald, Weimar

our of their badges) controlled the camp administration, and those in which it was in the hand of political inmates (called 'reds' after their badges).

One had to possess quite a degree of toughness and unscrupulousness to lend oneself to becoming a tool of the SS in this way, characteristics which are to be regarded as par for the course for a criminal. The only group among the politicals – to the extent that they really were politicals and not criminals whom the SS had awarded the red badge for some reason or other – to share these attributes were the Communists. I saw more than one of them become so completely absorbed in the camp ideology that, in his behaviour towards his fellow inmates, he could no longer be distinguished from a professional criminal."

Both for individuals and for entire groups, the holding of functions within the camp promised privileges with regard to provisions, accommodation, work assignments and liberties of one form or another. Already in the initial phase of Buchenwald, the inmate functionary hierarchy brought about the **social differentiation** within the camp that would later become much more pronounced. Survivors speak of a social hierarchy divided into an upper class, a middle class and a lower class within the camp. The upper class consisted of the camp seniors, the most important capos and a few block seniors, as well as a few barbers, tailors and trusties who worked in special areas. The members of this upper class were exclusively German. According to the recollections of Benedikt Kautsky, the members of the middle class included *"the barrack room duty workers, the foremen, the workshop workers and the junior clerks and functionaries of the administrative offices, the nurses, clerks and other functionaries of the infirmary, as well as less important capos and block seniors ... ."* The members of the lower class lived under 'normal conditions,' which meant they received normal rations, had to work outdoors and were constantly controlled by the inmate functionaries and the SS.

In Buchenwald, the SS assigned camp functions almost exclusively to political inmates and BV inmates. The reign of Com-

tations that usually accompany power. The block seniors and capos were lords over the life and death of the inmates entrusted to them, and they took advantage of this circumstance in numerous cases. I never heard of any case in which one of these inmate functionaries was called to account by the SS for having killed a fellow inmate. Thus it was in the very greatest conceivable interest of the inmates that this power was wielded by persons who did not abuse it to pursue their own personal objectives.

When this happened, the circumstances in the camp became completely unbearable. The SS had different methods in different camps, but in this respect the camps could essentially be divided into two groups: those in which criminal inmates (referred to in camp jargon as professional criminals or 'greens' after the col-

mander Koch came to be characterised by the spectacular rise and downfall of inmate functionaries and frequent changes in the occupancy of inmate offices. From the very beginning, he placed BV inmates in the key functions of camp seniors, i.e. the functions vested with control and penal authority.

Camp Senior One ("Lagerältester" or LA 1) held the highest function in the camp and was accountable to the SS command for the internal administration and daily general report. The assignment of the functions of block senior and capo were under his control. With regard to his fellow inmates, he possessed the power to decide over life and death. His deputies were Camp Senior Two (in charge of "labour allocation") and Camp Senior Three (in charge of enforcing the camp regulations). The camp seniors worked closely with the various offices of the general records department and, from early 1938 on, the labour administration office. There was later a special inmate labour detachment referred to as Camp Protection, which acted as a special police force for the camp seniors.

In his memoirs of Buchenwald and Auschwitz Concentration Camps, Benedikt Kautsky reports on the office of **block senior** as follows:

"The block senior held unlimited power within the block. He represented the block to the outside, which meant that twice a day he had to report on the number of occupants and the changes caused by death and illness, new admissions, releases and transfers to the general records department and at roll call; he was responsible for the attendance of all members of the block at roll call and for reporting punctually which inmate was missing. He also had to maintain internal discipline, see to cleanliness, supervise the distribution of rations, collect and distribute mail. The inmates had to obey him unquestioningly; he possessed absolute penal authority and the number of inmates who died at the hand of their block seniors doubtless amounts to thousands. It is needless to emphasise that the greens particularly excelled in this area ... "

Capos were inmates appointed by the SS to oversee labour detachments and carry out various duties within the camp. The term was probably derived from the French caporal (leader, captain) or from the Italian capo (head). Depending on the size of the labour detachment, there might also be a deputy capo and one or more foremen. The capo had the power of command over his labour detachment and could report inmates for punishment. He himself was not required to work but was obliged to drive the other inmates to work. Acts of violence carried out by capos against fellow inmates were usually tolerated or supported by the SS. There were capos who demanded payment or personal services from the inmates of their labour detachments in return for a bearable work regimen. The size and composition of the capo group changed in the course of the various periods of camp history. At the end of March 1945 there were altogether 245 capos (156 political "Reich Germans," 61 BV "Reich Germans," 8 ASR "Reich Germans," 1 "Bible researcher," 8 Poles, 10 Czechs and 1 Belgian) in Buchenwald and its sub-camps.

A bitter struggle was carried out over the occupancy of these functions, which were matters of life and death. Only two groups succeeded in organising themselves within this context: a group of BV inmates surrounding Hubert Richter and the Communists imprisoned in the camp. **Hubert Richter**, a former leader of a Berlin SA unit with a long police record, was the first Camp Senior One of Buchenwald; Paul Henning, a so-called habitual offender who had already been committed to Esterwegen Concentration Camp in 1936 was his deputy. The two of them ruled the camp with terror and blackmail until June 1938. The chaos of the construction phase was advantageous for them, providing them with opportunities for personal enrichment. Richter and the inmates who worked under him accordingly had little interest in making everyday life in the camp more predictable. Like the SS, they preferred violence as a means of enforcing subordination. Richter, a man feared throughout the camp, demonstratively acted as an executioner in the public hangings of 1938.

Illustration 88: General records department in Barrack 5, 1943
Source: Musée de la Résistance et de la Déportation, Besançon (SS Photo Album: "Buchenwald Jahresende 1943")

Camp Senior One in Buchenwald

July 1937 – March 1938	Hubert Richter (BV)
March 1938 – June 1938	Paul Henning (BV)
June 1938 – December 1938	Arthur Wyschka (polit./KPD)
December 1938 – January 1939	Hubert Richter (BV), killed on 3/23/1939
January 1939 – April 1939	Arthur Wyschka (polit./KPD)
April 1939 – June 1939	Karl Barthel (polit./KPD)
June 1939 – May 1940	Ernst Frommhold (polit./KPD)
May 1940 – November 1941	Ernst Busse (polit./KPD)
November 1941 – Spring 1942	Josef Ohles (BV), killed on 6/8/1942
Spring 1942 – Spring 1943	Fritz Wolff (polit.), denounced and deported to another camp in June 1943
Spring 1943 – November 1944	Erich Reschke (polit./KPD)
November 1944 – April 1945	Hans Eiden (polit./KPD)

Due to the BV inmates' lack of competence in carrying out organisational, office and administration work, the SS delegated these duties to political inmates from 1937 on. Whether Commander Koch wanted to provoke internal struggles between the "reds" and the "greens" over inmate functions, or whether it appeared to him to be advantageous to replace Richter and Henning due to their inability to deal with the overcrowding and extreme shortages of 1938, is a matter upon which we can merely speculate. In any case, the political inmates received the highest camp functions at the very point in time when they first became a camp minority as a result of the "Operation Work-Shy, Reich." Within a few months, however, they had been dismissed from their offices again. It was not until January 30, 1939 that Commander Koch ended "green" supremacy in the camp: on the night of January 19, the BV inmates around Richter – who had once again advanced to the position of camp senior – seriously questioned the camp regime by stealing the "cash donation box" from the Jewish special camp. In retaliation, Koch dismissed Richter and a large number of criminal block seniors and capos and, following excruciating tortures in the "black bunker" set up especially for this purpose, had them killed. The "black bunker" was a barrack on the muster ground whose windows were boarded up in early 1939 in order to torture inmates by making them live in total darkness under the most agonising conditions for weeks on end.

Because of the fact that the majority of the BV inmates were transferred to Mauthausen Concentration Camp in October 1938 or sent to Flossenbürg Concentration Camp as a construction labour detachment in April 1939, changes took place in the composition of the camp population, facilitating the appointment of "red" camp seniors, block seniors and capos in the spring of 1939.

Under the **"red" camp seniors** Karl Barthel, Ernst Frommhold and Ernst Busse, the camp functions were held primarily by Communists in the period between early 1939 and the autumn of 1941. The overall situation in the camp improved. The presence of the Communists was tolerated by the SS until October 1941, when they became politically vocal upon the arrival of a group of Soviet prisoners of war. At that point the SS appointed the BV inmate Josef Ohles as Camp Senior One. With a group of 76 BV inmates and the support of the second officer in charge of the preventive custody camp, he attempted to bring about the downfall of the most important

Communist functionaries. The prominent Communist infirmary capo Walter Krämer was shot to death, causing the internal struggle to escalate into an "inmates' war" over the occupation of powerful functions. The fact that, at this very point in time, the SS was in the process of murdering Soviet prisoners of war – among them a large number of Communist commissars – in a nearby stable made the situation all the more explosive.

In this war between Communist and BV inmates, conducted on both sides with every available means, the infirmary played an important role. Following the invasion of the Soviet Union, the murder of tuberculosis patients through the administration of lethal injections had become common practice, pursued unscrupulously by the SS doctors. Against this background, the Communist organisation bribed the camp physician Waldemar Hoven to kill the former White Guard officer Grigori Kuschnir, who had been charged with spying among the Soviet prisoners of war for the Gestapo, by the same means. Hoven advocated the appointment of Ernst Busse, who had been dismissed from his position as camp senior shortly beforehand, as the new infirmary capo. Under Busse, one of the three heads of the Communist organisation within the camp, the infirmary became the most important base in the "inmates' war," which reached its culmination between March and June 1942. The new Commander Pister settled the conflict under the changed circumstances that accompanied the beginning of the second phase of the camp's history.

The Daily Terror

"Whenever they were successful against their enemies, we had a hard time."

Paul Heller

The Penal System

Life in the camp was organised solely with the purpose of causing the greatest possible torment. Custody in the camp was not intended to bring about the quick death of the inmates, but to serve as an agonising process of destruction. In addition to the systematic everyday cruelty, the heavy labour and the miseries connected with malnutrition, inadequate clothing and unsuitable living quarters, the so-called **code of discipline and punishment** played a special role. It had been developed in 1933/

34 for the Dachau and Esterwegen Concentration Camps and later applied in all concentration camps. According to a testimony by Camp Commander Pister, *"all types of punishment [were formally] recorded in the service manual for concentration camps."* This manual stated that charges were to be brought against inmates in writing; the report served as the basis for the determination of the punishment. Already at this stage a grey zone of arbitrarily imposed and immediately executed reprisals emerged which not only every SS man but also capos, block seniors and inspectors ap-

Illustration 89: Karl Schulz: "Tree-Hanging," pen and ink drawing, 1943
Karl Schulz, German political inmate, 1938-1945
Source: Sammlung Gedenkstätte Buchenwald, Weimar

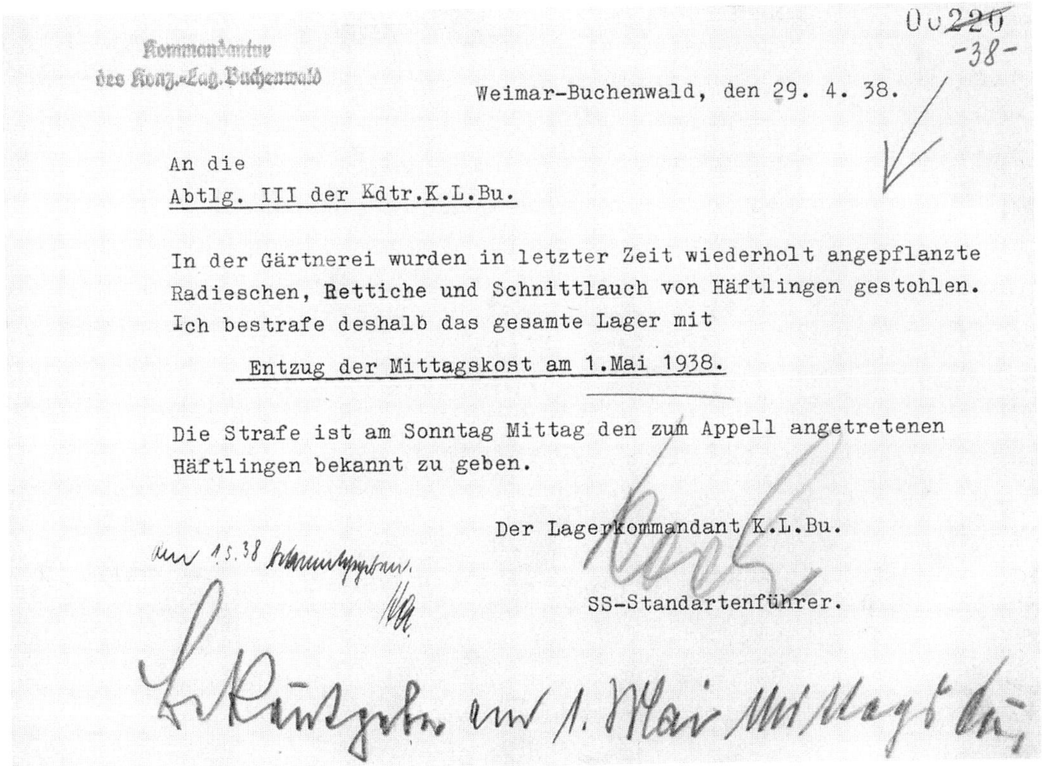

00220
-38-

Kommandatur
des Konz.-Lag. Buchenwald

Weimar-Buchenwald, den 29. 4. 38.

An die
Abtlg. III der Kdtr.K.L.Bu.

In der Gärtnerei wurden in letzter Zeit wiederholt angepflanzte
Radieschen, Rettiche und Schnittlauch von Häftlingen gestohlen.
Ich bestrafe deshalb das gesamte Lager mit

Entzug der Mittagskost am 1.Mai 1938.

Die Strafe ist am Sonntag Mittag den zum Appell angetretenen
Häftlingen bekannt zu geben.

Der Lagerkommandant K.L.Bu.

SS-Standartenführer.

Illustration 90: Punitive order issued by Camp Commander Karl Koch on Apr. 29, 1938: Collective deprival of food on May 1
Memo by Koch: "Bekanntgabe am 1. Mai Mittags" (to be announced at noon on May 1).
Source: Thüringisches Hauptstaatsarchiv, Weimar

pointed by the camp senior could take advantage of as it suited them. These measures included **harassments** such as standing to attention at the gate building, where the inmates received frequent blows, standing to attention for hours at roll call, pack drills and "sports," as the SS men referred to crawling, jumping and running on the muster ground. A particularly dreaded punishment was **"tree-hanging"**: The inmate's hands were tied behind his back; he was then hung from them and often left hanging until his arms had become dislocated. Martin Caspar recalls:

"When we had reached our destination I had to pile up bricks against a tree trunk. Then I had to stand on the bricks and wrap my arms around the tree trunk behind me. The SS man tied my hands together and lifted my arms with a jerk. Some object or force kept my hands raised. To my great dismay, the bandit then kicked the bricks away with his foot. There was a jolt and I was hanging from my arms in mid-air.
The beast disappeared, leaving me to my fate. The pain I felt in my arms and shoulders was indescribable. I tried to find something on the tree trunk to prop my feet on, but all my efforts were for nought; I kept sliding farther downward, which made the pain worse. ... I could no longer see anything, I blacked out and my ears were ringing, then I lost consciousness. When I came to, I was lying on the ground, being kicked by boots. The SS scoundrel yelled at me: 'Get to work!' I recognised the Scharführer, gathered all my strength and dragged myself away. I could no longer move my hands forward."

The extant **punitive reports** provide evidence of the fact that practically every act

Illustration 91:
Form for the
passing of a
flogging sentence
for Czeslaus P.,
Oct. 3, 1940
*Source: Buchen-
waldarchiv, Filme
der Hauptkom-
mission Warschau*

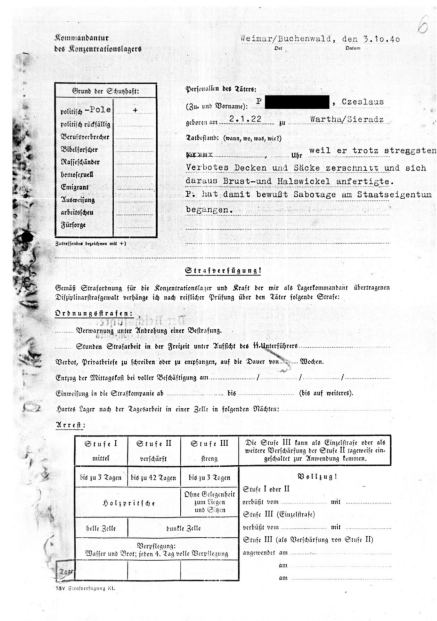

Illustration 91: Form for the passing of a flogging sentence for Czeslaus P., Oct. 3, 1940. Source: Buchenwaldarchiv, Filme der Hauptkommission Warschau

arising from personal initiative could be classified as insubordination or sabotage: failure to obey the salutation regulations, clothing regulations and other rules, the exchange of rations, the production of vital objects and pieces of clothing, illicit eating and smoking, illicit relieving oneself at a time when it was not permitted, etc. Banalities such as these – rather than serious offences such as stealing bread, attempting escape, resistance – most frequently led to punishment. The **sentence**, decided on by the camp commander, depended primarily on the position of the respective inmate in the camp hierarchy, secondarily on the graveness of the violation and finally on the number of previous punishments recorded in the inmate's file.

Körperliche Züchtigung:

Anzahl der Schläge *)	
5	
10	
15	*15*
20	
25	

*) Anzahl einsetzen.

Vorschriften:
Zuvor Untersuchung durch den Arzt! Schläge mit einer einrutigen Lederpeitsche kurz hintereinander verabfolgen, dabei Schläge zählen; Entkleiden und Entblößung gewisser Körperteile streng untersagt. Der zu Bestrafende darf nicht angeschnallt werden, sondern hat frei auf einer Bank zu liegen. Es darf nur auf das Gesäß und die Oberschenkel geschlagen werden.

Der Täter ist bereits körperlich gezüchtigt worden:	
am	Schläge

Ärztliches Gutachten:

Der umseits bezeichnete Häftling wurde vor dem Vollzug der körperlichen Züchtigung von mir ärztlich untersucht; vom ärztlichen Standpunkt aus erhebe ich keine Bedenken gegen die Anwendung der körperlichen Züchtigung.

~~Gegen die Anwendung der körperlichen Züchtigung erhebe ich als Arzt Bedenken, weil~~

Der Lagerarzt: *i.V. Wagner*
H. _____sturmführer.

Dienstaufsicht:

Der Vollzug der körperlichen Züchtigung wird im Hinblick auf die Tat und gestützt auf das vorliegende ärztliche Gutachten genehmigt — ~~nicht genehmigt.~~

Der Reichsführer-H
— Der Inspekteur der Konzentrationslager

H.-Gruppenführer.

1 2. Okt. 1940   19 30 Uhr

Ausführende:

Die Strafe der körperlichen Züchtigung haben folgende H.-Unterführer am _____ vollzogen.

eigenhändige Unterschrift | H. H.-Scharführer
 | H. _____führer

Zeugen und Aufsicht:

Als verantwortliche H.-Führer und Zeugen waren bei dem Strafvollzug zugegen:

eigenhändige Unterschrift | _____ Lagerkommandant
 | _____ Schutzhaftlagerführer
 | _____ Lagerarzt

Aktenvermerk:
1. Originalverfügung zu den Schutzhaftakten.
2. Abschrift zum Sammelakt: Strafen.
3. Abschrift an den Führer H.ZW/KL.

Der Lagerkommandant: _____
H. Standartenführer.

The torture multiplied with every new punishment. Within the course of three months in 1941, for example, the sixteen-year-old Polish boy Kasimier Klusek – who stole out of pure desperation – was punished on the "Bock" first with 5 strokes, then with transferral to the delinquent company, then with 10 strokes, then with 15 and finally, on December 12, 1941, with 25 strokes. He died two weeks later.

In the case of offences by Jewish inmates, the SS frequently punished the entire Jewish labour detachment or the entire barrack. During the construction years, one of the SS's favourite harassments was to make the inmates **work during** their **free time and on Sundays**. The tasks assigned as

Illustration 92: Flogging stand, replica, 1954
Catalogue 3/24
Photo: G. Krynitzki

punishment usually consisted of menial or particularly hard labour within the camp or in the vegetable garden. Especially during the period of Commander Koch, the SS also deprived inmates – often entire groups – of their rations as a form of punishment. On May 1, 1938, for example, Koch had the rations for the entire camp withheld because radishes had allegedly been stolen from the vegetable garden. The profits from such starvation days landed directly in Koch's pocket.

The public flogging of inmates was common practice at their places of work. For the execution of **floggings**, the SS had a wooden construction built, the so-called "Bock." Its function was to keep the inmate's legs and upper body from moving. The official code of punishment provided for the administration of five to twenty-five lashes; the number was often raised arbitrarily during the execution. Regularly during the evening roll call, an SS jailor –

usually the "Bunker boss" Martin Sommer – flogged his victim's naked buttocks with a whip before the eyes of the inmates standing at attention. Aside from deep humiliation, the inmates thus punished usually came away with open, bleeding wounds which took weeks to heal. Only the names of 241 inmates punished on the "Bock" in the first half year of 1938 are known. Ernst Frommhold writes in his memoirs:

"Two Scharführer grabbed the inmate, he had to put his feet into a block, his upper body was pulled over forwards and strapped down. Then each of the Scharführer took a whip, took several steps back from the Bock to the right and left, sliding the whips – long horsewhips filled with steel – through their hands with relish. Then they flung the whips through the air. The lashes followed successively. The SS had thought up a precise method. The lashes followed one another slowly; between each lash there was a relatively long

break. If the lashes had followed in quick succession, the recipient would have perceived them as a single pain. But this way there was a pause between each of the lashes, long enough to evoke in him a horrified wait for each new lash. ... Then the procedure was over. With a snarl, the general records department officer, SS Hauptscharführer Hackmann, generally referred to as 'Jonny,' called out 'Stop!'"

Illustration 93:
Martin Sommer
(1915-1988),
ca. 1935
Source: Bundes-archiv, Berlin

An inmate who had undergone flogging was usually assigned to the "**delinquent company**" immediately afterward. The SS punished those guilty of repeated violations against its regime by committing them to custody in the "delinquent company" (which existed from 1937 to early 1944). Inmates classified as "race defilers" and homosexuals as well as a proportion of the "recidivous" inmates remained there until their death. In 1942-43 the "delinquent company" comprised an average of 400 inmates and the so-called "**K Company**" 190. The latter was a special delinquent unit established in October 1939 for inmates reputed to be war saboteurs. The inmates in the delinquent companies worked in the quarry and the camp vegetable garden under the worst conditions – longer than all the others, with shorter breaks and on Sundays: they were literally worked to death. They were not permitted to receive money, were allowed to write only one letter in three months, received reduced rations, were isolated from the rest of the camp and subjected to constant harassment and brutal abuse. There was a phase in which the "K company" had to carry out a pack drill for two hours every evening after roll call on the commander's orders.

A punishment even worse than assignment to a delinquent company was **custody** in a cell at the "Bunker," where, until 1943, – entirely unhindered in his activities and usually without witnesses – the SS jailor Martin Sommer sadistically tortured inmates to death, hung them from the bars of the cell or killed them by means of phenol and air injections. The official code of punishment for the detention cells – three to forty-two days in the cell, individually or in groups, forced standing all day, nothing to

sit or lie on, to some extent in darkened cells, rations consisting of bread and water – hardly suffices to describe the degree of brutality that prevailed in the "Bunker." According to an SS investigation report of April 1944:

"Sommer doubtless devoted himself to his task as a torturer and executioner with great pride and much passion. He prided himself greatly on being the most dreaded and most hated person in the camp. He himself urged the doctors and inmates of the infirmary to administer toxic preparations and once even offered SS Hauptsturmführer Dr. Hoven 20,- Reichsmark for obtaining such preparations for him. ... [It] should not be overlooked that his many years of occupation in the detention cell building, execution of barbaric punishments and extortion of confessions from the inmates (according to Sommer sometimes as many as two thousand lashes per day) are what made him a monster."

The former Polish prisoner Richard Gritz recalls:

"In order to force a confession out of me, I was tortured in a manner no normal human being can even imagine. In the course of four weeks I received floggings at intervals of about ten to fourteen days, altogether 175 lashes on my backside. During the same period I was hung from my wrists ten times for twenty-five minutes each time. For four months I was

Illustration 94:
Rudolf Opitz
(1908-1939)
*Source: Sammlung
Gedenkstätte
Buchenwald,
Weimar*

from pacing in their cells. You had to stand ti attention, looking at the door, from five o'clock in the morning until ten o'clock at night. The peephole in the door contained a magnifying glass through which every movement could be closely observed. If you were caught, you received twenty-five strokes with a stick. If there was food, it was usually only half a ration."

Sommer tortured inmates on the basis of personal pleasure or on behalf of the commander or the Gestapo officers of the "Political Department." As in the case of the Protestant minister Paul Schneider in 1938-39 or that of the Communist Rudolf Opitz in 1939, the entire camp had to witness the agonising process of a death in the "Bunker." There were also numerous cases of inmates disappearing into the "Bunker," never to return. Leonhard Steinwender describes the circumstances surrounding the death of the Austrian Catholic priest Otto Neururer as follows:

supposed to sleep on the floor, dressed only in my shirt and underpants, with the window open; outside it was bitter cold. I shared the cell with a German Communist, Jakob Boulanger from Cologne, who gave me his suit out of pity for me, despite the fact that this was severely prohibited and he knew he was risking his life to do it. I was often desperate and wanted to hang myself; I refrained from doing so only because Boulanger told me I shouldn't be cowardly.

The day began with harassments at five a.m., especially when the notorious mass murderer Sommer was on duty. Because I slept in clothing I had to undress with lightning speed. Woe to him who did not run to the water faucet as soon as the cell was opened. And woe to him who was not back in his cell in half a minute. ... Sommer derived particular pleasure from driving all of the inmates into the 1.20-m-wide corridor, and making them do knee bends and jump until they collapsed from exhaustion. When the inmate was lying on the floor, he [Sommer] took to kicking him on the head with the heels of his boots until blood ran from the inmate's nose and ears. ... A look out of the window of the cell meant certain death. If Sommer caught someone doing that he beat him to death or gave him a deadly injection. ... The inmates were prohibited

"I can still clearly remember my last meeting with the kind-hearted, devoted Father Martin Neururer from Götzens in Tyrol. An inmate had approached him with the desire to be reconciled with the church or allowed to rejoin it. Neururer was not certain whether he had the necessary authority and wanted to confer with me about it. Because of the fact that every preventive custody inmate in the concentration camp was constantly in mortal danger, there could be no reasonable doubt. I asked my zealous comrade whether he was sure he knew who he was dealing with, whether someone could be laying a trap for him in order to gain some kind of advantage, or was perhaps planning something really terrible. Smiling, he looked at me with his faithful eyes and said, full of priestly fervour, full of joy over this great accomplishment of priestly effort, 'I am absolutely certain.' I wished him well, not suspecting that we were shaking hands for the last time. He had fallen into the hands of a provocateur.

Just a few days later he was called to the gate along with Father Spannlang of Upper Austria. Because there was no reason to believe otherwise, many friends hoped the hour of freedom had struck for the two of them. I had an uneasy premonition of their fate, which was confirmed within a few hours. They had been put in the Bunker, the notorious camp prison. Forty-eight hours later the news spread through the camp like wildfire: Father Neururer is dead. And one day later the same fate befell Father Spannlang."

Buchenwald was the first concentration camp in which the **death penalty** was executed publicly. On June 4, 1938 the inmate Emil Bargatzky, who had been recaptured following his escape, was hanged on the muster ground, followed by the inmate Peter Forster on December 21, 1938. The two had escaped together, killing an SS man in the process, and been sentenced to death by the special court of Weimar. From 1940 on, executions were generally carried out in the crematorium.

The Special Pogrom Camp of 1938

In the special camps set up by the SS on the muster ground in 1938 and 1939, the terror reached its most extreme form. The first of these camps was established after the anti-Jewish pogroms of November 9/10, 1938. In the days following the pogroms, by order of the Chief of the Security Police and the Security Service Reinhard Heydrich, the security police arrested some 30,000 Jewish males in Germany and deported 26,000 to concentration camps. This measure was intended as a means of forcing the Jews to relinquish their property and leave the country as quickly as possible. Between November 10 and 14, 9,828 Jews were committed to Buchenwald Concentration Camp. Gustav Beutler, who was deported to Buchenwald via Halle an der Saale, recalls:

"We had to jump off the vehicle and run to the gate of Buchenwald between two rows of SS thugs armed with sticks and iron rods. Many of us received severe beatings in the process. In front of me there was an older comrade from Halle by the name of Walter Schwabach, whose ear was beaten off. I received a blow to one eye, the consequences of which caused me to go blind in that eye. In front of the gate we were received by inmates who calmed us down, divided us up and led us onto the muster ground in groups. There we had to stand until the late hours of the night, because the barracks being set up especially for the Jews weren't finished yet. By evening, thousands of Jews had already been led through the gate and onto the muster ground. Indescribable scenes unfolded. …

After the first night, which we were forced to spend standing, we had to sit with a straight posture on the damp muster ground for days from morning to night and were not [allowed] to relieve ourselves, so that all these many persons had to walk around in their own excrement for weeks. As a special form of humiliation, the SS scoundrels had hit upon the idea of having several inmates slurp their cabbage soup out of a single tin bowl without spoons. During these 'meals' the guards would walk around poking fun at certain inmates. I remember, for example, the two Schloss brothers from Weissenfels being severely beaten and kicked daily by an SS Scharführer who was also from Weissenfels."

The **special pogrom camp** that stood to the west of the muster ground from November 1938 to February 1939 consisted primarily of five barn-like emergency barracks designated Barracks I A to V A. This special zone was separated from the rest of the barrack camp by means of barbed wire. On an area of some ten thousand square metres, in addition to these emergency barracks, there were two open latrines as well as a smaller building which had contained a provisional camp laundry until mid 1938. The emergency barracks were entirely different from the ordinary inmates' quarters. There were no partitions between the sleeping and day areas, no inside sanitary facilities, no heating, no windows, not even a foundation. The barracks had been constructed right on the bare ground, which turned to mud

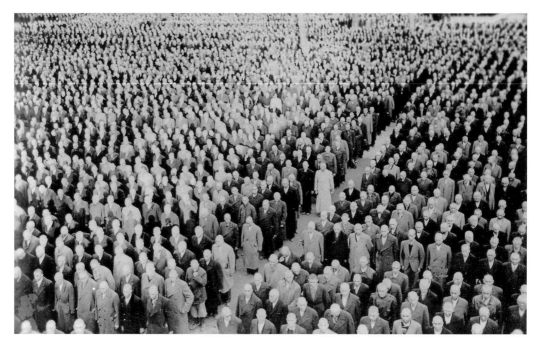

Illustration 96: Jews arrested following the pogroms; morning roll call in Buchenwald Concentration Camp, November 1938 (SS photo)
The SS took this photo from the observation deck of the main gate building.
Source: American Jewish Joint Distribution Committee, New York / USHMM

5122 -19

Konzentrations-Lager Buchenwald

Familienname: N a t h a n
Vorname: Hermann
geb. am 28.7.84. in Lohra /Marburg
Beruf: Kaufmann
Religion: mos. Staat: D
verh., led., gesch. Fr. Paula N., Lohra Lindenstr. 4
Kinder: 2

Jude Häftling Nr. 25 519
Block:

Schutzhaft angeordnet:
am: 10.11. durch (Behörde): Kassel
Bisherige Parteizugehörigkeit: keine
Vorstrafen: keine

Grund: „Judenaktion vom 10. 11. 38."

eingeliefert: 11.11.38.
entlassen: 7.12.38.

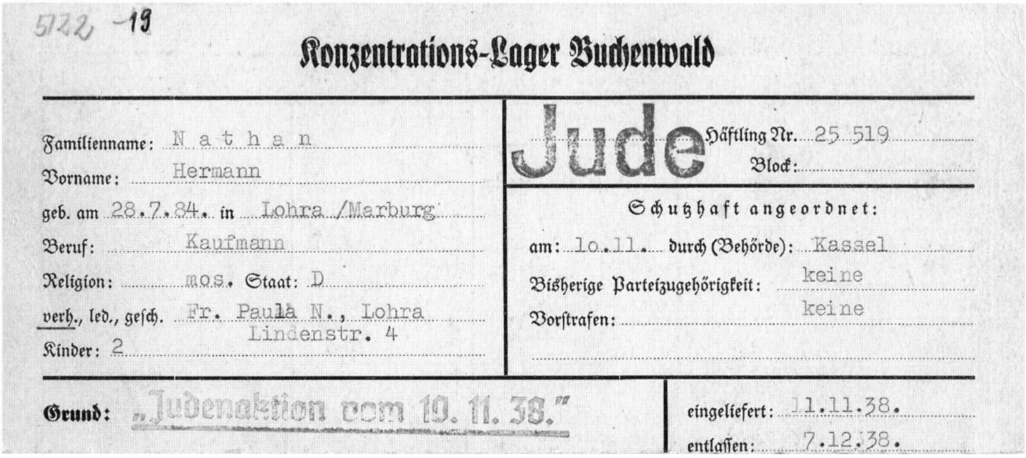

Illustration 97: Card from the special card file for inmates of the pogrom camp, 1938
Source: Buchenwaldarchiv, Weimar

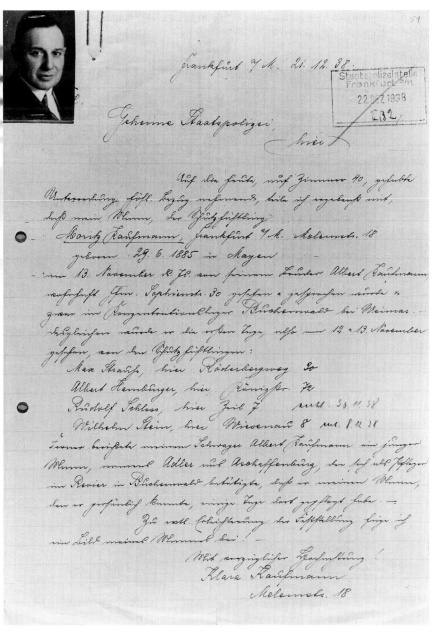

Illustration 98: Request from Klara Kaufmann to the Frankfurt am Main Gestapo concerning the whereabouts of her husband, Dec. 21, 1938

The SS in Buchenwald were not able to find Moritz Kaufmann. He had been cremated at the Weimar Crematorium as an "unidentified deceased person." In February 1939, one of the "unidentified deceased persons" recorded at the Weimar Registry Office received the name M. Kaufmann, date of death Nov. 18, 1938.

Source: Thüringisches Hauptstaatsarchiv, Weimar

Departure points of the 103 transports of Jewish inmates arriving at Buchenwald between November 10 and 13, 1938 (according to the daily revision reports)

10.11.38	Erfurt	185	**11.11.38**	Offenbach	27
	Zeulenroda	1		Halle	74
	Suhl	21		Magdeburg-	375
	Hildburghausen	19		Braunschweig	
	Mühlhausen	31		Sondershausen	12
	Blankenburg	2		Hannover	316
	Nordhausen	81		Meiningen	20
	Schwarza	1		Chemnitz	99
	Weimar	17		Meuselwitz	3
	Eisenach-Gotha	91		Nordhausen	8
	Langensalza	3		Tieburg	46
	Erfurt	3		Erbach	31
	Rudolstadt	3		Dessau	15
	Schmalkalden	34		Osnabrück	31
	Jena	16		Leipzig	153
	Salzungen	10		Groß Gerau	26
	Ellrich	1		(Darmstadt)	
	Geisa	14	**12.11.38**	Darmstadt	96
	Niederorschel	3		Frankfurt a. M.	581
	Kahla	3		Büdingen	48
	Themar	20		Osnabrück	29
	Buttstädt	3		Fulda	35
	Chemnitz	40		Friedberg	35
	Meiningen	42		Kassel	435
	Kelmerode	1		Offenbach	55
	Apolda	12		Friedberg	30
	Gera	32		Frankfurt a. M.	450
	Chemnitz	17		Frankfurt a. M.	451
	Arnstadt	11		Worms	37
	Zella-Mehlis	9		Aachen	55
	Dessau-Bernburg	70		Mainz	63
	Saalfeld	9		Oppeln	258
	Pößneck	8		Oppeln	388
	Chemnitz	15		Frankfurt a. M.	32
	Gießen	23		Breslau	811
11.11.38	Gießen	125		Altenburg	13
	Darmstadt	73		Sonneberg	3
	Schmalkalden	2		Würzburg	103
	Mainz	34		Halle	25
	Frankfurt a. M.	338		Halle	25
	Kassel	258		Bielefeld I	249
	Bad Nauheim	36		Osnabrück	31
	Friedberg	34		Eisenach	3
	Jena	2		Oppeln-Ratibor	57
	Tonndorf	1		Bielefeld II	157
	Worms	50		Leipzig	119
	Weimar	1	**13.11.38**	Frankfurt a. M.	432
	Breslau	963		Frankfurt a. M.	243
	Eisenach	18		Aachen	80
	Erfurt	9		Frankfurt a. M.	94
	Meiningen	29		Plauen	47
	Dresden	66		Zwickau	38
				Dresden	85

when it rained. The statements regarding their size differ greatly. Julius Feist, who arrived on November 10 and was thus one of the first inmates of the special zone, recalls:

"The building had only one door and its dimensions were as follows: 100 metres long, 12 metres wide and 5 metres high. To the right was a sleeping shelf, 2 metres deep with four compartments, each 50 centimetres high. There were posts at intervals of 1.35 metres; four men had to lie between them; that was only possible edgewise. There were no blankets, no straw. Past a corridor 1 metre wide came the next shelf 4 metres deep, in which people were accommodated from both sides, then another corridor, then another shelf ..."

All of the extremes of Buchenwald Concentration Camp – the crowdedness, the scarcity of water, the SS terror – multiplied in the special zone in the days following November 10, 1938. Although many of the inmates were soon released (by early 1939 9,400 had been set free on the condition that they would relinquish their property and leave Germany) 255 lives were lost between November 1938 and February 1939 due to terror, hunger and disease. Gustav Beutler writes:

"On January 7, 1939 I was sent to the Political Department outside the camp, where I had to stand in line with other comrades in the corridor. A high-ranking SS officer in patent leather boots paced back and forth in front of the rows of inmates, pouring out political threats to the effect that we would be released with the instruction to leave Germany immediately. ... Because I refused to set out on the indicated journey without my family, I was arrested again in Merseburg on February 1, 1939 and taken to Halle for an investigation concerning illegal political work. Later the Gestapo took my family and me to Hamburg, where we were put on the notorious Gestapo ship and sent to Shanghai. ..."

The Special Camp for Jews and Poles at the Beginning of the War

On September 7, 1939, Heydrich ordered the arrest of all Jews of Polish origin. Thousands of so-called "Ostjuden" (stateless Jews of Eastern European origin) were arrested in Vienna and interned in a stadium, 1,035 of them deported to Buchenwald in early October. When they arrived at the camp, the SS had already begun setting up the special zone. The first inmates were 110 Poles who arrived at the end of September and were tortured to death by the SS in the course of several weeks.

The SS called them the "**Bromberger Heckenschützen**" (Bromberg snipers). The designation was an NS propaganda invention referring to incidents which had taken place in Bromberg (Bydgoszcz) at the beginning of the war. On September 3, 1939, during a Polish troop retreat there, a number of gunfights had occurred, leading to the death of civilians belonging to the German minority. The NS propaganda dubbed the event "Bromberg Blood Sunday," a term synonymous with the assertion that the Polish population had carried out mass crimes against the German minority. The number of victims was multiplied in the propaganda accounts of the incident. This excessive exaggeration, as well as the rumour of the Poles' alleged bloodthirstiness, served as a justification for brutal retaliation measures and a pretext for the expulsion of Poles from the territories assigned to Poland by the 1919 Treaty of Versailles. In Buchenwald, the hysteria triggered by NS propaganda on "Bromberg Blood Sunday" led to the extermination of the first Polish inmates to arrive in the camp. They were locked up in a cage-like entanglement of barbed-wire and boards (called the rose garden or the dungeon) to starve and – unprotected from the cold that was setting in – freeze to death. Only one of them survived the winter.

According to eyewitness reports, the **special zone** had a surface area of 100 by 200 metres surrounded by a double barbed-wire fence 2.5 metres high. One section served as a muster ground, while another – soon covered with excrement and refuse like the remainder of the zone – was intended for those who no longer had the strength to appear at roll call. They were thrown into this enclosure even before they had died.

The SS jammed the 1,035 **Viennese Jews** – among them youngsters under eighteen years of age and old men over eighty-five – into a wooden barrack and four large tents, where they were temporarily joined by over 2,000 Poles. At the end of October 1939, a dysentery epidemic broke out in the tents.

Forced labour had to be discontinued. Beginning on November 2, all persons were prohibited from entering and leaving the special camp on penalty. On November 4 the demonstrative public flogging of every tenth special camp inmate was carried out because the prohibition had been violated. Beginning on November 9, the entire Jewish population of the entire concentration camp was refused food for several days in succession. The SS reduced the bread rations of all inmates who did not carry out

Illustration 99:
Newly committed
inmates undressing on the
Buchenwald
muster ground,
1939 (SS photo)
*Source: American
Jewish Joint
Distribution
Committee, New
York / USHMM*

Illustration 100:
Shearing and
disinfection of
newly committed
inmates in the
special zone, 1939
(SS photo)
*Source: American
Jewish Joint
Distribution
Committee, New
York / USHMM*

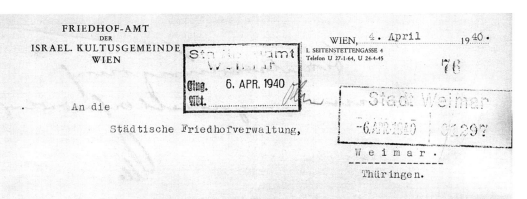

FRIEDHOF-AMT
DER
ISRAEL. KULTUSGEMEINDE
WIEN

WIEN, 4. April 19 40.

I. SEITENSTETTENGASSE 4
Telefon U 27-1-64, U 24-4-45

St... ...amt
W ...
Eing.   6. APR. 1940
Ubt. ....

76

Stadt Weimar
-6.APR.1940   01297

An die

Städtische Friedhofverwaltung,

W e i m a r .

Thüringen.

Ende Februar 1940 hat das Friedhofamt der Israel.Kultus-
gemeinde Wien über Ersuchen der Angehörigen die Urnen der nachstehend
genannten in Buchenwald Verstorbenen angefordert und die bezüglichen
Versandgebühren seinerzeit an die Stadthauptkasse Weimar überwiesen.

Name	geb.	gest.
Baruch Romze	geb.23.8.1889,	gest.22.2.1940
Ernst Feldsberg,	" 25.12.1896	" 24.2.1940
Osias Beer Fränkel,	" 26.6.1899,	" 27.2.1940
Lazar Ginsberg,	" 7.9.1884,	" 29.2.1940
Hermann Gross,r.Sonntag,	22.3.1922,	" 27.2.1940
Jakob Joel Gruber,	" 13.3.1884,	" 27.2.1940
Josef Bernhard Hafner,"	3.8.1895,	" 21.2.1940
Leib Israel Hass,	" 6.9.1897,	" 27.2.1940
Berisch Kanner,	" 16.12.1887,	" 15.2.1940
Leo Meisels,	" 1.9.1883,	" 23.2.1940
Salomon Schwarz,	59 J.alt	" 19.2.1940
Israel Tillemann,	" 1863,	" 23.2.1940
Paul Zygmann,	" 26.2.1923,	" 27.2.1940

Da die Zusendung der Urnen bis heute nicht erfolgt ist und
die Angehörigen die Bestattung veranlassen wollen, wird um ehemög-
lichste Uebersendung der genannten Urnen an die Verwaltung des Neuen
Israel.Friedhofes, Wien,XI.Zentralfriedhof, 4.Tor, neuerlich ersucht.

Der Friedhofamtsleiter:

Illustration 101: Cemetery office of the Jewish community of Vienna to the Municipal Cemetery Administration in Weimar, Apr. 4, 1940
Source: *Thüringisches Hauptstaatsarchiv, Weimar*

any form of labour from 200-300 grams to 165, then 100 grams per day, the soup ration from one litre to three quarters of a litre without potatoes and vegetables. Separated from the rest of the camp by barbed wire, the special zone became the scene of the first mass deaths of Jews and Poles in Buchenwald Concentration Camp, an incident bearing the attributes of deliberate mass murder. Within three months, over 400 Viennese Jews, over 100 Polish Jews and approximately 300 Poles – i.e. about forty percent of the special camp inmates – died as a consequence of terror and starvation. Only one in three lived to see the dissolution of the special camp in February 1940. Walter Poller, who entered the tents as a medical clerk following the many weeks during which the special camp had been isolated, recalls:

"When I entered the camp, about 400 inmates had already died. Despite this fact, the remaining inmates were lying in the tents, literally one on top of the other; they were allowed to leave the tent only to fetch their rations and relieve themselves. The living with the dead, the healthy with the mortally ill, the aged with the children, the fearful with the fatalists. Incredible stench of pestilence, indescribable filth, people rotting alive, madmen and lunatics, writhing with cramps, lying in comas … an apocalypse no mind is capable of thinking up, no feather capable of describing. … Eight days later I was in the special camp for the second time. I could not muster the courage to enter the tents. Rations were being distributed. This event proceeded much more calmly than it had before. The only ones to receive a portion were those who could fetch it themselves."

The Quarry

Abuse was part of the daily routine throughout the camp, but there was one place of work that was thought of as pure hell on earth: the quarry. It was here that most inmates had to spend their first few weeks and here that the delinquent companies worked. During the initial months of the camp's existence there were still two quarries, one of which the SS soon closed due to its lack of productiveness. What is more, the limestone extracted from the second quarry could not be sold to Weimar construction companies as had originally been planned, but was fit merely to serve as crushed stone, bottoming for paths and roads, or for the foundations of buildings constructed on the Ettersberg itself. The SS interest in the quarry's efficiency was therefore minimal. Until well into the war years, they put no machines into operation here, but had all of the work carried out solely by means of the physical strength of the inmates: the extraction and cutting of the stone, the loading and hauling of the dump cars, the transportation of the stones to the camp. The former Czechoslovakian prisoner Jaroslav Bartl recalls:

"The capos in the quarry were selected by the camp administration. They were always brutal killers. Although many of them wore the red triangle of the political inmates, they obeyed the orders of the SS to the letter. Labour in the quarry was carried out under unspeakable conditions, constantly under the rifles of the SS guards, accompanied by the screams and blows of the foremen. There were several accidents, mutilations, fatal injuries every day, and nearly every day at least one inmate was shot to death."

One of the many legionnaires interned in Buchenwald as political inmates was Johann Herzog, the quarry capo from 1941 to 1942. He had joined the foreign legion at the age of seventeen, served in Algiers, Morocco, Indochina and elsewhere until the mid 1930s and been taken into "preventive custody" upon entering Germany. He arrived in Buchenwald in 1939. Working first as a mason, then as a canteen salesman, he rose to become the capo in a sub-camp in 1940. As a foreman and capo in the quarry he earned the reputation of treating Jewish inmates, intellectuals and clergymen with particular brutality. Using sticks and shovel handles, he beat the inmates – who had to pull fifty heavily loaded dump cars from the floor of the quarry every day – into a state of utter collapse. In July 1941 he attacked a Catholic clergyman in front of his

Illustration 102: Quarry, 1943
In the background are the barracks of the Armed SS built in 1942.
Source: Musée de la Résistance et de la Déportation, Besançon (SS Photo Album: "Buchenwald Jahresende 1943")

"capo hut," killing him with blows. He drove a young Pole, who was suffering from dysentery, through the sentry line, where the latter was shot to death. The Gestapo released Herzog from the camp at the end of 1942.

The quarry was one of the SS's favoured places for killing inmates by "shooting during the attempt to escape." On November 9, 1939 the SS shot twenty-one Jewish inmates as an act of retaliation for the attempt on Hitler's life in the Bürgerbräukeller in Munich. When it became clear that the executions had not been ordered from above, a number of SS men refused to allow themselves to be registered as marksmen in the "escape register." Koch then had a survey carried out among the remaining men, asking who would like to sign up. The number of "marksmen" who reported was greater than the number of those murdered. The following description of the SS labour detachment officers assigned to the quarry is an excerpt from the 1945 report of the International Camp Committee:

"Hauptscharführer Blank, one of the greatest mass murderers of Buchenwald. On his command and with his active participation, the following persons were 'shot during the attempt to escape': the former Austrian minister of justice Winterstein. When Blank ordered him to go through the sentry line, Winterstein asked him if he could really assume responsibility for that; Blank answered by kicking him. Winterstein lit a cigarette and walked through the sentry line smoking. Blank went for a walk with the former Communist member of the Reichstag Werner Scholem and conducted a friendly conversation with him for ten minutes, then shot him down from the side with his revolver. The former Austrian military captain Stahl was also chased through the sentry line by special order of Blank, and his skullcap shattered by a dumdum bullet. The political inmate Rudi Arndt, who had twelve years of prison and concentration camp custody behind him, was also shot in the quarry on Blank's initiative, having been denounced by Jewish criminals with multiple previous convictions for allegedly carrying out political activities in the camp.

119

Illustration 103: Dr. Robert Winterstein (1874-1940)
Austrian Minister of Justice in 1935/36, "shot to death during an escape attempt" in the quarry on Apr. 13, 1940.
Source: Dokumentationsarchiv des Österreichischen Widerstandes, Vienna

Hauptscharführer Hinkelmann was another important player in this bloody drama. He was always running around drunk, had a hysterical woman's voice and carried out the foulest of business and profiteering transactions with the inmates. The deaths of several hundred persons who had to carry stones at a run the whole day through can be attributed to Hinkelmann. One of his favourite derisive comments was 'Run faster, and you'll be at your destination sooner', said with a grin to the exhausted, bleeding inmates. Hinkelmann, who was constantly in a state of drunkenness, was a veritable genius at thinking up torments. ... Hinkelmann forced old men to climb up the fir tree and then had the tree shaken, accompanied by his satanic laughter, until the poor devils fell to the ground, usually breaking their necks or injuring themselves so badly that they were committed to the infirmary, where they died a few days later.

Under Hinkelmann's direction, stone-hauler gangs had to carry stones from the quarry to the horse stables at a run for three weeks at a time. The construction of this three-to-four-hundred-metre-long road cost twenty-three lives."

Mass Murder, 1941-1943

"Where did you shoot them?"
"In the back of the head."

Member of the SS Horst Dittrich

The Murder of 8,000 Soviet Prisoners of War

The mass murder of Soviet prisoners of war carried out in the concentration camps between the summer of 1941 and the summer of 1942 was a crime planned in great detail. In March 1941, months before the attack on the Soviet Union, Hitler informed the NSDAP functionaries and commanders of the Wehrmacht of his intention to conduct the approaching war against the Soviet Union as an ideological war, in the course of which "the Jewish-Bolshevist intelligentsia, who had been the 'oppressors' of the people," would have to be destroyed. The so-called **commissar command** of June 6, 1941 ordered the commanders in chief of the Wehrmacht not to take political commissars prisoner but to shoot them to death immediately. In addition, special security police detachments embarked upon a protracted hunt for and singling out of "politically intolerable elements" in the prisoner-of-war camps.

In keeping with the guidelines issued by the Chief of the Security Police and the Security Service on July 17, 1941 (**Operational Order No. 8**) the search concentrated on state and party functionaries, political commissars, heads of high- and medium-ranking government agencies, leading figures of the economy, members of the intelligentsia and Jews, as well as all persons suspected of resistance. With **Operational Order No. 9**, the Gestapo offices were assigned the task of carrying out the selections in those of the prisoner-of-war camps that were under their jurisdiction, and of shooting the selected prisoners to death in the nearest concentration camp.

In early August 1941, the conversion of a barrack into a **shooting facility** got under way in Sachsenhausen Concentration Camp. The various rooms were set up as registration, examination and bath rooms, in which the prisoners were shot in the back of the neck through a slot in the wall. It was a smoothly running, reliable execution mechanism which could be set in motion at any time with relatively low personnel costs, and its existence proves that the SS expected the operation to continue for a long time. The killing facilities erected at Buchenwald – where the victims were shot through a slot in the measuring stick of the examination room – even received a special designation: "Genickschussanlage" (facility for shooting in the back of the neck).

These "facilities" existed only in Sachsenhausen and Buchenwald; in the Dachau, Flossenbürg, Groß-Rosen, Neuengamme and Auschwitz Concentration Camps the killings were carried out by different means. In Buchenwald, the executions of the first group of selected prisoners of war arriving in September 1941 took place on the firing range to the east of the Deutsche Ausrüstungswerke. The "Genickschussanlage" was constructed in a former stable outside the inmate area a short time later. In July 1945, Camp Commander Pister, then in prison, made the following statement on this subject:

"The stable bore the designation 99 after the extension number of the telephone in that building. This stable was no longer being used for horses and was divided into two sections. In the room to the right the prisoners had to undress. The room to the left was set up as a medical examination room. In this room there were blackboards with letters (large and small) on the walls in order to create the impression that an optical examination was to

Illustration 104:
Sketch of the
execution facility
in the stable, Apr.
21, 1945
Carolus is the
pseudonym of Karl
Feuerer, German
political inmate,
1939-1945.
*Source: Buchen-
waldarchiv,
Weimar*

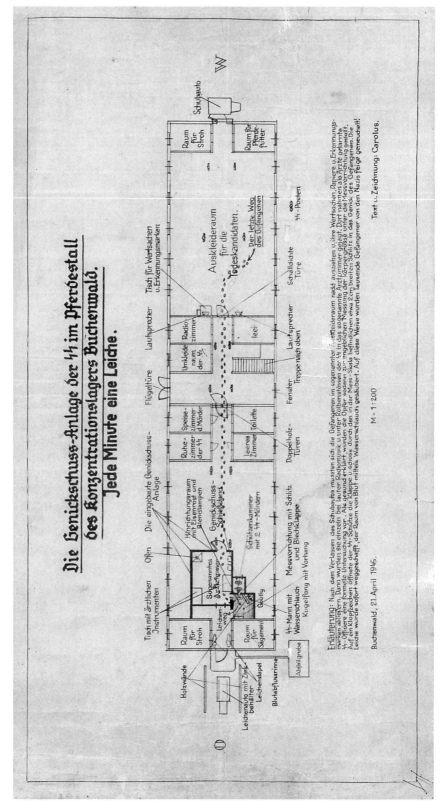

take place. *In a side room there was a measuring stick mounted to the wall, of the type used for physical examinations for military service. The sergeants – of whom there were eight or ten – were dressed in white coats of the kind worn by doctors, so that the prisoners naturally assumed they were going to be medically examined. Following the dental examination, a second sergeant listened to each prisoner's heart and lungs with a stethoscope. Then the prisoner had to enter another room and stand in front of a measuring stick that was mounted on the wall. In the midst of the act of measuring the prisoner's height, the sergeant tapped the wooden partition which separated the room from a small compartment behind the measuring stick.*

At the sound of the tap, a sergeant in the compartment shot the prisoner in the back of the neck. There was a long slit in the measuring stick so that the shot could be aimed at exactly the prescribed height. The corpse was then carried into an adjoining room by two further sergeants and the blood-covered floor was rinsed off with the aid of a hose."

From an organisational point of view, this mass murder system was made possible by the establishment of a specialised detachment, the so-called Commando 99, named after the telephone number of the stable. Commando 99 was constantly on call. During a hearing at the Dachau military tribunal in November 1947, Horst Dittrich, a member of the staff company, was interrogated on the procedure:

"After you entered the examination room for the first time, what happened there?"
"The Russian prisoner of war was then made to stand in this room with his back to the wall. This wall was about 2 metres high and numbers had been painted on it to the left and right to give the impression that the wall was used for measuring. Right in the middle of the wall was a slit about 8 to 10 cm wide. A man with a pistol stood behind this wall. The man who had led the prisoner to the wall tapped the wall with his foot to signal to the man standing behind the wall that he should fire his pistol."
"And you stood in this room for the first time and fired a shot?"

Identification tag

Parent camp	ID number	Hamburg Military District	Wietzendorf
STALAG	29276	X	D

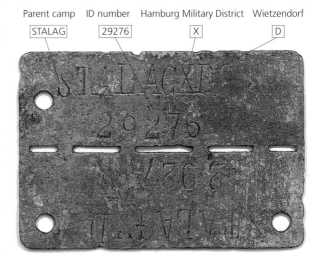

Illustration 105: Prisoner of war identification tag
Object found on the grounds of the Buchenwald Memorial
Catalogue 3/34
Photo: N. T. Salmon

Illustration 106: Corpse container, 1942
A number of sheet-metal-lined containers such as this one were built for the transport of corpses from the "horse stable" to the crematorium.
Catalogue 3/34
Photo: N. T. Salmon

"The first time, yes. In the end I fired eight shots."
"By that you mean that you fired eight shots, at eight different Russian prisoners of war?"
"Correct."
"Where did you shoot them?"
"In the back of the head."

The shootings – which according to the director of the crematorium numbered as many as four hundred per night – were carried out to the accompaniment of blaring marching music. Whereas in other camps the mass murders were terminated in the summer of 1942, Buchenwald remained a killing centre until at least 1943, due most likely to the fact that selections were continued at the Senne POW camp, located in the same district. Once the overall operation had been concluded in the summer of 1942, the numbers of prisoners destined for execution decreased, and the transports became irregular. This change in circumstances led the Buchenwald SS to cease operation of the "Genickschussanlage," and from 1943 on they killed prisoners of war by hanging them from hooks fixed to the walls of the crematorium cellar. Neither the total number nor the names of the victims can be ascertained, as no entries were made in the camp records and the deceased were cremated anonymously. The number is estimated at 7,000 or more. One inmate, whose duties put him in a position to witness and count the execution orders, recalled an overall total of 8,475.

The Selection and Killing of Inmates Deemed "Unworthy of Life"

From the very beginning, there were a number of mentally and physically **handicapped** persons among the inmates of Buchenwald Concentration Camp. A report from the year 1938 already describes a group of mentally handicapped, referring to them in camp jargon as a "Blödenkompanie" (idiots' company). There were a number of blind and deaf-mute inmates in Buchenwald as well. On July 15, 1940, for example, according to SS records, there were 67 "complete invalids" (48 who had already been handicapped upon arrival and 19 seriously ill persons) and 286 "semi invalids" (139 convalescents and 147 elderly) in the camp. These persons accounted for five percent of the 7,203 inmates counted that day. The new labour allocation officer Grimm viewed this state of affairs as a "co-

lossal burden," and in early 1941 he demanded with great insistence that disabled inmates be transferred to Dachau Concentration Camp.

An operation begun in 1941 and conducted under file number **14 f 13** was aimed at exterminating disabled Jewish and handicapped persons. SS Camp Physician Dr. Waldemar Hoven later testified:

"In 1941 I learned that the so-called 'Euthanasia Program' was being carried out in Germany with the aim of exterminating the imbeciles and cripples. Camp Commander Koch summoned all of the leading SS officers of the camp to a meeting and informed them that he had received secret orders from Himmler to the effect that all imbecile and crippled inmates were to be killed. The camp commander explained that by order of his superiors in Berlin all of the Jewish inmates in Buchenwald Concentration Camp were … to be included. In compliance with this order, 300-400 Jewish inmates of various nationalities were sent to the 'euthanasia station' in Bernburg for extermination. A few days later the camp commander provided me with a list of the names of the Jews exterminated in Bernburg, along with the order to forge their death certificates. I carried out this order. This special operation was carried out under the code name '14 f 13.'"

The exact date of the meeting alluded to in Hoven's statement is not known. It must have taken place during the first half of the year, probably in April or May of 1941. The first group of "euthanasia experts" arrived at Buchenwald Concentration Camp on June 16 or 17. They selected inmates who were taken to the Sonnenstein "euthanasia" facility in mid July and gassed to death. A second committee of "experts" appeared in Buchenwald in November 1941 and made selections primarily "on the basis of the files," i.e. without undertaking medical examinations. The extermination transports of exclusively Jewish inmates to the Bernburg "euthanasia" facility were carried out in March 1942. The following is an excerpt from a letter written on November 26, 1941 by one of the "experts", SS physician Dr. Friedrich Mennecke, to his wife:

"Then we continued the examinations until about four o'clock p.m. – more specifically, I examined 105 pat., Müller 78 pat. – so that 183 forms were completed, comprising the first instalment. The second lot followed, a total of 1,200 Jews, none of whom we 'examined' but for whom it suffices to copy the grounds for arrest (often quite extensive!) from their files onto the forms. Purely theoretical work, in other words, which is certain to keep us busy up to and including Monday, maybe even longer. Of this 2nd lot (Jews) I managed 17, Müller 15 today. At five o'clock on the dot we quit working and went to supper: a cold plate of fine salami (9 large slices), butter, bread, coffee! Price –.80 Mk without coupons!! At five-thirty got a ride back to Weimar in the car of a crim-assistant, SS Hauptscharführer (Leclair), who lives in Weimar but drives his own car every day."

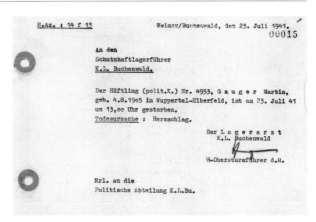

Illustration 107: Waldemar Hoven, SS camp physician, to the officer in charge of the preventive custody camp, under special file number 14 f 13, July 23, 1941
Source: Thüringisches Hauptstaatsarchiv, Weimar

The following **extermination transports** were sent from Buchenwald to "euthanasia" killing facilities in 1941-42:

7/13/1941	94 inmates to Sonnenstein (Pirna)
7/14/1941	93 inmates to Sonnenstein (Pirna)
3/2/1942	90 Jewish inmates to Bernburg
3/11/1942	90 Jewish inmates to Bernburg
3/12/1942	105 Jewish inmates to Bernburg
3/14/1942	99 Jewish inmates to Bernburg

Among the 571 victims there were 468 Jews.

The commencement of "Special Treatment 14 f 13" was accompanied by an increase in the **murder of sick persons through lethal injections** of phenol, hexobarbital or air. A method which had existed in the camp since 1940 but seldom been put into practise, it now began to take on a systematic character. At the Buchenwald Trial in Dachau, Dr. Eisele testified that in early July 1941 Commander Koch had ordered him to determine the identities of all persons afflicted with tuberculosis. Koch then came to him two weeks later and showed him a letter from Berlin in which

Illustration 108: Dr. Gotthard Martin Gauger (1905-1941)
Source: Sammlung Gedenkstätte Buchenwald, Weimar

"special treatment" (a Gestapo and SS term designating execution without legal formalities) was ordered for all tuberculosis patients, asocials and preventive cus-

Illustration 109:
SS camp physician
Waldemar Hoven to
Dr. Joachim Gauger,
July 27, 1941
Hoven had medical
records forged
by a nurse.
*Source: Thürin-
gisches Hauptstaats-
archiv, Weimar*

K.L. Buchenwald   Weimar/Buchenwald, den 27. Juli 1941.
    "Lagerarzt"   00044

              Betreff : Häftling (polit.), Nr. 4953, G a u g e r Martin,
                        geb. 4.8.1905 in Wuppertal-Elberfeld, gest.
                        23.7.1941 im K.L. Buchenwald.
              Bezug   : Ihre persönliche Unterredung mit dem Lagerarzt.
              Anlagen : 1

              Herrn
              Dr. Joachim G a u g e r ,
              Wuppertal - Elberfeld,
              Hopfenstraße 6.

                    Wie jeder andere Häftling wurde Ihr Bruder bei
              seiner Einlieferung in das K.L. Buchenwald am 12.6.1941
              einer eingehenden ärztlichen Untersuchung unterzogen. Bei
              derselben wurde eine starke Rechtsverbreiterung des Herzen
              festgestellt. Auf Grund dieses Befundes wurde Ihr Bruder
              von der Arbeit freigestellt und in ärztliche Behandlung
              genommen. Am 27.6.1941 wurde eine Röntgenaufnahme gemacht,
              von der Sie einen Abzug in der Anlage finden.
                    Am 23.7.1941, gegen 12,45, wurde Ihr Bruder von
              seinen Mithäftlingen in besinnungslosem Zustand in den
              Krankenbau eingeliefert. Die sofort einsetzende ärztliche
              Hilfe vermochte den Zustand des Patienten nicht mehr zu
              beeinflussen. Selbst eine intracardiale Verabreichung von
              Coramin blieb ohne Erfolg. Eintritt des Todes am 23.7.1941
              um 13,00 Uhr. Todesursache : Herzschlag.
                    Ich bedauere den plötzlichen Tod Ihres Bruders
              fern von seinen Angehörigen, umso mehr, da ärztlicherseits
              alles getan worden ist, um seine Gesundheit zu erhalten.
                                        Der L a g e r a r z t
                                           K.L. Buchenwald

                                        SS-Obersturmführer d.R.

tody inmates; then Koch commanded him to carry out this task. The first killing operation to take place in this context began with two transports from Dachau – on July 6, 1941 (1,000 persons) and July 12, 1941 (1,008 persons) – consisting primarily of sick men, to some extent invalids. The nurse Ferdinand Römhild later stated in this connection:

"We had a major operation in the camp; we had received a so-called invalid transport, from Dachau, and the camp was full of these people. Then in July an operation got under

way that was contrived solely by Dr. Eisen [He meant Eisele. – Author]. The inmates who could be or were identified as being infected with tuberculosis on the basis of their appearance were admitted to the infirmary when they came in for treatment and killed by means of hexobarbital injections. ... I can't state the exact number, but it may have reached 500. ... The percentage of those infected with tuberculosis was doubtless high, but by far the majority of these people were simply in poor condition, undernourished and worn out, and could certainly have been saved under better circumstances."

The Deportation and Extermination of Jewish Inmates

On January 19, 1942 the Concentration Camp Inspector ordered the transfer of all able-bodied Jews imprisoned in the German concentration camps to the POW camp "KGL Lublin." The postscript contained a reminder to equip the inmates with warm clothing, *"... as every measure must be taken to preserve the Jews' fitness for employment."*

This order cited instructions made in December 1941, while also making indirect reference to the list of "able-bodied Jews" drawn up by the "euthanasia" appraisers within the context of "Operation 14 f 13." Rumours of the impending transport of Jewish inmates had already circulated in the camp during the first few days of 1942. In retaliation, the SS had the Jewish inmate Oswald Alexander flogged in public in the second week of January. He died five months later.

Nevertheless, the rumours were based on reality. From the beginning of the war until late 1941, the NS regime had been undergoing a transition from the policy of forced deportation to that of the extermin-

ation of all Jews living within the territories under its power. All members of the Jewish population were systematically marked and assembled in ghettoes. From 1941 on, Jews in Germany had had to wear a yellow star sewn to their clothing. Beginning the same year, they were deported to camps and forced to live in ghettos on annexed Polish territory. Wherever the Germans gained direct control of foreign territory, Jews were massacred. In December 1941 the first extermination facility to make use of the experience gained in the "euthanasia" killing centres went into operation in Chełmno (Kulmhof).

Following the invasion of the Soviet Union, the crimes committed in concentration camps took on a new dimension. Both "Operation 14 f 13" and the mass shootings of the Soviet prisoners of war were characterised by the systematic manner in which the SS proceeded, the technical preparation of the procedures and the employment of specialised personnel. In the wake of the **"Wannsee Conference"** the same attributes also applied to the deportation and extermination of the Jewish populations of the European countries that had fallen under German control.

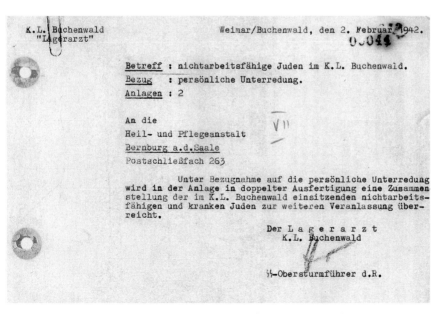

Illustration 110: SS camp physician Waldemar Hoven to Bernburg Sanatorium, Feb. 2, 1942
Source: Thüringisches Hauptstaatsarchiv, Weimar

The "Wannsee Conference" took place in a villa on Lake Wannsee in Berlin in January 1942. For the concentration camps, one consequence of the meeting was a temporary halt in the SS's deportation of Jewish inmates to Lublin. Independently of this decision, camp physician Hoven began making preparations for the murder of Jewish inmates following a "personal discussion" with the director of the Bernburg "euthanasia" killing facility. On February 2, 1942 he sent "a list, in duplicate, of the ill and disabled Jewish inmates of Buchenwald for necessary attention" to Bernburg. By mid March, the SS sent four transports containing altogether 384 Jewish inmates to this facility and had them gassed. Following these extermination transports there were still 836 Jewish inmates in the camp (as counted on March 16, 1942; total number of inmates: 8,117).

Because the SS apparently expected the remaining Jews to be deported without much delay, it was no longer important whether a Jewish inmate was also a "political inmate," a previously convicted, homosexual or "work-shy" inmate. The camp records now referred solely to "Jews," a group subdivided only by national origin, "Reich German," Czech and stateless Jews accounting for the majority. The newly

created SS Department of Economic Administration considered putting the Jewish inmates to work in the armament industry and in production, but these plans were thwarted in the fall of 1942. Hitler wanted the German Reich to be "Jew-free."

On October 5, 1942, SS Obersturmbannführer Maurer, head of Office D II of the SS Department of Economic Administration, informed all camp commanders of the following:

"The Reich Leader wants all concentration camps located on Reich territory to be made Jew-free. The Jews presently in your concentration camp are therefore to be transferred to Auschwitz or Lublin. I hereby request that the number of Jews serving sentences in your concentration camp be registered with me by the ninth of the month and that special attention be called to those inmates who are charged with duties which would not allow their immediate transfer."

On October 8, 1942, Buchenwald Concentration Camp command headquarters registered 405 Jewish inmates for transport to Auschwitz. Camp Commander Pister ordered ten goods cars and one passenger coach from the German Railway, making the transport officer personally responsible

Illustration 111: Bureau D, SS Department of Economic Administration, to the commanders of Buchenwald and Auschwitz Concentration Camps re the deportation of Jewish inmates, Oct. 12, 1942
Source: Thüringisches Hauptstaatsarchiv, Weimar

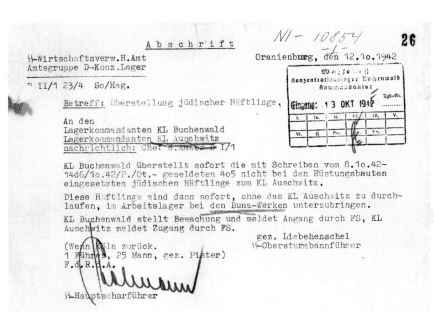

for seeing to it that "the cars are properly boarded up and sealed."

Two-hundred and thirty-four Jewish inmates remained in the camp, their deportation having been postponed because they were working for the "Construction Management Office / Jews" on the construction of a rifle factory, later "Gustloff-Werk II." For most of the Jews transported to the "IG-Farben" factory construction site at Auschwitz-Monowitz, Auschwitz meant death. Among the victims were the author Dr. Fritz Löhner-Beda, the former Landtag President of Vienna and chairman of the Viennese Social Democratic municipal councillors Dr. Robert Danneberg and the well-known Austrian lawyer and author Dr. Heinrich Steinitz. Only a very small number of these inmates survived to return on the evacuation trains in January 1945.

Illustration 112:
Dr. Fritz Löhner,
pen name: Beda
(1883-1942)
Source: Österreichische
Nationalbibliothek,
Vienna

Self-Preservation and Resistance

"All of my thoughts, all of my energy were focussed on the desperate struggle to survive the day, ward off my depressions, keep my spirit of resistance alive and obtain tiny advantages that might increase my chances of survival a little bit. Also, we constantly had to defend ourselves against the merciless SS men who tried to break the inmates' will to live. If I wasn't too exhausted or depressed from all of these efforts, I attempted to fathom out what was going on inside me and the others, because that interested me and was one of the few satisfactions the SS couldn't forbid."

Bruno Bettelheim

Resistance in the camp began with the **self-preservation** of the individual. The SS answered every attempt to raise an objection or rebel with brutal violence or murder. Mere suspicion was enough to put an inmate behind the bars of the "Bunker" cells. Emil Carlebach recalls the attempt of the Austrian Jew Edmund Hamber to bring charges against an SS murderer:

"The first case of open resistance against the murders committed by the SS took place in the fall of 1940. SS Oberscharführer Abraham drowned the Jewish inmate Hamber in a puddle of water. His brother, an eye-witness to the crime, was asked what the cause of death had been; he told the truth. Then the entire detachment was summoned to the gate, but naturally none of the others dared say he had seen anything. The foreman had to write down the names of his 28 men. ... The brother of the victim explained to me: 'I know that I will have to die for my statement, but maybe these criminals will be more careful in the future if they are in danger of being charged with murder; then I won't have died in vain.'"

During the first phase of the camp, due to various circumstances, the **attempt to escape** was doomed to failure: nearly all the inmates were concentrated in one place, the German public willingly supported all search measures and German troops occupied half Europe. All escapees were brought back to the camp, publicly punished and paraded and usually killed; what is more, an escape brought about the intensification of terror and privation for the entire camp. "Mutiny" carried the death penalty.

During this first period there were nevertheless conscious opponents to National Socialism – they formed a minority in the body of inmates – and a few outstanding examples of persons who maintained an upright stance and exhibited personal courage in their dealings with the SS. These persons were never forgotten by the inmates throughout the camp's existence. One of them was the pastor **Paul Schneider** who refused to salute the Nazi flag in April 1938 and then endured constant brutal mistreatment in the "Bunker" for many months until his death in July 1939. Particularly his sermons from inside his Bunker cell made a deep impression on the inmates falling in for roll call on the muster ground every morning and evening. Ernst Cramer, a Jew deported to the camp following the pogroms of November 1938, recalls:

"In the afternoon, when we were once again standing there, freezing, in rank and file, we experienced something very special. The roll call officer, obviously a Saxon, had growled out the order 'Silence, absolute silence' when a loud, woeful voice emerged from within the building which, as we had been told, contained the solitary bunkers. The words of the Sermon on the Mount rang out loud and clear: 'Blessed are they which are persecuted for righteousness' sake.'
'Shut that shaveling up,' the SS lieutenant called out angrily and soon thereafter everything was quiet. 'Blessed are they which suffer persecution,' a stranger next to me softly hummed the melody of the Gospel reading."

Among the Jewish inmates there was one block senior, **Rudolf Arndt** from Berlin, who spoke up so commendably for his fellow inmates in 1939-40 that he earned their great respect. During a conflict with "green" block seniors he was denounced and sent to the quarry. The SS, who referred to Arndt as the "Judenkaiser" (Jews' emperor) shot him there on May 3, 1940. Stefan Heymann recalls:

"After his arrival in Buchenwald Rudi was in a construction detachment for a short time. Later a special area was set up for the Jews and Rudi was appointed capo. Here he not only saved the lives of hundreds of Jews by wangling medicine with the aid of the Arian comrades in the main hospital, but also by leaving many inmates in the infirmary after the SS doctor had certified them as being fit for work. He hid them when the SS doctor was making his rounds and often kept them in the infirmary for weeks, without them having to go to work. He was aided especially by Walter Czolleck, who worked as a medical orderly, and Walter Blass, a clerk. Among the Austrian Jews, Rudi organised Block 22 of which he was the senior. I was his clerk. ... When a large number of Polish Jews from Germany were locked up in the so-called 'Little Camp' after the war began, Rudi saw to it that they received regular rations in that hell. ... Following the Jewish operation carried out on the occasion of the so-called assassination attempt in the Bürgerbräukeller, the treatment of Jews in the infirmary was prohibited. Rudi set up an infirmary service for the Jews in Block 22. Here the worst injuries were treated and bandaged. Rudi even gave injections with the most rudimentary means. His primary activity consisted in the organisation of good cultural work. He was the first person in Buchenwald to see to it that classical music was provided, receiving great support in this effort from Kurt Isaak."

On September 6, 1939, for reasons of religious conviction, the **Jehovah's Witnesses** unanimously refused to register for service in the Wehrmacht, defying the threat of death posed by the machine guns of the SS on the muster ground. The persistent observation of customary rituals such as the

Illustration 113: Rudolf [Rudi] Arndt (1909-1940), 1933
Source: Sammlung Gedenkstätte Buchenwald, Weimar

celebration of religious or political events also served to strengthen the will to survive, although it always represented a risk and, what is more, was often met with disapproval on the part of fellow inmates, as in the case of the fast carried out by the Viennese Jews on Yom Kippur, 1938.

The camp regime constantly corroded the foundations for human solidarity and

Illustration 114: Paul Schneider (1897-1939)
Source: Sammlung Gedenkstätte Buchenwald, Weimar

within that group the former members of left-wing parties, for the lighter labour detachments. The other side of this coin was always that the power of preferential treatment could also serve the purposes of the discrimination and harassment of irritating political opponents, and that the filling of positions within the inmate administration system came to be controlled by political cliquism. The conditions of life in the camp made it difficult to withstand these temptations, but they also appeared justified in the light of the Stalinist doctrine already in practise for many years in the German Communist Party, according to which political dissidents within the left wing were to be excluded and combated. Whereas these practises were somewhat modified in the early years through the presence and influence of eminent Communist members of the Reichstag such as Dr. Theodor Neubauer and Walter Stoecker, they played an increasingly significant role after the outbreak of war.

In the early period of Buchenwald there were also examples of **organised solidarity** that exceeded the limits of the group of "politicals." There are reports, for instance, of political inmates joining to help Jewish inmates following the pogrom of 1938. The political inmates also organised a "**Poles' school**" for Polish youths, tolerated to some extent by the SS. The Pole Henryk Sokolak taught there. One of the pupils, Jan Dubisz, recalls:

fostered a wolf's society in which only the stronger members were accorded chances of survival. According to the social Democrat Walter Poller, "the political first!" was an unwritten law among the political inmates, regardless of whether they were at enmity over old ideological conflicts. Above all, this meant *"that every political inmate in the camp who had proven not to be a son of a bitch enjoyed the preferential protection and help of all fellow political inmates."* And furthermore, *"... that vacant positions were to be filled by suitable political inmates."*

During the first phase of the camp's existence, these circumstances led to the selection of the non-Jewish politicals, and

"Thanks to this initiative a school was organised for the purpose of teaching the Polish youths German. ... When the coast was clear of SS, i.e. at the sound of the word 'fifteen,' Polish was also taught, but when the inmate on watch called out 'eighteen' (attention), we immediately continued the lesson in German. ... Those of us who took part in the lessons were all transferred to Block 50 and to the workshops of the DAW as metalworkers, electricians, joiners, tailors, shoemakers, painters, bricklayers and plumbers, our vocational qualifications and interests being taken into consideration."

There were also instances of political and humanitarian solidarity in the camp which had serious consequences for those who participated. In October 1941, for example, a group of 2,000 Soviet prisoners of war arrived in Buchenwald, dressed in rags and near starvation. Against the express orders of the SS and despite threats of heavy penalties, **spontaneous help** was organised. In retaliation, three prominent political block seniors – Josef Schuhbauer, Kurt Wabbel and Kurt Leonhardt – who had been or- dered by the SS to suppress all contact with the POWs – publicly received twenty-five strokes each on their bare buttocks, were demoted and assigned to a quarry detach- ment. Communist inmate functionaries in supposedly safe positions were also trans- ferred to the "delinquent company." The political inmates lost control of the pos- ition of Camp Senior One to the former convict Josef Ohles.

The Camp During the "Total War": 1942/43-1945

The Functions of the Camp are Expanded

"Pister declared: '… work, I want to see work!' The personal cruelties of the previous years, however, were only a fraction of the number that perished under his rule in the gradually developing sub-camps. The character of the camp changed. What had been a camp under construction was now a war production operation in which thousands and thousands of inmates performed forced labour. At the same time, the camp functioned increasingly as a parent and transit camp, through which hundreds of thousands were channelled under Pister's rule."

Report of the International Buchenwald Camp Committee

"Labour Allocation"

At the end of 1941, following the failure of the blitzkrieg in the East and the declaration of war by the United States, the hostilities took on the character of a world war. Alongside the functions it fulfilled in connection with the exclusion and extermination of entire groups of the population, the SS now saw the necessity and opportunity of emerging as an entrepreneur and economic factor. The growing need for soldiers and the expanding armament industry had led to a shortage of labourers to which the NS leadership responded with the recruitment and ruthless conscription of workers from the occupied countries of Europe. In March 1942, Hitler appointed one of his "Old Guard" – the Reichsstatthalter of Thuringia Fritz Sauckel – "Plenipotentiary for Labour Allocation," investing him with the authority to recruit an army of forced labour convicts several million strong.

The founding of the **SS Department of Economic Administration** in the same month marked the attainment of an analogous goal: the streamlining and centralisation of the SS bureaucracy. And whereas until this time forced labour had served as a means rather than as the purpose of concentration camp imprisonment, the camps were now to pursue their own economic activities as well as lease inmates to private industry. Within the course of a development that began with the incorporation of

Concentration Camp Inspection into the SS Department of Economic Administration as Bureau D, the economic organisation of the SS became a factor in the German war industry. In his report to Himmler on April 30, 1942, Oswald Pohl, the head of the SS Department of Economic Administration, stated:

"1. The war has brought about a perceivable change in the structure of the concentration camps and fundamentally changed their functions with regard to inmate exploitation. The detention of inmates solely for reasons of safety, for disciplinary or preventive purposes is no longer of primary importance. The emphasis has shifted to the economic aspect. The mobilisation of all inmate labour, initially for war-related tasks (accelerated armament) and later for peace-time tasks, is becoming the chief focus. …
3. I therefore called a meeting of all officers of the former Concentration Camp Inspection, all camp commanders and all factory directors on April 23-24, 1942, and presented the new developments to them in person. …
4. The transfer of Concentration Camp Inspection to the Department of Economic Administration has been carried out by mutual agreement with all of the departments involved. The cooperation between all administrative offices is entirely unproblematic; the elimination of the mutually unrelated coexistence of the concentration camps is generally accepted as a means of overcoming bonds which hinder progress."

134

Illustration 115: Aerial photograph, June 4, 1945
Source: Aerial photograph databank, H. G. Carls engineering firm, Würzburg

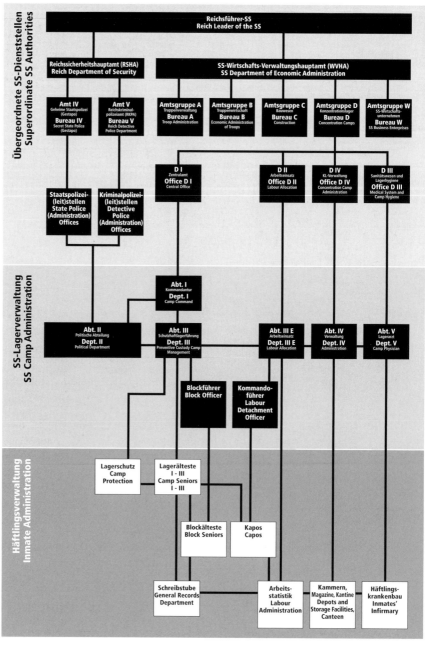

Organisational structure of camp administration from 1942 onwards
Source: P. Wentzler, Hinz & Kunst, Braunschweig

Illustration 116: Commander Hermann Pister (4th fr. l.) and Adjutant Hans Schmidt (far left) with works managers of the Gustloff-Werke, 1943
Source: Musée de la Résistance et de la Déportation, Besançon (SS Photo Album: "Buchenwald Jahresende 1943")

The slave army in the concentration camps grew steadily: from 88,000 in December 1942 to 224,000 in August 1943, 658,000 (187,000 women and 471,000 men) in late September 1944 and 714,000 in mid January 1945. The concentration camps, a long-accepted element of the societal norm, spread throughout Germany by means of a system of sub-camps. In April 1944 the concentration camp system comprised 20 parent camps and 165 sub-camps. At the beginning of 1945, Buchenwald was the largest camp complex still in existence.

The New SS Camp Administration

For the staff of the concentration camps, these circumstances led to a new manner of proceeding that was distinguished by cold-blooded planning and accounting and the purposive linking of "selection" with "labour allocation." The camps took on a new character. Former career climbers such as Buchenwald's Camp Commander Koch toppled because they could not adapt to the change; for others it was precisely these new circumstances which opened up new

career opportunities in the SS. Among the latter was Hermann Pister, whose assumption of duties in Buchenwald in January 1942 led to an increase in the role played by bureaucracy there. He had certain members of the command staff replaced and, unlike his predecessor Koch, attached importance to continuity in the higher offices. On April 30, 1942, Oswald Pohl wrote to the camp commanders to inform them of their new duties:

*"1.) The **command of a concentration camp** and all of the economic operations of the Schutzstaffel [SS] within its organisational sphere is the responsibility of the camp commander. He alone is accountable for securing the greatest possible productivity in the plants. ...*
*4.) The camp commander is solely responsible for the **allocation of the labourers**. This allocation must be exhaustive in the true sense of the word, in order to achieve the highest possible degree of productivity. ...*
*5.) **Working time** is not limited in any way. Its duration is dependent upon the operational structure of the camp and the type of work to be carried out and is to be determined solely by the camp commander.*

137

6.) *Circumstances which might reduce working time (meals, roll calls, etc.) are therefore to be reduced to an absolute minimum. Time-consuming falling-in procedures and midday breaks solely for the purpose of eating are prohibited.*

7.) *The former rigid organisation of the **guard** is to be relaxed and gradually flexibilised with a view to later peace-time duties. Mounted guards, the utilisation of watchdogs, mobile watchtowers and mobile obstacles are to be developed.*

8.) *The execution of this order places substantially higher demands on every camp commander than has hitherto been the case. Because of the fact that the camps are very different, no standardising regulations will be prescribed. The entire initiative is placed instead into the hands of the camp commander. He is required to link clear, specialised knowledge of military and economic matters with sensible, wise leadership of groups, and unite them in high performance potential."*

Within this context, the influence borne by the various departments within the command headquarters also changed. Particularly from 1943 on, after the SS Department of Economic Administration had issued orders to reduce the death rates in the concentration camps, Department V (camp physician) recorded a genuine increase in competence. Its cooperation with Department III E (labour allocation) was aimed both at assigning inmates to various labour areas in order to mobilise last reserves, and at sorting out the ill and weak for extermination. In the "Wechselbad," an infirmary bath facility, and sometimes in the cinema, SS doctors examined the new arrivals only briefly and then assigned them to categories of employability.

The SS physician Dr. August Bender, who according to his own testimony examined as many as 1,500 inmates per day in 1944, later spoke of ten categories – wisely refraining from mentioning the death transports to Auschwitz:

"1. Transportable (not under sixteen and not over sixty years of age, in good physical condition, therefore suitable for labour duty). (Their file cards were marked with a 'K.')

2. Limitedly transportable. Not in good physical condition, but capable of light labour, e.g. for specialised work (file card marked with 'X').

3. Camp labour: including inmates over sixty, but not under sixteen; good physical condition was a prerequisite, but with slight physical deficits (file card was marked 'L. A.').

4. Light camp labour: Less good physical condition, for example the task of breaking up wood into small pieces for burning (file card marked 'L. L.').

5. Useless: Mentally confused and physically deformed. Poor general physical condition which would soon make labour impossible; also tuberculars and persons who suffered from tumours (file card 'unbrauchbar' [useless] or 'B. B.' (an abbreviation for Bergen-Belsen).

6. Invalids: Very old persons, persons with arm amputations. Could work voluntarily, absolutely not transportable (file card 'Inv.').

7. Skilled work: Metal workers with leg amputations could work voluntarily; they never refused. Were never transported (file card 'B. A.').

8. Sedentary work: as in 7. Absolutely no heavy labour, for example optician, shoemaker, etc. (file card 'Sitzende Arbeit').

9. Trainee: Strong young people between fourteen and sixteen years or infirm elderly persons. Essentially no transport, trained as precision mechanics and assistants (file card 'L').

10. Careful handling: For all who had been dismissed from work (following illness). (File card 'Sorgfältige Behandlung')."

The infirmary submitted the results of the "examinations" – carried out in the form established in 1943 – to the labour administration office. There, under the orders of the SS labour allocation officer and in cooperation with the general records department, transport lists were drawn up, the inmates assigned to various labour duties and sub-camps. Inmates who had been labelled 'useless' usually only lived for a short time. While Buchenwald, unlike Auschwitz, possessed no extermination facilities, inmates were killed in the infirmary by means of injections; in camp jargon the term for this was "abspritzen" ("shoot down"). The Czech Jaroslav Bartl, a scribe in the infirmary from 1942 on, reports:

Illustration 117: Syringe
Catalogue 4/12
Photo: N. T. Salmon

"Most of the inmates knew what was in store for them when they entered OP II, where an SS man with a syringe was already sitting. There was not a single case in which an inmate resisted against the fatal injection. Perhaps it was the whole setting where it took place – the clean, white operating room, the polished instruments, the doctor in his white coat, who had a friendly look on his face and smiled encouragingly – perhaps it was due to all of these circumstances that at this moment the inmates – who knew about the murders in the infirmary – thought it could not be possible that here in this nice operating room, of all places, they, of all people, were going to be cold-bloodedly murdered. In the camp, the death of an inmate was almost always associated with cudgel blows, a rifle shot, the boulders in the quarry, the gallows, the Bunker, hunger – this here, this didn't look like Death… And they nevertheless landed on the floor of the crematorium on a heap along with those who had been shot to death in the quarry or had collapsed from exhaustion or under cudgel blows somewhere in the dirt…"

The Parent Camp

The transformation of the concentration camp on the Ettersberg to serve as a parent and transit camp began in 1942. Within the camp, in a double barrack built on the muster ground especially for this purpose, an experimental rifle assembly shop was set up. Outside, along the road to Weimar, other inmates were forced to build a number of production halls within a few short months. The construction of the rifle factory in 1942-43 had originated from the idea – concocted by the SS leadership – of setting up a camp armourer's shop. The

economic interests of the armament firms proved stronger, however, and the SS had to give up its plans. Even before their construction had been completed, the agreement was reached to lease the armament factory halls, complete with inmates, to the Weimar Fritz-Sauckel-Werk of the Wil-

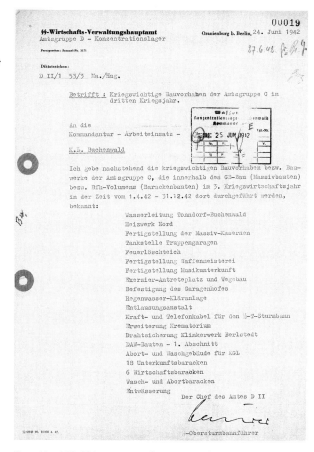

Illustration 118: SS Department of Economic Administration to Buchenwald Concentration Camp Command, June 24, 1942
Source: Thüringisches Hauptstaatsarchiv, Weimar

Illustration 119: Setting up machines in Gustloff-Werk II, Buchenwald, 1943 (SS photo)
Source: Sammlung Gedenkstätte Buchenwald, Weimar

helm-Gustloff-NS-Industriestiftung. In a draft of the lease of November 2, 1942, it was stated that:

"Drawing from the inmates of Buchenwald Concentration Camp, the leaser will place the labourers required for production at the lessee's disposal. It is assumed that approximately 6,000 labourers are required. None of the inmates assigned to the lessee's operation may be withdrawn without the lessee's consent except for reasons directly related to the grounds for

arrest. A separate agreement on the details pertaining to the transfer of the inmates will follow."

For the so-called **Gustloff-Werk II**, the SS had inmates build a **railway line** from Weimar station to Buchenwald within three short months. In June 1943 the SS celebrated its inauguration like a victory. The line had been built in such a makeshift fashion that it was constantly in need of repair, and another year passed before it could be used for the transport of passengers. These achievements of the new SS leadership claimed a large number of victims from among the inmates and contributed substantially to the high death rate during Hermann Pister's first year in Buchenwald, when one in three camp inmates died.

Construction work was also carried out inside the barbed-wire fence. In order to accommodate newly arriving mass transports, the barrack town was extended by two rows of wooden barracks on the northern edge – the so-called Little Camp. In order to check the spread of disease, new inmates were channelled through the **disinfection station**, a low building newly constructed in 1942 to the east of the depot and laundry. They handed in their clothing and all of their belongings, were shorn, im-

Illustration 120: Inmates at work constructing the Buchenwald railway line, 1943 (SS photo)
Source: Sammlung Gedenkstätte Buchenwald, Weimar

Illustration 121:
Buchenwald
railway line
unloading station,
1943
*Source: Musée
de la Résistance et
de la Déportation,
Besançon
(SS Photo Album:
"Buchenwald
Jahresende 1943")*

mersed in a disinfectant bath and herded, still naked, into the depot where they received camp uniforms and numbers. In the first quarter of 1944 alone, some 15,000 persons were subjected to this procedure in the disinfection station. In the summer of 1942 the SS also had the **crematorium** expanded substantially and equipped with cremation ovens developed especially for concentration camps by the company Topf & Söhne of Erfurt.

In 1944, approximately 4,500 inmates worked in the Gustloff-Werk II and the Deutsche Ausrüstungswerke adjacent to the camp. The SS demanded maximum productivity, cruelly goaded the labourers and punished every attempt to rest as an act of sabotage. In November 1943 the director of the SS Department of Economic Administration, Oswald Pohl, issued the order for all concentration camps:

Illustration 122:
Buildings of the
disinfection
station, 1943
*Source: Sammlung
Gedenkstätte
Buchenwald,
Weimar*

Illustration 123: Karol Konieczny: "In the Disinfection Building," watercolour, 1945
Source: Reproduction, Sammlung Gedenkstätte Buchenwald, Weimar

Illustration 124: Crematorium, 1943
Annex to left: dissecting room of pathology department.
Source: Musée de la Résistance et de la Déportation, Besançon (SS Photo Album: "Buchenwald Jahresende 1943")

"… that the required working time of eleven hours per day for inmates is also to be maintained during the winter months, with the exception of the external detachments (e.g. the construction projects) which must return to the camp on time in view of the brevity of the days and the early nightfall. On the other hand, the inmates employed in factory rooms or production halls are to be enlisted for eleven-hour shifts from Monday through Saturday. In cases of extreme urgency the inmates are also to work on Sundays, but only in the morning. To a significant degree, the work which is of relevance for the war and for victory is presently being carried out by inmates, and in view of this circumstance it is absolutely essential that daily working time amount to no less than eleven hours."

It was not long before SS terror proved unsuitable for the purpose of increasing efficiency, particularly within the context of more complex duties and those requiring specific skills. The attempts to adapt the punitive system to the new objectives remained superficial and had no substantial effect on the camp. In early December 1942, for example, Himmler ordered the camp commanders to employ flogging "in future as a last resort," when all other means of punishment had failed. His comment "that the real purpose of the most severe camp punishments has in most cases not been recognised," could hardly conceal the reality of the corporal punishment regimen in the camps, which was such a secure fixture in the daily routine of the SS that not even central orders had any effect on it. The only change brought about by the instruction was that the official execution of corporal punishment no longer took place publicly, before the assembled inmates, but in the cinema barrack and was banned entirely at the end of 1944 by order of Himmler. Commander Pister later had the "Bock" burned and evidence of corporal punishments removed from the inmates' files. In the 1945 report by the International Camp Committee it is stated:

Illustration 125: Crematory ovens manufactured by Topf & Söhne of Erfurt, 1943
The 1942 prototype of the crematory ovens used at Auschwitz-Birkenau.
Source: Musée de la Résistance et de la Déportation, Besançon (SS Photo Album: "Buchenwald Jahresende 1943")

"The face of the camp changed. The long roll calls were abbreviated in the interest of war production. The interminable standing during roll call – a torture which had been repeated twice a day for all inmates for many years – was reduced to a bare minimum."

Illustration 126: Return march of inmates from the Gustloff-Werk to the camp, ca. 1944 (SS photo)
Source: Sammlung Gedenkstätte Buchenwald, Weimar

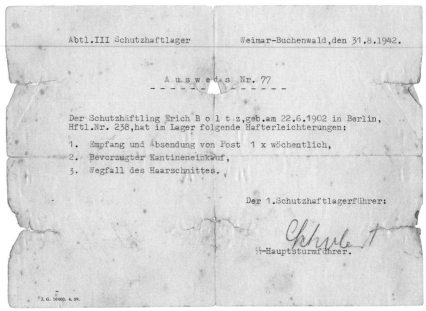

Beginning in 1942, long-term inmates and functionaries were granted so-called **special privileges** consisting of weekly mail correspondence and preferential canteen purchases. Inmates who possessed an appropriate identification card were also allowed to let their hair grow. In May 1943 the SS introduced a **bonus system**. For special performance at work, the SS distributed canteen coupons, the so-called camp money.

In March 1943, following a visit to Buchenwald, Heinrich Himmler criticised the absence of a **camp brothel** for the inmates. A visit to the brothel was to be used as a "means of incentive for higher performance." The bonus regulation laid down in

May 1943 by Oswald Pohl, the chief of the SS Department of Economic Administration, also provided for visits to the brothel "for good conduct and special labour performance."

On July 16, 1943 the SS brought sixteen female inmates between the ages of twenty and thirty from the Ravensbrück Concentration Camp to the "Sonderbau" ("special building"), as the SS referred to the brothel in Buchenwald. They had been promised improved rations, a quarter of the earnings and a speedy release (which they were never given). Each of the women had to place herself at the disposal of an average of five men per day. Inmates of the Little Camp, Jews, Sinti, Romani and Russians were prohibited from visiting the brothel. Others, primarily German, Austrian, Czech and Polish inmates could submit a written application for this privilege to the SS camp command by way of the officer in charge of their block. The authorisations were announced by the SS at the evening roll call. A visit to the brothel cost two Reichsmark, beginning in February 1944 only one Reichsmark. The brothel was closed when evening roll call was delayed, when there was a water shortage, and when Hitler's speeches were broadcast. The number of women changed only slightly; at the end of March 1945 there were still nine in the camp brothel.

The measures undertaken by the SS clearly led to further social differentiation within the camp, but not to the desired consequences. On the whole, the **general maintenance** of the inmates worsened steadily. Whereas the official rations had for the most part remained constant until 1942, that year marked a reduction of fat, meat, bread and potatoes. In May 1942, for example, the weekly ration of bread was reduced to 2,450 grams, meat to 280 grams and fat to 170 grams. The supply of potatoes – later replaced by turnips – was incumbent upon the respective camps and the local food and agriculture offices. The amount of food that ultimately reached the inmates was substantially lower than that available to the German public. Purely with regard to quantity, the camp average remained at approximately twenty-five

Illustration 129: Brothel ("special building"), 1943
Source: Musée de la Résistance et de la Déportation, Besançon (SS Photo Album: "Buchenwald Jahresende 1943")

percent below the national average. What is more, the food distributed to the inmates was often of poor quality or spoiled.

The SS received 4 to 6 Reichsmark per inmate and day for the lease of factory labourers, an income it was obliged to turn over to the Reich Treasury. In 1944 the camp administration estimated its daily expenses per inmate at 1.34 Reichsmark, comprising 30 Pfennig for accommodation, 39 Pfennig for clothing and 65 Pfennig for rations including the heavy labour bonus. Only 1.22 Reichsmark per day were calculated for female inmates.

Yet these official rates existed only on paper, for the majority of the inmates lived in ramshackle barracks, were dressed in rags and starving. According to a survey taken in March 1944 of the body weight of the inmates in the parent camp (who at that time accounted for only half of the inmates of Buchenwald Concentration Camp, the other half living under even worse conditions in the sub-camps) eighty-one percent, or 18,990 of approximately 21,500 persons, were undernourished.

Of the various deficiency diseases common among the inmates, **tuberculosis** was the most widespread. In mid 1944 approximately every tenth inmate in the Buchenwald parent camp suffered from open tuberculosis, a rate five times higher than that outside the camp. Only one fifth of the tubercular inmates were in the infirmary, however; the others performed heavy labour. Inmates with open tuberculosis were classified by the SS doctors under Category 5: "useless." Many of them were killed by means of injections.

The Infirmary and the Labour Administration Office

The appreciation in value of administrative and provision-related work as well as the new Camp Commander Pister's general interest in a well-functioning camp regime also determined the outcome of the "inmates' war" between the Communist and the BV inmates, a bitter struggle that began with the appointment of the BV inmate Josef Ohles as Camp Senior One in the autumn of 1941. The Political Department initially attempted to settle the differences in favour of the BV inmates around Josef Ohles, availing themselves of a method commonly used in the earlier years: the abrupt redistribution of the inmate functions. On March 26, 1942, following a denunciation by BV inmates, the department committed forty-eight political block seniors and capos to a **special detachment of the delinquent company** on charges of spreading the content of news heard on the radio. Four others, including the head of the illegal Communist party organisation Albert Kuntz, were put in the "Bunker."

Just a few weeks after the establishment of the special delinquent company detachment, Ohles was again dismissed from his function and replaced by the former cavalry captain Fritz Wolff, a political inmate and opponent of the Communists. On June 7, 1942 a political inmate made a declaration to the SS concerning Ohles' homosexual tendencies; the latter was dead the next day. At the same time, there was also an internal SS conflict of interests between the Political Department, with its objective of destroying the enemy, and the central command, concerned with the smooth functioning of the camp. In this conflict it was Commander Pister who established the priorities. On June 30, 1942, at the peak of the "inmates' war," Pister unexpectedly had the special detachment disbanded and re-

turned most of the Communist inmates to their former functions.

A period of **vehmic justice** followed until the spring of 1943, by which time all of Ohles' followers had been killed. During this period the illegal KPD leadership disciplined its own ranks, suppressed all forms of internal splitting and isolated members who failed to toe the party line. Within the context of these "purges," Camp Senior Two – Hans Bechert (KPD) – was ousted from his function and died on March 2, 1943 in the infirmary under mysterious circumstances. There are many indications that he was murdered. The last to topple was Camp Senior One Fritz Wolff in June 1943, after being accused of homosexuality.

Beginning in June 1943, shortly after the commencement of the large mass transports with which the SS filled the camp, the inmate administration in Buchenwald had an internal structure unequalled in any other camp within the concentration camp system. Virtually the entire functionary power in the camp – the three camp seniors, the infirmary, the labour administration office, the general records department, most of the block seniors, the most important capo positions – was monopolised by an illegal KPD party organisation that was centrally managed and disciplined with an iron hand. No inmate functionary could work against this grouping on his own initiative for any length of time. Newly formed in 1943, the "**triple head**" of the KPD organisation consisted of Walter Bartel, Harry Kuhn and the infirmary capo Ernst Busse. Kuhn led the "Abwehrapparat" (defence apparatus), a kind of secret service which saw to the maintenance of power and convicted real or alleged traitors, who died or were sent away on transports a short time later.

In mid 1942, in view of the rapidly increasing number of inmates, the SS consented to the activation of an inmate detachment for the purpose of guarding the storage facilities and depots and patrolling the camp at night. It was called **Camp Protection**. During the daytime it supervised camp cleanliness, investigated thefts and assisted in the maintenance of order when transports arrived. Formed after the

Illustration 130: Arm band for members of Camp Protection
In camp jargon, inmate functionaries were referred to as "armband wearers."
Catalogue 4/14
Photo: N. T. Salmon

inmates' war between the "greens" and the Communist inmates had reached its peak, the detachment was composed solely of political inmates and thus strengthened the position of the political camp seniors. With Camp Protection, the camp seniors had a kind of special police force at their disposal. Camp Protection was mentioned in the roll call lists for the first time on October 10, 1942, when it had twenty members; by the time of the air strike on August 24, 1944 the number had risen to fifty-one. After that attack the detachment was nearly doubled and became an international organisation. The existence of Camp Protection led to the reduction of SS presence in the camp. The detachment's activities limited SS terror, but were not themselves non-violent. It carried out special protection tasks on behalf of the Communist resistance organisation.

Under these circumstances, the **infirmary capo**, Ernst Busse, became the most influential inmate functionary in the camp. Not only did he belong to the political leadership of the Communists but, through his position in the infirmary, he wielded power over life and death, which he frequently exploited during the "inmates' war" of 1942/43. What is more, in the interest of its economic aspirations, the SS made the inmates' infirmary and the labour administration office the most influential positions of internal camp administration. In this second phase of the camp's

history, inmate doctors were permitted to practise their profession in the infirmary; they answered to the capo, who now held a purely administrative function. By mid 1944 the number of inmates working within the context of the infirmary had increased to ten times what it had been in 1938.

Busse came from a working class family from Solingen. A labour union functionary who had joined the KPD in 1919 at the age of twenty-one, he was elected to represent the KPD in the Reich parliament in 1932. He was arrested in 1933 and brought up for trial the following year on charges of "preparations for high treason." After spending two years in solitary confinement in the Kassel-Wehlheiden Prison, he was taken into "preventive custody" by the Gestapo and committed to Lichtenburg Concentration Camp. From there he was transferred to Buchenwald in early August 1937. In Buchenwald he was initially a block senior, from 1940 to 1941 a camp senior, and from 1942 on the capo of the inmates' infirmary. Due to the inherent contradictoriness of this position, he was committed in 1950 to the Soviet camp in Vorkuta, where he died in 1952.

Under the conditions of the mass transit camp, the administrative and order-maintenance competencies developed by the Communist inmate functionaries in the offices and the infirmary made them indispensable for Pister. There were several rea-

Due to their unconditional group cohesion in the occupation of these functions, they were increasingly able to ensure their survival as a group, protect their allies and strengthen the bonds with them. They created an internal order which made life in the camp more predictable for all of the inmates, a circumstance which accounts for the prestige they enjoy among the survivors. Nevertheless, in the extreme situation of a concentration camp, one group of persons could often be saved only at the cost of the others, the secret organisation be defended only with draconian measures. This led to the victimisation of other inmates, those who did not possess the privileges of the "inmate functionaries." In the process, German Communists became inextricably involved in the camp's racist SS hierarchy. Eugen Kogon recalls:

sons for this: they were Germans, but had contact to foreign inmates by virtue of their internationalist outlook. They were well familiar with camp practice and had experience in a number of trades. Thanks to a high level of discipline, they could rely on one another entirely, and they did not shy away from the ambiguous position of power between the SS and the other inmates.

"They only gradually developed an elite which placed emphasis on collaboration with others, though never exceeding a very sparse degree of joint activity of a sometimes highly remarkable character. The second stratum of camp Communists, who made up the main bulk and was unteachably stubborn, did not sanction such individual or collective solidarity under any circumstances. The third Communist stratum comprised the more active as

Häftlingskrankenbau   12.6.1944

    Arbeitsstatistik   Herbert

Anbei schicke ich Dir 2 Häftlinge
Nr. 53285 Valentin   2.Fi. re. amputiert 3+5. versteift.
Nr. 53801 Casse   re. Arm amputiert.
Die Häftlinge sind transportfähig geschrieben und wurden
bei der Massenuntersuchung(1000 Mann in 2 Stunden) unter-
sucht. Nach ihrer Angabe sind sie für Transportreserve C
bestimmt. Da kein Arzt z.Zt. hier ist, bitte ich, doch die
Häftlinge vom Transport abzustellen. Heute Nachmittag stel-
le ich sie dem Arzt vor, damit der sie abschreiben kann.
Bei solcher Arbeit kann einem der Hut hoch gehen.

                              Häftlingskrankenbau

well as the more passive opportunists who, as is often the nature of such people, were usually a hundred and fifty percent extremists.

The services of the Communists to the concentration camp inmates can hardly be overestimated. In many cases the camp inmates literally owed them their lives, even if the motives seldom arose from pure selflessness, but usually from the group's self-preservation instinct, from which the entire camp sometimes benefited."

The Little Camp

From 1938 on, the creation of special zones repeatedly served to cast the burden of overcrowding onto a smaller group of inmates in to ensure the camp's continued functionality. The logic of this method corresponded to that of the expulsion of the sick and the weak. Thus it is hardly astonishing that, beginning in 1943, the two functions – that of "quarantine" and that of selection for "labour allocation" – were assigned their own zone in which accommodation was minimised, rations

Illustration 133: Camp street in front of Little Camp latrine, May 1944 This photograph was taken illegally by Georges Angéli, who worked in the photography department. *Source: Georges Angéli*

Illustration 134: Little Camp quarantine area, May 1944 This photograph was taken illegally by Georges Angéli, who worked in the photography department. In the background is the tent camp that remained in use until the end of 1944. *Source: Georges Angéli*

Illustration 135:
View of the Little
Camp stable
barracks from
the upper floor
of the stone
Barrack 47, 1945
*Source: Sammlung
Gedenkstätte
Buchenwald,
Weimar*

reduced and hygienic conditions abominable: the so-called Little Camp on the northern edge of the barrack town.

The barracks there consisted of windowless Wehrmacht stables 40 metres long and 10 metres wide. In the interior, to the left and right of a corridor approximately 2 metres wide, rows of three- or four-level sleeping compartments had been installed. As Gerhard Harig recollects:

"They were large stables whose interiors were not divided into rooms. In the place of [man-sized] doors there was merely a [kind of barn door] ... at each of the narrow ends. Actually originally intended for use as stables, these wooden barracks had no windows and received light only through small wired-glass hatches. A narrow corridor had been left open down the middle of these stables; to its left and right, in place of stalls, compartments had been built three or four storeys high, large rectangular boxes made of raw wood. ... In order to wash or relieve oneself, one was required to leave the barrack. Initially there were rudimentary washroom facilities and even more rudimentary latrines outdoors and later in a drastically undersized lavatory facility in the centre of the Little Camp."

From 1943 on, all mass transports went through the Little Camp. Initially, the inmates stayed an average of four to six weeks there, and it was solely due to the rapid turnover that the zone was not characterised solely by rampant disease and death any sooner. Beginning in January 1945, however, in view of permanent overcrowding, those were the attributes it took on. The Little Camp left a deeply shocking impression on all who came to Buchenwald. The Dutchman Leo Kok recalls:

"As we were beaten out of the railroad cars with rifle butts at Buchenwald Station at the break of dawn on January 24, 1944, we were in a miserable condition after the terrible journey. There were three corpses in the car, and two who had lost their minds, in addition to the many who had lost consciousness. ... We finally entered the night, in wooden shoes, descending the high steps of the uniform depot into the dark, into the dirt, into the Little Camp, into Block 58, which was already full to capacity. ... Sixty men to a box, i.e. ten to each set of shelves, only possible if they arranged themselves like sardines in a tin. It was impossible to get undressed. Many decided it would be better to lie on a table or on the floor but that was prohibited after a few days. ...Going out to relieve oneself was ago-

ny; the latrine was either frozen over or flooded. It was located downhill from the block and special acrobatic talent was required to reach it. Nevertheless, it was continually full, for nearly everyone suffered from diarrhoea and dysentery. At night you had to grope for a free place with your hands, and then you usually ended up sitting down in another sick person's filth. When water was available, we had to go and wash in the washroom, which was usually quite a distance away, at five o'clock in the morning. Most people avoided going because it was excruciatingly difficult to get through the mud in wooden shoes and nobody, or almost nobody, had a towel. You hardly had the space and time to wash yourself properly anyway. We were yelled at everywhere we went and it took us days to figure out that the washroom attendants and the men on barrack duty, Camp Protection duty, etc. were inmates like us and not, as we had first thought, SS men. There were a few fortunate exceptions."

The **stables** were originally intended for fifty horses each. There is evidence of their accommodating as many as 1,960 human beings per barrack in Buchenwald. From May to December 1944, there was also a tent camp consisting of five army tents in the Little Camp. Kurt Mellach and Paul Springer wrote a joint report on this tent camp:

"In the summer of 1944, every barrack in Buchenwald Concentration Camp was overcrowded and 2,000 French inmates arriving from Compiégne were made to camp out on a vacant, barbed-wire-enclosed lot. Two days later the SS provided five tents with a capacity of 200 persons each. ... Tens of thousands of inmates passed through the tent camp, inmates of all European nationalities as well as American, English and Polish prisoners of war. Soon after its establishment, the tent

Illustration 136: Cup (aluminium), probably handmade
Found in the refuse dump downhill from the Little Camp. Engraving: "27. Juin 1943 G 14.862 M 1945 Konzentrationslager Buchenwald Weimar Guilleux Marcel"
Catalogue 4/6
Photo: N. T. Salmon

camp held 7 to 8 thousand inmates. Among them were numerous children of which the youngest were three years old. The five tents remained the only means of accommodation. ... Two to three hundred children, old people and gravely ill persons slept in the tent. All of the others had to sleep outside regardless of the weather conditions. Poorly clothed, insufficiently nourished, most of them without a blanket, in the stinging heat without water for drinking or washing. (In the beginning, after the completion of the plumbing, there was running water only on Sundays, later as much as one hour per day.) Or in the pouring rain for weeks on end, half-sinking into the soft clay ground, many barefoot and in insufficient, torn clothing. ... Already at the end of August, the five tents were supplemented by a barrack built of bed-boards gathered from all over the camp, and replaced in the autumn by Blocks 65, 66 and 67, built alongside them. Gradually the tents were taken down. The last of them disappeared at the beginning of January 1945."

New Inmates

"We asked ourselves what could be worse than this town, which was huge, but overpopulated, this town in which one suffocated and whose functioning was impossible to comprehend. When the block senior, a German inmate, said: 'All Frenchmen are crap,' those of the comrades who were not yet informed asked themselves what kind of huge trap they had stumbled into."

Robert Antelme

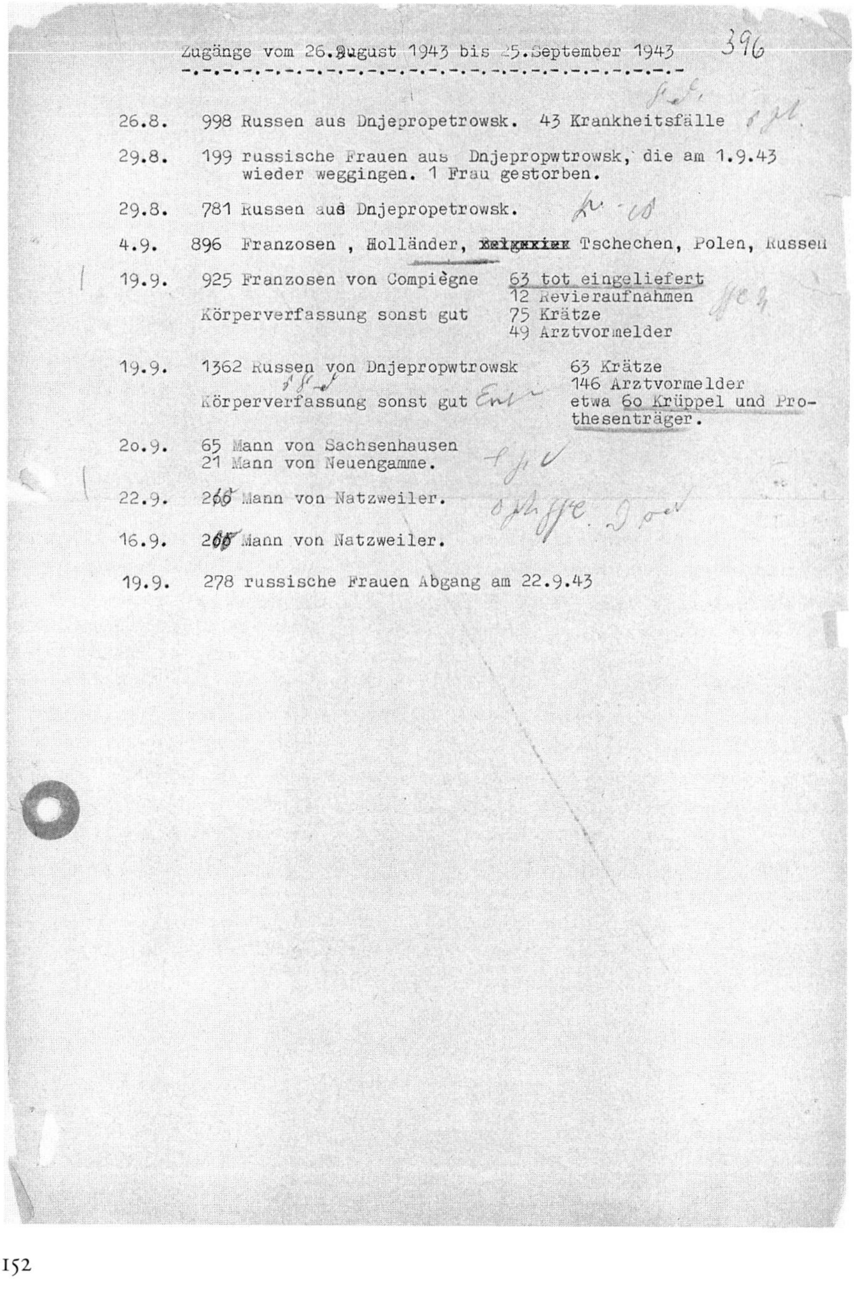

Illustration 137:
List of Transports,
August 26, 1943 –
September 25,
1943
The two transports
containing Russian
women were taken
to the Ravensbrück
Women's Concen-
tration Camp.
*Source: Thürin-
gisches Hauptstaats-
archiv, Weimar*

Zugänge vom 26.August 1943 bis 25.September 1943   396

26.8.	998 Russen aus Dnjepropetrowsk. 43 Krankheitsfälle
29.8.	199 russische Frauen aus Dnjepropwtrowsk, die am 1.9.43 wieder weggingen. 1 Frau gestorben.
29.8.	781 Russen aus Dnjepropetrowsk.
4.9.	896 Franzosen , Holländer, Belgier Tschechen, Polen, Russen
19.9.	925 Franzosen von Compiègne 63 tot eingeliefert
	Körperverfassung sonst gut 12 Revieraufnahmen
	75 Krätze
	49 Arztvormelder
19.9.	1362 Russen von Dnjepropwtrowsk 63 Krätze
	Körperverfassung sonst gut 146 Arztvormelder
	etwa 6o Krüppel und Pro-
	thesenträger.
2o.9.	65 Mann von Sachsenhausen
	21 Mann von Neuengamme.
22.9.	265 Mann von Natzweiler.
16.9.	265 Mann von Natzweiler.
19.9.	278 russische Frauen Abgang am 22.9.43

152

Mass Deportation

The number of inmates in Buchenwald Concentration Camp increased tenfold between April 1942, when the population was approximately 8,400, and the end of September 1944, when 84,505 inmates were counted. The basis for this mass subjection of human beings to the death mills of the camp was no longer formed solely, or even primarily, by the formal procedure of "preventive custody," although that basis still existed. The **apprehension practices** were continually **simplified** in a process which began with the outbreak of the war and were left increasingly to the discretion of the individual Gestapo offices or the commanders of the security police / security service units in the occupied countries. The longer the war dragged on, the more divergent the arrest practises from place to place became.

The first modifications consisted of the simplification of the registration and custody regulations for Soviet forced labour convicts, whose committal to the concentration camps was then carried out entirely outside the framework of the preventive custody directives; later the regulations applying to other inmate groups were also gradually abolished. This transformation, however, did not signify any gradual process of dissolving the concentration camps – the SS's strongest terror weapon – in favour of its entrepreneurial ambitions. On the contrary, as early as one year after the outbreak of war, Himmler had ordered the **division of the camps** into various levels, reflecting a form of graduated tyranny from camp to camp. According to this system, *"all lesser-incriminated preventive custody inmates clearly capable of reformation"* (Camp Level One) were to be committed to the Dachau, Sachsenhausen and Auschwitz I Concentration Camps. He designated the camps of Buchenwald, Neuengamme, Flossenbürg and Auschwitz II as being *"for heavily incriminated preventive custody inmates nevertheless educable and capable of reformation"* (Camp Level Two). All *"heavily incriminated, … virtually ineducable preventive custody inmates"* (Camp Level Three) were to perish in the camp at Mauthausen.

Illustration 138: Scene in front of a stable barrack in the Little Camp, May 1944
This photograph was taken illegally by Georges Angéli, who worked in the photography department.
Source: Georges Angéli

Illustration 139:
Pierre Mania: "In
the Railroad Car,"
drawing, 1943
*Source: Sammlung
Gedenkstätte
Buchenwald,
Weimar*

As is evident in numerous examples in the period until September 1942, this gradation remained in effect even when circumstances changed, although in the interest of "labour allocation" it was not so much the redistribution of the inmates to different camps that gained in significance, as the realisation of various camp levels through varying treatment within a single camp. In Buchenwald, for example, all three camp levels were in existence from 1943 on: Camp Levels One and Two in the parent camp as well as various subcamps, and Camp Level Three represented by the conditions of the tunnel construction detachments "Laura" and "Dora," in the Buchenwald quarry and in the subcamps with Jewish inmates. Level Three meant extermination through forced labour.

154

Until 1942, **mass committals** took place primarily in connection with political events such as the anti-Jewish pogrom of 1938 or the outbreak of war. In the period from 1943 to 1945 they became the rule, beginning with the deportation trains from the Soviet Union and Poland, later from Southern, Central and Western Europe as well as from camps which had to be evacuated due to the advancing fronts. Nearly every inmate who came to Buchenwald by these means received the red triangle combined with the initial of their country of origin. Jewish inmates also received a yellow triangle. Thus within a very short time, a camp initially distinguished to a great extent by the fact that the majority of its inmates were German became a reservoir for persons from all of the European nations occupied by Germany. Although nearly all the inmate groups introduced during the first period were still in existence after 1942, from 1943 on the inmate population of Buchenwald Concentration Camp was dominated chiefly by two inmate groups: forced labour convicts of Soviet or Polish origin and political inmates from occupied Europe. Not until mid 1944 were they joined by a third significant group: that of the Hungarian and Polish Jews.

In the course of the year 1944, **youths** under twenty-one years became the largest age group. The Reich Department of Security was not interested in the detention of children, as they were of no value as labourers, and in March 1943 the minimum age of eighteen for "Reich Germans" and sixteen for Poles and "Ostarbeiter" (forced labour convicts from the Soviet Union) was once again reconfirmed. The SS exploited this prescribed framework to the fullest and, beginning in 1943, young Poles and Russians were deported to the concentration camps in greater numbers than before. In December 1944, more than one third of the inmates of Buchenwald Concentration Camp – chiefly Russians, Poles and Jews – were minors under twenty-one years of age.

The age statistics in the year 1944 thus also reflect the consequences of targeted "selections" in reception camps, assembly camps and extermination centres as well as

Inmates according to origin							
Date	Total No.	Largest groups according to nationality *					
		Russians	Poles	Frenchmen	Jews	"Reich Germans"	Czechs
8/29/42	9,881	3,688 12 %	1,155 12 %	10 0,1 %	694 7 %	approx. 3,050 31 %	568 6 %
12/25/43	37,221	14,451 39 %	7,569 20 %	4,689 13 %	352 1 %	approx. 4,760 13 %	2,831 8 %
10/15/44	88,231	23,934 27 %	17,964 20 %	13,437 15 %	10,816 12 %	6,666 8 %	4,960 6 %

* Beginning in 1942, the SS subsumed all Jewish inmates under the category "Jews." This table accordingly does not reflect their countries of origin. The majority of them were from Hungary and Poland.

Age structure of the inmates, 1942/44									
Date	Total No.	Age groups							
		u. 20	20-30	30-40	40-50	50-60	60-70	70-80	o. 80
4/30/1942	6,558	142 2 %	1,286 20 %	2,158 33 %	1,899 29 %	874 13 %	188 3 %	11 0,2 %	–
12/30/1944	63,048	23,085 37 %	17,380 28 %	9,842 16 %	7,933 13 %	4,131 7 %	651 1 %	25 0,04 %	1

in Buchenwald itself. On October 7, 1944 Camp Commander Pister informed the SS Department of Economic Administration that the allocation of inmate minors could not be further increased at that point in time. Ten days earlier he had sent an extermination transport with 200 children and adolescents, exclusively Sinti and Romani, to Auschwitz.

Inmates from the Soviet Union

The number of inmates increased substantially in 1942 through the mass committal of Soviet and Polish forced labour convicts. These were persons who had been arrested by the Gestapo because they had escaped from their assigned workplaces in German industry or agriculture or had made themselves unfavourably conspicuous and

violated regulations. Between mid 1942 and early 1943 the Gestapo brought approximately 4,500 Soviet forced labour convicts to the camp from Thuringia, Hesse, Saxony and the Rhineland. They were treated by the SS with particular brutality, received drastically reduced rations (e.g. less than half the usual amount of bread), and were assigned almost exclusively to "Kommando X" (as the construction site for the new armament factory at the camp was called) or to the quarry. As early as August 1942, the camp physician proposed to the Political Department that, with regard to the Soviet forced labour convicts, the number of registered deaths be reduced to a minimum:

"According to an order issued last week, only one form is to be filled out. This is certain to save paper, but in view of the large proportion

Transports of Russians, Ukrainians, Czechs and Poles to Buchenwald

3/12/1943	1,000	Poles from Auschwitz
4/3/1943	968	Poles from Majdanek-Lublin Concentration Camp
8/4/1943	492	Poles from Majdanek-Lublin Concentration Camp
8/26/1943	998	Russians/Ukrainians from Dnepropetrovsk
8/29/1943	781	Russians/Ukrainians from Dnepropetrovsk
9/19/1943	1,362	Russians/Ukrainians from Dnepropetrovsk
9/30/1943	233	Russians/Ukrainians from Kiev
10/5/1943	604	Russians/Ukrainians from Nikolajev
10/10/1943	529	Russians/Ukrainians from Kirovograd
10/21/1943	300	Poles/Russians from Auschwitz
10/23/1943	1,539	Poles from Auschwitz
11/16/1943	318	Russians/Ukrainians from Kirovograd
11/27/1943	193	Russians/Ukrainians from Nikolajev
12/12/1943	200	Russians/Ukrainians from Auschwitz
3/24/1944	377	Russians/Ukrainians from Nikolajev
8/3/1944	73	Czechs from Gestapo Brünn (Brno)
8/13/1944	2,561	Poles from Warsaw
8/15/1944	1,999	Poles from Warsaw
10/1/1944	1,500	Poles from Auschwitz
10/12/1944	504	Poles/Russians from Auschwitz
11/4/1944	301	Poles from Auschwitz
12/7/1944	500	Poles from Auschwitz
12/18/1944	425	Poles from Auschwitz
1/22/1945	750	Poles from Auschwitz

of political Russians presently among the deceased, more paper, as well as time, could be saved if it were possible to cease registering these deaths altogether."

A short time later the SS also ceased entering the deaths of Soviet prisoners in the civil register.

In February 1943 the Reich Department of Security imposed a general ban on the release of "**Ostarbeiter.**" The head of Bureau D of the Department of Economic Administration informed the camp commanders that *"... in the interest of guaranteeing the armament programs being carried out in the concentration camps, the regulation hitherto in effect concerning the release of Ostarbeiter from the concentration camps after a certain period and their return to their old workplaces – having been originally established because of the disciplinary effect of this measure – will now be dispensed with."* Immediately afterward, the camp records reflected the existence of a new inmate category – the "Russian Civilian Workers" – comprising nearly all Soviet forced labour convicts previously registered as political inmates.

Ivan Alekseevic Borisov was brought to Germany by force in 1943 at the age of seventeen. He worked in a mine in Dortmund, escaped from there, was recaptured and escaped again in 1944, now from a prison camp where he had survived a typhoid fever infection. The second escape ended in the Gestapo prison in Münster. From there he was sent to Buchenwald, where he worked on the construction of the railway line and in the Gustloff-Werk II.

As a consequence of the German retreat which had begun in August 1943, a number of young Russians and Ukrainians came to Buchenwald on transports from Dnepropetrovsk, Kiev, Nikolajev and Kirovograd. Among them was Vladimir Mazijenko of Saporshje, Ukraine. He had been arrested at the age of fifteen and interned in the assembly camps of Dnepropetrovsk and Igren. In September 1943 he was deported from there to Buchenwald Concentration Camp, where he was initially forced to work in the Gustloff-Werk II, and was assigned in early 1944 to Block 8, the barrack for adolescents and children. He thus re-

Illustration 140: Cloth badge: "Ost" (east) Found in the detention cell building. The forced labour convicts deported to Germany from the USSR were required to wear this badge on the left-hand lapels of their jackets.
Catalogue 4/8
Photo: N. T. Salmon

Illustration 141: Ivan Alekseevic Borisov (1926), May 20, 1945
Source: Sammlung Gedenkstätte Buchenwald, Weimar

mained in the camp and lived to experience its liberation as a nurse in the infirmary.

By mid 1943, due to Gestapo arrests and transferral from "corrective labour camps," and above all as a result of the mass transports from the armament centres in the Ukraine, the Soviets had become the second largest inmate group after the political inmates. What is more, at the end of 1944 there were also 4,000 Soviet women in the Buchenwald sub-camps.

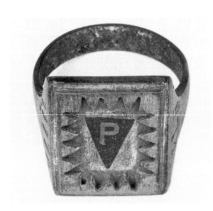

Illustration 142: Handmade ring with the identification symbol of the Polish inmates Found in the Little Camp. Catalogue 4/5
Photo: N. T. Salmon

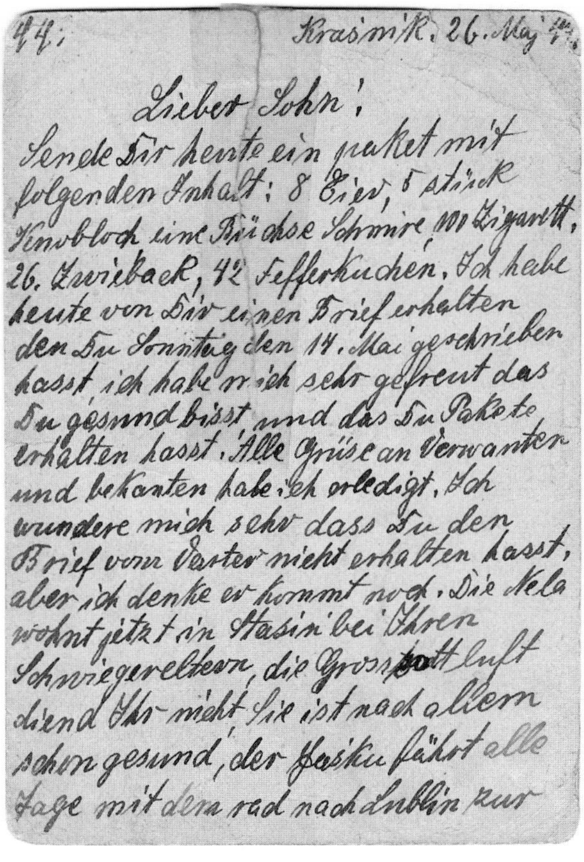

44; Krasnik. 26. Mai 44.
Lieber Sohn!
Sende Dir heute ein paket mit
folgenden Inhalt: 8 Eier, 5 stück
Knoblauch eine Büchse Schmire 100 Zigarett,
26. Zwieback, 42 Pfefferkuchen. Ich habe
heute von Dir einen Brief erhalten
den Du Sonntag den 14. Mai geschrieben
hasst, ich habe mich sehr gefreut das
Du gesund bisst und das Du Pakete
erhalten hasst. Alle Grüse an Verwanter
und bekanten habe ich erledigt. Ich
wundere mich sehr dass Du den
Brief vom Vater nicht erhalten hasst,
aber ich denke er kommt noch. Die Nela
wohnt jetzt in Stasin bei Ihren
Schwiegereltern, die Grosspott luft
dient Ihr nicht Sie ist nach allem
schon gesund, der Hesku fährt alle
Tage mit dem rad nach Lublin zur

Illustration 143: Letter to the Polish inmate Marian Tasiemski from his mother, May 26, 1944
All letters had to be written in German.
Source: Buchenwaldarchiv, Weimar

Polish Inmates

From May 1943 on, the Gestapo offices and commanding officers of the Security Police and Security Service in the occupied territories were no longer being required to apply to the Reich Department of Security for preventive custody orders, having been vested with the authority to decide locally on the committal of Poles to the concentration camps. As a result, there was a rapid increase in the number of Poles in Buchenwald. In addition, the SS had thousands of Polish inmates transferred from the Auschwitz and Majdanek Concentration Camps to Buchenwald for "labour allocation." There were 7,500 Poles in the camp at the beginning of 1944.

Until February 1944 most of the Polish inmates were classified under the inmates' group of the same name. Like the inmates from the Soviet Union, they were regarded as members of an "inferior race", granted a right to live only as cheap labour. In order to distinguish the Soviet and Polish inmates arrested by the SS merely to serve as slaves from those arrested for political reasons, the former were registered in the official camp records as "**Foreign Civilian Workers**" starting in early 1944. In mid April 1944, this new category comprised 22,120 inmates from Poland and the Soviet Union – more than half the entire camp.

The advancement of the Eastern front put an end to the transports from the Soviet Union. In August 1944, following the suppression of the Warsaw Uprising, the SS therefore quickly deported thousands of Poles to Buchenwald. By the end of 1944, there were nearly 6,500 Polish women in the women's sub-camps. As was the case for the majority of concentration camp inmates, Poles were no longer released and thus no longer had any means of leaving the concentration camp system alive. They

could only hope for liberation. They accounted for a large percentage of the escapees from the sub-camps. They were frequently recaptured and killed then and there without further ado, or hanged on one of the hooks in the wall of the Buchenwald crematorium cellar. The inmate hanged on the gallows by the SS in September 1944 – an event the entire camp was called together to witness on the muster ground – was a Pole.

Illustration 144:
Letter from the Czech inmate Alois Kröl to his wife, Jan. 9, 1944
Source: Buchenwaldarchiv, Weimar

Czech Inmates

The committal of inmates from the so-called Protectorate of Bohemia-Moravia to Buchenwald Concentration Camp began to increase in mid 1943. Before this point in time, Czechs had not played a significant role as an inmate group in the camp on the Ettersberg. The first of them came from Auschwitz in 1943. Committal directly from occupied Czechoslovakia began with the transport of 510 prisoners from Pilsen on July 22, 1943. Having been suppressed by means of massive terror following the assassination of Reinhard Heydrich in 1942, resistance in Czechoslovakia began to regain strength in 1944. Countermeasures became more severe in response, and the number of Czechs imprisoned in Buchenwald grew from approximately 600 in mid 1943 to nearly 5,000 in October 1944. Of all the concentration camps, Buchenwald was the one with the highest number of Czech inmates at the beginning of 1945.

Because the "Protectorate of Bohemia-Moravia" was considered territory annexed by Germany, the SS placed great emphasis on the issuance of differing badge colours. Over eighty percent of the Czechs were classified as political inmates and accordingly had to wear the red triangle. There were also groups of previously convicted persons (green triangle), so-called asocials (black), a few Jehovah's Witnesses (purple), emigrants (blue) and homosexuals (pink), as well as small groups of Czech Jews and Romani. Of the approximately 7,800 Czechs imprisoned in Buchenwald during the war, 773 died.

Deportation from France

Beginning in early 1944, the largest among the groups of political inmates from nearly thirty different countries were the French. Their deportation to Buchenwald was a consequence of the terror with which the

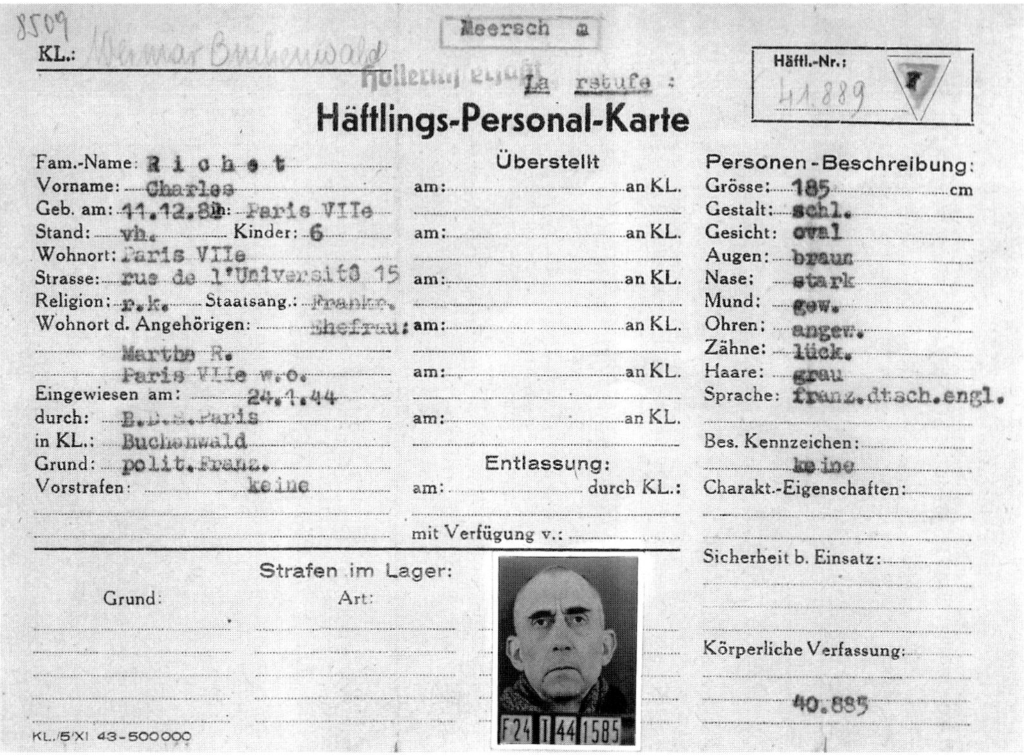

8509
KL.: Weimar Buchenwald
Meersch a
La rstufe :
Häftl.-Nr.: 41.889 F

Häftlings-Personal-Karte

Fam.-Name: Richet
Vorname: Charles
Geb. am: 11.12.82 in: Paris VIIe
Stand: vh. Kinder: 6
Wohnort: Paris VIIe
Strasse: rue de l'Université 15
Religion: r.k. Staatsang.: Frankr.
Wohnort d. Angehörigen: Ehefrau: Marthe R. Paris VIIe w.o.
Eingewiesen am: 24.1.44
durch: B.d.S. Paris
in KL.: Buchenwald
Grund: polit. Franz.
Vorstrafen: keine

Überstellt
am: an KL.
am: an KL.
am: an KL.
am: an KL.
am: an KL.
am: an KL.

Entlassung:
am: durch KL.:
mit Verfügung v.:

Personen-Beschreibung:
Grösse: 185 cm
Gestalt: schl.
Gesicht: oval
Augen: braun
Nase: stark
Mund: gew.
Ohren: angew.
Zähne: lück.
Haare: grau
Sprache: franz. dtsch. engl.
Bes. Kennzeichen: keine
Charakt.-Eigenschaften:
Sicherheit b. Einsatz:
Körperliche Verfassung:
40.885

Strafen im Lager:
Grund: Art:

F24 I 44 1585

KL./5/XI 43-500000

Illustration 145: The French physician Charles Richet's inmate's personal record card
Source: Gabriel Richet, Paris

German occupation forces sought to re-press the French Résistance, which had received impetus from the German defeat at Stalingrad. On April 10, 1942, the military commander in France, citing Hitler, had ordered *"that, in the future, for every assassination attempt, in addition to the shooting of a number of suitable persons, 500 Communists and Jews were to be transferred to the Reich Leader of the SS and the Chief of the German Police for deportation to the east."* In the camp at Compiègne near Paris, a "sufficient number of persons" were to be continually available. All arrests were therefore to be investigated with regard to *"whether transfer to Compiègne Camp for the purpose of deportation is advisable."*

During the occupation of France, **Compiègne** Camp was established north of Paris as "Frontstalag [front POW parent camp] 122." Beginning in mid 1941 it served as an internment camp for Jews, political prisoners, Russians and Americans. Jews and members of the Resistance were deported from Compiègne to Auschwitz. Later, until its dissolution in August 1944, the camp was a police detention centre of the commander of the Security Police and the Security Service. As Pierre Mania recalls:

Illustration 146: Boris Taslitzky: "Pierre Durand,"drawing, 1944
Source: Pierre Durand, Paris

"Compiègne was the antechamber, the waiting room, in which the member of the Resistance or patriot waited for a week, a month, sometimes longer, to be sent to Germany. He had been through Fresnes, Loos or Fort Baurrault and Montluc and sent to Compiègne thrashed, beaten, sometimes crippled. But nevertheless Compiègne was still France … and it still had at least the appearance of life. In Compiègne the Nazi German did not yet show his face, at least not all of it!"

Beginning in 1942, some 50,000 persons were deported from Compiègne to the concentration camps – initially Auschwitz, then others. Although the German occupying forces originally used the term "Deportation Communists" in this connection, the members of the Résistance sent to Buchenwald represented the entire political spectrum of the French Resistance movement:

Illustration 147: Maurice Hewitt's chess set, inmate handwork, 1944
Loan from Madame Berthin
Catalogue 4/6
Photo: N. T. Salmon

Illustration 148: A group of French inmates, front: General Louis Audibert, 1945 This photograph was probably taken in April 1945 as the sick and weak persons of the Little Camp were being taken to the SS barracks. *Source: Sammlung Gedenkstätte Buchenwald, Weimar*

The physician **Charles Richet**, a member of the Parisian Académie de Medicine and the head of the resistance group "Stephane Renault," was betrayed and arrested in 1943. Following detention in Fresnes Military Prison he was transported to Compiègne and from there to Buchenwald. He served as an inmate doctor in the Little Camp.

Henry Krasucki, a man of Jewish heritage, was arrested, interrogated and tortured by the French police in 1943 as the leader of the Parisian organisation of Communist youth. In 1943 he was deported to Auschwitz, in January 1945 to Buchenwald.

Julien Cain, the Administrator General of the French National Library, was arrested in February 1941 on suspicion of collaboration with the exile government in London. He was imprisoned in Romainville Camp for three years before being sent to Buchenwald in 1944.

Maurice Hewitt, a well-known musician, had smuggled members of the Allied paratroopers from France to Spain on behalf of the Résistance. He was sent on a mass transport from Compiègne to Buchenwald, where he joined Polish prisoners to form an illegal string quartet.

Pierre Durand, arrested at the age of twenty in the act of carrying out an assignment for the Résistance, was deported to Buchenwald in May 1944 following interrogation and solitary confinement.

The renowned aircraft designer **Marcel Bloch** (later Dassault) was sent to Buchenwald in 1944 after being turned over to the Gestapo. He turned down offers made by the German Air Force to work for the German aircraft industry.

Rene-Michel L'Hopital had been an adjutant to Marshal Foch during World War I and afterward. Following the occupation of France in 1940 he founded the resistance organisation "Armee volontaire." He was arrested in early 1942 in the wake of the "Nacht-und-Nebel-Erlass," interned for two years in Fresnes Military Prison and then sent to Buchenwald by way of the SS special camps of Hinzert, Wittlich and Trier and Sachsenhausen Concentration Camp.

The "**Nacht-und-Nebel-Erlass**" ("Night-and-Fog Decree") was the name of a secret order issued by the commander in chief of the German Wehrmacht, Wilhelm Keitel, on December 7, 1941 in reaction to the increasing activities of the French Résistance. It provided for the capital punishment of persons involved in these activities. Those members of the Résistance not or not yet sentenced to death after a summary trial

162

were to disappear in "night and fog," i.e. in nebulous obscurity, without the knowledge of their families. Some "Nacht-und-Nebel" (NN) inmates were sentenced to death and executed by special courts in Germany. Beginning in mid June 1943, non-convicted persons as well as those who had already served their sentences were turned over to the Gestapo. In September 1944 the supreme command of the Wehrmacht ordered the discontinuation of all legal proceedings in progress at the time and handed 24,000 NN prisoners over to the Gestapo. The majority of them were taken to concentration camps.

Between June 1943 and August 1944, altogether more than 13,000 persons – primarily Frenchmen on the verge of physical collapse – were brought by train from Compiègne to Buchenwald. French prisoners also came on SS transports from Toulouse, Paris, Belfort, Grenoble and Auschwitz. Each time a transport train arrived, the scene described in the memoirs of Jacques Lusseyran was repeated:

"Then the doors opened. We were there. Several of us screamed in German: 'Trinken! Bitte, trinken!' Blows fell amongst the people in the railroad car: clubs, rifle butts. Those standing too close to the door rolled out.
We had to line up in rank and file and march very fast. We were surrounded by dogs that bit those who lagged behind. It was nearly impossible because of our swollen legs. It was like walking on knives.
We were sporadically attacked by the SS."

The number of Frenchmen deported to Buchenwald is estimated at approximately 25,000. At the end of 1944, there were in addition more than 1,000 Frenchwomen in the women's sub-camps. Frenchmen accounted for a large share of the initial inmate populations of the sub-camps "Dora" and "Laura," where they had to work on the construction of tunnels. Many of them suffered injury and illness; thousands died. The most influential group among the foreign political inmates, they played a significant role in the inmates' resistance movement.

Italian Inmates

Immediately following the September 1943 armistice agreement between Italy and the Allies, the first Italian political inmates were transported to Buchenwald from the prison at Sulmona, a city east of Rome. Further transports of political prisoners followed in 1944, many of them by way of the notorious **police detention camp La Risiera** in San Sabba near Trieste. Having been set up in an unused rice mill in the first half of 1944, this camp was under the jurisdiction of the Security Police in the "Adriatic Coastland Operation Zone". Members of the Resistanza from all over Northern Italy were placed in custody there. Between June and November 1944 the SS brought 1,290 Italians to Buchenwald from La Risiera. Other Italians, including members of the International Brigades active in the Spanish Civil War, came on transports from Compiègne.

A group of approximately 1,000 Italian military internees whom the Wehrmacht had turned over to the SS enjoyed a somewhat special status. They were transferred from POW camps to the "Dora" and "Laura" sub-camps in October/November 1943. They had separate quarters and were not

Italian inmates 1943/44					
	Total no. of Italians (not including military internees)	No. of political inmates included in total: men/women	Jews	Romani	Others
12/31/43	376	376 / –	–	–	–
10/15/44	1,347	1,333 / –	–	2	12
10/31/44	1,141	1,092 / 38	–	2	9
12/30/44	1,535	1,461 / 35	26	2	11

classified as preventive custody inmates although they performed the same heavy labour and essentially shared the same lot as the other inmates.

Like many of the inmates from Southern France, the Italians were unable to adapt to the harsh climate that was typical of the Ettersberg; many new arrivals contracted pneumonia. Of the approximately 3,500 Italians deported to Buchenwald Concentration Camp by the SS between the autumn of 1943 and the beginning of 1945, nearly one third perished.

Yugoslav and Croatian Inmates

In the camp records kept by the SS, a distinction was made between Yugoslavs and Croatians. The first Yugoslavs were committed to the camp in the summer of 1941. At first their number was quite small: 15 Yugoslavs and 3 Croatians by mid August 1942. A transport from Flossenbürg in October 1943 brought the number of Yugoslavs up to 759 by the end of 1943. In mid July 1944 there were 575 Yugoslavs and 327 Croatians in Buchenwald. Rudi Supek, a Yugoslav political inmate, reports:

"According to the result of the inquiries, the Buchenwald administration recorded the passage of some 3,900 Yugoslavs, the large majority of whom were assigned to the two hundred existing labour detachments. ...

Most importantly, it must be pointed out that the Yugoslavs formed a group of quite unusual heterogeneity, not only with regard to language and religion but also to the cultural milieu from which they came. Behind every 'J' [for the German word 'Jugoslav'] were members of various Yugoslav peoples. The largest share were Slovenes, then the Croatians, then the Serbs, finally the Montenegrins. There were also Mohammedans [Muslims] from Bosnia and the Yugoslav regions on the border to Albania. The only people missing were the members of the fifth Yugoslav nationality – the Macedonians. ...

Furthermore, the fact should not be overlooked that the Yugoslavs were not only divided into five large groups nationally but also differed from one another with regard to creed, forming three large groups, Orthodox, Catholics and Mohammedans, all having developed under extremely divergent religious and cultural influences.

From the point of view of social origins and life circumstances, the differences were also substantial. There were peasants from regions of Carniola and all other regions all the way to the fertile lowlands of Voivodina, men who had fought in the NOV – the People's Liberation Army – or helped the partisans, labourers who had followed the call of the Communist Party and joined in the struggle for national and social liberty, members of the middle class, civil servants, office workers, businessmen, members of free-lance professions, professors, teachers, agronomists, etc. ... The largest group consisted of adolescents. ... All of these colourful shades of landscape and character ... were carried and safeguarded in the hearts of these people and in their spent bodies, each a universe of history and emotion in its own right."

Jewish Inmates from Auschwitz

Once the majority of Jewish inmates had been transported away from Buchenwald in October 1942, the small number still in the camp remained relatively constant for a period of nineteen months. The demand for skilled construction workers kept many of them from being sent to Auschwitz, but the SS nevertheless upheld its plan to deport all Jews. There were Jewish residents of Germany who were initially exempted from deportation to the extermination camps (in 1941-42) due to the fact that they were citizens of allied or neutral states, but this privilege was intended only as a temporary measure. Between October and December 1943 they accounted for an increase in the number of Jewish inmates to nearly 400, or approximately one percent of the entire camp population.

At the beginning of 1944, the "Judenreferat" (Jewish Department) headed by Adolf Eichmann planned the eradication of the last remaining Jewish communities in occupied Europe, leading to the deportation of 400,000 Hungarian Jews to

Transports of Frenchmen, Italians and Yugoslavs to Buchenwald

5/21/1943	50	from Compiègne via Mauthausen Conc. Camp
6/27/1943	962	from Compiègne
9/4/1943	900	from Compiègne
9/18/1943	989	from Compiègne
10/21/1943	506	from Flossenbürg (Yugoslavs)
10/30/1943	911	from Compiègne
12/16/1943	921	from Compiègne
1/19/1944	1,939	from Compiègne
1/24/1944	1,990	from Compiègne
1/29/1944	1,580	from Compiègne
5/14/1944	2,052	from Compiègne
5/14/1944	1,677	from Compiègne via Auschwitz Conc. Camp
6/24/1944	172	from Trieste
7/1/1944	120	from Trieste
7/3/1944	395	from Paris/Grenoble
7/14/1944	108	from Trieste
7/24/1944	95	from Trieste
8/3/1944	79	from Trieste
8/5/1944	25	from Verona
8/6/1944	1,080	from Paris
8/20/1944	1,650	from Paris
8/21/1944	72	from Trieste
8/22/1944	1,246	from Paris
9/8/1944	96	from Trieste
9/9/1944	176	from Dijon/Belfort
9/12/1944	32	from Trieste
9/25/1944	59	from Trieste
10/6/1944	70	from Trieste
10/14/1944	78	from Trieste
10/23/1944	51	from Trieste
11/4/1944	103	from Trieste
11/19/1944	139	from Trieste
12/30/1944	400	Yugoslav prisoners of war

Auschwitz between May and July of the same year. Two thirds of these persons were killed in the gas chambers. At the same time, however, the "Jägerstab" (Fighter Staff) preparing for the transfer of the aircraft industry to bombproof underground facilities was in urgent need of labourers, so that, beginning in May 1944, tens of thousands of Hungarian Jews in Auschwitz-Birkenau were exempted from immediate extermination. They were sent instead to concentration camps in the so-called Old Reich, where the SS assigned them to the heaviest labour duties, performed under conditions which inevitably led to debilitation and death. Arriving in Buchenwald on May 24, 1944, the very first transport of Hungarian Jews comprised 1,000 persons, of whom one third were under twenty years of age and more than 30 were children. The SS sent them on to the tunnels of "Dora" almost immediately. According to László Kovács:

"The door of the railroad car is pushed open and on the ramp, hastened by blows, rows of

five are formed, then our group starts moving, accompanied by SS men with dogs and machine guns. ... The group stops in front of a large building. It is the bath. We must undress in the front room, then our hair is removed and we bathe. In a corridor, everyone must stop and wait, our personal data is recorded, we are photographed from all sides, our height measured. All of this accompanied by blows. Then we receive our clothing. I received a prison uniform with the number 56,582, wooden clogs, a cap, a spoon and a red enamel soup dish. ...

A small grey-haired man asks us about ourselves in German. When he hears that I am not even thirteen years old and have come here alone, without any friends or family, he offers to help me, tells me that I can go and work, just get out of here as quickly as possible ... 'This is Buchenwald; here terrible things await everyone,' he informs me. 'If they ask you how old you are, tell them you're seventeen.'

The same day a drill of several hours. To become acquainted with the orders, everything serving the one goal of subordination. Roll call! Attention! Cap off! Cap on! etc. Under the threat of blows the drill goes better and better. In the evening, barrack duty."

The Jews sent from Auschwitz usually remained on the Ettersberg for only a short time. The first sub-camps with Jewish inmates were established as early as June 1944 in Bochum, Magdeburg and Rehmsdorf. By December 1944 the number of sub-camps with populations consisting primarily or exclusively of Jewish inmates had risen to twelve men's camps with 15,000 Jewish men and boys and fourteen women's

Transports of Jews, Sinti and Romani to Buchenwald Concentration Camp

4/17/1944	883	Sinti and Romani from Auschwitz
5/24/1944	1,000	Hungarian Jews from Auschwitz
6/2/1944	1,000	Hungarian Jews from Auschwitz
6/6/1944	2,000	Hungarian Jews from Auschwitz
6/18/1944	1,000	Hungarian Jews from Auschwitz
7/16/1944	2,500	Hungarian Jews from Auschwitz
8/3/1944	918	Sinti and Romani from Auschwitz
8/5/1944	1,459	Polish Jews from Auschwitz
9/9/1944	544	Polish Jews from Kielce
10/30/1944	150	Jews of various nationalities from Auschwitz
11/4/1944	301	Hungarian Jews from Auschwitz
11/9/1944	615	Hungarian Jews from Budapest
11/19/1944	778	Hungarian Jews from Budapest
11/19/1944	283	Jews of various nationalities from Auschwitz
11/27/1944	1,000	Jews of various nationalities from Stutthof
12/3/1944	354	Polish Jews from Plaszow
12/6/1944	1,997	Jews, Sinti, Romani, etc. from Dachau
12/14/1944	2,496	Jews, Sinti, Romani, etc. from Dachau
12/24/1944	916	Polish Jews fr. Tschenstochau (Częstochowa)
12/25/1944	1,913	Hungarian Jews from Budapest
1/18/1945	2,740	Polish Jews fr. Tschenstochau (Częstochowa)
1/20/1945	1,446	Polish Jews fr. Tschenstochau (Częstochowa)
1/22/1945	2,224	Hungarian and Greek Jews from Auschwitz
1/23/1945	916	Polish und Hungarian Jews from Auschwitz
1/26/1945	3,935	Jews of various nationalities from Auschwitz
2/10 – 2/12/1945	6,804	primarily Jews and Poles from Groß-Rosen

Illustration 149: Hungarian Jews in Auschwitz, Summer 1944
Source: Auschwitz Memorial Archives, Oświęcim

camps with 11,500 Jewish women. Poorly clothed, weakened by hunger and illness, they were assigned to labour which meant constant agony to the point of death, but at the same time represented the only chance of survival. As long as the gas chambers in Auschwitz were still in operation, Jewish inmates too ill and weak to work were sent back for immediate extermination; there were over 2,000 such cases from Buchenwald alone. On the other hand, due to the evacuation of Jewish forced labour camps in occupied Poland and the dissolution of the Auschwitz and Gross-Rosen Concentration Camps, the Jews accounted for the largest inmates' group in Buchenwald at the beginning of 1945.

Illustration 150: Radio message from the Auschwitz camp administration to the commander of Buchenwald, June 5, 1944
Source: Thüringisches Hauptstaatsarchiv, Weimar

Sinti and Romani from Auschwitz

The deportation of Sinti and Romani from Germany to ghettoes and concentration camps in occupied Poland began soon after the war broke out. Approximately 5,000 chiefly Austrian Romani and Sinti were deported to the ghetto of Łódz (at that time called Litzmannstadt) at the end of 1941 and killed in gas cars in Chełmno (Kulmhof) soon thereafter. Furthermore, beginning in that year, thousands of Romani fell victim to shootings carried out by task forces of the Security Police, the Security Service, the Regular Police and the Wehrmacht in the USSR, Poland and Serbia, or were gassed to death.

In compliance with an order issued by Himmler on December 16, 1942, the SS assembled some 23,000 Sinti and Romani from several European countries, among them over 13,000 from Germany and Austria, in a separate barrack camp in Auschwitz-Birkenau. Many died as a result of the wretched conditions that prevailed there. This "Gypsy Camp" was eventually disbanded, but not before the SS had killed the majority of its inmates. By early September 1944, approximately 1,800 Sinti and Romani – including many adolescents – were transported from Auschwitz to the men's camps at Buchenwald, as well as some 800 women to the women's sub-camps. Many did not survive the hard labour and terror in the tunnels of the underground detachments. Particularly in the sub-camp "Dora," which would later become the independent Mittelbau Concentration Camp, hundreds were worked to death.

Operation "Gitter" ("Gewitter"), 1944

In Germany, the NS regime responded to resistance with sheer violence. The attempts of the students' group "Weisse Rose" (White Rose) to rouse the Germans were brutally suppressed, as were the activities of the Communist resistance groups, the anti-authoritarian youth opposition movement "Edelweisspiraten" in Cologne and others. Former Buchenwald inmates

such as Walter Husemann, Theodor Neubauer and Arthur Hoffmann also died on the guillotine for pursuing their resistance activities after their release from the camp.

No sooner had Hitler's war intentions become obvious than an initially small group of officers began making plans to overthrow him. After the outbreak of hostilities, they made contact with other opponents of Hitler. The so-called "Kreisauer Circle" (named after its meeting place in Silesia) consisted of high-ranking officers and civil servants, politicians of the Weimar Republic and trade unionists as well as Protestant and Catholic clergymen, who joined to develop a strongly Christian and socially-oriented common platform. The members of this group grew in number as military defeat became more and more imminent. The attempt to assassinate Hitler on July 20, 1944 failed, and the regime took bloody revenge on the conspirators.

Until that time the Gestapo had imagined the majority of potential political opponents to be safely in the concentration camps and prisons or under its surveillance, and the assassination attempt took it completely by surprise. In August 1944 it hastily took action all over Germany with the intention of forestalling every attempt at resistance through the preventive arrest of alleged activists. Between August 22 and 24, 1944, within the framework of an arrest operation under the code names "Gitter" and "Gewitter," the various Gestapo headquarters committed altogether 742 former **members of the Reichstag** and well-known members of political parties of the Weimar Republic to Buchenwald. Among them were the former member of the Reichstag Fritz Soldmann (SPD), Alfred Hamann (KPD), Gustav Schumann (SPD), Otto Schieck (KPD), Ernst Hörnicke (KPD) and Peter Knab (KPD). Further victims of this operation were the reform educationalist Dr. Kurt Adams of Hamburg, who died in the camp on October 7, 1944, and the Social Democrat Dr. Fritz Behr, who had been a municipal councillor in Weimar for many years.

The committals carried out in connection with Operation "Gitter" were interrupted by the air attack of August 24, 1944 on Buchenwald, not to be resumed until

Illustration 151: Hamburg Gestapo to the Hamburg Board of Education re the death of Dr. Kurt Adams in Buchenwald, Nov. 2, 1944
Source: Staatsarchiv Hamburg

September. After that the camp received only isolated arrestees from interim detention centres such as the "Messelager" in Cologne. Among these persons was Otto Gerig, a member of the Reichstag from the Centre Party, who died in Buchenwald. Peter Schlack, another Centre Party member of the Reichstag, was kept in custody by the Gestapo in the Cologne sub-camp of Buchenwald Concentration Camp for quite a long period. The "operation" met with the disapproval of the public, as many of those arrested were advanced in age and had done nothing to warrant suspicion apart from having held offices in government for more than a decade. Therefore most of them were released following fruitless interrogations by the Weimar Gestapo. Fritz Soldmann remained in the camp until the end and died after liberation as a result of his imprisonment.

The Transfer of Judicially Imprisoned Individuals to Facilities for "Extermination through Labour"

At a conference held in Himmler's field quarters on September 18, 1942, the SS and the justice system agreed that inmates of penitentiaries be turned over to the concentration camps "for extermination through labour." The measure was to apply without exception to "... preventive custody inmates, Jews, gypsies, Russians and Ukrainians, Poles with sentences of over three years, Czechs and Germans with sentences of over eight years according to the decision of the Reich Justice Minister." As a note taken by Reich Justice Minister Otto Thierack during the negotiations indicates, an agreement was reached to the effect that

"... in consideration of the aims established by the heads of state for the settlement of the Eastern question, in future Jews, Poles, Gypsies, Russians and Ukrainians are no longer to be sentenced by regular courts of law in criminal cases, but to be attended to by the Reich Leader of the SS."

Along with the punishment of so-called "dangerous habitual offenders", "**security detention**" as defined by Article 42 e of the penal code was (and today still is) imposed by court decision. The court also had the authority to determine the duration of this measure and investigated each case every three years. The prisons and mental hospitals comprised security detention departments. Nevertheless, beginning in late 1942, "security detention inmates" were turned over to the SS, and by February 1943, this category had been introduced to the camp records. Of the approximately 2,300 "security detention inmates" (SV) who had been sent to Buchenwald by the end of 1944 and assigned to the heaviest labour detachments, half died within the same period.

Political prisoners who had narrowly escaped the death sentence and were serving long-term prison sentences were also turned over to the concentration camps. The most eminent of these persons to be committed to Buchenwald were the former members of the Reichstag Dr. Hermann Brill and Albert Kayser.

Temporary Detention II

At the end of 1944 the SS introduced the inmate category "Temporary Detention II." By March 1945, military tribunals turned over at least 800 Wehrmacht soldiers from military prisons to the SS. There is no question as to how the latter intended to deal with them in view of the fact that they were immediately sent on to Mittelbau Concentration Camp, from which no return was provided for. According to the report by the International Camp Committee:

"In November 1944 the first inmates of a new category – 'Temporary Detention II' arrived. These were members of the Wehrmacht, most of whom had been sentenced to long prison terms on charges of desertion or absence with-

Illustration 152: Hermann L. Brill (1895-1959), after 1945
Source: Sammlung Gedenkstätte Buchenwald, Weimar

out leave and had now been taken out of the penitentiaries and military prisons within the context of the investigation of their sentences and sent to the concentration camps for labour allocation in 'temporary detention'; according to Himmler's plans they would serve the remainder of their prison terms after the war. By the highest orders of the highest offices in Berlin, they all had to be sent to Mittelbau Concentration Camp, i.e. to 'Dora.' ... These

Change in percentage of "Reich Germans" (Germans and Austrians) in the camp, 1942/44						
Date	Total no. in camp	Total no. of "Reich Germans"	Major sub-groups within group of "Reich Germans" according to size (percentage of total no. in camp)			
			Political	BV/SV	ASR	Bible res.
8/29/42	9,881	approx. 3,320 34 %	1,692 17 %	741 8 %	approx. 450 5 %	245 3 %
10/15/44	88,231	7,042* 8 %	2,629 3 %	2,032 2 %	492 < 1 %	287 < 1 %
* All groups including German Jewish inmates, of whom there were less than 100 until the autumn of 1944.						

temporary detainees were not only Reich Germans but also citizens of other nations who had joined the German Wehrmacht voluntarily. Likewise during these months Himmler also began to commit members of his own SS units to the concentration camps to the extent that they were guilty of some crime. In December 1944 and January-February 1945, smaller transports of Croatians, members of a Mohammedan [Muslim] SS formation and Frenchmen, some of them in SS uniforms, came to the camp as inmates."

Illustration 153: Personal record card of Stanley Booker from the prisoner-of-war camp Stalag Luft III, 1944
Following detention in Buchenwald, the Allied airmen – among them Stanley Booker – were taken to this POW camp.
Source: Stanley Booker

Members of the Allied Forces

In August 1944 the commander of the Security Police and the Security Service in France had the police detention camp at Compiégne and the detention centres in Paris evacuated in view of the advancing Allies. Most of the inmates were deported to Buchenwald on August 20, 1944, among them 167 Allied airmen who had been shot down over France. This group comprised 82 Americans (U.S. Air Force), 48 Britons (Royal Air Force), 26 Canadians (Royal Canadian Air Force), 9 Australians (Royal Australian Air Force), 2 New Zealanders (Royal New Zealand Air Force) and 1 Jamaican (Royal Air Force). For quite a while it remained uncertain what was to be done with these "terror airmen" as they were referred to by NS propaganda. On October 19, 1944 the majority were taken to the prisoner-of-war camp of the German Air Force, "Stalag Luft III" in Sagan. **Levitt C. Beck**, an airman of the U.S. Air Force shot down over France in June 1944 and betrayed to the Gestapo, was gravely ill and remained in Buchenwald. He died in the infirmary on November 29, 1944.

Among the Gestapo inmates who arrived on a transport from France on August 17, 1944 were 37 members of Allied secret services who had been arrested in connection with activities they carried out in occupied France. On orders by the Reich Department of Security, they were to receive "special treatment". Between early September and mid October, 34 of them were hanged in the cellar of the crematorium. Only 3 of them were saved.

Illustration 154: Levitt C. Beck (1920-1944), ca. 1943
Source: Sammlung Gedenkstätte Buchenwald, Weimar

Belgians, Dutch and Luxembourgers

The first **Luxembourgers** in Buchenwald were 26 members of a voluntary Luxembourg police company. In August 1941, in the Weimar police barracks, they had refused to allow themselves to be trained to combat partisans. In their joint report, Aloyse Ehlinger and Léon Bartimes wrote:

"The news spread through the camp like wildfire: Luxembourg police officers who had been stationed in Weimar months earlier had been committed to the concentration camp. During their six-month stay in the barracks in Hardtstrasse, Weimar, an inmate shoemaker and tailor detachment from Buchenwald had

worked in the cellar there. The Luxembourgers saw these poor devils when they arrived and when they were driven back again. There were gratings on the windows of the cellar rooms in which they worked. A policeman was stationed in front of the locked door. During this period, a large proportion of the soldiers' rations and now and then a few cigarettes they had received from home wandered through the grated windows to these inmates. The latter now showed their gratitude, informed them about life in the camp and its dangers. They then received a guarantee from the block senior and the foreman of the quarry, to which the delinquent company had been assigned, that none of the Luxembourgers would be harmed."

There had been a number of Dutch inmates in the camp since 1940; they had been sent on small transports or individually, usually from workplaces in Germany. The increasing committal of **Belgians** and Dutchmen in 1944 was primarily a result of the intensified reprisals carried out by the Security Police in The Hague and Brussels against the Dutch and Belgian resistance movements. There were a small number of Belgians among the "Nacht-und-Nebel" inmates. Like **Jean Fonteyne**, most had been members of the resistance. A father of four, Fonteyne had lived underground since 1941 and was a member

Illustration 155:
Jean Fonteyne's
inmate jacket
Loan from the
family
Catalogue 4/9
Photo: N. T. Salmon

Illustration 156:
Lucien van Beirs
and Jean Fonteyne
at the time of their
departure from
Buchenwald, 1945
L. to r.: Lucien van
Beirs, Raphael
Algoet (war
correspondent),
Jean Fonteyne,
Paul Levy (war
correspondent).
*Source: Fonteyne
family*

of the Resistance movement "Front de l'Independance." He was arrested as a member of a military unit of the "Armée belge des partisans" and initially placed in custody, like many others, in the Breendonk Police Detention Camp, one of the most deplorable in Western Europe. From there he was deported to Buchenwald in May 1944, where he was the cofounder of the Belgium support committee whose other members were a Catholic, a Liberal, a Communist and a Social Democrat. **Georges de Bleser**, who belonged to the police resistance organisation "Milice patriotique" as well as to the "Front de l'Independance," was also sent to Buchenwald following one year of solitary confinement in Breendonk. **Lucien Aphonse Constant Van Beirs**, a royal public prosecutor, was arrested in the attempt to emigrate to Spain. In Buchenwald he was forced to work as a load hauler and was sent to the dreaded "S III" sub-camp.

The largest transport from the **Netherlands** came from the Amersfoort Transit Camp on April 19, 1944. The talented young writer **Vincent Weijand** came to the camp by way of Bergen-Belsen Concentra-

Illustration 157: Lucien van Beirs a few days after his return from Ohrdruf (S III) Sub-Camp, April 1945
Source: Sammlung Gedenkstätte Buchenwald, Weimar

tion Camp. He had refused to betray friends of his who had gone underground. He died in Barrack 45 on February 21, 1945.

Illustration 158: Vincent Weijand (1921-1945)
Source: Sammlung Gedenkstätte Buchenwald, Weimar

Belgians, Dutchmen and Luxembourgers 1943/44			
	Belgians	Dutchmen	Luxembourgers
1/2/1943	15	325	8
1/1/1944	218	512	47
4/30/1944	1213	984	60
11/15/1944	2354	595	82

Danish Policemen

On October 15, 1945, the Danish government issued an official memorandum concerning the crimes committed by Germans in the process of occupying Danish territory. There it is stated:

"Due to the fact that the Germans had not succeeded in gaining any influence over the Danish police – neither the officers nor the ordinary policemen – the German military authorities began to fear the police in the late summer of 1944. Pancke [the Senior SS and Police Commander] explained that General Hanneken [the commander of the German troops in Denmark] and he were afraid that the police, a force of eight to ten thousand well-trained men, would attack the Germans in the case of an invasion. ... On September 19, 1944, at eleven o'clock in the morning, the Germans set off a false air-raid alarm. Immediately afterwards, [German] police soldiers forced their way into the police prefecture of Copenhagen and all the other police stations in the city. Several policemen were killed. The operation was carried out uniformly throughout the country. The majority of policemen on duty were arrested. From Copenhagen and other large cities the prisoners were transported

Illustration 159: Dr. Svend Aaage Schaldemose-Nielsen (1900-1944), 1944
Source: Buchenwaldarchiv, Weimar

to Germany on ships sent for this purpose by Kaltenbrunner, or in freight cars."

At the end of September / beginning of October, 1,953 Danish police officers were deported to Buchenwald via Neuengamme Concentration Camp. At Buchenwald,

Illustration 160: Report on scarlet fever epidemic in the Little Camp, Nov. 24, 1944
Source: Thüringisches Hauptstaatsarchiv, Weimar

L. II. Scharlach. 24.11.44.	
Gesamtbestand :	178
Davon erkrankt:	178
In verdacht :	56
Bestimmt :	122
Neue Fälle :	2
Tote :	1

Bemerkungen:

Davon sind 150 Dänen

Der Tote war Scharlach positiv

und Nephritis

L. II . 24.II . 44.	57
Im Kl. Revier liegen : 220 Dänen,	
Da von Erysepel 39	
Phlegmonen : 5	
Innere : 26	
Scharlach :150	

Die Meningitis ist verstorben.

most of them lived in Block 57 of the Little Camp, where a scarlet fever epidemic broke out. Among the dead was the police president of Odense, **Dr. Svend Aaage Schaldermose-Nielsen**, who died in the Little Camp on November 26, 1944. In mid December, Himmler ordered that the police officers be treated as prisoners of war. They were taken to other camps immediately afterward. The months in Buchenwald had claimed sixty lives.

Norwegian Students

On November 20, 1943, approximately 1,250 students from the University of Oslo were arrested and taken to a camp in Norway. They had protested repeatedly against the Nazification of the university, and were apparently taken into custody in order to undergo a kind of exemplary "re-education." On January 13, 1944, 348 of them were transferred to Buchenwald, where they were isolated from the other inmates and subjected in vain to "SS education." The Norwegian students received Red Cross packages which they shared with the other inmates, and were extremely popular on account of their attitude of solidarity. The Dane J. Nybe Frederiksen reports:

"A few days later the Danish Red Cross arrived with a new load of packages. We were very happy because, particularly at that time, it was extremely important for us to get good, sol-

Illustration 161: The Danish inmate Hendrik Jensen's bowl and spoon
Engraving: "J H, 86.273, 7 Nov. 44"
Catalogue 4/9
Photo: N. T. Salmon

id food. The Norwegian students also received Red Cross packages from Denmark, which further strengthened our friendship with them. … We had good, edifying conversations with those intelligent fellows. … Among the Norwegians there were several whose medical training was nearly complete; from them we received much help and support."

The Norwegian students left Buchenwald between July 1944 and March 1945. On their odyssey through various camps, 17 died, some of them in Buchenwald.

Transports of Norwegians, Dutchmen, Belgians, Luxembourgers and Danes to Buchenwald

Date	Number	Description
1/14/1944	348	Norwegian students from Oslo
4/19/1944	499	Dutchmen from Amersfoort Transit Camp
5/8/1944	967	Belgians, etc. from Breendonk Transit Camp and elsewhere
5/23/1944	891	Belgians, etc. from Security Police / Security Service in Brussels and elsewhere
6/19/1944	574	Belgians, etc. from Security Police / Security Service in Brussels and elsewhere
7/19/1944	70	Dutchmen from Security Police / Security Service in The Hague
8/10/1944	827	Belgians, etc. from Security Police / Security Service in Brussels and elsewhere
9/29/1944	1,480	Danish policemen
10/5/1944	473	Danes

The Sub-Camps

"Leipzig
We arrive there on July 21 towards the end of the day. The camp appears to be small (5,000 women). Factories everywhere, barbed-wire everywhere … High smoking chimneys. Here it doesn't smell of burnt flesh, though, but of work."

Suzanne Orts

Men's Sub-Camps

In the early years of Buchenwald, the SS operated on the principle that the work gangs had to march back into the camp on the Ettersberg every evening. In the fall of 1942 this state of affairs began to change – gradually at first, and then, under the influence of the German defeat at Stalingrad, radically. The "inmates' construction brigade", sent to Cologne at the end of 1942, formed the first large detachment outside the parent camp. The inmates had to clear away rubble and blind shells in the bomb-stricken cities. On November 3, 1942 Himmler ordered that "in all cases, to the extent permitted by the circumstances, advantage be taken of the possibility of allocating concentration camp inmates and prisoners of all kinds" for this perilous

work. The intention was thus clearly stated from the start: inmates were to put their lives at risk for the performance of tasks which involved danger, time and effort; they were to work fast, cost-efficiently and without being seen. In addition to the economical aspect of cheap labour, the fact that the SS thus also possessed a means of driving thousands of people to their deaths unhindered played a major role in the establishment of the sub-camps.

Controlled and managed by the parent camp, the sub-camps accounted for half of Buchenwald's inmates by as early as 1943. By the spring of 1945 the increase in the number of sub-camps essentially mirrored the increase in mass committals, the latter being directly related, in turn, to the course of the front line and the SS demand for labour. Transports from Auschwitz as well

Illustration 162: Inmates with defused bomb, Kalkum Bomb Disposal Squad, 1943/44
Source: Norbert Krüger, Essen (Ruhrlandmuseum Essen)

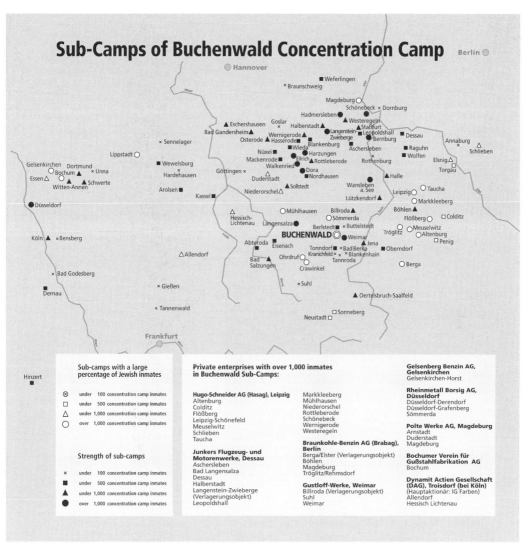

Sub-Camps of Buchenwald Concentration Camp
Source: P. Wentzler, Hinz & Kunst, Braunschweig

Sub-camps (male inmates), 1943 bis 1945					
Date	No. of inmates	No. in parent camp	No. in sub-camps	No. of sub-camps	Parent camp %
1/1/43	9,028	8,186	842	2	91
6/1/43	13,746	11,887	1,859	6	87
12/1/43	34,653	18,706	15,947	12	54
3/15/44	42,566	21,498	21,068	22*	51
8/15/44	74,915	31,491	43,424	64*	42
2/1/45	62,792	26,075	36,712	60	42
2/1/45	79,361	30,405	48,956	75	38
3/1/45	84,651	36,083	48,568	62	43

* Six new sub-camps established in March 1944; eighteen new sub-camps established in August 1944.

Illustration 163: Inmates of SS Construction Brigade III at work clearing rubble in Cologne, Oct. 23, 1943
Source: Hist. Archiv Stadt Köln, Nachlaß Peter Fischer F 400/17

```
Aussenkommandos
      28.10.44              A
   Sonneberg                 280
   Baubrigade III            996
   Baubrigade IV             826
   Baubrigade V              648
   E.Baubrigade I            514
   E.Baubrigade II           498
   Bochum    Eisen.          652
   Bochum    Verein          937
   Annener   Gußstahl        677
   Napola    Bensbg.          13
   Essen                     149
   Düsseldorf                141
   Berta+Bors.654+294=       948
   Köln St+Fo. 34+ 44=        78
   Köln      Deutz           195
   Kalkum                     52
   Godesberg                   1
   Wewelsburg                 42
   Kassel+Ar.169+122=        291
   Giessen                    77
   Schwerte                  688
   Richard   Wernig.         789
   Julius    Schöneb.       1149
   Emil      Leipzig        1074
   A 2       Ju-Ascher       488
   A 4       Hans+Ago        945
   A 5       Heinrich        385
   A 6       Wilhelm         595
   Mansfd.   Biber II        283
   Mansfd.   Rothenbg.        80
   Ju-Dessau                  50
   Ju-Thyra                  467
   Ju-Halberstadt            821
   Ju-Niederorschel          276
   Mala+Mai.2979+198=       3177
   B11+Dora586+24265=24851
   B 3       Anhyd.         2053
   Laura                     568
   Martha    Mühlhs.         541
   Emma+Ant. 382+244=        626
   Wille     Zeitz          4129
   Jena+Taucha550+700=1250
   Böhlen                    990
   Langensalza               145
   Plömnitz                 1490
   Schlieben                1922
   Siebel    Halle           936
   Lützkendorf               919
   Reh       Staßfurt        484
   Magdeburg                1199
   Blankenburg               500
   Osterode                  272
   Gandersheim               199
   Gazelle                   472
   Hecht                     250
   Rebstock                  205
   ─────────────────────────────
   Zusammen                63283
```

Illustration 164: List of sub-camps, Oct. 28, 1944
Source: Buchenwaldarchiv, Weimar

as the evacuation of the SS-controlled Jewish forced labour complexes in Skarzysko-Kamienna, Tschenstochau (Częstochowa) and Piotrków led to the establishment in 1944 of sub-camps with exclusively or primarily Jewish inmates. The founding of seventy-six new sub-camps between July and December of 1944 corresponded directly to the mass transports carried out in the summer of that year. In late October 1944, the largest sub-camp – "Dora," which itself already had a number of sub-detachments – became an independent concentration camp by the name of Mittelbau. In February 1945 Buchenwald's sub-camp system reached the peak of its expansion, with eighty-seven men's and women's camps.

Buchenwald inmates worked for SS companies and SS construction detachments, construction units of the "Organisation Todt," offices of the SS, the Wehrmacht, the police and the NSDAP, armament manufacturers, the German Railway, municipal administrations and enterprises considered "essential to the war effort". After the construction projects of Bureau C of the Department of Economic Administration, the armament combines such as Hugo-Schneider AG ("Hasag") – where the anti-tank rocket launcher was manufactured – and the Junkers aircraft and engine works took the greatest advantage of inmate labour, occupying thousands. Buchenwald's sub-camp system stretched from the Rhine River to the Land of Saxony.

Though they were similar in certain basic respects – rows of rude barracks surrounded by barbed wire and guarded by SS – there were considerable differences between the various sub-camps. Particularly in the **underground detachments** and in the SS construction detachments – which from June 1944 on included a number of the existing sub-camps for Jewish inmates – work and terror took on an intensity so great that the camps could no longer be regarded as anything but extermination instruments. In connection with one of the first large-scale projects of prime significance, – for example the relocation of the so-called "V-Waffen" ("retaliatory weapon") production to underground sites – the SS already proved rigorous with regard to the lives of the inmates. During the first months of tunnel construction at the sub-camp "**Dora**" in Mount Kohnstein near Nordhausen (southern Harz Mountains), the Buchenwald Concentration Camp death rate shot up to a previously unheard-of level. Of the 3,122 inmates who died in Buchenwald and its sub-camps between mid December 1943 and mid March 1944, 1,976 died in "Dora" alone. Every fourth victim in "Dora" was Russian; a further twenty-five percent were French. Georges Desprez recalls:

"We arrive in Dora on September 3, 1943. Standing in mud, we wait several hours. Then we go in the direction of a tunnel. Fifty metres past the first entrance we pass through a second gate; through the leaden haze we can hardly see ten metres in front of us. The smell of burnt powder chokes us and the muffled sound of explosions fills us with terror. Driven on by a riding whip, we stumble through the semi-darkness of these catacombs beneath the hardly visible light bulbs to Tunnel 45, where our sleeping quarters are located. … But we

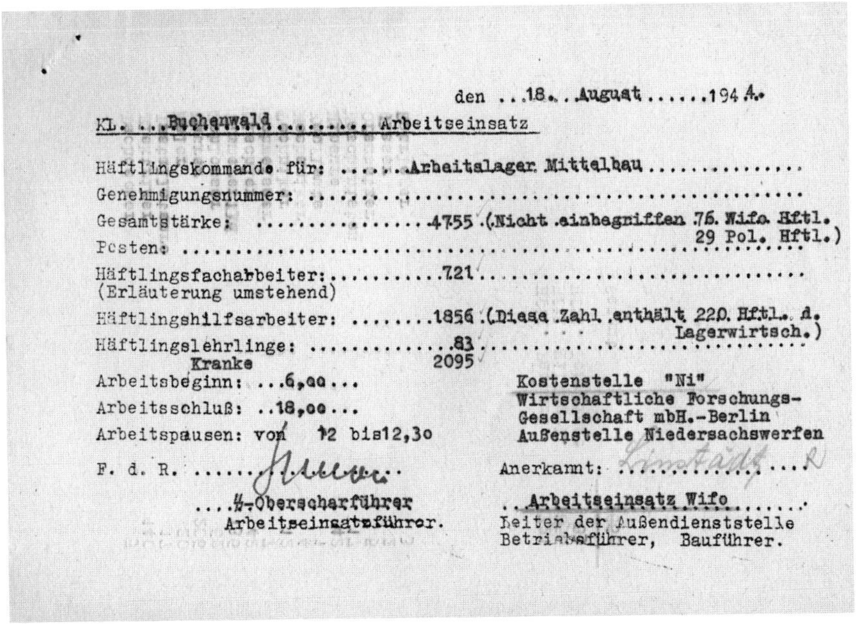

den ..18...August......1944.

KL. ...Buchenwald......... Arbeitseinsatz

Häftlingskommando für: ....Arbeitslager Mittelbau..............

Genehmigungsnummer: ....

Gesamtstärke: ....4755 .(Nicht einbegriffen 76. Wifo. Hftl. 29 Pol. Hftl.)

Posten: ....

Häftlingsfacharbeiter:...........721.........................
(Erläuterung umstehend)

Häftlingshilfsarbeiter: ....1856 .(Diese Zahl enthält 220. Hftl. d. Lagerwirtsch.)

Häftlingslehrlinge: ....83............................

Kranke 2095

Arbeitsbeginn: ...6,00...

Arbeitsschluß: ..18,00...

Arbeitspausen: von 12 bis12,3o

Kostenstelle "Ni"
Wirtschaftliche Forschungs-Gesellschaft mbH.-Berlin
Außenstelle Niedersachswerfen

F. d. R. ....

....SS-Oberscharführer
Arbeitseinsatzführer.

Anerkannt: ....

..Arbeitseinsatz Wifo........
Leiter der Außendienststelle
Betriebsführer, Bauführer.

Illustration 165:
Daily report from Mittelbau Sub-Camp, Aug. 18, 1944
Source: Buchenwaldarchiv, Weimar

hardly have time to lie or squat down when we are driven forth under blows with a stick. Without a break, we are led to other tunnels. Some are assigned to the drills, others to the job of stone-breaking or of loading and pushing the carts. We sleep right there. Only after three days do we finally receive a piece of bread and a litre of water with turnips which we gobble down, sitting or crouching between the dead and dying."

Matters did not begin to improve until after the first tunnel construction phase. Alexij V. Nikolajev reports:

"The move from the tunnel to the barracks somewhat relieved our terrible circumstances. For one thing we could bathe and remove the lice from our clothing – for the first time. Secondly, a cast iron oven was burning in the barrack, radiating heat. Thirdly, we could wash ourselves once a day. Fourthly, there was no longer a tunnel over our heads – dusty, dirty, mixed with bad air."

On the other hand, a modern armament factory now went into operation in the tunnels using slave labour. Roman Kornejev recalls:

"The production was highly advanced. The people worked on production lines, assembling V1s and V2s, welding the rocket bodies together ... The components were delivered for assembly ...; the production line never stood still."

Under the pressure to produce, the number of accidents increased. The SS responded to every form of refusal to work and sabotage with brutal violence. At Christmas 1944 the Italian inmate Carlo Slama wrote in his secret diary:

"You can't visit the Bunker – i.e. the camp prison – unless you've got a strong stomach. A place of torture, of butchery, of hanging – in other words of indescribable suffering. Within only five months, 300 internees have been hanged in the Bunker at Dora."

One who survived is the Frenchman Herman Rols. He was arrested in March 1943 for evading recruitment for forced labour. In September 1943 he was deported from Compiègne to Buchenwald. In January 1944 he was sent on to "Dora" where he broke his shin in an accident while working on rocket assembly. Following his release from the inmates' infirmary he was sent to a bomb disposal unit near Osnabrück. During the evacuations of April/May 1945 he suffered a shot in the head; he also survived a typhus infection contracted after the liberation.

One of the many Frenchmen who did not survive "Dora" was **Robert Bourgeois**. He came from Besançon, where he had been a Catholic priest and a teacher at the Grand Seminaire since 1938. He was arrested in 1943 as a member of the Résistance and sent from Buchenwald to "Dora" in March 1944. Less than a month later, the work in the tunnels and the terror had debilitated him to such a degree that the SS

Illustration 166: Robert Bourgeois (1910-1944)
Source: Buchenwaldarchiv, Weimar

sent him on a transport of sick persons to Bergen-Belsen Concentration Camp where he died shortly thereafter. By the time of the liberation, about one third of the approximately 60,000 inmates of "Dora" (later transformed into the Mittelbau Concentration Camp) and its sub-detachments had died.

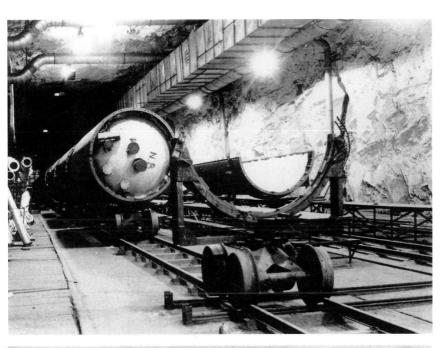

Illustration 167: Assembly track for A4 rocket in Tunnel B of Mittelbau Concentration Camp, 1945 *Source: Sammlung Gedenkstätte Buchenwald, Weimar*

0∪092

Der Standortarzt der Waffen-SS Weimar-Buchenwald, den 11.April 1944
W e i m a r

Betreff: Besuch im Aussenkommando Dora am 8.4.44

A k t e n n o t i z

Das Krematorium, das besichtigt wurde, arbeitet reibungslos. Die Frage der Entfernung von Zahngold verstorbener Häftlinge wurde mit SS-Hauptsturmführer Bremmer besprochen und geregelt. Dann erfolgte eine Besichtigung im Stollen und der dort eingebauten und teilweise schon betriebsfertigen Spül-Klosettanlagen.
Im Krankenbau sind keine besonderen Ereignisse eingetreten, die Röntgeneinrichtung ist noch nicht eingetreffen, jedoch ist zum Einbau alles vorbereitet. Der Operationssaal ist noch nicht völlig fertiggestellt. Nach Rücksprache mit dem Lagerarzt SS-Obersturmführer Kahr sollen in der nächsten Zeit noch einige Häftlingsärzte zur Verstärkung des Revierpersonals nach dort überstellt werden, in erster Linie ein Chirurg und ein Hautarzt und wenn möglich zwei erfahrene praktische Ärzte.
Es wurden ferner noch verschiedene Unstimmigkeiten bereinigt, die bei der Bearbeitung der neuerdings dort erstellten Totenpapiere entstanden waren.

Der Standortarzt der Waffen-SS Weimar

SS-Hauptsturmführer d.R.

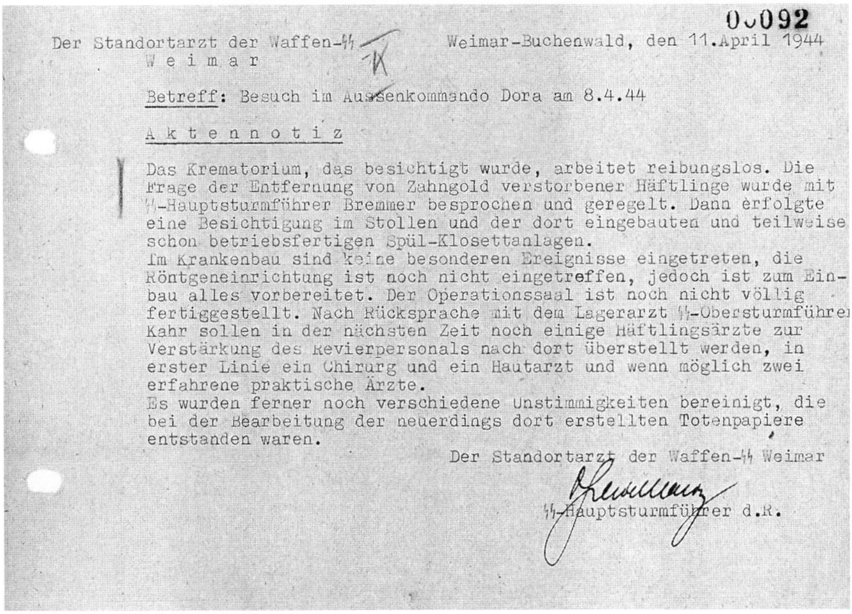

Illustration 168: File memo by garrison physician, SS Hauptsturmführer Dr. Schiedlausky, concerning a visit to Dora Sub-Camp, Apr. 11, 1944 *Source: Thüringisches Hauptstaatsarchiv, Weimar*

Victims of "Dora" construction phase, September 1943 to March 1944					
Russians	Frenchmen	Poles	Germans	Italians	Other nationalities
839	708	407	373	264	295

"Dora" was the most dreaded of the underground factories, but many victims were claimed by all of the **construction units of the SS and the "Organisation Todt.**" (The latter was a central state construction organisation of the German Reich, named after its chief, Fritz Todt.) Ill-famed sub-camps of this kind were located in Ellrich, Rottleberode and other sub-camps of Mittelbau-Dora Concentration Camp, in Lehesten near Saalfeld, Thuringia (code name "Laura"), Langenstein-Zwieberge and near Halberstadt (code names "Malachit," "Makrele I and II," "Maifisch"), in Springen near Bad Salzungen,

Thuringia (code name "Heinrich Kalb"), Berga/Elster (code name "Schwalbe V"), Rehmsdorf (code name "Wille"), Ohrdruf, Thuringia (code name SIII), Wansleben am See (code name "Biber II"), Weferlingen (code name "Gazelle"), Westeregeln (code name "Maulwurf"), Plömnitz (code names "Leopard" and "Leau") and elsewhere.

The **Ellrich Sub-Camp** was established in the Harz Mountain community of the same name on May 1, 1944. From late October 1944 on it belonged to Mittelbau Concentration Camp. Its code name was "Erich." By November 1, 1944, i.e. by the time of its incorporation into the Mittelbau camp system, the number of inmates at Ellrich had grown from the initial 196 to 8,002. The inmates – a large proportion of them Sinti and Romani who had been brought from Auschwitz to Buchenwald – had to perform hard labour on the construction of new tunnel facilities in the eastern section of Mount Kohnstein and in the Himmelberg, a mountain near Woffleben. The tunnels were constructed for the purpose of moving armament production underground. The Sinto Willi Ernst recalls:

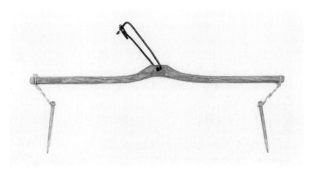

Illustration 169: Handmade bread scales from Springen underground detachment
The bread scales were used to ensure the fair distribution of the bread rations.
Loan from Kreisheimatmuseum Dermbach
Catalogue 4/16
Photo: N. T. Salmon

"Whereas my brother stayed in Buchenwald, my father and I were sent to Dora and from there to Ellrich and Harzungen; ... in the so-called Tunnel Detachment B11 we had to dig the entry tunnels. That was extremely dangerous work. The tunnels were blasted deeper and deeper into the heart of the mountain and many inmates were killed in the process. ... As time went on, you became quite indifferent, because as an inmate you had to witness so many cruelties every day and naturally tried to survive somehow or other. I received countless blows; death was the order of the day."

Inmates in Mittelbau Concentration Camp and its parent camp "Dora," 11/1/1944		
	Mittelbau (total)	Parent camp "Dora"
Russians	9,481	4,051
Poles	8,347	3,883
Frenchmen	5,114	2,373
Germans	2,114	1,185
Belgians	2,047	217
Sinti and Romani	1,185	377
Hungarian Jews	1,170	472
Czechs	1,078	557
Italians	500	275
Yugoslavs	494	180
Dutchmen	141	28
Others	804	140
Total	32,475	13,738

In April 1945 the camp was evacuated, the inmates being sent in the direction of Oranienburg and Bergen-Belsen.

The code names **S III** and **"Olga"** stood for the SS's special project for the construction of emergency underground quarters for the NS leadership in Jonastal between the Thuringian cities of Arnstadt and

Ohrdruf. A labour camp with concentration camp inmates was officially opened there on November 6, 1944. By mid December 1944, the SS had assembled over 12,000 inmates there from the Buchenwald, Sachsenhausen, Stutthof, Płaszow, Dachau and Auschwitz Concentration Camps. They were made to subsist in miserable conditions, performing extremely heavy labour in the construction of railway lines and tunnels. The inmates had their living quarters in four camps in Ohrdruf, Crawinkel (underground shelters and tents) and Espenfeld. High time pressure, terror and disease claimed many lives. The dead were brought to Buchenwald twice a week. Eugen Kogon writes:

Illustration 170: Sign: "Mützen ab" (caps off) from Ellrich Sub-Camp
Loan from Deutsches Historisches Museum Berlin
Catalogue 4/21
Photo: N. T. Salmon

"The corpses were dirty, lice-infested and wasted beyond all measure. Their average weight was rarely more than forty kg; they were lumped together and it was almost impossible to separate them. Almost without exception, the autopsies revealed such a high degree of consumption that a runny nose would have sufficed to knock these people over."

Illustration 171: Sleeping quarters in "Gazelle" underground detachment, Weferlingen
Source: Sammlung Gedenkstätte Buchenwald, Weimar

Having operated independently at first, the camp was taken over by the Buchenwald administration in mid January 1945, at which time its inmate population numbered over 9,000. By March 26, 1945, the number had risen to 13,726. In early April the SS evacuated approximately 9,900, sending them on marches to the parent camp and killing hundreds along the way.

The number of deaths that occurred in S III can only be estimated. It is likely that 4,000 people died during the detachment's five-month existence. In February and March 1945 the SS deported 2,884 sick persons to Bergen-Belsen Concentration Camp.

On May 6, 1944, during an inspection of the inmates in the sub-camp "**Laura**" – a tunnel construction project for "retaliatory weapon" production near Lehesten (Thuringia) – Camp Physician Schiedlausky noted the following:

"It was just possible to select the desired number of 200 deployable inmates. General debility and suspected consumptive diseases

such as TB and heart disease were determined in 248 cases. In the infirmary and in convalescence there are altogether 95 ill persons likewise unavailable for labour allocation until further notice. The only other still completely deployable inmates are to be found in the administration and camp personnel detachments – they number 72 – as well as in the operation detachment which it was also possible to inspect. The ratio is particularly unfavourable in the case of the Italian prisoners of war; here there are 21 fit for employment – several of whom, however, appear to be only partially deployable – as compared to 65 debilitated inmates who will soon no longer be fit for employment."

Illustration 172:
Page 1 of the
death report from
S III Sub-Camp,
Mar. 17, 1945
*Source: Thüringisches
Hauptstaatsarchiv,
Weimar*

```
K.L.Buchenwald
"Lagerarzt"                          Weimar/Buchenwald, den 17.März 1945   00191

Betreff: Verstorbene Häftlinge im Aussenkommando S III.

An die
Politische Abteilung
K.L.Buchenwald.

1.  ?            109150   Aschermann Salamon        1.9.08     ?
                 +19.2.45 um 16,00 Uhr an Kollaps
2.  ?            27581    Radowanowitsch            24.11.22   ?
                 +19.2.45 um 17,00 Uhr an inf. Magen-Darmkatarrh
3.  ?            9607     Kanos Sianisador          19.10.24   ?
                 +19.2.45 um  8,00 Uhr an Herzkreislaufversagen
4.  ?            111231   Wessolkin Peter           16.3.25    ?
                 +19.2.45 um  6,00 Uhr an Herzkollaps
5.  ?            117341   Zadoronij Wiktor          23.6.26    ?
                 19.2.45  um 12,00 Uhr an inf. Magen-Darmkatarrh
6.  Russe        101587   Ruszynyuk Michal          29.4.19  Dubuza
                 +19.2.45 um 16,00 Uhr an Herzschwäche b.allg.Körperschwäche
7.  Franz.       112278   Allemaz Luwien            6.2.21    Feillons
                 +19.2.45 um 16,00 Uhr an Herzschwäche b.allg.Körperschwäche
8.  Russe        1870     Sulima Iwan               7.1.00   Poloniackop
                 +19.2.45 um  8,30 Uhr an Herzschwäche b.Oedemkrankheit
9.  ?            117562   Kaufmann Johann           30.4.01    ?
                 +19.2.45 um  6,00 Uhr an Herzklappenfehler
10. Jugosl.      55737    Chripsek Wladislaw        24.6.07    ?
                 +19.2.45 um 17,00 Uhr an Fleckfieber
11. Pole         969      Nowak Stefan              ?9.2.45    ?
                 +19.2.45 um 15,00 Uhr an inf. Magen-Darmkatarrh
12. Ital.        85741    Cipriand Guido            7.7.17    Piere St.Stepano
                 +20.2.45 um  6,00 Uhr an inf. Magen-Darmkatarrh
13. ?            73853    Iwanow Alexander          ?          ?
                 +20.2.45 um 10,00 Uhr an Gehirnblutung, Schädelbasisbruch
14. ?            73957    Skorobahutka W            ?          ?
                 +20.2.45 um 10,00 Uhr an Stirnbeinbruch, Gehirnblutung
15. Ital.        109504   Lewakowitsch Lionello     1.9.06   Porpetto
                 +20.2.45 um 23,00 Uhr an Herzschwäche b.allg.Körperschwäche
16. Gr.Jude      120755   Otkunis Mos.              28.5.09   Saloniki
                 +20.2.45 um 17,00 Uhr an inf. Magen-Darmkatarrh
17. Franz.       53382    Denis Claude              1.7.23    Chantellevault
                 +20.2.45 um 17,00 Uhr an Kollaps
18. Jugosl.      109289   Kudek Josef               9.3.02    Zagreb
                 +20.2.45 um 17,00 Uhr an Asthenie
19. Russe        37034    Awdinschenko Mivhael      15.9.27   Alexieczke
                 +20.2.45 um  5,00 Uhr Freitod durch Erhängen
20. Ung.Jude     112245   Adler Dezsö               4.4.04    Komjadi
                 +20.2.45 um  8,50 Uhr an Sepsis b.Phlegmone li.Brustseite
21. pol!Tsch.    136163   Zizka Ludwig              17.4.09    ?
                 +20.2.45 um  7,00 Uhr an Herzmuskelschwäche b.Fleckfieber
22. Ital.        94467    Boldini Bruno             5.2.08    Udine
                 +20.2.45 um 14,00 Uhr an inf. Magen-Darmkatarrh
23. Tsch.        59666    Veseli Jaroslav           1.5.03    Prag
                 +20.2.45 um  6,00 Uhr an Herzschwäche b.Darmkatarrh
24. polit.Jude   104767   Lindenbaum Walter         11.12.07  Wien
                 20.2.45  um  ,00 Uhr an Bronchitis, inf.Magen-Darmkatarrh
25. Ung.         119248   Toth Imre                 10.11.10  Batmonostor
                 20.2.45  um  8,30 Uhr an akutem Magen-Darmkatarrh, Abszess
                          li. O-Schenkel
```

Many of the sub-camps which received their supplies from the parent camp lacked clothing, footwear and underwear. An SS hygienist inspected the sub-camp "Dora" in 1944, ascertaining that only every ninth inmate possessed a mess kit and every third inmate a spoon. On August 11, 1944, the SS officer in charge of the disinfection station labour detachment reported to the SS camp physician of "Dora," Dr. Kahr:

"I have determined that the underclothing and clothing articles of the inmates are in a completely tattered and soiled state. This is primarily to be attributed to the work carried out in the tunnels with tools and at machines and to the fact that the inmates have no work uniforms at their disposal. The issue of articles of clothing and underclothing by the inmates' clothing depot can, according to the employees there, no longer be carried out because the

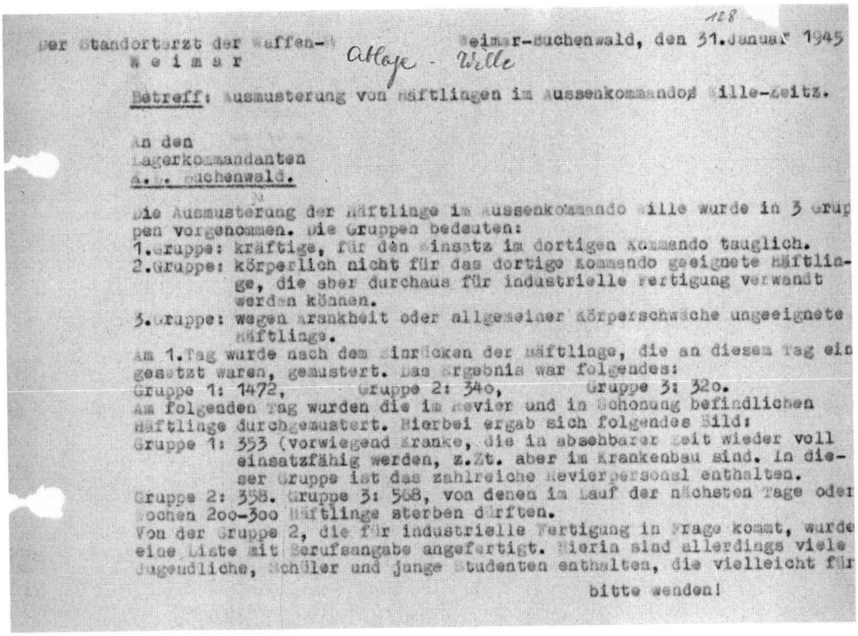

Illustration 173: Memo from garrison physician, SS Hauptsturmführer Dr. Schiedlausky, to camp commander concerning inspection of the inmates of "Wille" Sub-Camp, Jan. 31, 1945
Source: Thüringisches Hauptstaatsarchiv, Weimar

der Standortarzt der Waffen-
Weimar   Weimar-Buchenwald, den 31.Januar 1945
Anlage - Wille

Betreff: Ausmusterung von Häftlingen im Aussenkommando Wille-Zeitz.

An den
Lagerkommandanten
d.K. Buchenwald.

Die Ausmusterung der Häftlinge im Aussenkommando Wille wurde in 3 Gruppen vorgenommen. Die Gruppen bedeuten:
1.Gruppe: kräftige, für den Einsatz im dortigen Kommando tauglich.
2.Gruppe: körperlich nicht für das dortige Kommando geeignete Häftlinge, die aber durchaus für industrielle Fertigung verwandt werden können.
3.Gruppe: wegen Krankheit oder allgemeiner Körperschwäche ungeeignete Häftlinge.
Am 1.Tag wurde nach dem Einrücken der Häftlinge, die an diesem Tag eingesetzt waren, gemustert. Das Ergebnis war folgendes:
Gruppe 1: 1472,   Gruppe 2: 340,   Gruppe 3: 320.
Am folgenden Tag wurden die im Revier und in Schonung befindlichen Häftlinge durchgemustert. Hierbei ergab sich folgendes Bild:
Gruppe 1: 353 (vorwiegend Kranke, die in absehbarer Zeit wieder voll einsatzfähig werden, z.Zt. aber im Krankenbau sind. In dieser Gruppe ist das zahlreiche Revierpersonal enthalten.
Gruppe 2: 358. Gruppe 3: 568, von denen im Lauf der nächsten Tage oder Wochen 200-300 Häftlinge sterben dürften.
Von der Gruppe 2, die für industrielle Fertigung in Frage kommt, wurde eine Liste mit Berufsangabe angefertigt. Hierin sind allerdings viele Jugendliche, Schüler und junge Studenten enthalten, die vielleicht für
                                                           bitte wenden!

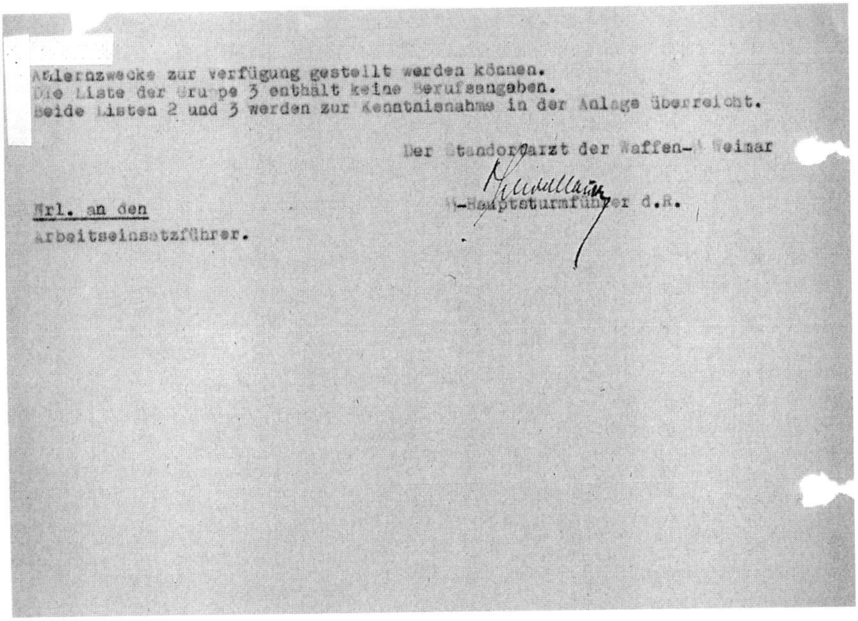

Anlernzwecke zur Verfügung gestellt werden können.
Die Liste der Gruppe 3 enthält keine Berufsangaben.
Beide Listen 2 und 3 werden zur Kenntnisnahme in der Anlage überreicht.
                              Der Standortarzt der Waffen- Weimar
                              SS-Hauptsturmführer d.R.
Mrl. an den
Arbeitseinsatzführer.

supply is exhausted. A regular change of underclothing is not possible, because there is no reserve supply. Foot cloths and socks are in a similar state of disrepair. After bathing, the inmates are thus compelled to put on the same clothing, which is in a soiled state, again. For drying, one towel is available for every two to three inmates. These circumstances are entirely incompatible with a hygienic camp order, and make it extraordinarily difficult to combat vermin and disease. There is imminent danger of the camp soon being infested with lice and exposed to other contagion hazards."

The facilities in **Gleina, Tröglitz, Rehmsdorf (code name "Wille") and Berga/Elster** were among the sub-camps consisting almost exclusively of Jewish inmates. In

Illustration 174: Michael Rozenek, after liberation in 1945
From l.: Michael Rozenek; Arno Bach who hid him during the final stage of the war; Jurek Rozenek, his brother.
Source: Sammlung Gedenkstätte Buchenwald, Weimar

May 1944, following Allied air attacks on the Zeitz Works of the Braunkohle-Benzin AG ("Brabag" – brown coal and petroleum company), the company management and the SS reached an agreement on the deployment of concentration camp inmates for the removal of the damages. On June 4, 1944 the first 200 prisoners arrived at the Gleina camp from Buchenwald. Following a second transport, this time of 1,000 Hungarian Jews, a crude tent camp was set up in Tröglitz, directly alongside the factory. At the end of September 1944, the two camps had a combined population of 4,164 Jewish inmates. The circumstances in which they were compelled to live were extremely poor: open latrines, no wastewater disposal facilities, outside washing facilities, insufficient medical care, along with heavy physical labour and hunger. Of the nearly 1,000 Jewish inmates who were sent back to Buchenwald in September because they were "unfit for work," a large majority were sent on to Auschwitz for extermination. In the winter the SS had a barrack camp built in Rehmsdorf. There the inmates had to clear a tract of land for the Brabag. The Polish Jew Michael Rozenek recalls:

"The work at Brabag was more than hard, and particularly difficult for us inmates. We were employed primarily for transport and rail tasks. Moreover, we had to get up very early and march the entire way from the camp to the factory site, a distance of approximately

three kilometres. Thus in addition to a twelve-hour working day it took us approximately three hours to walk from the camp to the site and back. In view of the weather conditions, the cold and the snow, and our shabby clothing, that was especially difficult for us. Every day we had to pull a large cart along in order to transport the inmates who had died doing the heavy work and on the march back to the camp. The task of pushing this cart was tantamount to a death sentence, because we were hardly able to stay on our feet ourselves.... . I was convinced that not one of us would be able to survive this daily routine for more than a month."

Of the Hungarian and Polish Jewish inmates in Rehmsdorf, 203 died in January 1945 alone. On April 6, 1945 the SS evacuated the inmates, sending them in open coal cars in the direction of the Erz Mountains. Michael Rozenek, whose parents and all of his siblings except for one brother had been killed, was thirty years old at the time; he and his brother succeeded in escaping from an evacuation march in April 1945. A German family hid them until liberation.

Women's Sub-Camps: Female Inmates in the Armament Industry

The camp of the Hugo Schneider Company ("Hasag") of Leipzig, already temporarily administered by Buchenwald in the summer of 1944, was one of the first sub-camps with female inmates. On September 1, 1944 Buchenwald took official charge of all sub-camps of the Ravensbrück Women's Concentration Camp located within its range of authority. In mid January 1945, these sub-camps accounted for nearly 25,500 female inmates working exclusively in armament industry operations. They were primarily young women, whom the SS offered to the armament manufacturers as labourers. During their imprisonment, many of them bore children who had no chance of surviving.

The procedures for placing the female inmate labourers at the disposal of the various armament companies were investigated and heard during the Nuremberg trials in the case against the **Krupp Company**. Krupp had applied to the Department of Economic Administration for 2,000 male inmates for its factory in Essen, but had not received them. On July 4, 1944, Pister travelled to Essen with his labour allocation officer Albert Schwartz to offer the company 2,000 female inmates by way of substitution. As they toured the rolling mill, where the labourers were needed, it became obvious that the work could not be performed by women and Pister promised to place 2,000 Hungarian Jews at the disposal of Krupp-Essen at the next opportunity. During this visit the price per inmate (4 Reichsmark per day) was nevertheless agreed upon, and various arrangements for their accommodation, guarding and provisions were discussed. In August, the Krupp company informed the SS Department of Economic Administration that it now needed 500 female inmates after all. During the Krupp trial, Albert Schwartz further testified that:

"In response to the report by Commander Pister, the Department of Economic Administration approved the deployment of the female inmates to the Krupp company in Essen and authorised the Krupp company to select them from an existing sub-camp in Gelsenkirchen (Gelsenberg Benzin AG), where later a representative of the Krupp company actually selected the 500 strongest women, who were then transported to Essen."

Rachel Grünebaum, one of these Jewish women, recalls:

"I was born in Sighet, Romania, on December 9, 1923. At that time Sighet was the administrative centre of a district, with a population of twenty-four thousand, of whom approximately half were Jews. In 1944, Ger-

man soldiers and Hungarians set up a ghetto in the city. We had to leave our homes and live with two sisters, complete with their families (altogether twelve persons, including seven children) in a single room in the house of friends. The ghetto was dissolved after about four weeks and everyone living there was transported on three transports to Auschwitz. I was on the first transport. Each of us was allowed to take along one small knapsack containing clothing. We were crowded into the large synagogue and registered. At dawn we were put into cattle cars, 90 persons to a car. The transport lasted approximately two days and three nights; then we were in Auschwitz-Birkenau. The selection took place on the ramp. Dr. Mengele selected those who were fit for employment. I was separated from my kin, who were sent from there to the gas chambers.

I was in Auschwitz-Birkenau for about six weeks and had to endure countless selections. Then I was deported to Germany with a group of approx. 2,000 women and put in the sub-camp in Gelsenkirchen. There I had to work clearing up the rubble of bombed buildings. It was heavy physical labour and we were fed only once a day. Later, 520 of the strongest women were selected by the Krupp company and taken to Essen. That was work that had never before been performed by women. In April we were taken by train to Bergen-Belsen via Buchenwald. At the time of my liberation I weighed twenty-five kg and had typhus. I had to stay in a hospital until August 1945."

The largest **women's sub-camp – Hasag Leipzig**, with over 5,000 female inmates – was under the command of the former second officer in charge of the preventive custody camp at Buchenwald, Wolfgang Plaul. The **Hugo-Schneider AG (Hasag)** had become an armament combine in the course of the war. Founded in 1863 as a lamp factory, it began producing armaments

Age of female inmates, 12/30/1944						
Total number	Age groups, number and percentage of total					
	under 20	20-30	30-40	40-50	50-60	60-70
24,210	6,765 28 %	10,455 43 %	4,706 19 %	1,961 8 %	305 1 %	18 0.07 %

Illustration 175: Suzanne Orts, née Pic (1927), before her arrest
Source: Suzanne Orts

in 1936. In 1940 it took over confiscated plants in Tschenstochau (Częstochowa) and Skarzysko-Kamienna. At the Jewish forced labour camp in Skarzysko-Kamienna, selections and mass murders took place with the participation of the plant security force. Following the evacuation of this camp, Buchenwald sub-camps were established at Hasag branches in Altenburg, Meuselwitz, Schlieben, Taucha, Colditz and Flössberg with more than 13,000 female and male inmates. Of all the business enterprises in which concentration camp inmates were exploited, it took fourth place after the construction units of the SS, the IG Farben AG and the "Hermann Göring" Reich factories.

The first women in Hasag's Leipzig camp were Poles from Majdanek Concentration Camp. They were followed by Jewish women from the Skarzysko-Kamienna forced labour camp which had been evacuated by the SS in July 1944, and other female political prisoners from several European countries. Suzanne Orts, who belonged to a Gaullist sub-group of the Résistance, recalls:

"When we departed from Romainville, our transport consisted of 60 women. Most of them were members of the Résistance: Gaullists, Communists, several victims of police raids and common offenders (theft, black marketing), one prostitute. Their professions were: labourers, students, teachers, 2 doctors, 1 lawyer – no declared Jews, but Jewish members of the Résistance."

Illustration 176: Danuta Brzosko-Medrik, née Brzosko (1921), winter 1942
Source: Danuta Brzosko-Medrik

Illustration 177: Bonus coupon from Buchenwald garrison canteen for Hasag-Leipzig Sub-Camp, 1944
Source: Danuta Brzosko-Medrik

188

The women in the sub-camps generally worked between ten and twelve hours a day. They worked in shifts, usually performing heavy physical labour. Suzanne Orts, reporting on Hasag:

"Twelve hours of work, one week by day, one week by night; Sunday is a day of rest. Added to this the roll call ceremony every morning and evening. They wake us at four o'clock. We produce seven-kg antiaircraft grenades. They arrive in a neighbouring building in the form of metal plates; there they are processed, rolled out, formed and cast by women inmates. We finish them: the floor, the acid bath, the electrolysis bath. The final step in the process: with one of our comrades we lubricate them before they are stacked up in carts. All day long these seven kilos have to be moved, taken from a table, held up around a rotating brush, rubbed with a grease-soaked rag and then placed into the cart. The whole business, two, three, four hundred times a day. The cycle is accelerated. The shells pile up. The master yells. The female SS overseer deals out blows —

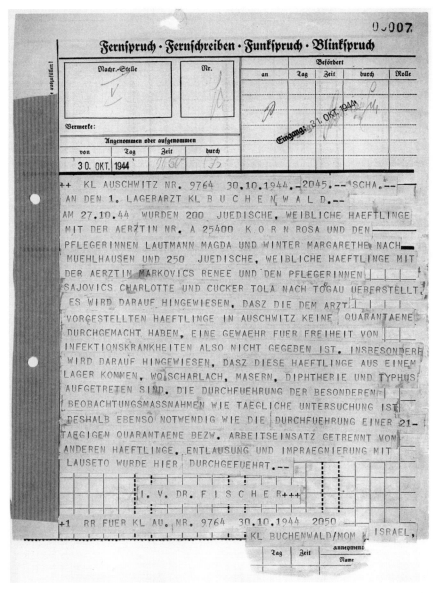

Illustration 178: Teleprint message from Auschwitz Concentration Camp to the chief camp physician at Buchenwald Concentration Camp concerning the transport of two hundred Jewish women to Mühlhausen Sub-Camp, Oct. 30, 1944

Source: Thüringisches Hauptstaatsarchiv, Weimar

189

under circumstances such as these it's not hard to learn the profession."

The SS and the female overseers who had been trained in Ravensbrück Concentration Camp used every conceivable means of raising the women's productivity. The Polish inmate Danuta Brzosko-Medryk reports:

"Plaul turned up at roll call. Smiling. In his hands coupons bearing the label of the SS garrison canteen, Buchenwald, sub-camp, stamp one Reichsmark. In a flowery, grandiloquent speech he thanked us on Hitler's behalf for our work and promised us compensation in the form of coupons for which we could buy anything our hearts desired in the camp canteen. This 'anything' was a stinking snail salad with spoiled vegetables ... . Many

hands reached out. But none of the women from Majdanek touched the compensation. Other former inmates of other camps also refused it. First puzzled, then furious, the commander ordered a special roll call as a punitive measure for those who had not reached for the coupons."

In a number of factories – at Hasag, for example, as well as in the army ammunitions establishment and at the explosives factories of Hessisch-Lichtenau, Westfälisch-Anhaltinische Sprengstoff AG and Dynamit Nobel in Allendorf – women had to handle nitrate compounds without any form of protection. These substances dyed their hair and skin a yellowish green to bronze and led to liver poisoning with jaundice and irreversible damage to the lungs.

Illustration 179: Women in the Buchenwald Sub-Camp Penig after liberation, 1945
Source: Sammlung Gedenkstätte Buchenwald, Weimar

Committal for Execution

"Again and again, people from outside the camp were brought in, or inmates were summoned to the gate, led straight to the crematorium and slaughtered there, always in the presence of the camp physician and a representative of the camp command, regardless of the inmate's age, gender, status and nationality."

Eugen Kogon

During the war, the Reich Department of Security could order the execution of any person in police custody – or correct their court decisions accordingly – without legal proceedings or a formal death sentence. This procedure was referred to as "**Sonderbehandlung**" ("**special treatment**"). It was applied to recaptured inmate and forced labour convict escapees who had stolen clothing and food in order to survive while they were at large. Poles were also often committed for special treatment" for having had illicit relationships with German women.

The executions did not usually take place in front of the inmates, but in the firing range of the Deutsche Ausrüstungswerke, at times in the dog kennels at command headquarters, and most often in the courtyard or cellar of the crematorium. For this purpose the walls of the cellar bore forty-eight hooks, arranged in the manner of a butcher's shop. Testifying on the execution procedures, SS labour detachment officer Hermann Helbig later stated:

"The two German inmates were there as well. The noose was laid around his neck, the two of them lifted him up, the noose was slung over the hook and then the inmate was dropped."

Illustration 180: Execution cellar in crematorium, April 1945
Before they retreated, the SS had most of the wall hooks used for execution by hanging torn out of the walls.
Source: Sammlung Gedenkstätte Buchenwald, Weimar

Illustration 181: The public execution of 20 Polish inmates near Poppenhausen (Thuringia), May 11, 1942 Photo taken by an onlooker. The Buchenwald SS carried out the execution with the aid of the "transportable gallows." Source: *Thüringisches Staatsarchiv Meiningen*

The doctor did not pronounce the inmate dead until thirty-five to forty minutes had passed. When asked whether the people being brought in for execution had to witness the deaths of the others, Helbig answered:

"They were brought down one by one. They presumably saw the others hanging there."

Questioned further, Helbig stated that he had personally hanged approximately 250 persons. Eugen Kogon estimates the number of men and women killed in the crematorium cellar at 1,100.

Only once, in September 1944, did the SS hang a Pole on the muster ground in front of the entire assembly of inmates. Public executions are known to have taken place primarily in sub-camps, for example "Dora," Langenstein-Zwieberge and Wernigerode. Hermann Pister stated in this connection:

"The inmates were usually led past the hanged person. As a deterrent. In the case of sub-camps the hanging was carried out by the responsible Gestapo office, or a detachment from Buchenwald betook itself to the sub-

camp with a portable gallows to carry out the execution."

In the autumn of 1944 the SS hanged 34 Frenchmen, Belgians, Englishmen and Canadians who were members of the Allied secret services. One of them was the French technical designer and racing driver **Robert Benoist**. In the mid 1930s he had raced regularly for Bugatti Automobiles and won the Grand Prix de Picardie and the Le Mans twenty-four-hour race as well as setting six world records in 1936. After the war broke out he was an officer in the French air force; later he escaped from a German POW camp and joined the Résistance. On September 10, 1944 he was hanged on a wall hook in the cellar of the crematorium. August Favier drew a portrait of him during his last hours. Christian Pineau later reported:

"I recall 37 French, English and Canadian paratroopers who came to Block 17 one day. Favier went there to draw their portraits. He drew fast, for all of them wanted to sit for him. Several weeks later, 34 of these comrades were hanged by the Nazis. In the months

following the executions we often looked at the portraits of these people in the evenings."

There are also eye-witness reports of the execution of Polish officers in 1943. They were brought in two prison vehicles directly from the railway station in Weimar to the courtyard of the crematorium. There they had to line up. They were wearing uniforms. The camp adjutant read out a kind of pronouncement of judgement; the execution on the gallows was carried out in his presence. The most well-known victim of the executions in Buchenwald was the member of the Reichstag and chairman of the KPD Ernst Thälmann, who was shot to death on the night of August 17, 1944 at the entrance to the oven room.

Illustration 182: Auguste Favier: "Robert Benoist," drawing, Sept. 10, 1944
Robert Benoist was one of the thirty-four members of the Allied secret services who were hanged in September 1944 in the cellar of the crematorium. He sat for this portrait on the day of his murder.
Source: Sammlung Gedenkstätte Buchenwald, Weimar

Illustration 183: Ernst Thälmann (2nd from r.) at a congress of the executive committee of the Communist International in Moscow, November/December 1926
Source: Ernst Thälmann. Eine Biographie, Berlin, 1980.

Special Prominent Inmates

In Buchenwald there were a number of small sites that were isolated from the main inmates' camp and used for internment purposes. One such site was the "Fichtenhain" special camp right in the midst of the SS area. The persons imprisoned here were registered and treated differently from the camp inmates. The first prisoners were a group of Romanians from the "Archangel Michael" Legion (Iron Guard) who had fled to Germany. They moved into the wooden barracks at the end of 1942 and remained there until the late summer of 1944. At the beginning of January 1943 the "legionnaires" numbered 130, by the end of March, 225.

Illustration 184: Isolation barrack adjacent to "Fichtenhain Special Camp", 1943
Source: Musée de la Résistance et de la Déportation, Besançon (SS Photo Album: "Buchenwald Jahresende 1943")

Adjacent to the "Fichtenhain" special camp was an **isolation barrack** surrounded by a wall. Here the former chairman of the SPD Reichstag group Dr. Rudolf Breitscheid, his wife Tony, and Mafalda of Hesse, the wife of the Chief President of Hesse-Nassau and daughter of the Italian king, were kept in custody.

Located between the SS barracks and the armament factory, "Fichtenhain" was destroyed during the air attack of August 24, 1944. Breitscheid was killed immediately; Princess Mafalda of Hesse died as a result of insufficient treatment of her injuries. Tony Breitscheid recalls:

"In the summer of 1944 an open approach trench was dug alongside the barrack – our only protection against aerial bombs. The camp was overflown more and more frequently; large war-industry operations were located only five minutes from our barrack. On August 24, a long, violent air battle took place above us. We got into the trench. We had no sooner climbed in when the bombs began to drop. The burning barrack collapsed onto the trench. …
My husband was dead. I was not informed of that fact until three days later. I had severe burns myself, but had to remain alive."

Beginning in February 1945, the SS also held special prisoners from the Reich Depart-

Illustration 185: Princess Mafalda of Hesse (1902-1944)
Source: Heinrich Prinz von Hessen: Der kristallene Lüster. Meine deutsch-italienische Jugend 1927-1947, München, Zürich: Piper, 1994.

Illustration 186: Rudolf Breitscheid with Léon Blum (l.), ca. 1933
Source: *Gilbert Ziebura: Léon Blum. Theorie and Praxis einer sozialistischen Politik, Vol. 1, Berlin, de Gruyter, 1963.*

Illustration 187: Barracks of the Armed SS in Buchenwald, 1943
In the cellar of one of these barracks were the SS detention cells in which Dietrich Bonhoeffer and others were imprisoned. The troop barracks, of which there were four altogether, were constructed as part of expansion projects in 1942.
Source: *Musée de la Résistance et de la Déportation, Besançon (SS Photo Album: "Buchenwald Jahresende 1943")*

ment of Security in "**SS Detention**," a row of cells in the cellar of one of the troop barracks. The Protestant theologian Dietrich Bonhoeffer, the military intelligence captain Ludwig Gehre and General Friedrich von Rabenau were in custody there. On April 3 they were taken to Flossenbürg, where they were killed on April 9, 1945.

From the spring of 1943 to April 1945 the **falcon lodge** on the Buchenwald falcon yard – a facility built by the SS for representational purposes – also served as a place of special confinement. After the occupation of the "free zone" in Southern France, former members of the French government were interned there. Léon Blum, the former premier minister of the People's Front government, was kept in custody the longest. He later wrote:

"I was in the hands of the Nazis. For them I was more than just a French politician; I also embodied the very thing they hated most in the world: I was a democratic Socialist and a Jew. But the very aspects that made me a particularly despised enemy also raised me to the status of an especially important hostage. … We were aware that we would be treated carefully in order to make a deal of that kind, possibly at the last minute. …

In Buchenwald we had already felt the presence or sudden approach of death a year earlier. I am referring to the morning in July when, by personal order of Himmler, the Weimar Gestapo came to take poor Georges Mandel away from the house in which we had lived together for fifteen months. … We helped him pack his bag and the blankets the freezing man would need for the flight he was about to embark on. We accompanied him all the way to the gate of the barbed-wire enclosure that separated us from the rest of the world. …

The severity of our isolation explains a fact which is incomprehensible at first; I mean our long-lasting ignorance of the unutterable horrors that took place only a few hundred metres from where we were. The first inkling we had of this was the strange smell that often came through the open windows in the evening and pursued us the whole night when there was a constant wind from the same direction: it was the smell of the crematorium ovens."

In February 1945, following its reconstruction, the isolation barrack was used to imprison **"kinship inmates,"** members of the families of the officers and politicians who had participated in the assassination attempt on Hitler, as well as the kin of other eminent persons who had fallen out of favour with the regime. Isa Vermehren recalls the circumstances in her memoirs:

"It took us a few days to get our bearings among these large families – there were ten representatives of the name Stauffenberg alone … eight Goerdelers, Frau von Hofacker with her two eldest children, Baroness von Hammerstein with her two youngest, the wife of Pastor Schröder with her three under-age children of ten, seven and four. Further, the elderly Fritz Thyssen and his wife were there; what is more, we were able to celebrate a reunion with Mrs. Halder and two inmates we knew from Potsdam. The daughter of Ambassador von Hassell, Fey Pirzio-Biroli, Mrs. Kaiser, her daughters, her brother Mr. Mohr and his wife, the wife of General Lindemann from Hamburg, Miss Gisevius and her cousin Major Schatz and the Kuhn couple from Berlin were also there. Living under this friendly roof there were moreover eight Hungarians, the last regular Hungarian government, who had been kidnapped after Admiral Horthy had entered into armistice negotiations with Russia. …

It would be going too far to describe each of these persons in detail, but it is important to note that the criteria according to which these people had been selected will presumably always remain inexplicable. Certainly, the reasons are quite obvious in the case of the two large families Stauffenberg and Goerdeler.… . The confusing thing, however, was the fact that by no means all of the Goerdelers, for example, were assembled here – the burgomaster's wife and children to be sure, and his brother, but only one and by no means all of his nieces and nephews; due to the fact that the only member of Mr. Gisevius' family who was found was his sister, they also took a cousin of his into custody, a dedicated Nazi of all people, and an enthusiastic active front officer."

By the end of March the number of inmates in the isolation barrack had reached

Illustration 188: Dietrich Bonhoeffer (1906-1945), Tegel Prison, 1944
Source: Reproduction, Sammlung Gedenkstätte Buchenwald, Weimar

Illustration 189: Friedrich von Rabenau (1884-1945)
Source: Referat Gedenkstätten, Berlin

Illustration 190: Georges Mandel (1885-1944) in Buchenwald
This photo was taken by Léon Blum in the Buchenwald falcon yard.
Source: Archives Nationales, Paris

57. On April 3, they were sent in the direction of Southern Germany. Fey von Hassell recalls:

"The rumbling of artillery could now be heard in Buchenwald as well. Our nerves were so on edge that we could hardly bear it, particularly as the rumour was circulating that we were to be transported off again – and on April 3 the order really came: pack your things. You may take with you only what you can hold on your knees.
The Stauffenbergs left many suitcases behind in the camp. But I simply could no longer take the order seriously and I dragged my suitcase along, even if I couldn't hold it on my knees. … Somehow we all managed to get a seat, some of us on the laps of others. … The three busses started off and kept going until the following morning. … Once when we stopped we noticed that we were being followed by a car carrying two persons under SS guard. We recognised Léon Blum, the former French premier minister, and his wife; they waved to us inconspicuously. Behind them was a 'Black Maria.'"

Members of the French government in the SS falcon yard of Buchenwald, 1943-45

4/4/1943 Édouard Daladier (French premier minister, 1940), Maurice Gamelin (Commander in Chief of the French and British armed forces, 1940) und Léon Blum (French premier minister, 1936-1938) are brought to Buchenwald following the occupation of the free zone in France.

5/2/1943 Édouard Daladier and Maurice Gamelin are transported by car from Buchenwald to Itter Castle in Tyrol, where they are liberated by the Americans on 5/5/1945.

5/11/1943 Paul Reynaud (last premier minister before surrender of France, 1940) is taken from a location in the vicinity of Berlin to Itter Castle. He spends one day in Buchenwald along the way.

End of May 1943 Georges Mandel, minister of the interior in the last cabinet of Paul Reynaud, is brought from Sachsenhausen Concentration Camp to Buchenwald.

End of June 1943 Léon Blum marries Jeanne Levylier, his secretary to whom he is distantly related, in Buchenwald, thus saving her from deportation to a sub-camp.

7/4/1944 Georges Mandel is taken away by the Gestapo and turned over to the militia of the Vichy regime as a hostage. Three days later, while travelling in a car in the vicinity of Paris, he is shot to death by the driver.

4/3/1945 Along with the other special inmates, Jeanne and Léon Blum are taken to the prison in Regensburg. They are liberated in Niederndorf, Tyrol on 4/29/1945.

Illustration 191: Markwart (l.) and Otto-Philipp von Stauffenberg after liberation, 1945
Source: Fey von Hassell: Niemals sich beugen. Erinnerungen einer Sondergefangenen der SS, München, Zürich: Piper, 1991.

Medical Experiments

At quite an early stage, SS doctors treated inmates as experimental material with the intent of gaining professional distinction. They tried out various forms of surgical intervention, tested various treatment methods and caused human beings to suffer in order to carry on their studies on pathological processes. The first pharmaceutical company to show an interest in the test results obtained in Buchenwald were the Behring works in Marburg/Lahn, a subsidiary of IG Farben AG, in 1939.

Whereas at this point in time there were only a few isolated contacts, regular collaboration with the SS commenced at the end of 1941. In view of large-scale typhus epidemics in the prisoner-of-war camps, the SS offered to test various serums on inmates. On the basis of joint agreements between the SS, IG Farben AG, the Wehrmacht and certain government offices, the preparations for this undertaking were carried out in Buchenwald at the end of 1941/beginning of 1942.

No sooner had the first experiments been concluded in early 1942 than the SS set up a permanent experimental laboratory in Block 46, where by the end of the war experiments had been carried out with nearly all epidemic diseases. Inmates who left this block alive were usually seriously ill, lost their hair and teeth or were later killed in order to obtain comparative medical material for the clients. From 1943 on, Buchenwald accommodated the "Department of Epidemic Typhus and Virus Research" of the Hygiene Institute of the Armed SS, expanded by the addition of a "Serum Institute" in Block 50. The building housed a guest laboratory for physicians working for the Wehrmacht, the Armed SS and the Robert Koch Institute of Berlin, who participated in the experiments on human beings carried out in Block 46. During one epidemic typhus therapy experiment with acridine granulate and rutenol, produced by the Hoechst company, 21 of the 39 inmates involved, died. The SS kept precise records of their symptoms. In the report of June 1, 1943 it is stated:

"Indications that the substance relieved the symptoms, shortened the term of illness or lowered the fever were not observed.
Among the 39 persons, all of whom were in a state of more or less reduced NPC [nutritional and physical condition], the following observations were made:

in	30	cases	*flushed face*
"	37	"	*bloated face*
"	39	"	*conjunctivitis*
"	9	"	*shivers*
"	38	"	*headache*
"	39	"	*exanthema*
"	38	"	*haemorrhagic exanthema*
"	33	"	*yellowing of the hands*
"	1	case	*subcutaneous phlegmon above the larynx*
"	8	cases	*tinnitus*
"	11	"	*impairment of hearing*
"	16	"	*swollen tongue*
"	6	"	*nose-bleeding*
"	4	"	*speech impairment*
"	4	"	*syncopal attacks*
"	39	"	*insomnia*
"	10	"	*muscular twitching*
"	16	"	*muscular pain*
"	2	"	*cramps*
"	10	"	*shaking of the hands*
"	2	"	*paralytic symptoms*
"	3	"	*exophthalmos*
"	10	"	*benumbedness*

"	*9*	*"*	*apathy*
"	*36*	*"*	*deliria*
"	*2*	*"*	*Catalonian stupor*
"	*1*	*case*	*gangrene of one lower leg*
"	*39*	*cases*	*splenic enlargement*
"	*14*	*"*	*tenderness of the spleen*
"	*35*	*"*	*subicterus*
"	*2*	*"*	*vomiting (control group)*
"	*15*	*"*	*constipation*
"	*12*	*"*	*diarrhoea*
"	*1*	*case*	*intestinal haemorrhaging*
"	*13*	*cases*	*tracheitis*
"	*15*	*"*	*bronchitis*
"	*1*	*case*	*bronchopneumonia*
"	*1*	*"*	*pyelitis*
"	*1*	*"*	*pyelitis and urethritis*
"	*1*	*"*	*nephritis*
"	*2*	*cases*	*rheumatic pains*
"	*5*	*"*	*numbness in the extremities*

In addition, the following post-illness symptoms were observed:

in	*1*	*case*	*urticarial rash*
"	*3*	*cases*	*decubitus ulcer*
"	*3*	*"*	*furunculosis*
"	*1*	*case*	*parotitis*
"	*7*	*cases*	*profuse perspiration*
"	*5*	*"*	*post-illness fever*
"	*15*	*"*	*ataxia*
"	*3*	*"*	*dizziness*

During the illness
36 patients urinated and
11 patients defecated in their beds.

The mortality amounted to 55.5 % of the control group
53.3 % of the group receiving acridine granulate
53.3 % of the group receiving rutenol

6/1/1943"

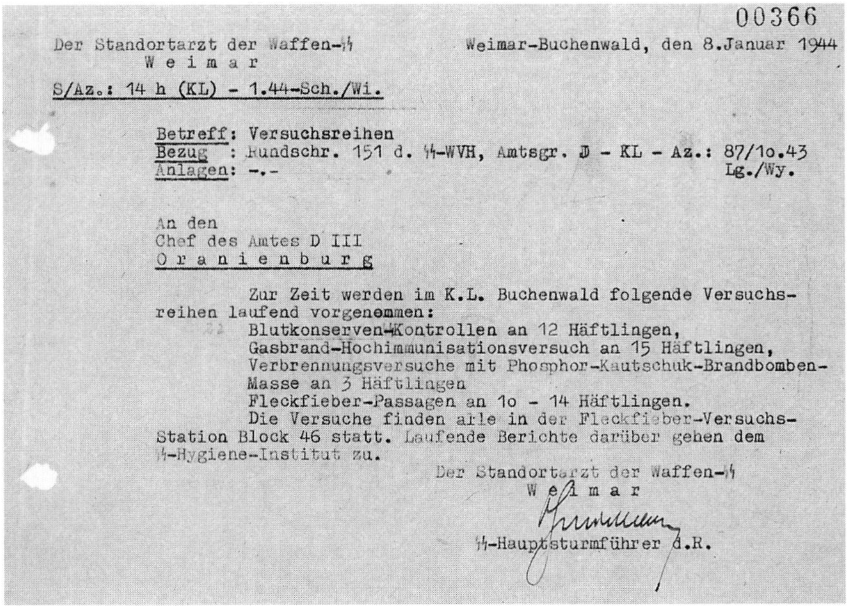

00366

Der Standortarzt der Waffen-SS
Weimar

Weimar-Buchenwald, den 8.Januar 1944

S/Az.: 14 h (KL) - 1.44-Sch./Wi.

Betreff: Versuchsreihen
Bezug : Rundschr. 151 d. SS-WVH, Amtsgr. D - KL - Az.: 87/1o.43 Lg./Wy.
Anlagen: -.-

An den
Chef des Amtes D III
Oranienburg

Zur Zeit werden im K.L. Buchenwald folgende Versuchsreihen laufend vorgenommen:
Blutkonserven-Kontrollen an 12 Häftlingen,
Gasbrand-Hochimmunisationsversuch an 15 Häftlingen,
Verbrennungsversuche mit Phosphor-Kautschuk-Brandbomben-Masse an 3 Häftlingen
Fleckfieber-Passagen an 1o - 14 Häftlingen.
Die Versuche finden alle in der Fleckfieber-Versuchs-Station Block 46 statt. Laufende Berichte darüber gehen dem SS-Hygiene-Institut zu.

Der Standortarzt der Waffen-SS
Weimar
SS-Hauptsturmführer d.R.

Illustration 192: The garrison physician, SS Hauptsturmführer Dr. Schiedlausky, to the chief of Bureau D III re medical experiments, Jan. 8, 1944
Source: Thüringisches Hauptstaatsarchiv, Weimar

The SS used a number of inmates as so-called passages, i.e. as living cultures for pathogens. Their blood was used for the artificial infection of others. Not one of these inmates survived. According to the journal of the "Department of Epidemic Typhus and Virus Research", thirty-five series of experiments were carried out between August 1942 and October 1944. The majority were experiments with epidemic typhus serums but investigations were also carried out on gas gangrene, therapeutic agents for the treatment of typhus and epidemic ty-phus, tolerance for serums against small-pox, typhus, paratyphoid fever types A and B, cholera, diphtheria and yellow fever. SS doctors also experimented with various poisons, tested the preservability of blood serum and inflicted burns upon inmates in order to test treatment methods. In 1944, with Himmler's support, Dr. Carl Vaernet carried out experiments and gland operations on 5 homosexual inmates. Altogether at least 1,000 served the SS as test objects; an unknown number of them died as a result.

Illustration 193:
Vaccine for the
Armed SS from the
production of the
"Serum Institute"
in Block 50, 1944
Catalogue 4/36
Photo: N. T. Salmon

The 1944 Bomb Attack
on the Armament Factory Adjacent to the Camp

"Even more far-reaching than the considerable material damage and loss of life caused by this event were the indisputable consequences it had on life in the camp. Everything was different after that. The SS, who were in a state of total confusion on that day, had been disrupted in their all-too-perfectly regulated former habits. … They had lost their footing; they no longer seemed able to cope with the situation."

Roger Arnould

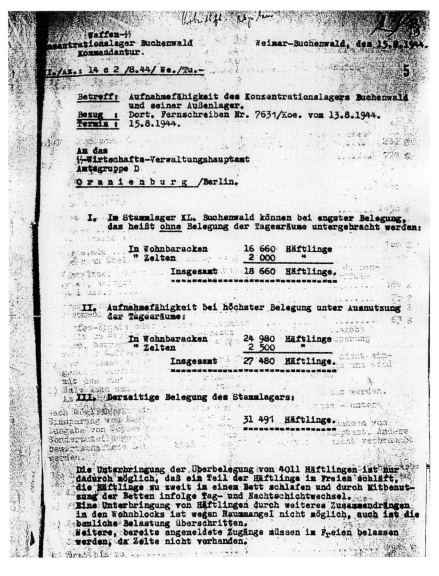

Illustration 194:
Report on the capacity of Buchenwald Concentration Camp nine days before the air attack, Aug. 15, 1944
Source: Thüringisches Hauptstaatsarchiv, Weimar

Armament Production in the Gustloff-Werk II

In certain phases, as many as 3,500 inmates worked in Buchenwald's Gustloff-Werk II. Beginning in the spring of 1944 a corporate group operating under the code name "Mibau" produced control components for the "V2" rocket. Arms production had been carried out in Buchenwald since 1943 by technically advanced methods. The results failed to meet expectations, however, due in part to conflicts of authority between the SS and the plant management, but also to acts of sabotage by the inmate workers. Perhaps even more significantly, the contradiction between the modern nature of the production and the savage force by which the camp was ruled was never resolved. As the Polish Jew Leon Weissmann testified at the Buchenwald trial held in Dachau in 1947, the labour detachment officers employed brutal methods. Weissmann reports:

"One day my capo ordered me to work for some Germans in the Wilhelm Gustloff Works. I refused, and for doing so I had to report to [SS Hauptscharführer] Jakobs. He screamed at me, beat me and kicked me several times. He added that he would think about my punishment. I should report to him the following morning. When I reported to him the next morning everyone was sent away and Jakobs ordered me to jump into a pit of ice-cold water with all my clothes on. Three times I was forced to stay under water till I could no longer hold my breath. He threatened to kill me if I ever mentioned the occurrence to any-

one. *When I was finally permitted to climb out of the pit Jakobs beat me and kicked me for another half hour; I was not allowed to change my wet clothing or even just take it off."*

The inconsistency was also apparent in the guidelines for inmates of the Gustloff-Werk issued by Camp Commander Pister at the end of November 1943.

"1. From 11/29/43 on, a performance sheet will be kept for every inmate, indicating the degree to which he achieves the performance of a free worker in percent. As far as possible, the work is to be expressed in numbers of units. If he achieves this number / exceeds the minimum, he receives a performance bonus at the end of the week.
Anyone who does not succeed in performing his work or produces a lot of botch has the disadvantage of having to do additional work during his free time or being deprived of rations as a punishment.
2. No inmate may leave his place of work without reporting to the master, capo or foreman. Conversation during working time is prohibited. During working time, every distance must be walked at a fast pace.
3. Lack of discipline or the refusal to work will entail punishment of the severest nature.
4. The capos and foremen are to be distributed throughout the halls in such a way that each of them has a specific control area. The supervisor is answerable for any complaints pertaining to his area. He is also responsible if inmates not belonging to the detachment are present in his area. …
8. The performance sheets with favourable and unfavourable remarks are to be submitted to the labour allocation officer once a week for assessment. The result is reported to the camp commander.
9. Every inmate's attitude and performance count towards the assessment regarding his release. Diligence shortens the term of imprisonment."

Pister was naturally well aware that, at the end of 1943, very few of the inmate arms production labourers from the Soviet Union, Poland and France had any chance of being released.

Illustration 195:
Tool chip from Gustloff-Werk II
Found object
Catalogue 4/41
Photo: N. T. Salmon

The Air Strike

The carefully prepared attack by the First Bomber Division of the Eighth U.S. Air Fleet on Buchenwald on August 24, 1944, was aimed at the Gustloff-Werk II, the Deutsche Ausrüstungswerke and the SS facilities. It heralded the final phase in the history of Buchenwald Concentration Camp. No damage occurred within the inmates' living area. The inmates' camp was struck only in the section directly adjacent to the Deutsche Ausrüstungswerke; there were damages to the crematorium, the laundry and the disinfection building as well as depot barracks in which winter clothing was stored.

At the time of the attack, the camp – with over 31,000 inmates – was at the limit of its capacity. A large number of inmates were compelled to remain near the factory during the strike; 2,000 were injured and

Illustration 196: Destroyed halls of Gustloff-Werk II after air attack, Aug. 24, 1944
Source: F.N.D.I.R.P., Paris

Illustration 197: Inmates clearing rubble from an SS shelter after the air attack, Aug. 24, 1944
Source: F.N.D.I.R.P., Paris

many died. The Luxembourger Nicolas Spielmann describes the situation:

"There was only one air raid shelter in the entire camp area, and it was intended for the SS. The inmates were permitted to leave the factory in the event of danger, but had to remain within the sentry line and thus were standing around the plants unprotected.

In the wonderfully clear sky they were able to watch their friends flying by. A grey column of smoke could be seen. That was a sure sign of an attack. Yet only a very few inmates understood that sign. Warnings to flee into the nearby forest were not heeded. But only for a short time.

A deafening whir in the air and then, twice, a terrible crash. That must have been somewhere close by; they distinctly felt the air pressure. In wild leaps, they all fled to the forest that was about twenty metres from the garage. Here approach trenches had been dug out a short time earlier. They crouched down inside these trenches. They were not permitted to go deeper into the forest, for the sentry line was standing right next to them, the safeties of their rifles released. No sooner had

the crowd disappeared in the trench then a deadly hissing, wailing and crashing commenced.

With our heads pressed tightly into the clay soil and our eyes closed, we could distinctly hear the large building barracks falling down. Now dust, stones and debris rained upon them. The trench had already half collapsed. Many were buried. ...

The entire area was black with dust and smoke. Where seconds earlier buildings had stood, there was now nothing but heaps of rubble. Many had found their grave there. The entire garage complex had disappeared. There were huge bomb craters everywhere. The trucks had been knocked askew like toys."

By November 1944, altogether 388 inmates had lost their lives as a result of the air strike. Over one hundred SS men and members of their families died as well. The SS attempted to resume production in the Gustloff-Werk II after the attack. In view of the enormous destruction in the factory, however, they attained only a fraction of the previous level of production, which had been low to begin with.

Illustration 198: Destroyed house in the SS Officers' Colony I, Aug. 24, 1944
Source: F.N.D.I.R.P., Paris

Survival Strategies and Resistance

"You couldn't even begin to think about resistance unless you ... had attained a labour assignment with which the most pressing problems could be overcome. In order to gain the support of like-minded persons for an act of resistance, they first had to be helped to living conditions that protected them from chronic hunger. In every camp, the prerequisite for group activity was getting your brother-in-arms into a better labour detachment."

Hermann Langbein

Illustration 199: Henri Pieck: "So mußten sie neben Toten leben" (they had to live alongside the dead), charcoal drawing 1944
Source: Henri Pieck: Buchenwald. Reproduktionen nach seinen Zeichnungen aus dem Konzen-trationslager, Berlin, Potsdam, 1949. Sammlung Gedenkstätte Buchenwald, Weimar

Illustration 200:
Comb, made
by hand from
a plastic ruler
Found object
Catalogue 3/43
Photo: N. T. Salmon

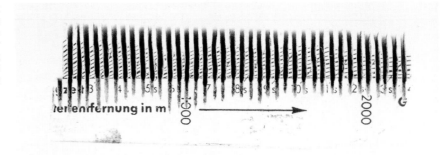

Illustration 201: Handmade aluminium spoon
Found object
Catalogue 3/43
Photo: N. T. Salmon

The concentration camp inmates did not form a community based on their common misfortune. Forced into a racist hierarchy by the SS, the struggle for survival was carried out alone or in groups. In the Little Camp and the newly established subcamps – where the threat to life and sanity was immediate – the first few weeks following committal were devoted solely to **self-preservation**. This involved not only the daily competition to obtain the vitally essential food rations and secure clothing and a place to sleep, but also the struggle to maintain rudimentary civil habits and patterns of social behaviour.

A prime expression of self-preservation was the effort of the individual to find a means of carrying out the simplest actions – cutting one's hair, brushing one's teeth, eating, etc. – in an atmosphere of complete desolation. The inmates fashioned combs, toothbrushes, spoons and game pieces from scraps of metal or animal bones. The Hungarian László Kovács recalls:

"A knife was a forbidden object! The inmates hammered their spoon handles flat and sharpened them. Those of us who worked at the appropriate workplaces were able to manufacture knives from steel sheeting and saw blades. One day a Lithuanian comrade asked me to make knives in the workshop. At the first opportunity it was possible to make two knives, later three knives each time. We smuggled them into the camp in the lapels of our coats. The operation was repeated several times; I only learned later who received the knives ..."

The attempt to maintain **religious practices** – using the most rudimentary of means – also strengthened the will to survive and helped forge social contacts. Albert Simon, who had been arrested and deported to Buchenwald in 1943 at the age of nineteen for his activity in the resistance organisation "Forces Françaises Combattantes," recalls:

"Everyone knew that I was a Jociste (member of a Christian party). I had the Holy Communion with me. In other words I had a wafer with me which had been consecrated as such, a small piece of wafer in a piece of white paper folded three times. Many of my religious comrades who knew that I had the Holy Communion wanted it from me. On Christmas 1944/45 I slipped into the infirmary

secretly and distributed approximately forty Hosts to my comrades. That was strictly prohibited. I risked my life. I would have been hung on the hook."

The rare **cultural events** – joint music-making events, chess tournaments and theatrical performances organised by individuals or groups – constituted a further means of self-preservation.

Among the inmates there were trained artists and gifted amateurs who attempted to document everyday life in the camp with the means at their disposal. In 1944/45, inmates sketched scenes of the conditions in the "Little Camp," usually on waste paper. Others wrote in journals in order to be able to testify to the crimes at some later date. The Frenchmen Pierre Mania, Boris Taslitzky and Auguste Favier, for example, sketched many facets of life in the camp. On the production of his wooden sculpture "Das letzte Gesicht" (the last face), Bruno Apitz writes:

"In August 1944 American bombers destroyed the armament plants located just outside the camp. The spreading flames damaged the Goethe Oak, a declared natural monument located within the camp.
By order of the fascist camp command, the tree was felled and sawed for firewood in the wood yard. I obtained a piece of the wood and hid it in the barrack of my detachment at the time, the pathology facility.
In a safe corner of the barrack I then hewed the death mask out of the wood. That was quite risky, for if I had been caught I inevitably would have 'gone up.' That would have meant Bunker and death. Other inmates from the detachment stood watch as I worked. Another inmate stood beside me and swept up the sawdust as it fell, while others were constantly in readiness to hide the piece of wood and the tools immediately in the event of danger. I worked hastily, and my haste is apparent in the coarse cut.
At our detachment there were a large number of plaster casts – so-called death masks – taken from inmates who had died. They served me as models. Thus from the many faces of our dead, a single one emerged, which I called 'Das letzte Gesicht.'"

Illustration 202: Albert Charles Simon (1925), 1945
Source: Albert Charles Simon

Illustration 203: Handmade altar, 1943
Inscriptions: "Weihnachten 1943 Hoffnung Glaube" (Christmas 1943 Hope Faith).
Maurice Hewitt, French political inmate in 1944-1945, took the altar with him when he left the camp.
Loan from Madame Berthin
Catalogue 3/50
Photo: N. T. Salmon

209

Another form of documentation was the taking of **personal notes**. The Italian Alberto Berti, for example, used remnants of old cement sacks in order to keep a secret diary. Berti had been arrested as a partisan and for that reason he was taken to one of the most appalling sub-camps: Langenstein-Zwieberge.

In the concentration camp – the "society systematically constructed as an inferno" (Robert Antelme) – there were many instances of **help and solidarity**, as confirmed by many inmates' reports. Groups were

formed by virtue of common nationality, dedication to a political outlook or religious belief, and various forms of organised self-help developed within these groups. In 1943-44, inmates of various nations formed "**Hilfskomitees**" (support committees) in order to aid fellow countrymen. Nearly all of the larger national groups represented in the camp had organisations of this kind by mid 1944. Among the first to be founded – in October 1943 – was the Polish secret committee, organised separately from the Communist group. In 1944 the two joined to form the "**Provisional Polish Cooperation Committee**."

In early June 1944, French inmates founded the **Comité des Intérêts Français**. It was present in all areas of camp life and coordinated help provided to French nationals. The **Dutch committee** was formed the same month, comprising representatives of the Anti-Revolutionary Party, Liberal Democrats, Catholics, Social Democrats, Communists and political independents. In addition to improving the circumstances of the Dutch inmates, they also discussed the future political challenges of post-war society. The **Italian solidarity committee** was established in October 1944. In this context, Renato Bertolini reports:

"In October 1944 – previous activity had developed only sporadically – the Italians succeeded in forming a solidarity committee consisting of the Communist Zidar and the Christian Democrats Pecorari and La Rocca. Anyone could join, without any distinctions being made and without refusal of membership. Dr. Pecorari was the cashier and distributor of the donations collected by the other two members of the committee.

There was a confidential agent in every block containing Italians, particularly in the Big Camp where the majority of the inmate population was more constant, whereas in the Little Camp it fluctuated much more strongly. They collected 'marks' (special money that was approved for circulation in the camp), cigarettes and tobacco. You could buy beer (war beer) and tobacco.

The ration the inmates were permitted to purchase got smaller and smaller until it

Illustration 204: Bruno Apitz, "Das letzte Gesicht" (the last face), oak treated with clear varnish, 1944
Loan from Deutsches Historisches Museum
Catalogue 3/46
Photo: N. T. Salmon

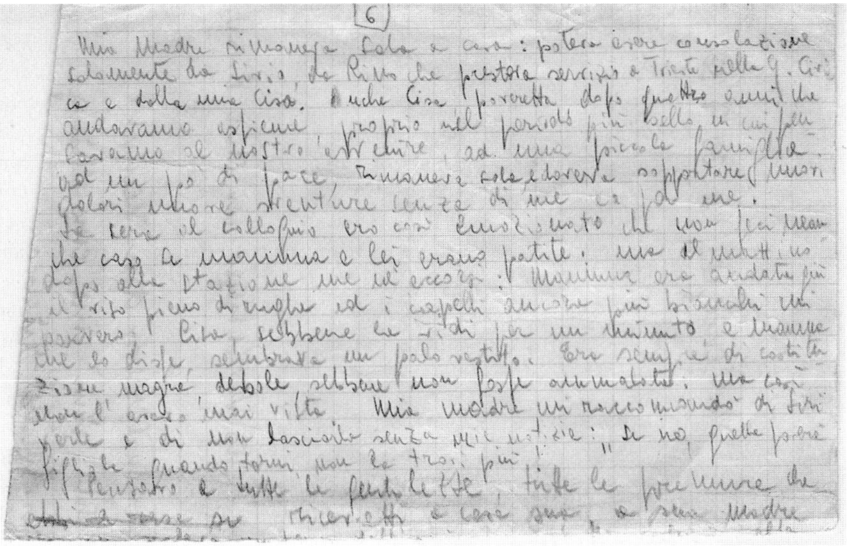

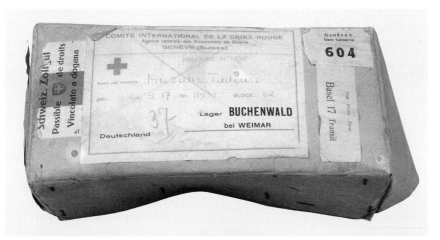

Illustration 205:
Personal notes by
Alberto Berti, 1945
*Source: Gedenk-
stätte Langenstein-
Zwieberge*

finally ended at one cigarette per day. Thus it is all the more understandable how much of a sacrifice the donors of the Big Camp were making for the benefit of those in the Little Camp, where nothing was handed out and nothing could be purchased. There was an average of 200-300 Italians in the Big Camp. They collected an average of 40 marks, 30 cigarettes and 50 grams of tobacco per week. For each block a detailed list of each collection and distribution was drawn up, copied six times and circulated among all Italians for the purposes of mutual control. Almost every-one in the Big Camp participated. Altogether twenty collections were carried out, with a total sum of 769 marks, 612 cigarettes and 600 grams of tobacco. This represented about 2,000 donations, which were passed on to the inmates of the Little Camp, sick persons and Jews, whom the Nazis refused the right to to-bacco."

The extent of the misery was so great that the committees could do little to provide relief. Ther means were further limited by the social hierarchy which had become established in

Illustration 206:
Red Cross package
Catalogue 3/60
Photo: N. T. Salmon

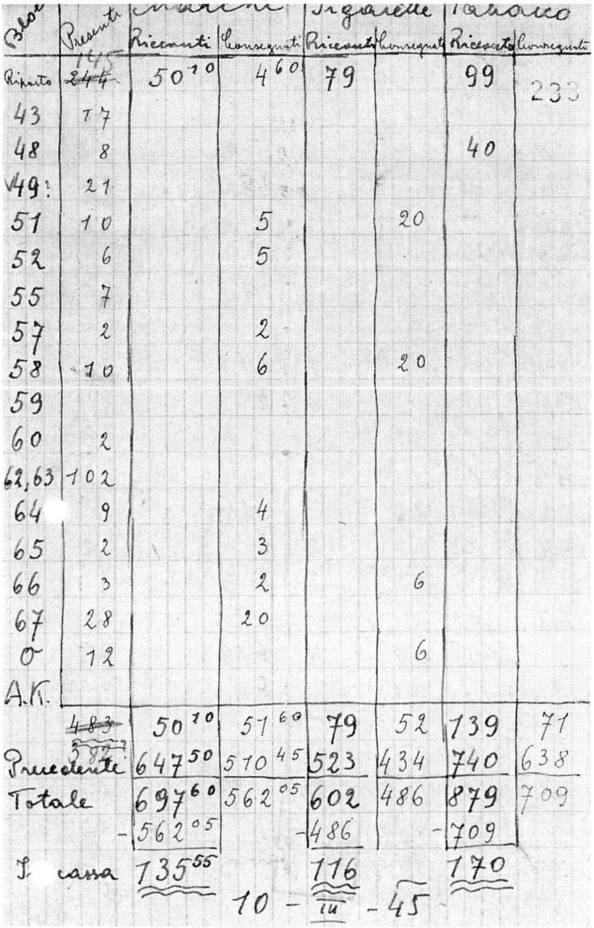

(handwritten collection list table)

Blocco	Presenti	Marmell... Ricevuti	Consegn.	Sigarette Ricevuti	Consegn.	Tabacco Ricevuti	Consegn.
Riparto	244	50 10	4 60	79		99	233
43	77						
48	8					40	
49:	21						
51	10			5		20	
52	6			5			
55	7						
57	2			2			
58	10			6		20	
59							
60	2						
62,63	102						
64	9			4			
65	2			3			
66	3			2		6	
67	28			20			
O	12					6	
A.K.							
483		50 10	51 60	79	52	139	71
Precedente		647 50	510 45	523	434	740	638
Totale		697 60	562 05	602	486	879	709
			-562 05		-486		-709
I. cassa		135 55		116		170	
		10		-14		-45	

Illustration 207: Collection list of the Italian committee "Italian Solidarity,"
Mar. 10, 1945
Source: Buchenwaldarchiv, Weimar

portion to the entire camp, block by block, this act of solidarity was greatly appreciated. The actual distribution, however, was a scandal for weeks inasmuch as, for example, only one single package was allotted to every ten Frenchmen in the so-called Little Camp – who were in particularly dire circumstances, as discussed in greater detail below – whereas the inmates entrusted with the distribution, assisted by certain Frenchmen, reserved entire stacks of packages for themselves or used them for their 'prominent friends.'"

Some inmates attempted to evade the labour in arms production forced upon them by the SS. There were isolated cases of open protest, which usually ended in death. On December 15, 1943, for example, a group of Italian military internees who had been deployed for tunnel construction in "Dora" protested against unequal treatment. They demanded the same extra provisions received by the other inmates working in the tunnels and cited the Geneva Convention, according to which prisoners of war could not be made to work for the war industry. The inmate capo reported them for refusal to work. Without further hearings, 7 Italians were shot to death by the SS. In a report of July 29, 1944 on the field fortifications work of the SS construction brigades in the West, it is stated:

"The punctual completion of these special structures was only made possible by constantly keeping the inmates hard at work. Due to the given circumstances (invasion, air raids, etc.) the inmates proved undisciplined and very unwilling to work. Severe measures had to be taken, particularly with the Polish inmates, as in several cases they persuaded the other inmates to refuse to work; they are also usually responsible for cases of escapes and, above all, instigated the biggest assault on the Wehrmacht guards."

Clandestine sabotage also took place in the Gustloff-Werk II. Even in the factory construction unit "Kommando X," the motto "Kommando X – Rabota nix" (work nix) circulated among the Soviet inmates. Valentin Logunov recalls:

the camp, a factor which made itself felt, for example, when there were Red Cross packages to be distributed. Eugen Kogon writes:

"As the provisions in the camps became increasingly worse in 1944, the Red Cross began sending mass shipments to national groups in the camps, particularly to the French, Danes and Norwegians. The SS men enriched themselves shamelessly from aid operations such as these from abroad. ...
Among the inmates themselves, these packages and their magnificent contents understandably evoked strong antagonism. When the French comrades declared their intention of passing on a considerable pro-

"In the range halls, the sights of completed rifles are raised imperceptibly, trigger springs are damaged; ground glass which has been added to the oil is poured into inaccessible parts. Hydrochloric acid is added to the lubricating oil used in the assembly of the ten-shot automatic rifles in Hall Three. During testing at the firing range the rifle functions trouble-free but after a few weeks damages occur in the cartridge magazine and the ejector and all ten cartridges fly out one after the other."

No action contrary to SS intentions, no attempt to limit the SS's absolute power was conceivable without reliable support. The most effective forms of organisation and resistance activity were developed by groups which had gained experience in resistance before their arrests, i.e. primarily political inmates of various nationalities. The German Communists' monopoly on jobs in the inmates' administration in Buchenwald was the major factor leading to the development of the largest **Communist underground organisation** in the SS camp system.

From the point of view of the German Communists, the struggle against the "greens" – which reached its climax in the inmates' war of 1941-1943 – was a form of resistance. Based on the experience gained in the inmates' war, the safeguarding of one's own organisation, the fight against political "deviationists" and the granting of privileges to one's own followers were means of combating the SS. Reporting on the selection principles, Benedikt Kautsky writes:

"Only those who were either convinced, true-to-the-line Communists, or whom one was absolutely sure would later follow the instructions of the Communist party unreservedly without being Communists themselves – only those persons were considered valuable. In order to save the lives of those inmates, a well-thought-out organisation was created, by means of which these personalities got the best possible treatment with regard to the choice of work and, what is more, in times of food shortage, received better provisions than the rest of the camp.

This was not made possible in the manner frequently practised in the blocks administered by criminals – where the rations of the entire block population were reduced – but through connections to people in the kitchen, in the infirmary, in the workshops and institutions under SS authority – such complex connections that a small circle of adherents could be relatively well provided for without limiting the general rations."

Already during the "inmates' war," the German Communists sought allies among the Communists of other countries. In July 1943, after they had succeeded in taking over the most important functions in internal camp administration, they arranged a clandestine meeting of representatives of various Communist parties. In the course of the year 1944 further meetings took place and the circle expanded. The Germans dictated the time and place. The participants worked on reconciling the differences between the national groups represented in the camp, finding means of taking their various interests into account, coordinating aid operations and taking measures to integrate foreign political inmates into camp detachments.

Due to the dominant position of the German Communists in internal camp administration, the group of persons who constituted the illegal **International Camp Committee** were able to contribute greatly to the avoidance of open conflicts between the national groups and to saving the lives of members of Communist parties and of resistance organisations. At the same time, the committee saw to it that the German Communists were able to remain in inmate offices at a time when Germans accounted for only a very small minority in the camp.

Representatives of the following Communist parties belonged to the committee: Walter Bartel, Ernst Busse, Harry Kuhn (Germany), Domenico Ciufoli (Italy), Henri Glineur (Belgium), Jan Haken (Netherlands), Otto Horn, Franz Schuster (Austria), Emil Hršel, Kvetoslav Innemann, Alois Neumann (Czechoslovakia), Jan Izydorczyk (Poland), Nikolaj Kjung, Ivan Smirnov, Nikolai Simakov (USSR),

Illustration 208: Plan drawn up by the military groups of the International Camp Committee, assignment of areas in case of occupation of the grounds, early 1945
The plan exhibited four sectors distinguished by colour: Slavic sector (I/red – Soviet inmates and Czechs), Southeast sector (II/green – Poles and Yugoslavs), Romance sector (III/blue – Frenchmen, Italians, Spaniards and Belgians), Centre sector (IV/yellow – Germans, Austrians, Dutch).
Source: Buchenwaldarchiv, Weimar

gians, Soviet political inmates and prisoners of war, all of whom maintained contact with one another. Thanks to courage and inventiveness, 91 carbines, 1 light machine gun, 20 pistols and 16 German stick hand grenades were obtained as a means of defence if the occasion arose. Fritz Jehle reports:

"In addition to 24 hand grenades which we had managed to get from the armoury, we produced 60-70 hand grenades ourselves. In the pathology station, Comrade B. carried out preparations for the production of the explosive in collaboration with the Austrian Comrade W. Cotton and other required chemical substances were obtained in all manner of roundabout ways, and guncotton produced."

The secret Communist organisation concentrated primarily on its own supporters until well into the final year of the war. Whereas in the support committees of the French, Italians and other nations, persons of differing political viewpoints often worked together from the very beginning, it was not until August 1944 that the Social Democrat Hermann Brill gathered members of various parties from among the German political inmates to form the German **"Volksfrontkomitee"** (**People's Front Committee**).

Brill initiated this group in February 1944. As a "prisoner incapable of reformation", Brill had been transferred to Buchenwald from the Brandenburg-Goerden

Marcel Paul (France), Rudi Supek (Yugoslavia).

This secret organisation acquired illegal information and began to make preparations and form military groups so as to be in a position to prevent the imminent final massacre by the SS in the event of the NS regime's defeat. The members of the International Camp Committee's military organisation were Dutchmen, Austrians, Germans, Spaniards, Italians, Yugoslavs, Poles, Czechs, Frenchmen, Bel-

Illustration 209: Guncotton for the manufacture of explosive devices, 1945
Catalogue 3/55
Photo: N. T. Salmon

Illustration 210:
Otto Roth and his
family before his
arrest in 1939
The German
political inmate
Otto Roth
(electrician's
detachment) was
one of the leaders
of the underground
military organisation
of the International
Camp Committee.
*Source: Buchen-
waldarchiv, Weimar*

prison, where he had had to serve a twelve-year sentence as one of the heads of the resistance group "Deutsche Volksfront" (German People's Front).

For his plans to found a committee, he gained the support of the Social Democrat Ernst Thape and the Centre Party politician Werner Hilpert (both of whom had been in Buchenwald since 1939), the Communist Walter Wolf and several French Socialists. They drew up "an interpretation of the People's Front idea, expanded and deepened in several respects" (Brill). In April 1944 they summarised this interpretation in the paper referred to as the Buchenwald Platform, consisting of six points concerning, among other things, the elimination of National Socialism and the creation of a new democratic republic. On this basis, an illegal committee was formed under Brill's leadership in early July 1944 and was in existence until the end of that year. Its primary task was to discuss the policy foundations for a democratic post-war Germany. The group meetings had to be discontinued following a Gestapo operation in late 1944.

Collaboration also took place in connection with aid provided to **children and adolescents** in the camp. Through the es-

tablishment of two children's barracks – Block 8 (1943) and Block 66 (1945; Little Camp) –, it was possible to protect at least some of the children and adolescents in the parent camp from heavy forced labour and thus to ensure their survival. In the report written about the children in April 1945, it is stated:

Illustration 211: Wood carving
Found in the attic of the depot.
Catalogue 3/59
Photo: N. T. Salmon

Illustration 212: Wilhelm Hammann (1897-1955)
Source: Reproduction, Sammlung Gedenkstätte Buchenwald, Weimar

"The number of child inmates in Buchenwald Concentration Camp amounts to approximately 900. Their national categorisation is as follows:

Children in Buchenwald

Poland	*288*
Czechoslovakia	*270*
Hungary	*290*
Yugoslavia	*42*
Soviet Union	*6*
Austria	*6*
Germany	*2*
Total	***904***

The age group of 14-18 accounts for approximately eighty-five percent of the total number of children. The youngest, a 3-year-old child, is of Polish nationality."

At the beginning of April 1945, Wilhelm Hammann – the last block senior of the children's Block 8 – saved many Jewish children from the death march by denying their presence in the barrack during an SS operation to deport all Jewish inmates. For this act the Yad Vashem Memorial in Israel honoured him as "One of the Righteous Among the Nations."

There were isolated cases, such as the **rescue** of three secret service members in the autumn of 1944, in which the Communist inmate functionaries cooperated with non-Communists like Eugen Kogon. Kogon recalls:

"Rescue was only possible if the persons in danger died officially and their names and numbers were exchanged for those of persons who had really died. … Naturally, only a limited number of the endangered persons could be taken into consideration. It was a tragic moment when Squadron Leader Dodkin of the Royal Air Force … went about making the selection in a certain sequence. … Only three of them could be rescued: in addition to Dodkin the Englishman Captain Peuleve and Lieutenant Stephane Hessel from the secret service of General de Gaulle. … In Block 17 [arrival block] we triggered an alleged typhus epidemic pro forma, and isolated the three officers; we had to keep the news of this from spreading in the camp, in Block 46 [the epidemic typhus experimentation block]. … Within the same few days, 'like a gift from heaven,' a transport carrying dozens of Frenchmen afflicted with epidemic typhus arrived in Buchenwald from Cologne. … Then, because of the fact that the three officers were known in the camp, we set about smuggling them – now with the identities of a carpenter, a policemen and a student – into sub-camps under the guise of specialists. How do you think we felt as we pulled the wool over people's eyes – people in the general records department, the labour administration office, the depot – removed obstacles and eliminated possible opponents? Our necks always in several nooses at once!"

Illustration 213: Child survivors of the Little Camp, April 1945
Stefan Zweig, born in 1941, (seated, l.) was the youngest survivor of Buchenwald.
Source: Reproduction, Sammlung Gedenkstätte Buchenwald, Weimar

Death and Survival, 1944/45

Mass Death

"Here, every man has to fight for himself and not think of anyone else. Even his father. Here, there are no fathers, no brothers, no friends. Everyone lives and dies for himself alone."

Elie Wiesel in a text on the Little Camp

Extermination Transports

Beginning with the deportation of the sick and handicapped as well as Jewish inmates to euthanasia killing facilities in 1941-42 – for which the term "Himmelfahrtstransporte" was coined in the camp ("Himmelfahrt" meaning "ascension" in the Christian sense) – it had become common practise for the SS to get rid of ill or weak inmates by transferring them to other camps or killing them by means of phenol, hexobarbital or air injections. "The SS themselves used ... the expression 'Verschrottung' [scrapping]," as we learn from the report of the International Camp Committee. The initial destination was Majdanek Concentration Camp outside of Lublin. On January 15 and February 6, 1944 the SS transferred altogether 1,888 sick and enfeebled inmates there from the sub-camp "Dora." Between December 1943 and April 1944 similar transports were sent to Majdanek from the concentration camps in Dachau, Flossenbürg, Mauthausen, Neuengamme, Auschwitz, Ravensbrück and Sachsenhausen. Between March 1944 and March 1945, thousands of ill and debilitated persons were also deported to Bergen-Belsen Concentration Camp.

On August 24, 1944, Richard Glücks, the head of Bureau D (concentration camps) of the Department of Economic

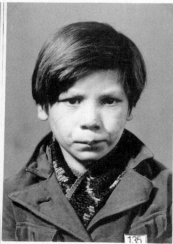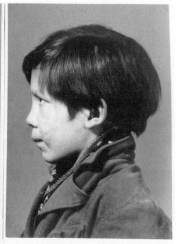

Illustration 214: Albert W. (1931-1944), ca. 1939
The photographs of Albert W., Bruno Z. and Egon P. were in the card index of the "Eugenic Research Department" of the Reich Board of Health. The three Sinto boys were sent from Auschwitz-Birkenau to Buchenwald in August 1944. On September 26, 1944 the SS sent them back to Auschwitz-Birkenau on an extermination transport.
Source: Bundesarchiv Koblenz

Illustration 215: Bruno Z. (1930-1944), ca. 1939
Source: Bundesarchiv, Koblenz

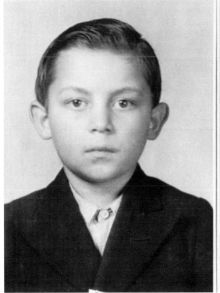
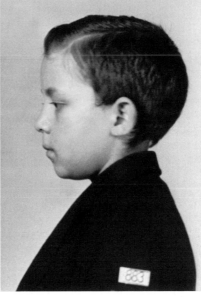

Illustration 216:
Egon P. (1930-
1944), ca. 1939
*Source: Bundes-
archiv, Koblenz*

Administration, ordered the transfer of all debilitated Jews to Auschwitz. On August 28, an initial transport carrying 72 pregnant women, mothers and children left the sub-camp of the Hugo-Schneider AG in Leipzig. Upon their arrival, only 25 of them received inmate ID numbers; the others were taken straight to the gas chambers. A transport of 200 Sinti and Romani – almost exclusively children and adolescents – followed on September 26. In this connection, Eugen Kogon writes:

"Even hardened men were deeply moved when in the autumn of 1944 the SS suddenly picked out Jew children and all of the gypsy boys, herded them together and used loaded and machine guns to round up the screaming, crying children – some of whom would have given anything to go back to their fathers and inmate

Illustration 217:
Memo from the
SS Department
of Economic
Administration
to the camp
physicians, notifying
them of an order
providing for the
"return transfer" of
Jewish inmates,
Aug. 25, 1944
Source: Thüringisches Hauptstaatsarchiv, Weimar

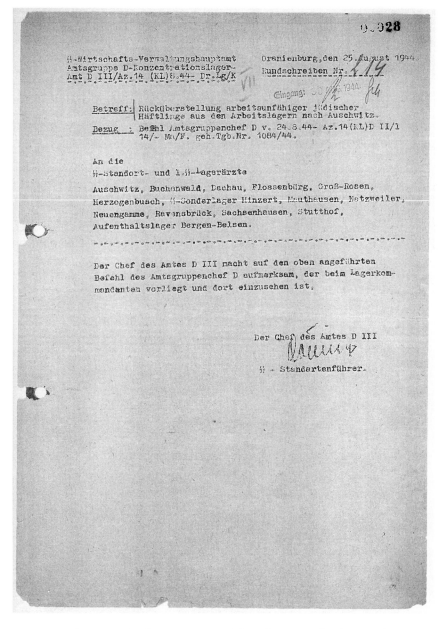

protectors in the various detachments – in order to send them to Auschwitz to be gassed."

In the September 1944 report of the inmates' infirmary it is stated:

"On 9/23/44 1,000 Jews returned from the Wille-Zeitz detachment, on 9/27/44 600 Jews from the Magdeburg detachment. The large majority of these inmates are no longer likely to be considered for labour allocation."

The selection took place in the cinema barrack at the end of September. One of these 1,600 Jews – Eugene (Jenö) Heimler – writes about the event in his memoirs:

"Up to this point the SS doctor had been sitting with his back to me and I hadn't been able to see his face. But when it was my turn and I stepped in front of him and looked him in the face, a cold shudder ran through me. … During that fraction of a second in which

Illustration 218:
Interior of the cinema
barrack, 1943
In October 1944,
this was the setting
for a "selection" of
Jewish inmates sent
back from Magde-
burg and Rehmsdorf
Sub-Camps due to
illness and weakness.
*Source: Musée de
la Résistance et de la
Déportation,
Besançon (SS Photo
Album: "Buchenwald
Jahresende 1943").*

Illustration 219: Eugene (Jenö) Heimler (1922-
1990)
*Source: Eugene Heimler: Bei Nacht und Nebel.
Autobiographischer Bericht, Berlin: Hentrich,
1993.*

*our eyes met, only my subconscious was work-
ing. My conscious mind wanted to inform
him that I had tuberculosis, but in reality I
answered his question by saying that I had a
bladder infection. He repeated mechanically:
'bladder infection.' 'Yes, sir.' His hand*

*reached for my slip of paper and put it on the
smaller pile. 'Dismissed.' I was convinced that
my faltering voice had cost me my life, for I
was certain that the smaller pile meant death.
I couldn't sleep for two nights and I asked
myself why I hadn't said tuberculosis. …
The next morning the inmates of the Upper
Camp told us what had happened to our comrades. They had been taken into the forest of
Buchenwald on a train. Eighty to a hundred
men, sick men and malingerers, had been
packed into each car. Then the cars had been
sealed. The sealed cars stood in the forest for
an entire day; then they rolled off towards
Auschwitz."*

This "Selektion" in the cinema barrack was
followed in early October by the largest
extermination transport that ever left Buchenwald. It took 1,188 Jews to the gas
chambers. In the last quarter of 1944, the
SS sent a total of over 2,000 Jews, Sinti and
Romani to Auschwitz for extermination.

Evacuation from Auschwitz and Groß-Rosen

In late 1944, the Red Army approached the
concentration and work camps in occupied
Poland and in the eastern regions of the
German Reich. The SS sent the inmates of

221

```
                                                                    0J002
   ...dortarzt der "affen-ϟϟ            Weimar-Buchenwald, den 31. März 1945
        W e i m a r

  S/Az.: 14 h 8 /3.45 - Sch/Wi.


           Betreff: Vierteljahresbericht über den San.-Dienst für die Zeit vom
                    1.Januar 1945 bis 31.März 1945.
           Bezug  : Dort.Rundschreiben v.27.12.44, D III/Az.14 (KL) 12.44 Lg/K.


           An den
           Chef des Amtes D III
           O r a n i e n b u r g
```

1. Durchschnittlicher Lagerbestand 77 390
    Frauen in Aussenkommandos am 31.3.45   23 289

2. Todesfälle im KL. Buchenwald und den Aussenkommandos
    eines natürlichen Todes   Januar 1945   1959
                               Februar 1945   3709
                               März 1945   4617   1o 285

    eines unnatürlichen Todes Januar 1945   18
                               Februar 1945   397
                               März 1945   52   467

    Frauen
    eines natürlichen Todes   Januar 1945   28
                               Februar 1945   17
                               März 1945   25   7o
    eines unnatürlichen Todes keine Frau.

    Lager S III:
    eines natürlichen Todes   v.12.12.44 - 4.2.45 1506
                               bis 31.3.45   843   2 349
    eines unnatürlichen Todes v.12.12.44 - 4.2.45   18
                               bis 31.3.45   16   34

    Die hohe Zahl der Häftlinge, die im Februar im KL. Bu-
    chenwald eines unnatürlichen Todes starben, erklärt
    sich aus dem feindlichen Bombenangriff auf die Gust-
    loff-werke Weimar sowie aus Tieffliegerbeschuss von
    Transportzügen.

3. Stationäre Behandlung (im Tagesdurchschnitt)

    im KL. Buchenwald   2264
    Männer in Aussenlagern (einschl. S III)   21o6
    Frauen in Aussenlagern   492   4 862

4. Ambulante Behandlung (im Tagesdurchschnitt)

    im KL. Buchenwald   2332
    Männer in Aussenlagern (einschl. S III)   4144
    Frauen in Aussenlagern   1589   8 o65

5. Im Laufe der Berichtszeit wurde eine Unfruchtbarmachung
    vorgenommen.

6. Infektionskrankheiten im KL. Buchenwald

    Fleckfieber (am 29.3.45 25 von Bad Sulza übernommen)   28
    Ruhr...   9o
    Ruhrverdacht   114
    Scharlach   21
    Lungentuberkulose 41o
    Erysipel 1o4
    Trachom   7

7. Allgemeine Lagerhygiene

    Im Verlaufe des Berichtsvierteljahres wurde das Bild des Lagers

Illustration 220: Quarterly medical service report by the garrison physician, SS Hauptsturmführer Dr. Schiedlausky, Mar. 31, 1945
Source: Thüringisches Hauptstaatsarchiv, Weimar

$0000

vor allen Dingen durch den starken Zuzug aus evakuierten Lagern
bestimmt. Es handelte sich vor allem um Häftlinge aus den Lagern
Auschwitz, Gross-Rosen und Stutthof, die regelmässig in sehr ge-
schwächter Verfassung hier ankamen und sowohl einen grossen Be-
standteil der angestiegenen Sterbeziffer wie des Krankenstandes
ausmachten. Im einzelnen handelte es sich um folgende grössere
Transporte:

am 26.und 27.1.45 2750 Mann von Auschwitz (Zustand schlecht)
am 6.2.45:   2500 Mann vom KL. Sachsenhausen (Zustand schlecht)
am 1o.2.45:   2400 Mann von Auschwitz über Grossrosen (Zustand
                       sehr schlecht),
am 11.2.45:   2000 Mann von Auschwitz über Grossrosen (sehr schlecht)
am 12.2.45:   2500 "   "   "   "   "   "   ("   "   ")
am 7.3.45:   1000 Mann von Grossrosen (Zustand sehr schlecht)

Trotzdem die Zugänge regelmässig in stark verlaustem Zustand hier
ankamen, konnte die Gefahr der Fleckfieberverseuchung durch genaue
Kontrollen und sofortige Isolierung vereinzelter Fälle behoben werden.
Neuerdings hat sich die Zahl der Fleckfieberkranken wieder gehoben,
da von Bad Sulza eine Reihe von Fleckfieberkranken übernommen wurden.

Die Zahl der Durchfallkranken war unter den Neuzugängen aus den evakuierten Lagern sehr hoch und führte zu einem Ansteigen der Ruhrver-
dachts- und Ruhrfälle. Jedoch ist mit dem Beginn der wärmeren Jahres-
zeit ein Absinken der Zahlen beobachtet werden. Das gleiche gilt
von der Zahl der Erysipelkranken.

Durch den Bezug einer neuen Revierbaracke, die als Tbc-Station dient,
ist die Möglichkeiten geboten, in erhöhtem Masse Tbc-Verdächtige zu
isolieren. Auch der Bau neuer Wohnbaracken dient dazu, die sanitären
Verhältnisse vor allem im sog. kleinen Lager zu heben, wo die Überfül-
lung der Blocks unübersichtliche Zustände geschaffen hat.

Transportschwierigkeiten wie Materialknappheit sind die Ursache, dass
von der Genehmigung der Erdbestattungen neuerdings weitgehend Gebrauch
gemacht wird. Das gleiche ist in den Aussenkommandos der Fall.

In der Berichtszeit wurden verschiedene Aussenkommandos zurückgezogen:

am 7.1.45 das Aussenkommando Schwerte
am 16.2.45 die Aussenkommandos Magdeburg-BRABAG und Eisenach-BMW
am 9.3.45 das Aussenkommando Halle-Siebel,
am 1o.3.45 das Aussenkommando Düsseldorf und in den letzten Tagen im
Zuge der militärischen Entwicklung die Aussenkommandos Kassel und Arols
und vorher die beiden Aussenkommandos in Bochum.

II. T r u p p e

1. Stärke der Truppe 52/7494
2. Todesfälle   5
3. Revierkranke im Tagesdurchschnitt .... (KL!Bu.)   26
4. Ambulante Behandlung (im Tagesdurchschnitt) (KL. Bu.) 93

5. **Infektionskrankheiten am 31.3.45**

   Go.   1
   Erysipel   3

III. Russisches Kriegsgefangenenlager

1. Belegstärke am 3o.3.45:
   im KL. Buchenwald   89o   in S III   368
   im Aussenkommando Malachyt   24
   im Aussenkommando Schwalbe   19   1301

2. Todesfälle im Vierteljahr 1.1.45-31.3.45   7
3. Revierkranke im Tagesdurchschnitt   72

these camps off towards the west on foot or by train. The evacuation of Auschwitz began in January 1945, then of Groß-Rosen Concentration Camp (Silesia) a few weeks later. More than 10,000 completely exhausted and enfeebled persons, the majority of them Jews, arrived in Buchenwald. The SS had driven them long stretches on foot through the ice-cold winter or jammed them into unroofed freight cars. Many starved or froze to death along the way; others were shot to death by the SS. Upon their arrival, the cars were full of dead persons whose identities were never determined. Josua Ron reports:

"In mid January 1945 – we were in Buna-Monowitz (Auschwitz III) at the time – we heard the rumbling guns of the advancing Soviet army. On January 18 we were taken from our barracks and sent off on the road to Gleiwitz [Gliwice] at a trot – the march now known as the 'death march.' This 'excursion' lasted sixty hours. To this day I still dream of those horrible hours and see the dead before me – people who could not cope with the terrible strain and were shot to death. In Gleiwitz, those of us who had survived were jammed into a huge hall in order to be 'loaded' onto coal cars the next day. We were taken through Eastern Czechoslovakia to Buchenwald. On this trip we experienced a bit of humanity. Hundreds of Czechs stood on the bridges under which our train slowly passed and threw black bread and other food down to us. That saved many of us from dying of starvation, and enabled some of us to reach Buchenwald alive. Today we know that 16,000 persons had left Auschwitz and only about 5,000 reached [Buchenwald]. It snowed almost incessantly throughout that ice-cold January and we were in open, jam-packed freight cars. We received neither food nor drink in the course of this five-day 'journey.' There were many dead bodies lying beneath us on the floor."

Between mid January and April 1945, there were constant masses of human beings camping out in the open air in front of the disinfection station, gravely ill and dead persons among them. Half dead from thirst and hunger, they flung themselves onto the food cauldrons. The report of the International Camp Committee states:

"In the bathroom itself, the most horrible injuries could be seen. From one transport that came from Auschwitz in open cars, thousands of hands and feet had gotten frostbite. When people took the socks or dirty foot rags from their feet, their skin often stuck to the rag and came off with it. Bullet wounds from shots fired by the guards for no reason began to bleed again. The people could hardly move or be driven forward in the interest of the others who were still lying on the street."

Those who had survived the trip were crammed into the "Little Camp," which had already become a slum. The SS granted them no respite, but sent most of them on to sub-camps, of which new ones were still being founded during the very last weeks of the war.

Place of Death: Little Camp

In December 1944 the SS had the "Little Camp" expanded to comprise seventeen barracks; the tents were taken down. Once the evacuation trains began to arrive, the number of persons accommodated in each stable rarely sank below 1,000. It was nothing unusual for 1,800 to 1,900 inmates to be assigned to a barrack five hundred square metres in size. Whereas the population of the "Little Camp" had numbered 6,000 at the beginning of January 1945, it rose to 17,100 by the eve of the evacuation. Hunger, filth, desperate struggles for survival and contagious diseases ruled the slum of the Buchenwald barrack town. Fred Wander, who had come on one of the transports from Auschwitz, writes in his book The Seventh Well:

"I walked down the long rows of wooden partitions in which human beings were lying. Something had sharpened my gaze, shown me faces I never saw otherwise. Distorted faces, faces swollen by wounds, scabs and abscesses, faces which nevertheless had all retained something of their special quality: pride and spoiledness, arrogance and a final trace of bet-

ter days. *Here someone stretched his head out, the head of a saint, watching everything with naïve curiosity. There someone crouched with a peculiar contortion of his long, horribly thin limbs and prayed, his eyes closed, his whole body shaking ecstatically, his hands beating his breast. Elsewhere someone lay, moving his hands as though making signs to an invisible demon – convulsions of death. And someone was caught in a waking dream, a pained smile framing his mouth. There lay the dead among the living; no-one paid them any attention. Death was alone in the midst of an insane mass of human beings. Many lay there rigid, their eyes open, outcasts, anonymous, like deserters: deserters from a wonderful existence.*"

Illustration 221: Name plaque
Found in Little Camp.
Inscription: "Jozef Szternberg, KL 20253, geb.6.VI.1925 in Bensburg."
Jozef Szternberg arrived in early March 1945 on an evacuation transport from Groß-Rosen. Nothing is known of his further fate.
Catalogue 5/3
Photo: N. T. Salmon

Mass death was the result, a death which claimed some 5,200 victims in less than a hundred days. The corpses of the deceased were thrown out of the barracks by night in order to make room for the living. This number also included the dead from Barrack 61, an epidemic block which had been part of the inmates' infirmary since the beginning of 1945. It was there that, following the arrival of the mass transports from Auschwitz, the SS began killing people

Illustration 222: Auguste Favier, "In the Little Camp," drawing, 1945
Source: Reproduction, Sammlung Gedenkstätte Buchenwald, Weimar

with contagious diseases and the so-called "Muselmänner" – who staggered into the camp as skeletons – by means of injections. Jaroslav Bartl, an infirmary nurse at the time, recalls that

"... the liquidation of inmates by means of injection was transferred from the infirmary to Block 61 of the Little Camp, which had been set up as an infirmary station. ... The [SS] medical orderly Wilhelm killed weak and ill inmates right at the entrance to the barrack – many of those who had been sent to

Block 61 on grounds of illness died without ever having seen the barrack."

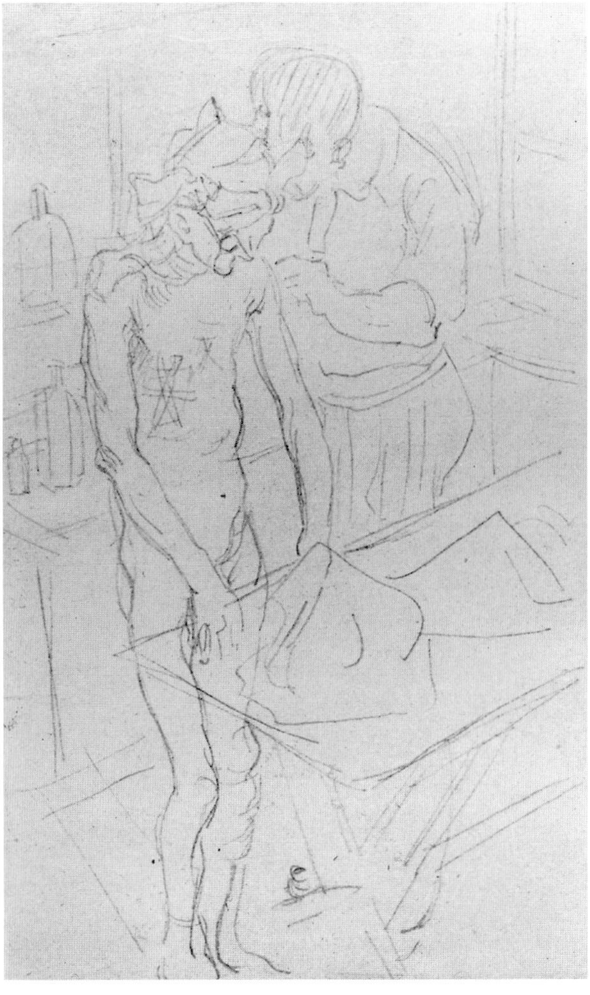

Inmates who worked in the infirmary were also involved in these killings. In early 1945, the "Little Camp" – as a camp for the infirm and the dying – was the prime place of death in the Buchenwald complex, followed by SS tunnel construction projects such as Ohrdruf (S III), Berga/Elster and Langenstein-Zwieberge. Between the beginning of January and April 11, 1945, 13,969 human beings died in Buchenwald and its sub-camps.

The bodies were cremated until March 1945. After 1943 urns were available only for the mortal remains of deceased "Reich Germans" and a small number of foreign inmates (Norwegians, Danes). Beginning as early as 1943, the SS had the ashes of most of the deceased dumped in the manner of refuse. In February 1945 the crematorium failed to receive its fuel supply; the corpses piled up and the rat population grew. With Himmler's approval, "emergency burials" began in March in mass graves on the south slope of the Ettersberg.

Illustration 223: Boris Taslitzky: "Maurice Halbwachs Waiting to Have his Bandages Changed," drawing, 1945
Maurice Halbwachs (1877-1945), president of the Institut francais de Sociologie, vice president of the Société de Psychologie, professor at the Collège de France, died on Mar. 15, 1945 in the Little Camp.
Source: Reproduction, Sammlung Gedenkstätte Buchenwald, Weimar

The End

Evacuation

From the beginning of 1945 on, the gradual dissolution of the concentration camp system dominated nearly all areas of everyday life for the inmates of Buchenwald, finding expression in uncontrolled surges of mass committals of inmates from evacuated camps. Regardless of these circumstances, the SS continued in the very same months to expand the sub-camp system to its maximum size. Even as the Allied forces approached, the SS never considered dissolving the camp by releasing some or all of the prisoners. Camps were evacuated in Western and Eastern Europe, their inmates being singled out and incorporated into the labour potential of the still-existing camps. Usually only the more able-bodied survived the actual evacuation. A strategy had thus been introduced which would also prove decisive for Buchenwald. There is evidence that during the first days of April 1945 the SS command temporarily considered surrendering the camp to the Allies, an idea they rejected again just as quickly. As the front advanced, it began to reach the sub-camps, and the return transport of inmates from those locations had already begun in March. The result was a sharp rise in the population of the parent camp to approximately 48,000 (on the evening of April 6).

As late as April 3, Hermann Pister declared his intention to surrender the camp. His audience in the cinema hall was the "rescue team," a group of primarily German and Austrian inmates to be activated in the event of an air raid. In a letter to Pister from four inmates – the French politician André Marie, the Dutch officer Pieter Cool, the Belgian politician Eugène Soudan and the British officer Christopher Burney – reference was made to this announcement; the writers offered to speak out in Pister's favour later on if he kept his word to surrender the camp. The inmates from the sub-camp at Ohrdruf began arriving on April 4. The SS had driven them along the roads to the point of complete exhaustion, shooting many to death along the way.

On April 5 the SS began making preparations for the evacuation of the parent camp. The Gestapo drew up a list of 46 inmates whom they apparently suspected were the leaders of the illegal resistance, ordering them to report to the camp gate on April 6. The wanted persons went underground in the camp; not a single one of them was turned in. The illegal Camp Committee instructed all of its agents to delay the evacuation.

Himmler gave the order to evacuate the camp on April 6. By this time the SS had already rounded up more than 6,000 Jewish inmates in the Deutsche Ausrüstungswerke. Others managed to hide in non-Jewish barracks, tear off their badges or go underground in the "Little Camp."

Commissioned by the illegal resistance organisation, two electricians – the Pole Gwidon Damaszyn and the German Social Democrat Armin Walther – had built a transmitter and installed it in the cinema barrack. Late on the morning of April 8, 1945, the above-quoted message was transmitted twelve times. The transmitter was then destroyed.

The attempt to smuggle the Austrian Eugen Kogon out of the camp was successful; on the same day he sent a fabricated letter to Pister from Weimar:

Illustration 224:
List of forty-six
inmates who were
ordered to report
to the camp gate
on Apr. 6, 1945
According to
Eugen Kogon, the
aircraft designer
Marcel Bloch
(Dassault) was also
on the list. He was
the only one to
report to the gate
on Apr. 6, 1945,
but was sent away
again by the SS.
Source: Buchen-
waldarchiv,
Weimar

75 — 2

Material Halle 23   Abschrift

Buch...chiv
Sign. 75 0-2

Liste der 46 Antifaschisten

Heilmann	Paul	Dt.
Lewit	Achim	Österr. J.
Siewert	Robert	Dt.
Busse	Ernst	Dt.
Kipp	Otto	Dt.
Sitte	Kurt	T.
Hauptmann	Hein	Dt.
Bokowski	Karl	Dt.
Dietsch	Artur	Dt.
Piók	Harry	H.
Apitz	Brunno	Dt.
Löser	Kurt	Dt.
Eul	Theo	Dt.
Przybolowski	Marian	P.
Leitner	Franz	Ö.
Großkopf	Richard	Dt.
Bräuer	Heinrich	Dt.
Senkel	Paul	T.
Wehle	Willi	Dt.
Schulz	Karl	Dt.
Grosse	Otto	Dt.
Berndt	Walter	Dt.
Schalker	Jan	H.
Gadzinski	Artur	P.
Kogon	Eugen	Ö.
Neumeister	Hans	Dt.
Seifert	Willi	Dt.
Wolf	Ludwig	Dt.
Robert	Jan	H.
Frenzel		Dt.
Gärtig	Karl	Dt.
Gründel	Paul	Dt.
Schilling	Paul	Dt.
Lingen		H.
Müller	Alfons	Dt.
Mühlenstein	Nuchem	T.
Tressor		H.
Jellinek	Wilhelm	T.
Cohn	August	Dt...J.
Wojkowski	Paul	Dt.
Drewnitzki	Viktor	Dt.
Behrens	Paul	Dt.
Kuntz	Albert	Dt.
Scherlinski	Alfred	Dt.
Boulanger		Dt.
Carlebach	Emil	Dt.J.

Die Obengenannten stehen am 6.4.45 um 8 Uhr am Schild III

"Commander!

Transports are leaving Buchenwald. They are death transports – like the one from Ohrdruf! The terrible tragedy of Ohrdruf must not be repeated.

Dispatched by air to carry out special missions, we have seen with our own eyes the victims of the escort guard units and agitated members of the population along wide stretches.

Woe to Thuringia, and woe to the commanders in Buchenwald, if that is repeated! The era of Koch, the Commander of Atrocities, by whose virtue the name of this camp has come to be abhorred by the entire civilised world, would thus be restored.

Much has improved under your rule. We know that. Like the rest of the country, you may be in difficulties today – difficulties from which you see no other escape than to send thousands on their way. Stop! Stop immediately!

Our tank commanders are on their way this very minute to settle accounts: You still have a chance.

James Mc Leod
Major
War Office, London."

Camp Commander Pister rigorously followed the orders of the SS command until the end of Buchenwald and even afterward, in his position as the Inspector of the Concentration Camps of the South, to which he had been provisionally assigned by Himmler. He began the evacuation of the parent camp on April 7. The evacuation destinations were the Theresienstadt ghetto and the concentration camps at Dachau and Flossenbürg. On the same day, a memorandum was issued by Glücks, the Inspector of the Concentration Camps, to the effect that the remaining camps in Southern Germany could take on an additional 20,000 inmates. On that basis, Pister had almost precisely the same number of inmates sent by force on marches to Southern Germany, as well as a large majority of the Jewish inmates to Theresienstadt. Camp survivors assume that the entire camp would have been evacuated had the inmates not refused to cooperate by every means at their disposal. The disobedience and resistance of the inmates saved thousands from the death marches. Robert J. Büchler recalls:

"On April 10, 1945, when the American troops were positioned only a few kilometres

Illustration 225:
Eugen Kogon
(1903-1987)
*Source: Repro-
duction, Sammlung
Gedenkstätte
Buchenwald,
Weimar*

from the camp, we suddenly heard the dreaded order again: all Jews to the muster ground immediately! In the tense atmosphere that dominated the camp at the time, this order had the effect of a huge bomb explosion. We were horrified. Every one of us tried to reach our block as quickly as possible. We had already gathered experience, and although our superiors were not in the block, we knew what had to be done.

```
                                                    86

                    Buchenwald,7.Mai 1945.


     Wir haben am 3.Mai d.J. in Lehnstedt bei Weimar auf einem
Acker verscharrt die Leichen von 16 Kameraden aus Buchenwald
vorgefunden,die laut Aussagen der Bevölkerung am 7.April d.J.
beim Durchmarsch von der SS erschossen bezw.erschlagen zurück-
gelassen wurden.Folgende Nummern waren noch feststellbar:

     19047 Borisenko Wasil,polit.Russe geb.3.2.18  Bujwolowo
     38663 Lang Ladislaus,ungar.Jude     " 28.4.06  Beleszno
     59822 Tischler Ernö,    "      "    " 30.12.18.Maszod
     83981 Wajsbrod Arje,polnisch.Jude   " 11.2.01  Sandomierz
     92580 van Alphen Mattheus,Holländer" 8.10.09Segreeveldminkapelle
     19188
     26524
     65481

     Die Angeführten Namen wurden auf Grund der angegebenen Nummern
nach der Kartei des Krankenbaues ermittelt.Zu den letzten 3 Num-
mern waren Karten nicht vorhanden.

                    (gez.) Victor Heinz 9151
                       "   Flamm Sigmund 3320
```

Illustration 226:
Former Buchenwald
Concentration
Camp inmates'
investigations of
murders executed
during evacuation
march of Apr. 7,
1945, May 7, 1945
*Source: Thüringi-
sches Hauptstaats-
archiv, Weimar*

Illustrations 227-
231: Evacuation
train immediately
after liberation,
1945
According to J. R.
Büchler, Israel,
the pictures show
inmates from
Buchenwald.
*Source: Moreshet
Archives, Givat
Haviva, Israel, D. 4*

This time it was not members of Camp Protection who broke into the block, however,
but an entire unit of heavily armed SS men
who tried to chase us out with blows. They
were in a great hurry and wanted to carry out
their work thoroughly. It was clear to us that
we couldn't hold out for long and if you wanted to save yourself you had to try to leave the
block immediately. After a raging scuffle of
about thirty minutes, the SS henchmen had

tight hold of us and were able to lead us to the
muster ground. Only a few of us succeeded in
hiding somewhere."

On altogether sixty marching routes, some
by rail, most on foot, insufficiently dressed
and almost without food provisions, in
April 1945 approximately 28,000 inmates
of the parent camp and at least 10,000 inmates of the sub-camps were en route on

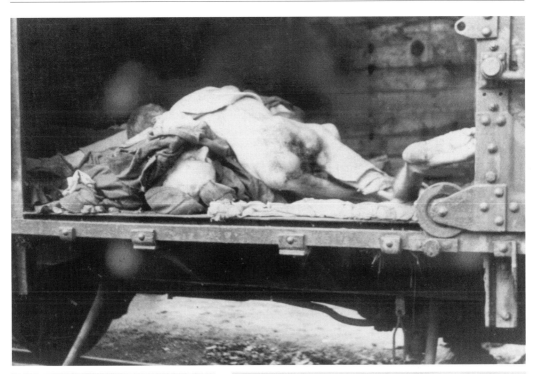

marches justifiably referred to as death marches. Probably about one in three inmates either died along the way, of exhaustion immediately after their arrival, or was shot to death by the SS escort units. Rudolf Kychler reports:

"On April 10, 1945 we passed through the gate of Buchenwald at six o'clock in the evening. Josef Tesla and Jaroslav Mikula were with us; they had been commissioned by the illegal organisation to act as leaders. Much has been written about such death routes; this one was no different. We slept on the floor of the railway station in Weimar; at four o'clock the next morning we left on cattle cars. Near

Großschwabhausen we were stopped by low-flying aircraft. They had shot through the locomotive boiler. Buchenwald was about fourteen km away from where we stopped. The SS men were at a loss to know what to do. They drove back to get orders and that afternoon we set off towards Dachau on foot. We kept to the back. The strategy of slowing down the transport was in effect here as well. Through Jena, and on to Gera via Eisenberg. Near Grossen the American army carried out a sudden tank attack. The transport was broken up; the entire group of Ostrauers remained in the forest by Grossen. And it was there that, on the following day (the third day of the march), the Hitler Youth attacked us and killed nineteen of our comrades. Then an officer of the Protective Police transported us back to Eisenberg, where we were liberated on April 13, 1945. Two days later we were once again summoned back to Buchenwald."

Liberation from the Outside; Liberation from Within

On the first days of April 1945, U.S. Army troops reached the sub-camp at Ohrdruf, whose last remaining inmates had been killed by the SS before their retreat. On April 11, U.S. armoured units advanced towards the SS garrison of Buchenwald. Thomas Geve reports:

"*Towards noon we heard a wailing like we had never heard before. The Germans called it the 'Tank Alarm Siren.' The decisive moment had come. We searched the valley below us. On the periphery of the forest we saw a party of greycoats with steel helmets running, SS guards who had retreated with cases of ammunition and machine guns. Later on we saw more of them; they were running faster but only a few of them were armed with rifles. Then the surrounding area was quiet again and the uncertainty dragged on.*"

American troops ended SS rule on the Ettersberg. As inmates recorded in Camp Report No. One, on the evening of April 11 1945 the first two American tanks approached the quarry from the north at 1 p.m. An hour later, twelve tanks reached

the stalls in the northern section of the camp and engaged the SS in heavy combat. At about 2:30 p.m. they overran the SS area. A short time later – at 2:45 – the inmates began an operation to disarm the remaining SS men and take control of the camp. Several inmates, including Otto Roth, proceeded to the camp gate, where Watchtower One was located, meeting no resistance. Otto Roth later reports:

"*…with the support of several electricians, a ladder was brought there in order to climb up Watchtower One. The SS had already cleared the watchtower; only one SS Oberscharführer retreated from the detention cell building in the direction of the stable.*
Immediately following the occupation of the main gate, the camp senior Hans Eiden followed and raised the white flag on the tower. The central loudspeaker system was put back into operation and in a short address the entire camp was informed that the control of the camp had been taken over by the International Committee.
The group standing ready at the south-western corner of the camp forcibly opened the entry gate between Towers Two and Three and was able to take the SS man withdrawing from the detention cell building as their first prisoner.
In front of the main gate there stood a member of the Wehrmacht, armed with a Carbine 98 and six ammunition pouches on his belt. Comrade Roth summoned him to surrender his weapon and ammunition. After he refused, his rifle and ammunition were taken from him on the spot. The soldier then retreated towards the east."

At about the same point in time, the German political prisoner Fritz Freudenberg came to the camp gate, where he encountered Otto Roth:

"*On the watchtower over the camp gate there was an LMG [light machine gun] on the stand as always, and no SS men. I told my comrades I was going to go and get it! I hesitated briefly and then took hold of a ladder and ran to the gate building, lay down on the ground and waited, but nothing happened. […] Then I jumped up again, leaned the lad-*

der against the wall, climbed up to the roof like lightning, lay down flat again and looked over the ridge of the roof into the command area. There was nothing to be seen. So as not to expose myself to the command area side, I climbed through a window that was opened toward the camp side, into the uppermost room of the interior. I then descended the winding staircase on tiptoe, armed with a sharpened three-sided file. In this room were three long crates with anti-tank rocket launchers in them. As I had never held such an object in my hand, I stopped for a moment to consider its function. Suddenly I heard steps, and two legs came down the winding stairs – our detachment blacksmith, Comrade August Bräucker! That gave me a terrible scare! In a whisper he explained the function of the anti-tank rocket launchers to me. With the thing under my arm, I then descended the next flight of stairs. On this floor were the labour service officer's room and the exit. The labour officer's room was empty! Very slowly I proceeded to the exit door. It was unlocked; I searched the surrounding area through a narrow crack, but discovered nothing. When I finally ventured out, a man in uniform was suddenly standing there below the detention cells. I screamed: 'Hands up!' He obeyed my order. He was unarmed. In answer to my question as to where he had come from and

Illustration 232: Corpses of murdered inmates found by U.S. Army troops in Ohrdruf (S III) Sub-Camp in early April 1945
Source: Reproduction, Sammlung Gedenkstätte Buchenwald, Weimar

Illustration 233: Ohrdruf Sub-Camp: A former Dutch inmate shows the gallows to General Eisenhower (r.), the commander-in-chief of the Allied troops, and his general staff (Gen. Bradley, Gen. Patton and others), Apr. 12, 1945
Source: Archiv für Kunst und Geschichte, Berlin

233

Illustration 234: Flag of the French "Brigade d' Action Libératrice"in Buchenwald Camp, 1945
The flag of the French resistance groups was manufactured illegally in the camp before liberation.
Catalogue 5/13
Photo: G. Krynitzki

Illustration 235: Marcel Paul (1900-1982), one of the leaders of the French resistance organisation in the camp
Source: Sammlung Gedenkstätte Buchenwald, Weimar

of the Wehrmacht and I, were now standing in front of the camp gate.

Suddenly our electrician, Comrade Otto Roth, was standing at the inner gate. He was armed with a pistol. He instructed me to reach through the window of the guard station and press the button beneath the windowsill. This triggered the electric lock and the camp gate opened. Comrade Roth ran immediately towards the command area.

Now that the camp gate stood open, the inmates came running towards it, first singly, then in larger masses. Several of them had rifles! The stream of inmates poured onto the barrack grounds and took possession of the rifles and ammunition that were to be found there. At that very moment, American tanks and a line of vehicles, coming along the road from Hottelstedt, crossed the barrack grounds in the direction of Weimar."

Florréal Barrier, a member of the French "Brigade d' Action Libératrice," reports:

"I belonged to the unit that was the first to leave the camp. As I went through the gate, the camp had already been liberated. The combat patrol had cleared the gate and we armed ourselves with weapons which had just been confiscated from the SS areas. Then, with the group I belonged to – there were about fifteen of us; we belonged to several of the original groups of five –, we set off in the direction of Weimar. By way of Caracho Path and the road through the factory area, we

where he was going he told me that he was from the Wehrmacht and was stationed near Hottelstedt / Ettersberg. His group had split up and each was seeking refuge somewhere on his own. From him we learned that American tanks had already been on their way over the Ettersberg towards Weimar for an hour. The three of us – Comrade Bräucker, the member

234

went to the very outermost edge of the camp, where the Bismarck Tower was located at the time, and today the memorial. There we encountered the first units of the American army."

In the course of the hours that followed, the inmates took seventy-eight fleeing members of the SS prisoner. On the same afternoon, Lieutenant Emmanuel Desard of the U.S. Army, who along with Sergeant Paul Bodot was one of the first members of the Allied forces to enter the camp, transferred the administration of the camp and the responsibility for the 21,000 survivors to Camp Senior One, Hans Eiden. At about the same time, a reconnaissance troop of the Sixth Armored Car Division of the Third U.S. Army was present in the camp. Paul Bodot reports on this first encounter:

"On April 6th we learned in Gotha of the existence of the camp in Ohrdruf, which had been liberated by our Fourth Division. We were met there by a vision of horror: a large number of corpses, reduced to skeletons, had been killed – shot at the base of the skull – by the SS, who had resolved to liquidate all witnesses before fleeing. There was nevertheless one single survivor: a young, seventeen-year-old Russian who had managed to hide underneath a barrack. At the edge of the forest we were horrified by a certain smell, which came from two pyres of charred corpses and a large heap of corpses. Very soon we learned of the existence of other camps.
After Erfurt, Lieutenant Desard and I left our line of vehicles in search of the Buchenwald camp. After we had driven about ten km, we came across a strange group: armed civilians were guarding prisoners. The leader of this group, a Belgian deportee by the name of Leopold Hansen, told us that the inmates had liberated themselves a few hours before, and that patrols like his had set off in pursuit of fugitive SS men and guards. He offered to serve us as a guide and climbed up onto the hood of the jeep. At the edge of the forest, below the camp, we crossed the guard path. We were surprised at its length, and at the number of survivors (more than 20,000). When we drove into the camp in the jeep,

Illustration 236: Auguste Favier: "Frédéric Henri Manhès," drawing, December 1944
Colonel Henri Manhès [named Frédéric] (1889-1959) was one of the co-founders of the French support committee in the camp and led the "Brigade d'Action Libératrice" along with Marcel Paul.
Source: F.N.D.I.R.P., Paris

Leopold began to shout and wave: 'The Americans! But the first of them are French!' The scene that followed was overwhelming and unforgettable: hundreds of deportees came towards us like a tidal wave, shouting with joy, and tore down the rows of barbed wire erected by the SS. We were met by members of the international liberation committee, who had succeeded in enforcing strict discipline, which the internees obeyed to a T. As the Lieutenant wrote his report, I went to the barrack for those with contagious diseases to bring the sick inmates the news of their liberation. Only two or three deportees had the courage to accompany me and I understood immediately: I could hardly believe my eyes. The air here was unbreathable; mistrustful

235

Illustration 237: Sergeant Paul Bodot in the jeep in which he and Lieutenant Emmanuel Desard drove to Buchenwald on Apr. 11, 1945, early April 1945
Source: M. Eyben

Illustration 238: Group of inmates (3rd from r. with rifle) in the vicinity of the camp, Apr. 11, 1945
This photo was taken by Sergeant Bodot.
Source: M. Eyben

gazes turned toward me. In the semi darkness I saw deportees staggering along a corridor, others were sitting on the floor, most of them were lying in groups of four or five on plank beds intended for one inmate each. The misery of the entire world could be read in their gazes. Many of them were not even conscious of the fact that they had been liberated. But slowly a spark brightened their faces. They wanted to convince themselves that it was not a dream, and tried to touch my uniform. Soon things were in a state of turmoil, eyes filled with tears, some dropped to their knees ... The sick people reacted more slowly but they also stretched out their shaking, imploring hands. I went to them so that they could touch my uniform. I couldn't stop myself from shaking many hands, although my escorts advised me not to. I had the feeling of gratification at a job well done: my presence alone had given most of them new courage, for many of them had wished for one thing only: a quick death. I had entered a camp for incurables; when I left, it was buzzing like a beehive.

A camp committee took charge of the camp, which was still a battlefield. In Camp Report No. One of April 11, 1945 it is stated:

"Resolution passed to form a camp council of representatives of all nations. Representation ratio: one representative to 1,000 inmates of one nation.
The Camp Senior in office to date will take over the function of camp commander. For the execution of immediate measures, a camp executive board will be formed with representatives of all nations.
This committee consists of Kalcin (USSR), Manhes (France), Bartel (Germany), Frank (CSR) and Ciufoli for the remaining Romance nations.
Further resolution passed for the formation of the following commissions:
1) Security commission
2) Rations commission
3) Medical commission
4) Clothing commission
5) Camp administration commission
6) Information service commission.
... The camp is under the firm control of the

former inmates. The camp administration functions are to be carried out by our own institutions. The camp is to be protected externally against the SS, internally against bandit elements. It is of utmost importance that we face the Allies as disciplined, free human beings."

During the days that passed until the Americans assumed the administration of the camp on April 13, the fundamental structures for order and provisions were maintained and first-aid measures commenced, being of vital importance for the majority of the inmates. Hundreds still died within the first few days. By April 16, 1945, there were 20,000 of the approximately 21,000 persons liberated on April 11 left in the camp, divided into the following nationalities:

French	2,900
Poles	3,800
Hungarians	1,240
Yugoslavs	570
Russians	4,380
Dutch	584
Belgians	622
Austrians	550
Italians	242
Czechs	2,105
Germans	1,800
Spanish and others	1,207
	20,000

There were 4,000 Jews among the survivors.

Everyday Life in the Camp after Liberation

The confrontation with the circumstances and the supply situation in Buchenwald was a shock for the American soldiers. They had liberated a camp inhabited by 21,000 human beings of which many were languishing away, a camp that was also full of corpses. Inmates would continue to die by the hundreds as a result of hunger and the disastrous hygienic conditions. William Kolbe, a U.S. Army officer at the time, recalls:

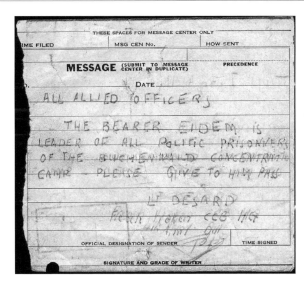

Illustration 239: Slip of paper identifying Camp Senior One Hans Eiden as the leader of the political inmates.
This slip of paper was written and signed by Lieutenant Emmanual Desard on the afternoon of Apr. 11, 1945.
Source: Buchenwaldarchiv, Weimar

Illustration 240: Hans Eiden (1901-1950)
Camp senior, 1944-1945.
Source: Sammlung Gedenkstätte Buchenwald, Weimar

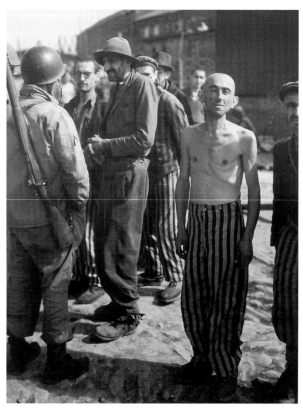

"My first impression was one of disbelief in view of the emaciated people in striped uniforms, their sunken eyes; you could feel the horror these individuals had experienced. And then I saw the red brick ovens in which there were still human skeletons, and hooks outside for the bodies. As I looked around some more, I saw the shelves on which the prisoners had had to sleep; the most horrible scene, however, was that of the flat quarry carts with hundreds of corpses piled up on them and covered with lime in an out-of-the-way corner of the complex … a completely unbelievable scene which I will never forget."

The American chaplain Rabbi Herschel Schacter had similar experiences:

"From the floor to the ceiling there were hundreds of men and many boys, hanging over thin straw sacks and looking down at me, looking down at me with confused eyes … I remember their eyes, the way the looked down, looked down with big, big eyes – all I saw were eyes – hunted, crippled, paralyzed with fear. They were emaciated skin and bones, half insane, more dead than alive. And I stood there and called out in Yiddish 'Shalom Aleichem, Jews, you are free!' 'You

Illustration 241: After April 11, 1945, liberated inmates
Source: National Archives and Record Administration, Washington D. C.

Illustration 242: After April 11, 1945, wagon containing corpses in the courtyard of the crematorium
Source: National Archives and Record Administration, Washington D. C.

Illustration 243:
After April 11, 1945,
in the Little Camp
*Source: National
Archives and Record
Administration,
Washington D. C.*

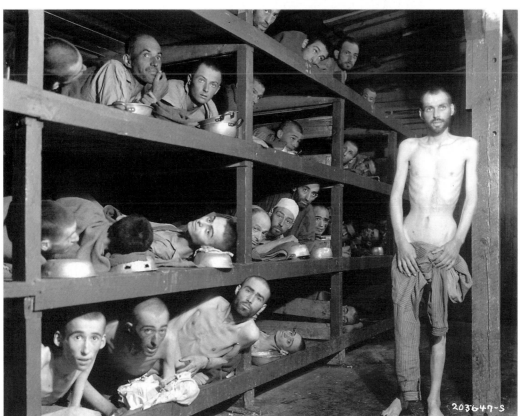

Illustration 244: After April 11, 1945, in the Little Camp
Source: National Archives and Record Administration, Washington D. C.

Illustration 245: Members of the U.S. Army taking sick persons from the Little Camp to the barracks
Source: Yad Vashem, Jerusalem

are free.' The more courageous of them came towards me slowly ... to touch my army uniform, to look at my Jewish clerical insignia, and asked me in disbelief: 'Is it true? Is it over?'"

Following liberation, the gates of the "Little Camp" initially remained closed. Edward R. Murrow, reporting from there for the BBC on April 15, 1945:

"As I entered, I was surrounded by men who tried to lift me up on their shoulders. They were too weak. Many of them could not even get out of bed. I was told that this building had once accommodated eighty horses; now there were 1,200 human beings in it, 5 to every sleeping place. The stench was beyond imagination ...
As I went through to the end of the barrack, I was applauded by the men who were too weak to get up. It sounded like the clapping of babies' hands, they were so weak."

The U.S. Army left the order and control of the camp to the inmates' self-administration. Arms were turned in by order of the American commander.

On April 12, the French doctor Dr. Joseph Anselme Brau became the chief medical officer of the liberated camp. Within the first few days, the 120th U.S. Army Evacuation Hospital moved 4,700 sick persons from the camp barracks to the former SS barracks. At least one in four of them died in the weeks that followed. Hospitals in the vicinity also took in ailing survivors. All available energy was invested in the attempt to save lives, and – in view of the daily heaps of corpses in the courtyard of the crematorium – those in charge were thus compelled to continue the burial of the dead in the craters on the southern slope of the Ettersberg. From the end of April on, the dead were buried below the Bismarck Tower, i.e. at a site on the southern slope.

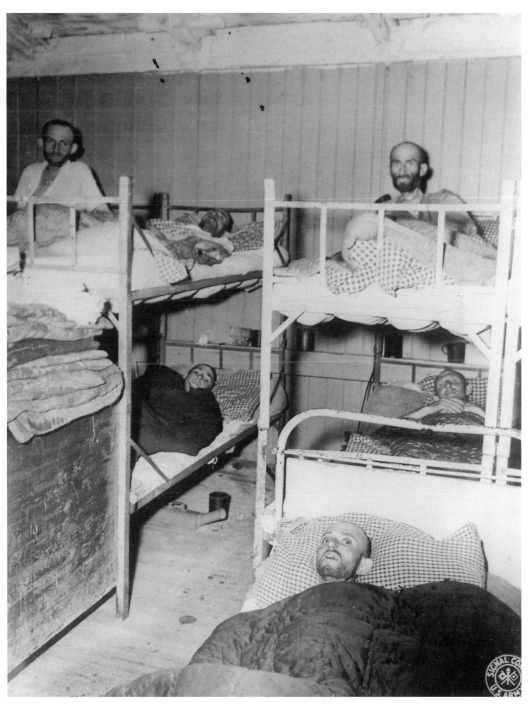

Illustration 246: Scene in inmates' infirmary barrack after liberation
Source: National Archives and Record Administration, Washington D. C.

Illustration 247: Joseph Anselme Brau (1891-1975)
Beginning on April 12, 1945, this former French political inmate was the chief physician of the liberated Buchenwald camp.
Source: F.N.D.I.R.P., Paris

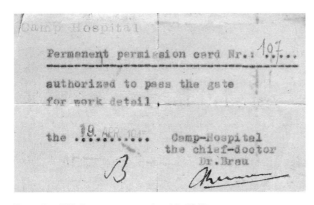

Illustration 248: Permanent pass, Apr. 19, 1945
Source: F.N.D.I.R.P., Paris

Publicity and Legacy

Buchenwald was one of the first concentration camps in which, at the time of its liberation by American troops, the evidence of the crimes had not yet been destroyed. On the contrary, the image of the overcrowded mass camp, slowly drowning in chaos, with all the consequences and all the corpses, was still immediately apprehensible. For this reason, Buchenwald was a primary focus for Western European and American press coverage of the camps. On April 16, 1945, citizens of Weimar were forced to tour the camp and bury corpses. The initial impression was strongly influenced by photos of the Little Camp, of emaciated figures, of the mountain of corpses in the crematorium, of the SS's medical specimens, tanned human skin and shrunken heads.

For the people in the camp, the liberation was like a rebirth. The political programmes drawn up there during the very first weeks are an expression of the desire for a better society. On April 19, at a commemoration ceremony for the dead held on the Buchenwald muster ground, liberated inmates read out a pledge that came to be known as the Oath of Buchenwald.

On April 13, 1945, at an assembly of Austrian Socialists and members of the SPD, Hermann L. Brill read out his "Manifesto of the Democratic Socialists of the Former Buchenwald Concentration Camp." The meeting was attended by French, Belgian, Dutch, Danish, Polish and Czech Social Democrats. A few days later, a revised version of the manifesto – signed by a number of Germans and Austrians, two Czechs, a Dutchman and a Belgian – was submitted by a commission whose members included the Austrian Social Democrat Benedikt Kautsky. The manifesto was based on the points listed in the Buchenwald Platform written by the People's Front Committee in 1944 and formulated the programme for a new democratic post-war society in seven points: the destruction of fascism, the establishment of a people's republic, liberation of labour, socialisation of the economy, peace and justice, humanity, Socialist unity.

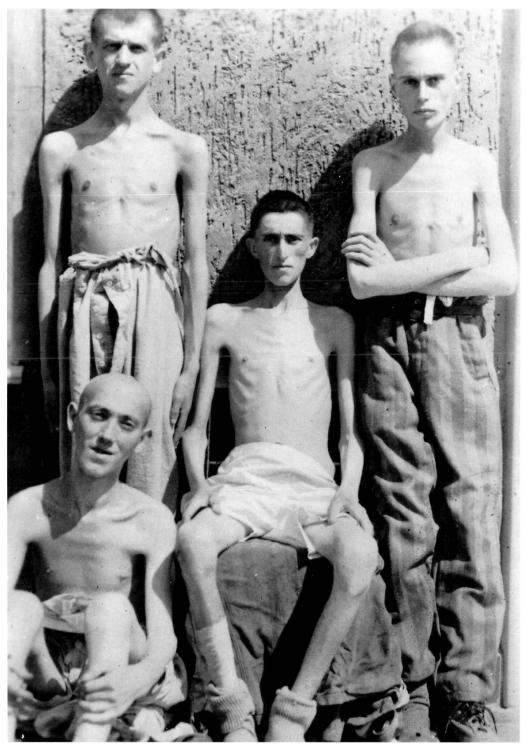

Illustration 249: Liberated youngsters, after April 11, 1945
This photo was one of a series taken and reproduced by the German political inmate Eberhard Leitner.
Source: Sammlung Gedenkstätte Buchenwald, Weimar

Illustration 250: Jacques Rancy with a "shrunken head" found in 1945 in the house of an SS physician. Photo caption: "Tête réduite d'un détenu trouvée dans la villa d' un médecin SS de Buchenwald. Photo prise entre le 11 et le 15 avril 1945." This photo was one of a series taken by the Frenchman Jacques Rancy, a former political inmate, after the liberation of the camp. Primarily during Koch's term as camp commander, the SS produced "shrunken heads" from the scalps of murder victims and distributed them among the SS as presents.
Source: Jacques Rancy

Illustration 251: Citizens of Weimar ordered to tour the concentration camp, here in the courtyard of the crematorium. A rag doll representing an inmate is hanging from the "transportable gallows", Apr. 16, 1945. Photo caption: "German civilians from Weimar were brought by U.S. military police to nearby Camp Buchenwald, nazy [sic] horror prison, to view evidence of atrocities. When Gen. Patton's U.S. Third Army seized the camp, this body of a prisoner was found dangling from a hook in the yard."
Source: National Archives and Record Administration, Washington D. C.

Illustration 252: Citizens of Weimar ordered to tour the concentration camp, Buchenwald, Apr. 16, 1945. Photo caption: "German Atrocities. German women exhibit varied expressions as they witness atrocity horrors in Camp Buchenwald at Weimar, taken by Gen. Patton's U.S. Third Army. Citizens from Weimar were put under Military Police escort and marched through the camp by U.S. authorities."
Source: National Archives and Record Administration, Washington D. C.

Illustration 253: Members of an American congressional committee viewing a heap of corpses in the courtyard of the crematorium, Apr. 24, 1945. Photo caption: "Senator Alben W. Barkley of Kentucky, a member of a congressional committee investigating Nazi atrocities, views the evidence at first hand at Buchenwald concentration camp."
Source: National Archives and Record Administration, Washington D. C.

Illustration 254:
Wooden obelisk
made for the
memorial service of
Apr. 19, 1945
Photo: Eberhard
Leitner
*Source: Sammlung
Gedenkstätte
Buchenwald,
Weimar*

Illustration 255: May 1, 1945 edition of the Spanish Communists' camp newspaper
Source: Buchenwaldarchiv, Weimar

Antifascist committees were involved in the denazification process and the organisation of administration in the Weimar region. The former political inmate Hermann Louis Brill became the first minister-president of Thuringia. The International Camp Committee gathered reports that served as a basis for Eugen Kogon's book *Der SS-Staat*. Most of the survivors were released after May 8, 1945, the end of the war. Gradually they set off on journeys back to their native countries. Rolf Kralovitz recalls his return to Leipzig:

"It was already evening when we arrived in Leipzig. Because the Americans had ordered a curfew, we spent the night in a bus station in the suburb of Lindenau.
The non-Jewish inmates were picked up by their families and friends the next morning. But for the four of us there was nobody. Bruno Gewürtz, who acted initially as our spokesman, suggested: 'We should go to the Americans. They'll help us.'
So we took the tram, which was already back in operation in mid May, to the city centre. The American military administration was in Auenstrasse 14.
I knew the building very well. It was the former Jewish home for the elderly, an endowment of the Ariowitsch Family. After the eighty-five inhabitants of the home had

Ansprache in französischer, russischer, polnischer, englischer
und deutscher Sprache auf der Trauerkundgebung
des Lagers Buchenwald am 19. April 1945

Kameraden!

Wir Buchenwalder Antifaschisten sind heute angetreten zu Ehren der in
Buchenwald und seinen Aussenkommandos von der Nazibestie und ihrer Helfers-
helfer ermordeten

        51 000 Gefangenen !

51 000 erschossen, gehenkt, zertrampelt, erschlagen, erstickt, ersäuft,
       verhungert, vergiftet - abgespritzt -

51 000 Väter, Brüder - Söhne starben einen qualvollen Tod, weil sie
       Kämpfer gegen das faschistische Mordregime waren.

51.000 Mütter und Frauen und hunderttausende Kinder klagen an!

Wir lebend gebliebenen, wir Zeugen der nazistischen Bestialitäten sahen
in ohnmächtiger Wut unsere Kameraden fallen.

Wenn uns ein's im Leben hielt, dann war es der Gedanke:

       Es kommt der Tag der Rache !

<u>Heute sind wir frei !</u>

Wir danken den verbündeten Armeen, der Amerikaner, Engländer, Sowjets und
allen Freiheitsarmeen, die uns und der gesamten Welt Frieden und das Leben
erkämpfen.

Wir gedenken an dieser Stelle des grossen Freundes der Antifaschisten
aller Länder, eines Organisatoren und Initiatoren des Kampfes um eine neue,
demokratische, friedliche Welt.

       F.D. R o o s e v e l t .

Ehre seinem Andenken !

Wir Buchenwalder,

Russen, Franzosen, Polen, Tschechen, - Slovaken und Deutsche,
Spanier, Italiener und Oesterreicher,
Belgier und Holländer, Engländer,
Luxemburger, Rumänen, Jugoslaven und Ungarn

kämpften gemeinsam gegen die SS, gegen die nazistischen Verbrecher, für
unsere eigene Befreiung.

Uns beseelte eine Idee: Unsere Sache ist gerecht -

       Der Sieg muss unser sein !

Wir führten in vielen Sprachen den gleichen, harten, erbarmungslosen,opfer-
reichen Kampf und dieser Kampf ist noch nicht zu Ende.
Noch wehen Hitlerfahnen!
Noch leben die Mörder unserer Kameraden!
Noch laufen unsere sadistischen Peiniger frei herum!
Wir schwören deshalb vor aller Welt auf diesem Appellplatz, an dieser Stätt
des faschistischen Grauens:

       Wir stellen den Kampf erst ein, wenn auch der
       letzte Schuldige vor den Richtern der Völker steht!

Die Vernichtung des Nazismus mit seinen Wurzeln ist unsere Losung.
Der Aufbau einer neuen Welt des Friedens und der Freiheit ist unser Ziel!.
Das sind wir unseren gemordeten Kameraden, ihren Angehörigen schuldig.

Zum Zeichen Eurer Bereitschaft für diesen Kampf erhebt die Hand zum Schwur
und sprecht mir nach: W I R   S C H W O E R E N !

==

Buchenwaldarchiv
Sign. Nt 488

Illustration 256: Inmates' pledge taken on Apr. 19, 1945 (Oath of Buchenwald)
Source: Buchenwaldarchiv, Weimar

Illustration 257: Funeral procession to the south slope of the Ettersberg, second half of April 1945
Photo: Lee Miller
Source: © Lee Miller Archive, Chiddingly, England

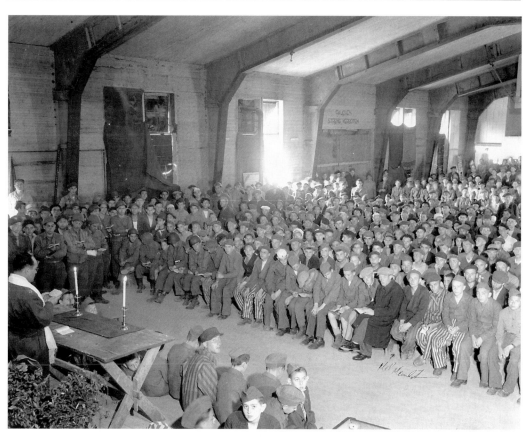

Illustration 258: Shavuot celebration in the cinema, May 1945
The sermon was held by Chief Rabbi Herschel Schacter.
Source: National Archives and Record Administration, Washington D. C.

been deported in September 1942, the Secret State Police took over this building as its chief headquarters. After the liberation of Leipzig it served as a headquarters first for the American, then – following the change of occupation – for the Soviet military administration. After 1948 it was directed back to its originally destined purpose as a home for the elderly.

An American captain who spoke German welcomed us in the 'Military Government Office' and listened to our story attentively. We explained to him that what we needed above all was a place to stay, and asked him to help us. He answered: 'The mayor we have appointed to office will be here in a little while: surely he can solve your problem.'

When the mayor came, we told him our concern. He reacted defensively, however: 'Leipzig was badly bombed. I can't offer you a room.' I said to him: 'Are you aware of the fact that, as Jewish survivors of the concentration camp, we are returning to our native city? We can hardly believe that you can't even find a room for us. In Weimar, they offered inmates entire flats.' He replied dryly: 'So why don't you go back to Weimar?'

I was naturally quite angry about this, and the Americans standing nearby were grinning broadly. He realised he had made a mistake and he said: 'Alright then. My car is downstairs. Come with me!'

We drove to the town hall. There was a long queue of refugees and former citizens of Leipzig who had returned home, all of them also looking for a place to live. But we, we didn't have to go to the back of the queue; we were taken right into one of the offices. There the mayor declared: 'They all get rooms!' And suddenly we were even allowed to choose the

Illustration 259: Departure by plane of the first liberated Frenchmen, Apr. 18, 1945
Left: Frédéric Henri Manhès; to his right: Julien Cain (director of the national library), to the rear with bag: the musician Maurice Hewitt.
Source: Sammlung Gedenkstätte Buchenwald, Weimar

Illustration 260: Departure of children and adolescents for France, June 5, 1945
Source: Willy Fogel, Paris

Illustration 261: Children and adolescents liberated from concentration camps, on their way to France, June 1945
Source: National Archives and Record Administration, Washington D. C.

neighbourhood we wanted to live in. I requested: 'If possible in Fregestrasse, because that's where I grew up.'
And I was actually assigned a room in Fregestrasse 26, only two houses away from the house in which I had lived with my family when I was young.
I rang at the home of the Schumann family on the third floor and showed my allotment slip from the housing office. Frau Schumann led me into a small room; it was her husband's office: 'As you can see, there's nothing to sleep on here, only this short sofa.' I said: 'That doesn't matter to me in the least. I'll put a chair at the end of the sofa and put my legs on that. If you only knew how much worse I had slept in the past years.'
That was how I took up residence in my first room in freedom. I was a civilian again.'"

Buchenwald served temporarily as a displaced persons' camp until the last former inmates left it in conjunction with the withdrawal of the U.S. Army from Thuringia. At the beginning of July 1945 the Americans vacated the camp and turned it over to the Soviet troops.

Illustration 262: Liberated Buchenwald inmates on their way home to Leipzig, 1945
In the door of the bus, second from left: Rolf Kralovitz
Source: Sammlung Gedenkstätte Buchenwald, Weimar

Officially registered deaths at Buchenwald Concentration Camp (men)					
Year	No. committed	No. deceased	No. released or transferred	Average camp population	Camp population at year-end
1937	2,912	48	303	2,200	2,561
1938	20,122	771	10,884	7,420	11,028
1939	9,553	1,235	7,539	8,390	11,807
1940	2,525	1,772	5,120	8,290	7,440
1941	5,890	1,522	3,897	7,730	7,911
1942	14,111	2,898	9,607	8,784	9,517
1943	42,177	3,516	10,859	20,414	37,319
1944	97,867	8,644	63,494	58,334	63,048
1/1 to 3/31/45	43,823	13,056	13,379	82,322	80,436 (end of March)
Total	238,980	33,462			

The Dead

Between July 1937 and the end of March 1945, 238,980 male inmates were committed to Buchenwald. By the end of March, 33,462 deaths had been officially registered in the camp records.

A further 913 inmates died between April 1 and 10, 1945, so that the number of recorded victims totals 34,375. Thus in relationship to the average camp population of 22,654 inmates, one and a half times the yearly population died within the nearly eight years of the camp's existence. Of the approximately 27,000 female inmates in the twenty-eight women's sub-camps, 335 died. The SS also shot approximately 8,000 Soviet prisoners of war to death and hanged approximately 1,100 persons in the crematorium; the identities of those persons were never determined. Along with the anonymous deceased brought on the death transports from the camps in the East and the evacuation marches of April 1945, which claimed an estimated 12,000 victims, the total number of deaths attributable to Buchenwald Concentration Camp is estimated at approximately 56,000.

Epilogue

The Buchenwald Trial, Dachau, 1947

The U.S. Army began investigating the crimes immediately following the liberation of the camp. Having carried out a number of interrogations in the liberated camp, Egon W. Fleck (Civ. and First Lt.) and Edward A. Tenenbaum (Intelligence Team of the Psychological Warfare Division of the Twelfth U.S. Army Group) submitted their first report on April 24, 1945. When the American troops left Thuringia in July 1945, they took nearly all of the evidence (reportedly three tons of files) with them. The leadership of the SS command staff had also been captured by the Americans. Between mid 1945 and the end of 1946, over 6,000 suspects were examined and hundreds of statements by former inmates put on record. The 793 persons arrested within this context were being held in the internment camp in Dachau.

On April 11, 1947, two years after the liberation of the camp, the Buchenwald Trial commenced. The defendants included the former Senior SS and Police Chief of the SS district of Fulda-Werra, SS Obergruppenführer Josias Erbprinz zu Waldeck und Pyrmont, and thirty further persons. Of the SS command staff officers, only the Chief of the Political Department and SS Garrison Physician Dr. Schiedlausky was missing. He had already stood trial before a British military tribunal and been sentenced to death. In addition to Dr. Hanns Eisele, Dr. August Bender, Dr. Werner Greunuss and SS Sanitätsdienstgrad Friedrich Wilhelm, however, a number of other persons responsible for the dire medical conditions and the murder of ill persons sat on the interrogation bench. The only woman among the defendants was Ilse Koch. Aside from the members of the SS, four inmates were also on trial on charges of crimes committed against fellow inmates. All of the defendants pleaded "not

Illustration 264:
Buchenwald Trial
before the military
tribunal in Dachau.
The defendant Ilse
Koch, wife of the
Buchenwald
Concentration Camp
commander Karl
Koch, testifying
before a map of the
concentration camp,
July 8, 1947
*Source: Archiv
für Kunst und
Geschichte, Berlin*

guilty." The trial ended on August 14, 1947 with the pronouncement of the sentence: twenty-two persons were sentenced to death by hanging, five to life imprisonment and four to prison terms of ten to twenty years. Following this main trial, twenty-five further trials concerned with crimes committed in Buchenwald were held before the U.S. military tribunal in Dachau, the subjects of the charges being the abuse of inmates, the mass murder of Soviet prisoners of war and crimes committed in the sub-camps and on the evacuation marches.

All of the sentences pronounced during the Buchenwald Trial were subsequently re-examined on the basis of the extensive records. On June 8, 1948, the commander in chief of the armed forces, General Lucius D. Clay, confirmed fifteen of the death sentences and commuted seven into life imprisonment. Ten former members of the SS command had been executed by 1951. Camp Commander Pister died in prison. The remaining sentences were reduced to minor offence punishments following the second amnesty. With the exception of Ilse Koch, who was sentenced to life imprisonment by the Regional Court

of Augsburg in 1951, the defendants had all been set free by the mid 1950s.

Members of all strata of German society called for the release of the SS criminals, one such petition being signed by the entire population of a village. Far from the scenes of the crime, the defendants were known simply as good neighbours and fathers. Nobody could imagine them as perpetrators of mass crimes. For many, their appearance seemed more credible than the testimony of the survivors.

Between 1949 and 1965, thirteen further trials took place in the Federal Republic of Germany in connection with crimes committed in Buchenwald; in two cases the defendants were inmate capos. The lawsuits against Ilse Koch and Martin Sommer (in 1958 before the Regional Court of Bayreuth) were those which most strongly attracted public attention. In the German Democratic Republic (Eastern Germany), the legal proceedings against the former SS Hauptscharführer Wilhelm Schäfer were followed with particular interest by the public. Schäfer was sentenced to death by the Supreme Court for participation in the murder of Soviet prisoners of war and executed.

"We, the resurrected ..."

"We, the resurrected, all looked more or less the way the archive photos of April and May 1945 showed us: skeletons revived with Anglo-American canned corned beef; shaven-headed, toothless ghosts, useful merely for the purpose of testifying and then making off for the places where we really belonged. But we were 'heroes,' at least if we could believe the banners stretched across our streets and bearing the words: Gloire aux Prisonniers Politiques!"

Jean Améry

For many of the camp survivors, the way back to freedom was hard. Deeply wounded by the experiences of torture and degradation, they found themselves in post-war societies which offered no assurances that damaged life would not be injured anew, nor guarantees that the crimes could not be repeated. Most people had lost members of their families, many their homes. For many of the surviving Polish Jews, there was no return. Their world had been obliterated, their friends and relatives killed. In June 1945, with the support of the American authorities in Egendorf near Weimar, former Jewish inmates of Buchenwald Concentration Camp founded the "Buchenwald Kibbutz." They were among the first survivors of the Nazi camps to go to Palestine in 1945. Others waited in displaced persons' camps for opportunities to leave Germany in order to begin a new life elsewhere, usually outside Europe.

The world to which the survivors returned knew little of the reality of the camps. Society stood at the threshold of a new era, and reminders of the trauma were bothersome. "Society is concerned merely with its own safety and won't trouble itself with damaged life: it is looking forward, at best to make sure the same things won't happen again", Jean Améry remarked bitterly. Only for "one brief hour of the world" had he been able to believe that "everything had changed completely". The image of a "new world of peace and liberty" (the oath of the survivors) which had arisen in this "one brief hour" remained a utopia.

The integration of the concentration camp victims into German post-war reality was also not without stipulations. They were not free to move as they wished within society's new normality. They were the living witnesses to a history, the guilty conscience of a German society which wanted nothing more than to forget the role it had played as a "people's community".

Throughout the world, there were survivors who attempted to spread the insight they had gained, and to emphasise it through their efforts. It was the insight which Primo Levi, on the basis of his experience in Auschwitz, expressed as follows:

"It happened, and therefore it can happen again. It can happen everywhere."

Illustration 265-266: Jószef Szajna: "Roll Call", installation in the permanent exhibition on the history of Buchenwald Concentration Camp, 1995

Prof. Jószef Szajna, born on March 13, 1922 in Rzeszów, was active in the resistance group "Zwiazek Walki Zbrojnej" at the age of seventeen. In 1940, during an attempt to escape from the Gestapo, he was arrested by the Hungarian border patrol and turned in. From 1941 to January 1944 he was an inmate of Auschwitz Concentration Camp. In January 1944 he was transferred to Buchenwald, from there to the Junkers-Werke Sub-Camp in Schönebeck. He succeeded in escaping from an evacuation march in April 1945. Today he lives and works in Warsaw as an artist, writer, stage director and stage designer.

Photo: G. Krynitzki

Appendices

Notes on Sources and Publications

Though many files were lost in the air attack of August 24, 1944 on Buchenwald (files from the Political Department, the Hollerith card file, the picture archive) and in the destruction of files that took place in April 1945 (SS personnel matters, Political Department, Hygiene Institute of the Armed SS, death register original), considerable portions of the **Buchenwald Concentration Camp administrative files** have been preserved, particularly those of Department III (preventive custody camp), III E (labour allocation), IV (administration) and V (camp physician). Today they are essentially distributed among three archives: the Buchenwald records held by the Red Cross International Search Service, the NS 4/Buchenwald records at the Thüringisches Hauptstaatsarchiv Weimar (formerly located in the Bundesarchiv in Koblenz) and the Buchenwald Concentration Camp archive held in the same location. The United States Army placed the largest set of files at the disposal of the Internationaler Suchdienst (International Search Service) in Arolsen, Germany. The main collection consists of 488 files and 67 books, comprising a total of over 104,000 sheets (1957 inventory) and has been systematically supplemented as other materials have been collected. Since these files have not yet been made available for scientific evaluation (it was only in 1997 that the first one percent of the files were opened for study), the work on the permanent exhibition was based primarily on the smaller sets of records in the collection of the Thüringisches Hauptstaatsarchiv Weimar. An overview of the scale and nature of these sources is provided in Heinz Boberach (ed.), *Inventar archivalischer Quellen des NS-Staates: Die Überlieferung von Behörden und Einrichtungen des Reichs, der Länder und der NSDAP. Teil 2: Regionale Behörden und wissenschaftliche Hochschulen für die fünf ostdeutschen Länder, die ehemaligen preußischen Ostprovinzen und eingegliederte Gebiete in Polen, Österreich und der Tschechischen Republik mit Nachträgen zu Teil 1*, München, New Providence, London, Paris: Saur, 1995, pp. 96-98 (*Texte und Materialien zur Zeitgeschichte*, Vol. 3/2).

We also worked from records held in the archive of the Archivum Glownej Komisji Badania Zbrodni Przeciwko Narodowi Polskiemu (Main Commission for the Elucidation of Crimes against the Polish People) in Warsaw, which are available on microfilm in the picture archives at Buchenwald Memorial (32 rolls). The following are the most important of the other archives that made sources available for our work:

– the archive of Panstwowe Muzeum Oswiecim Brzezinka (the Auschwitz-Birkenau Memorial in Oswiecim);
– the Bundesarchiv in Berlin-Lichterfelde, comprising records formerly in the Berlin Document Centre (including personnel files for members of the command staff), the Zentraler Staatsarchiv der DDR, Abteilung I (Central State Archives of the German Democratic Republic, Department I), Potsdam, and from Koblenz (including SS Wirtschaftsverwaltungshauptamt);
– the Stadtarchiv Weimar (Weimar Municipal Archives) on the connection between the camp and the town;
– the collection of the Musée de la Résistance et de la Déportation, Besançon;
– the archive of the Fédération Nationale des Déportés et Internés Résistants et Patriotes, Paris, for biographical details on French nationals at Buchenwald;
– the archive of the Ministère des anciens combattants et victimes de guerre in Caen;
– the archive of the United States Holocaust Memorial Museum, Washington;
– the National Archives and Record Administration, Washington;
– Yad Vashem. Martyrs' and Heroes' Remembrance Authority, Jerusalem.

One special category of source material only partially investigated for the permanent exhibition is to be found in the document collections, interrogation transcripts and statements under oath produced in preparation for, and in the course of, **legal proceedings.** A substantial stock of such documents is constituted by the volumes of documents produced by the International Military Tribunal: Trial of the Major War Criminals, Nuremberg, 14 November 1945-1 October 1946, published in accordance with the direction of the International Military Tribunal by the secretariat of the tribunal under the jurisdiction of the Allied Control Authority for Germany, 1947. In addition, by way of preparation for the permanent exhibition, we evaluated the documents and testimonies made at the Nuremberg successor trials (in particular Case I, Case IV, Case VI) and documents from the 1947 Buchenwald Trial in Dachau (National Archives and Record Administration, Washington, Record group 153, Records of the Judge Advocate General [Army], U.S. v. Prince zu Waldeck et al.,

War Crimes Case N. 12-390) that are stored on microfilm (13 rolls) in the Buchenwald Archive at the Buchenwald Memorial. The trial against the former Buchenwald detention cell building warder, Martin Sommer, heard before the Landgericht Bayreuth in 1958 is documented in: H. G. van Dahm, Ralph Giordano (eds.), *KZ-Verbrechen vor deutschen Gerichten: Dokumente aus den Prozessen gegen Sommer (KZ Buchenwald), Sorge, Schubert (KZ Sachsenhausen), Unkelbach (Ghetto in Czenstochau)*, Frankfurt am Main: Europäische Verlagsanstalt, 1962, pp. 9-149. Other trials brought before German courts are summarised in: *Justiz und NS-Verbrechen: Sammlung deutscher Strafurteile wegen nationalsozialistischer Tötungsverbrechen 1945-1966*, processed by the Seminarium voor Strafrecht en Strafrechtspleging Van Hamel of the University of Amsterdam. 22 vols. Amsterdam 1968-1981 (particularly Nos. 145, 188, 214, 262, 281, 358, 376, 377, 464, 616, 779).

The **unpublished memoirs** of former inmates used for the permanent exhibition are taken from the Buchenwald Archive and the archive of the Yad Vashem Memorial.

Of the numerous **published memoirs**, the present exhibition catalogue quotes from the following: Jean Améry, *Jenseits von Schuld und Sühne: Bewältigungsversuche eines Überwältigten*, Stuttgart: Klett-Cotta/DTV, 1988. Robert Antelme, *Das Menschengeschlecht: Als Deportierter in Deutschland*, München: DTV, 1990. *Das war Buchenwald!: Ein Tatsachenbericht*, Leipzig, 1945. Julius Freund, *O Buchenwald!*, Klagenfurt: Selbstverlag, 1945. Thomas Geve, *Geraubte Kindheit*, Konstanz: Südverlag, 1993. Fey von Hassell, *Niemals sich beugen: Erinnerungen einer Sondergefangenen der SS*, München, Zürich: Piper, 1991. Bruno Heilig, *Menschen am Kreuz*, Berlin: Neues Leben, 1948. Eugene Heimler, *Night of the Mist: Bei Nacht und Nebel*, Berlin: Hentrich, 1993. Benedikt Kautsky, *Teufel und Verdammte: Erfahrungen und Erkenntnisse aus sieben Jahren in deutschen Konzentrationslagern*, Wien: Wiener Volksbuchhandlungen, 1961. Friedrich Kochheim, *Bilanz: Erlebnisse und Gedanken*, Hannover: Culemann, 1952. Rolf Kralovitz, *ZehnNullNeunzig in Buchenwald: Ein jüdischer Häftling erzählt*, Köln: Walter-Meckauer-Kreis, 1996. Jacques Lusseyran, *Das wiedergefundene Licht: Die Lebensgeschichte eines Blinden im französischen Widerstand*, München: DTV, 1993. Walter Poller, *Arztschreiber in Buchenwald: Bericht des Häftlings 996 aus Block 36*, Offenbach am Main: Verlag das Segel, 1960. Christian Pineau, "'Ceux' qui ont vécu 'ça'", in: id. (ed.), *Buchenwald: Scènes prises sur le vif des horreurs Nazies. 78 planches couleurs et noir dessinées par André Favier, Pierre Mania*, Lyon, 1946. Jorge Semprun, *Was für ein schöner Sonntag*, Frankfurt am Main: Suhrkamp, 1980. Leonhard Steinwender, *Christus im Konzentrationslager: Wege der Gnade und des Opfers*, Salzburg: Selbstverlag, (1946). Isa Vermehren, *Reise durch den letzten Akt: Ravensbrück, Buchenwald, Dachau. Eine Frau berichtet*, Reinbek: Rowohlt, 1994. Fred Wander, *Der siebente Brunnen: Erzählung*, Berlin, Weimar: Aufbau, 1982. Elie Wiesel, *Die Nacht zu begraben, Elischa*, Frankfurt am Main, Berlin: Ullstein, 1996. Moritz Zahnwetzer, *KZ Buchenwald: Erlebnisbericht*, Kassel-Sandershausen: Zahnwetzer, (1946).

Passages from the treatise by the psychoanalyst Bruno Bettelheim, *Aufstand gegen die Masse. Die Chance des Individuums in der modernen Gesellschaft*, Frankfurt am Main: Fischer, 1995, to the extent that they relate directly to his imprisonment in Dachau and Buchenwald Concentration Camps in 1938/39, were treated as memoir literature and cited as such.

There is no detailed account of the history of the Buchenwald Concentration Camp. The salient publications in this context are listed in the **bibliography** compiled by Michael Ruck, *Bibliographie zum Nationalsozialismus*. Köln: Bund-Verlag, 1995, pp. 449-476. Rosemarie Hofmann and Wolfgang Röll provide a list of all relevant works published up to the beginning of the 1980s in their *Bibliographie zur Geschichte des faschistischen Konzentrationslagers und der Nationalen Mahn- und Gedenkstätte Buchenwald. Teil 1: Deutschsprachige Literatur. Teil 2: Fremdsprachige Literatur*, 2 vols. Weimar: Gedenkstätte Buchenwald, 1985-1986 (*Buchenwaldheft* 23/24 and 25).

Eugen Kogon's documentary report, *Der SS-Staat: Das System der deutschen Konzentrationslager*, München: Heyne, 1993 (26th edition) occupies a special position between the memoirs and the **documentations**. Large sections of this work, which is one of the first analyses of the concentration camp system, are still considered relevant today. Eugen Kogon worked from material compiled by political inmates upon request by the Intelligence Team of the Allied Forces Supreme Headquarters Psychological Warfare Division immediately after liberation. The materials were only edited, however, after the permanent exhibition was opened: David A. Hackett (ed.), *Der Buchenwald-Report: Bericht über das Konzentrationslager Buchenwald bei Weimar*, München: Beck, 1996. There is a relatively large fragment of this report in the Buchenwald Archive at the Memorial, and for the purposes of the present catalogue, the accounts comprised within that fragment were drawn from and quoted. A far shorter work than Kogon's analysis is an evaluation of the report produced by German political inmates, published about a year after the camp was liberated and entitled *KL Bu. Konzentrationslager Buchenwald:*

Bericht des Internationalen Lagerkomitees, Weimar: Thüringer Volksverlag, (1946).

Since the appearance of the first edition of the documentation published by the International Buchenwald-Dora Committee – *Buchenwald: Mahnung und Verpflichtung. Dokumente und Berichte,* Berlin: Kongreß, 1960 – a number of similar documentations have been published in various languages. The following were resourced directly for this work: Léon Bartimes, Eugène Bauler, Albert Beffort, Victor Holper, Léon Reuter, Michel Schaffner, *KZ Buchenwald 1937-1945. Das SS-Konzentrations-Lager bei Weimar in Thüringen,* Luxembourg: Imprimerie Saint-Paul, 1985. Pierre Durand, *Les armes de l'espoir: Les Français à Buchenwald et à Dora,* Paris: Éditions sociales, 1977. Erich Fein, Karl Flanner, *Rot-Weiß-Rot in Buchenwald. Die österreichischen politischen Häflinge im Konzentrationslager am Ettersberg bei Weimar 1938-1945,* Wien, Zürich: Europaverlag, 1987. Daniel Rochette, Jean-Marcel Vanhamme, *Les Belges à Buchenwald et dans ses kommandos exterieurs,* Bruxelles: de Méyère, 1976.

The documentation *Der "gesäuberte" Antifaschismus: Die SED und die roten Kapos von Buchenwald. Dokumente,* Berlin: Akademie, 1994, edited Lutz Niethammer (who also wrote the forward), was used as a necessary supplement to the other source books, which rarely mention the issue of Communist inmate functionaries in Buchenwald.

Aside from the above-mentioned protocols of the Nuremberg Trials, the present volume also quotes from: Ludwig Nestler (ed.), *Die faschistische Okkupationspolitik in Frankreich (1940-1944),* Berlin: DVW, 1990 (series: *Europa unterm Hakenkreuz. Die Okkupationspolitik des deutschen Faschismus (1938-1945, Vol. 4).* Peter Chroust (ed.), *Friedrich Mennecke: Innensichten eines medizinischen Täters im Nationalsozialismus. Eine Edition seiner Briefe 1935-1947,* 2 vols., Hamburg: Institut für Sozialforschung, 1988.

For the work with biographical sketches, we drew from original sources as well as from: Manfred Overesch, *Hermann Brill in Thüringen 1895-1946: Ein Kämpfer gegen Hitler und Ulbricht,* Bonn: Dietz, 1992. Martin Schumacher (ed.), *M.d.R. Die Reichstagsabgeordneten der Weimarer Republik in der Zeit des Nationalsozialismus: Politische Verfolgung, Emigration und Ausbürgerung 1933-1945. Eine biographische Dokumentation,* Düsseldorf: Droste, 1992.

Of the various **publications** we drew upon for the compilation of this catalogue, the first to be mentioned are the reports produced by the Institut für Zeitgeschichte for the Auschwitz Trial in 1964: Hans Buchheim, Martin Broszat, Hans-Adolf Jacobsen, Helmut Krausnick, *Anatomie des SS-Staates.* München: DTV, 1994 (6th edition). The following is a listing of only the most important monographs from among the wide selection of publications we used:

For the history of the first concentration camps, the birth of the concentration camp system and the background history to Buchenwald, the monographs by: Klaus Drobisch, Günther Wieland, *System der NS-Konzentrationslager 1933-1939,* Berlin: Akademie, 1993. Johannes Tuchel, *Konzentrationslager: Organisationsgeschichte und Funktion der "Inspektion der Konzentrationslager" 1934-1938,* Boppard am Rhein: Boldt, 1991 (*Schriften des Bundesarchivs,* 39). Idem, *Die Inspektion der Konzentrationslager 1938-1945. Das System des Terrors,* Berlin: Hentrich, 1994 (*Schriftenreihe der Stiftung Brandenburgische Gedenkstätten,* No. 1). Other studies on the structure of the SS: Heinz Höhne, *Der Orden unter dem Totenkopf: Die Geschichte der SS,* Bindlach: Gondrom, 1990. Tom Segev, *Die Soldaten des Bösen: Zur Geschichte der KZ-Kommandanten,* Reinbek: Rowohlt, 1992. Bernd Wegner, *Hitlers politische Soldaten: Die Waffen-SS 1933-1945. Leitbild, Struktur und Funktion einer nationalsozialistischen Elite,* Paderborn: Schöningh, 1990.

Characteristically, in the years during which Buchenwald Concentration Camp was established, its population did not comprise primarily political prisoners – as had been the case with previously existing camps – but rather those arrested within the framework of the police operations conducted in 1937 and 1938 against what were termed "habitual criminals" and the "work-shy". A fundamental publication in this context is: Detlev Peuckert, *Volksgenossen und Gemeinschaftsfremde. Anpassung, Ausmerze und Aufbegehren unter dem Nationalsozialismus,* Köln: Bund-Verlag, 1982. The monographs on the strategy of "general racial prevention" were not published until after the permanent exhibition had been opened: Wolfgang Ayaß, *Asoziale im Nationalsozialismus,* Stuttgart: Klett-Cotta, 1995. Ulrich Herbert, *Best: Biographische Studien über Radikalismus, Weltanschauung und Vernunft, 1903-1989,* Bonn: Dietz, 1996. Patrick Wagner, *Volksgemeinschaft ohne Verbrecher: Konzeption und Praxis der Kriminalpolizei in der Zeit der Weimarer Republik und des Nationalsozialismus,* Hamburg: Christians, 1996 (*Hamburger Beiträge für Sozial- und Zeitgeschichte,* Vol. 34).

Our account of the persecution of Sinti and Romani peoples is based primarily on Michael Zimmermann's monograph, *Rassenutopie und Genozid: Die nationalsozialistische "Lösung der Zigeunerfrage,"* Hamburg: Christians, 1996 (*Hamburger Beiträge für Sozial- und Zeitgeschichte,* Vol. 33).

The Memorial has published its own works on the subject of the internment of Jews and homosexuals at Buchenwald Concentration Camp: Wolfgang Röll, *Homosexuelle Häftlinge im Kon-*

zentrationslager Buchenwald, Weimar: Gedenkstätte Buchenwald, 1991. Harry Stein, *Juden in Buchenwald 1937-1942*. Weimar: Gedenkstätte Buchenwald 1992.

We used the documentation by Wolfgang Schumann, Ludwig Nestler et al. (ed.), *Europa unterm Hakenkreuz. Die Okkupationspolitik des deutschen Faschismus (1938-1945). Achtbändige Dokumentenedition*, Vols. 1-6, Berlin: DVW/ Akademie, 1988-1992 for an overview of persecution and deportation as it was practised in countries under German occupation.

The research results of Falk Pingel, *Häftlinge unter SS-Herrschaft: Widerstand, Selbstbehauptung und Vernichtung im Konzentrationslager*, Hamburg: Hoffmann und Campe, 1978 and Wolfgang Sofsky, *Die Ordnung des Terrors: Das Konzentrationslager*, Frankfurt am Main: Fischer, 1993 was fundamental to our depiction of the situation of the inmates. We drew from the work of Hermann Langbein, *...nicht wie die Schafe zur Schlachtbank: Widerstand in den nationalsozialistischen Konzentrationslagern 1938-1945*, Frankfurt am Main: Fischer, 1988 with regard to the issue of resistance.

There are very few individual studies on the day-to-day lives of the inmates of Buchenwald Concentration Camp: Georg Kühn, *Die Verbrechen der SS-Ärzte im Häftlingskrankenbau des Konzentrationslagers Buchenwald und die hygienischen Bedingungen im Lager*, Weimar: Gedenkstätte Buchenwald, 1988 (*Buchenwaldheft*, 30), and for a more general overview: Klaus Drobisch, *Widerstand in Buchenwald*, Berlin: Dietz, 1987.

For the role of forced labour and the commercial ambitions of the SS: Enno Georg, *Die wirtschaflichen Unternehmungen der SS*, Stuttgart: Deutsche Verlagsanstalt, 1963 (*Schriftenreihe der Vierteljahreshefte für Zeitgeschichte*, 7). Ulrich Herbert, *Fremdarbeiter: Politik und Praxis des "Ausländer-Einsatzes" in der Kriegswirtschaft des Dritten Reiches*, Berlin, Bonn: Dietz, 1986. Hermann Kaienburg, *"Vernichtung durch Arbeit": Der Fall Neuengamme. Die Wirtschaftsbestrebungen der SS und ihre Auswirkungen auf die Existenzbedingungen der KZ-Gefangenen*, Bonn: Dietz 1990. Walter Naasner, *Neue Machtzentren in der deutschen Kriegswirtschaft 1942-1945: Die Wirtschaftsorganisation der SS, das Amt des Generalbevollmächtigten für den Arbeitseinsatz und das Reichsministerium für Bewaffnung und Munition/Reichsministerium für Rüstung und Kriegsproduktion im nationalsozialistischen Herrschaftssystem*, Boppard am Rhein: Boldt, 1994 (*Schriften des Bundesarchivs*, 45).

Our depiction of the sub-camps draws from the account published in the fourth edition of the documentation *Buchenwald: Mahnung und Verpflichtung* (1983; see above), which is based upon *Verzeichnis der Haftstätten unter dem Reichs-*führer-SS (1933-1945): Konzentrationslager und deren Außenkommandos sowie andere Haftstätten unter dem Reichsführer-SS in Deutschland und deutsch besetzten Gebieten, Arolsen: Internationaler Suchdienst, 1979. Insight is also provided by: Gudrun Schwarz, *Die nationalsozialistischen Lager*, Frankfurt am Main, New York: Fischer, 1990. Martin Weinmann (ed.), *Das nationalsozialistische Lagersystem (CCP)*, Frankfurt am Main: Zweitausendeins, 1990.

There is no complete account of the system of sub-camps at Buchenwald Concentration Camp. There are, however, analyses which cover several of the sub-camps: Laurenz Demps, *Zum weiteren Ausbau des staatsmonopolistischen Apparates der faschistischen Kriegswirtschaft in den Jahren 1943 bis 1945 und zur Rolle der SS und der Konzentrationslager im Rahmen der Rüstungsproduktion, dargestellt am Beispiel der unterirdischen Verlagerung von Teilen der Rüstungsindustrie*, doctoral thesis, Berlin: Humboldt-Universität, 1971, and Christa Naumann, *Das arbeitsteilige Zusammenwirken von SS und deutschen Rüstungskonzernen 1942-1945, dargestellt am Beispiel der Außenkommandos des Konzentrationslagers Buchenwald*, doctoral thesis, Berlin: Humboldt-Universität, 1973.

For our description of Dora Sub-Camp, the later Mittelbau Concentration Camp, we made use of the following: Manfred Bornemann, *Geheimprojekt Mittelbau: Vom zentralen Öllager des Deutschen Reiches zur zentralen Raketenfabrik im Zweiten Weltkrieg*, Bonn: Bernard & Graefe, 1994. Idem, *Aktiver und passiver Widerstand im KZ Dora und im Mittelwerk: Eine Studie über den Widerstand im KZ Mittelbau-Dora*, Berlin, Bonn: Westkreuz, 1994. Angela Fiedermann, Torsten Heß, Markus Jaeger, *Das Konzentrationslager Dora-Mittelbau: Ein historischer Abriß*, Bad Münstereifel: Westkreuz, 1993. Alvin Gilens, *Aufbruch und Verzweiflung: Dimensionen von Dora*, Berlin, Bonn: Westkreuz, 1995. Also worthy of mention is the work of Joachim Neander, *Das Konzentrationslager "Mittelbau" in der Endphase der nationalsozialistischen Diktatur: Zur Geschichte des letzten im Dritten Reich gegründeten selbständigen Konzentrationslagers unter besonderer Berücksichtigung seiner Auflösungsphase*, Clausthal-Zellerfeld: Papierflieger, 1997. Our account of Ellrich Sub-Camp is based on: Manfred Bornemann, *Chronik des Lagers Ellrich 1944/45: Ein vergessenes Konzentrationslager wird neu entdeckt*, Nordhausen: Landratsamt, 1987.

Of the individual treatises appearing in the 1990s on the subject of the sub-camps in the Buchenwald system, not all were taken into consideration, since many were published too late for inclusion. The most important of them, however, deserve mention: Frank Baranowski, *Geheime Rüstungsprojekte in Südniedersachsen und Thüringen während der NS-Zeit*, Duderstadt: Mecke 1995. Karola Fings, *Messelager Köln:*

Ein KZ-Außenlager im Zentrum der Stadt, Köln: Emons, 1996. Martin Grieger, Klaus Völkel, *Das Außenlager "Annener Gußstahl" (AGW) des Konzentrationslagers Buchenwald September 1944-April 1945*, Essen: Klartext, 1997. Karl Hüser, *Wewelsburg 1933-1945: Kult- und Terrorstätte der SS. Eine Dokumentation*, Paderborn: Bonifatius 1982. Bernd Klewitz, *Die Arbeitssklaven der Dynamit Nobel*, Ramsloh: Engelbrecht, 1986. Idem, *Die Münchmühle. Außenkommando des Konzentrationslagers Buchenwald*, Marburg: Landkreis 1988. Martina Riese, *Die Geschichte des Außenkommandos des Konzentrationslagers Buchenwald im Reichsbahnausbesserungswerk Schwerte-Ost 6.4.1944-29.1.1945*, Schwerte 1989. Dieter Vaupel, *Das Außenkommando Hessisch-Lichtenau des Konzentrationslagers Buchenwald 1944/45: Eine Dokumentation*, Kassel: Gesamthochschulbibliothek, 1984. Bernd Joachim Zimmer, *Deckname Arthur: Das KZ-Außenkommando in der SS-Führerschule Arolsen*, Kassel: Gesamthochschulbibliothek, 1994.

There are at present only sketchy discussions of the women's sub-camps and the evacuation marches from Buchenwald Concentration Camp: Renate Ragwitz, *Die Frauenaußenkommandos des KZ Buchenwald*, Weimar: Gedenkstätte Buchenwald, 1982 (*Buchenwaldheft*, 15). Christine Schäfer, *Evakuierungstransporte des KZ Buchenwald und seiner Außenkommandos*, Weimar: Gedenkstätte Buchenwald, 1983 (*Buchenwaldheft*, 16).

The unpublished study by Werner Scherf, *Die Verbrechen der SS-Ärzte im KZ Buchenwald – der antifaschistische Widerstand im Häftlingskrankenbau. 2. Beitrag: Juristische Probleme*, doctoral thesis, Berlin: Humboldt-Universität, 1987 was particularly helpful in our treatment of the post-war trials conducted before Allied courts.

The minutes of the international academic conference held in Weimar in 1995, which sought to take stock of the status of research up to that point, were published after the present text had already been concluded: Ulrich Herbert, Karin Orth, Christoph Dieckmann (eds.), *Die nationalsozialistischen Konzentrationslager – Entwicklung und Struktur*, 2 vols. Göttingen: Wallstein, 1998.

Permanent exhibition, Section 4. 1: Deportation to Buchenwald, 1942-1945
Photo: G. Krynitzki

Ground Floor

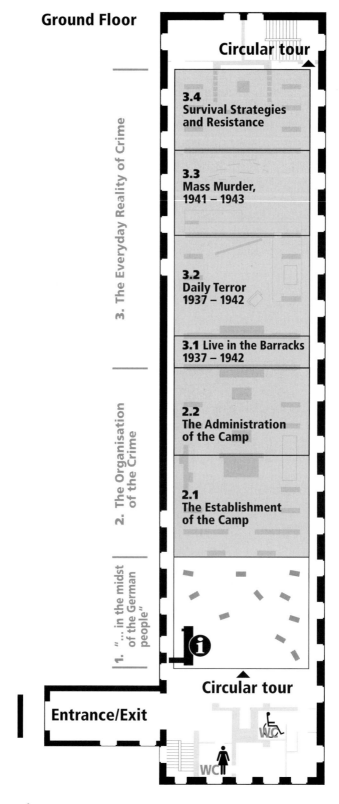

Circular tour

3. The Everyday Reality of Crime

3.4
Survival Strategies
and Resistance

3.3
Mass Murder,
1941 – 1943

3.2
Daily Terror
1937 – 1942

3.1 Live in the Barracks
1937 – 1942

2. The Organisation of the Crime

2.2
The Administration
of the Camp

2.1
The Establishment
of the Camp

1. "… in the midst of the German people"

Circular tour

Entrance/Exit

WC

WC

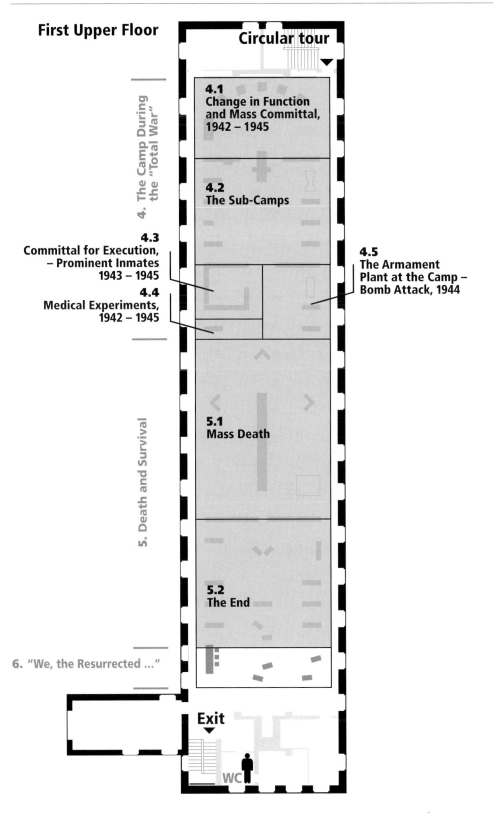

First Upper Floor

Circular tour

4. The Camp During the "Total War"

4.1
Change in Function and Mass Committal, 1942 – 1945

4.2
The Sub-Camps

4.3
Committal for Execution, – Prominent Inmates 1943 – 1945

4.4
Medical Experiments, 1942 – 1945

4.5
The Armament Plant at the Camp – Bomb Attack, 1944

5. Death and Survival

5.1
Mass Death

5.2
The End

6. "We, the Resurrected ..."

Exit

WC

The Permanent Exhibition on the History of Buchenwald Concentration Camp

Opened: April 8, 1995

Scientific direction:
Dr. Harry Stein

Idea and conception:
Rikola-Gunnar Lüttgenau, Dr. Harry Stein

Scientific assistants:
Rikola-Gunnar Lüttgenau (2.2/4.3/6)
Dr. Vera Neumann (5.1/5.2)
Wolfgang Röll (4.1/4.2/4.5)
Dr. Irmgard Seidel (women's sub-camps)
Friedbert Staar (2.1)
Dr. Sonja Staar (3.1)
Sabine Stein (3.4)
Dr. Harry Stein (1/3.2/3.3/3.4)

External scientific assistants:
Dr. Klaus Drobisch (research on SS)
Karola Fings (research on Sinti and Romani)
Franka Günther (research on French and Belgians in Buchenwald)
Video production: Dr. Wilhelm Rösing, Frankfurt am Main
Chronos Film GmbH, Kleinmachnow

Exhibition design and reconstruction of former depot:
Architekturbüro Kleineberg, Braunschweig
Uwe Kleineberg, B.Eng. – Axel Pohl, B.Eng., Architects
Assistants:
Manuela Heller, B.Eng., Architect
Ralf Schönhoff

Glass case construction:
Firma Glasbau Hahn, Frankfurt am Main

Exhibition design and graphic design:
Hinz & Kunst – Graphische Werkstatt und Verlags GmbH, Braunschweig
Peter Wentzler
Assistants:
Antje Koos
Dirk Laube

Artistic installations:
Józef Szajna, Warsaw
Ohannes Tapyuli, Braunschweig

Catalogue:
Dr. Harry Stein (text and editing)
Sabine Stein (exhibition register)
German-English translation: Judith Rosenthal, Frankfurt am Main
Editing of English version: Katie Machalek

Permanent exhibition, Section 5. 2: Liberation
Photo: G. Krynitzki

Permanent exhibition, Section 1: "in the midst of the German people"
Photo: G. Krynitzki

The dimensions of the exhibition objects are listed in the following sequence: length × height × width.

1. "… in the midst of the German people."

1/1 The Defeat and the Legend of the Reich
Image/text collage

1/2 The Economic Crisis
Image/text collage

1/3 Consensus and Participation
Image/text collage

1/4 Resistance
Image/text collage

1/5 Anti-Semitism
Image/text collage

1/6 The Persecution and Extermination of the Jews
Image/text collage

1/7 The Persecution and Extermination of the Sinti and Romani
Image/text collage

1/8 The Meritocratic Community
Image/text collage

1/9 Terror, Social Racism, Forced Labour, Extermination – The Concentration Camps
Image/text collage

1/10 Weimar
Image/text collage

2. The Organisation of Crime

2.1 The Establishment of the Camp

Weimar-Buchenwald-Weimar
2/1 "Ettersberg Concentration Camp" – The decision concerning the location
Theodor Eicke to the Thuringian Ministry of the interior re construction of a new concentration camp in Thuringia, Oct. 17, 1936; DIN A 4; ThHStA, KZ Bu 19, Bl. 21. Hellmuth Gommlich to the Thuringian Geological Land Inspection re construction of a new concentration camp in Thuringia, Apr. 24, 1937; DIN A 4; ThHStA, KZ Bu 41, Bl. 8. Ettersberg, 1933; photo; 17.3 × 12.8 cm; *Kampf und Sieg in Thüringen*, Weimar, 1934. Theodor Eicke to Heinrich Himmler re the name of the concentration camps, July 24, 1937; DIN A 4; ThHStA, KZ Bu 19, Bl. 156. Karl Koch to the Thuringian State Ministry of the Interior re change of name to Buchenwald Concentration Camp, Post Weimar, July 28, 1937; 21 × 15 cm; ThHStA, KZ Bu 19, Bl. 22. Hellmuth Gommlich; passport photo; 4.5 × 6.5 cm; ThHStA, PA 2740.

2/2 Weimar
City map, 1939, 46.5 × 56 cm, Stadtmuseum Weimar. Button for May 1, 1934; ⌀ 3 cm; SGB. Gang of inmate labourers in Gaberndorf near Weimar, 1939; photo; 6 × 6 cm; Rolf Lange, Gaberndorf. Leaflet "Besucht Thüringen – Das Grüne Herz Deutschlands" (Visit Thuringia – The Green Heart of Germany), 29 × 20 cm; Stadtmuseum Weimar.

2/3 Residential addresses and restaurants
Commander's Office Order No. 13, May 31, 1941; DIN A 4; BwA, HKW-Film 1. Commander's Office Order No. 6, Feb. 28, 1941; DIN A 4; BwA, HKW-Film 1. Commander's Office Order No. 158, June 10, 1940; DIN A 4; BwA, HKW-Film 1. Official telephone directory, Reich Postal Directorate Erfurt (Centre), 1943; 40 × 30 cm; SGB.

2/4 Bus connection
Omnibus schedule, 1942; 20 × 29 cm; SGB. Signpost Buchenwald bus stop, 1939; photo; 6.5 × 10 cm; SGB. Commander's Office Order No. 91, Apr. 17, 1939; DIN A 4; BwA, HKW-Film 1. Commander's Office Order No. 171, Oct. 8, 1940; DIN A 4; BwA, HKW-Film 1.

2/5 Cremation of inmates' corpses in the Weimar Municipal Crematorium
Chapel and crematorium on the Main Cemetery of Weimar; photo; 13 × 6.9 cm; Lehrmann, A., *Neue Stadtbaukunst*, Weimar, Berlin/Leipzig/Vienna, 1928, p. 30. Weimar Crematory; photo; 13.4 × 10 cm; Lehrmann, A., *Neue Stadtbaukunst*, Weimar, Berlin/Leipzig/Vienna, 1928, p. 33. Cross section of Weimar Crematorium; photo; 8.2 × 7 cm; Lehrmann, A., *Neue Stadtbaukunst*, Weimar, Berlin/Leipzig/Vienna, 1928, p. 33. Copy of an instruction from the chief burgomaster of the City of Weimar re the cremation of dead inmates in the Municipal Crematorium, Aug. 4, 1937; DIN A 4; ThHStA, NS 4 Bu 35, Bl. 2. Municipal Bureau of Cemeteries to an inmate's relative (draft), Oct. 24, 1938; DIN A 4; Stadtarchiv Weimar, 6-66-78/1. Cemetery Office of the Jewish community of Vienna to the Municipal Cemetery Administration of Weimar re the shipment of urns of deceased Jews, Apr. 4, 1940; DIN A 4; Stadtarchiv Weimar, 6-66-78/5. Urn lid, Weimar Crematorium; ⌀ 11.5 cm; SGB.

2/6 Weimar Department of Works
Weimar Dept. of Works to the General Inspection for Water and Energy re supply of power to Gustloff-Werk II, Aug. 11, 1942; DIN A 4, 2 sheets; BwA, 44-2-3. Fritz Sauckel, Reich Defence Commissary in Thuringia, to the Weimar Dept. of Works re supply of power to Buchenwald, Mar. 27, 1943; DIN A 4; BwA, 44-3-2.

2/7 SS funeral in Weimar
Thüringer Gauzeitung, May 19, 1938; 48 × 65 cm; Stadtarchiv Weimar. *Das Schwarze Korps*, May 26, 1938; SGB. SS Section XXII to Heinrich Himmler, June 2, 1938; DIN A 4; BwA, HKW-Film 1. Buchenwald Commander's Headquarters to Weimar Cemetery Administration, July 13, 1939; DIN A 4; BwA, 45-1-7, Bl. 7. Weimar Cemetery Administration memo re grave maintenance costs, July 18, 1939; DIN A 4; BwA, 45-1-7, Bl. 8.

A Concentration Camp near Weimar
2/8 Drawing board plans
Design for a concentration camp in the rural district of Weimar, June 1, 1937; photocopy; 78 × 69 cm; SGB. Entrance to "Ettersberg Concentration Camp" construction site, July 9, 1937; photo; 17.5 × 12.5 cm; SGB.

2/9 First inmate transports
Construction of the first barrack foundations by members of the SS, July 9, 1937; 4 photos; 17.5 × 12.5 cm; SGB. Assembling the barrack segments, July 15, 1937; 2 photos; 17.5 × 12. 5 cm; SGB. Committal of the first inmates from the disbanded Lichtenburg Concentration Camp for the construction of "Ettersberg Concentration Camp," July 15, 1937; 2 photos; 17.5 × 12.5 cm; SGB. Inmate transport from the disbanded Sachsenburg Concentration Camp for the construction of "Ettersberg Concentration Camp," July 27, 1937; photo; 14 × 9 cm; SGB.

2/10 Inmates' camp: construction begins
Field forge and barrack furnishings, July 23, 1937; photo; 17.5 × 12.5 cm; SGB. Field kitchen, July 23, 1937; photo; 17.5 × 12.5 cm; SGB. Surveying work and foundation construction, July 23, 1937; photo; 17.5 × 12.5 cm; SGB. Excavation for the first SS "Hundertschaft" barracks, Aug. 4, 1937; photo; 17.5 × 12.5 cm; SGB. View of camp from provisional watchtower, Aug. 4, 1937; photo; 17.5 × 12.5 cm; SGB. Foundations of Barracks 13 and 15, Aug. 20, 1937; photo; 17.5 × 12.5 cm; SGB. Completed Barracks 1 to 6, Aug. 20, 1937; photo; 17.5 × 12.5 cm; SGB. Work on muster ground, Aug. 20, 1937; photo; 17.5 × 12.5 cm; SGB. Heinrich Himmler re inmate committals to concentration camp, Sept. 20, 1937; 2 DIN A 4 sheets; ThHStA, KZ Bu 19, Bl. 130.

2/11 SS area: construction begins
Skeleton structure of first SS "Hundertschaft" barrack, Aug. 20, 1937; photo; 17.5 × 12.5 cm; SGB. Foundations for second and third SS "Hundertschaft" barracks, Aug. 20, 1937; photo; 17.5 × 12.5 cm; SGB. Completed SS "Hundertschaft" barracks, Nov. 10, 1937; photo; 17.5 × 12.5 cm; SGB. Former SS "Hundertschaft" barracks, 1994; photo; 12 × 9 cm; SGB. Construction of commander's mansion, Sept. 30, 1937; 2 photos; 17.5 × 12.5 cm; SGB. Report by Richard Seifert,

1965; DIN A 4; BwA 52-11-699. Punitive report, Nov. 17, 1937; DIN A 4; BwA. Machine gun watchtower at camp entrance, Sept. 7, 1937; photo; 17.5 × 12.5 cm; SGB. Construction of main gate building, Nov. 10, 1937; photo; 17.5 × 12.5 cm; SGB. Construction of Watchtower 1 on main gate building, Nov. 10, 1937; photo; 17.5 × 12.5 cm; SGB. Construction of road through command area to main gate building ("Caracho Path"), Spring 1938; photo; 18 × 13 cm; SGB. Petrol tank for headquarters filling station, spring 1938; photo; 18 × 13 cm; SGB. Chief of SS administration to Reich governor of Thuringia re acquisition of land, Mar. 3, 1938; DIN A 4; ThHStA, KZ Bu 19/1, Bl. 130. Commander's Office Order No. 124, Oct. 20, 1939; DIN A 4; BwA, HKW-Film 1.

2/12 Construction plan, 1937
Map of Buchenwald Concentration Camp, July 23, 1937; photocopy; 74 × 61.5 cm; SGB.

2/13-2/14 Camp fence
Concrete fence posts, 1937; 415 cm; SGB. Special Commander's Office Order, Aug. 14, 1939; DIN A 4; ThHStA, NS 4 Bu 33. Watchtower 23 at eastern gate, 1945; photo; 22 × 17 cm; SGB. Commander's Office Order No. 99, July 23, 1942; DIN A 4; ThHStA, NS 4 Bu 33. Fragment of an M 35/I submachine gun, 1937; 60 cm; SGB. Fragment of an MG 34 machine gun, 1937; 126 cm; SGB. Machine gun belt, 1937; Ø 30 cm; SGB. Camp fence at Watchtower 18, 1939; photo; 22 × 17cm; SGB. 7 porcelain insulators, 1938; SGB. Barbed wire from the camp fence, 1938; 20 remnants 30-80 cm; 3 Rosenthal-brand porcelain insulators, 1939; SGB. Rosenthal-brand porcelain cup from the SS casino, 1938; SGB. Advertisement for Rosenthal porcelain; photo; 13 × 18 cm; *Kunst im Dritten Reich*, Year 2, 1938.

2/15 Power supply system
M.A.N. diesel emergency set with generator, 1939; 350 × 190 × 150 cm; SGB. Plan for radio, telephone and signal cables for inmates' camp and SS command area, Sept. 28, 1939; photocopy; 80 × 55 cm; SGB. Power supply plan, June/July 1940, supplemented Aug. 17, 1942; photocopy; 83 × 50cm; SGB. Power supply plan, Oct. 15/16, 1940, supplemented Aug. 17, 1942; photocopy; 90 × 68 cm; SGB. Letter from SS administration chief to the Thuringian State Ministry of the Interior re power supply contract for Buchenwald Concentration Camp, Dec. 16, 1937; 15 × 21 cm, 2 sheets; BwA, 44-3-2. File memo re power supply to Buchenwald Concentration Camp until 1953, Aug. 14, 1942; DIN A 4; BwA, 44-3-2.

Buchenwald Concentration Camp Construction Phases
2/16-2/17 Construction phases (model with diagram/photo)

Buchenwald 1937/1941/1944; 3 diagrams; 80 × 65 cm. Bornems Lenart, "Roll Call Buchenwald," 1944; India ink drawing; 61.4 × 30.8 cm; SGB. Camp model; SGB. Garden lot, 1944; photo; 12 × 9 cm; SGB. Disinfection station, 1944; photo; 12 × 9 cm; SGB. Crematorium, 1942; photo; 12 × 9 cm; SGB. Crematorium courtyard, 1945; photo; 12 × 9 cm; SGB. Laundry and depot building in inmates' camp, 1945; photo; 12 × 9 cm; SGB. Entrance to Fichtenhain Special Camp, 1944; photo; 12 × 9 cm; SGB. Inmate roll call, 1944; photo; 12 × 9 cm; SGB. Army stables as inmate accommodation in Little Camp, 1942; photo; 12 × 9 cm; SGB. View of Little Camp, Block 52 (stable barrack), from stone Block 47, 1945; photo; 12 × 9 cm; SGB. Former inmates' canteen, 1994; photo; 12 × 9 cm; SGB. Cinema barrack in inmates' camp, 1945; photo; 12 × 9 cm; SGB. Brothel in inmates' camp, 1943; photo; 12 × 9 cm; SGB. Camp road to inmates' infirmary, 1945; 2 photos; 12 × 9 cm; SGB. Tent camp in Little Camp, 1945; photo; 12 × 9 cm; Georges Angéli. Inmates' infirmary, 1944; photo; 12 × 9 cm; SGB. Motor winch in Quarry II, 1944; photo; 12 × 9 cm; SGB. Ramp in Quarry II, 1945; photo; 12 × 9 cm; SGB. Main entrance to Gustloff-Werk II, 1943; photo; 12 × 9 cm; SGB. Gustloff-Werk II civilian labourer barracks, 1943; photo; 12 × 9 cm; SGB. Construction of Gustloff-Werk II fire pond, 1944; photo; 12 × 9 cm; SGB. Gustloff-Werk II, Hall 7, 1944; photo; 12 × 9 cm; SGB. Construction of track system for Buchenwald Station, 1944; photo; 12 × 9 cm; SGB. DAW G.m.b.H workshop barracks in the camp, 1942; photo; 12 × 9 cm; SGB. Queue of inmates on Caracho Path, 1944; photo; 12 × 9 cm; SGB. SS Department of Economic Administration to command headquarters of Buchenwald Concentration Camp, June 24, 1942; DIN A 4; ThHStA, KZ Bu 18/1, Bl. 19. Building of SS music band and armoury, 1943; photo; 12 × 9 cm; SGB. Riding hall stable, 1945; photo; 12 × 9 cm; SGB. Riding hall, 1945; photo; 12 × 9 cm; SGB. SS barracks at Quarry II, 1944; photo; 12 × 9 cm; SGB. Mansion of Camp Commander Koch, 1942; photo; 12 × 9 cm; SGB. Eagle house of SS falcon lodge, 1945; photo; 12 × 9 cm; SGB. Main gate building, 1945; photo; 12 × 9 cm; SGB. Signpost in command headquarters area, 1941; photo; 12 × 9 cm; SGB. Signpost for zoo; photo; 12 × 9 cm; SGB. Bears' cave at Buchenwald Zoological Garden, 1939; photo; 12 × 9 cm; SGB. Signpost at Buchenwald bus stop, 1939; photo; 12 × 9 cm; SGB. Construction office following air attack on Aug. 24, 1944; photo; 12 × 9 cm; SGB. Signpost to Buchenwald Concentration Camp, 1945; photo; 12 × 9 cm; SGB.

SS Production Plants in Buchenwald

2/18 Quarry

NSDAP regional headquarters of Thuringia to Regional Department for Four-Year Plan, Nov. 2, 1937; DIN A 4; ThHStA, KZ Bu 18/1, Bl. 182. Thuringian Regional Department for Four-Year Plan to camp commander of Buchenwald, Dec. 22, 1937; DIN A 4; ThHStA, KZ Bu 18/1, Bl. 183. Quarry I, Sept. 7, 1937; photo; 17.5 × 12.5 cm; SGB. Quarry II, Sept. 7, 1937; photo; 17.5 × 12.5 cm; SGB. Limestone from Quarry II, 30 × 15 × 15 cm; SGB.

2/19 German Erd- und Steinwerke G.m.b.H. (DEST) Berlstedt Sub-Camp

Oswald Pohl to Bank der Deutschen Arbeit AG re financing of a clinker plant near Weimar, May 4, 1938; 2 DIN A4 sheets; BwA, 4-41-10. Commander's Office Order No. 147, Mar. 22, 1940; DIN A 4; BwA, HKW-Film 1. Accident report from Berlstedt Brickworks Sub-Camp, Dec. 9, 1938; DIN A 4; ThHStA, KZ Bu 12, Bl. 110. DEST business report, Weimar plant, 1940; 35 × 26 cm; BA Potsdam, Film 11135. Floor clinker from Berlstedt Brickworks Sub-Camp; 24 × 3 × 11 cm; SGB. Brick from Berlstedt Brickworks Sub-Camp; 25 × 12 × 6 cm; SGB. Vase model; DEST Berlstedt, 1939; 18 × 5 cm; SGB. 5 flower pots, DEST Berlstedt, 1939; 10 × 6 cm; SGB. Clay urns, DEST Berlstedt, 1944; SGB.

2/20-2/21 German Ausrüstungswerke G.m.b.H. (DAW)

Oswald Pohl to camp commander re future tasks to be carried out by concentration camp repair workshops, July 11, 1942; 2 sheets DIN A 4; ThHStA, KZ Bu 18/1, Bl. 15 and 16. SS Department of Economic Administration to commander of Buchenwald Concentration Camp re production of skis, July 20, 1942; DIN A 4; ThHStA, KZ Bu 18/1, Bl. 9. Hermann Pister to SS Department of Economic Administration, July 20, 1942; DIN A 4; ThHStA, KZ Bu 18/1, Bl. 8. Landscape, 1940 (inmate work); oil on cardboard; 39 × 33 cm; SGB. Franz Ambrasath, "Fisherman," 1939; oil painting; 23 × 22 cm; SGB. Cigarette case, 1939 (inmate work); lime wood; 9 × 14 × 2.5 cm; SGB. Owl, 1940 (inmate work); lime wood, dyed; 5.5 × 12.5 × 5 cm; SGB. Cog, 1939 (inmate work); lime wood; 40 × 45 × 17 cm; SGB. Jewellery box, 1940 (inmate work); beechwood; 17 × 4.5 × 11 cm; SGB.

The SS Totenkopf Squadrons

2/22 The SS Totenkopf regiments

Regiment Order of the Day No. 87, Apr. 30, 1938; DIN A 4; ThHStA, KZ Bu 18/1, Bl. 226. Age structure of the SS Totenkopf squadrons, Dec. 31, 1938; *Statistisches Jahrbuch der Schutzstaffel der NSDAP*, Berlin 1938. Regiment Order of the Day No. 88, May 3, 1938; DIN A 4; ThHStA, KZ Bu 18/1, Bl. 227. Commander's Office

Order No. 136, Dec. 18, 1939; DIN A 4; HKW, KL Buchenwald, sygn.2, str.132. SS Totenkopf Regiment "Thüringen" in Weimar (Karlsplatz) on Thuringian NSDAP Gautag, Nov. 7, 1938; photo; 22 × 14; *Der Führer in Weimar* 1925-1938 (brochure), Weimar, 1938, p. 66. SS Totenkopf, 1938; 3 cm; SGB. 2 SS collar patches, 1938; SGB. SS identification tag, 1938; 7 × 5 cm; SGB. SS Hauptscharführer service and dress uniform, 1938; SGB. SS helmet, 1938; SGB. SS dagger, 1938; 37.5 cm; SGB. SS belt buckle, 1938; 6.3 × 4.8 × 1.7 cm; SGB. Wilhelm Burböck to Philipp Grimm re Yuletide, Dec. 20, 1941; DIN A 4; ThHStA, NS 4 Bu 36. Philipp Grimm to Wilhelm Burböck, Dec. 23, 1941; DIN A 4; ThHStA, NS 4 Bu 36. Yule candelabra, 1939; clay; Porzellanmanufaktur Allach; 22 × 12 × 12 cm; SGB. Special Commander's Office Order, Mar. 8, 1940; DIN A 4; HKW, KL Buchenwald, sygn.3, str. 20. Bulletin re "Pol. Gemeinschaftsstunde" (Polish community hour), May 5, 1942; DIN A 4; BwA, Majdanek – Film.

2/23 Leisure time and sports
Folder "Körperschule – Der Energiemensch" (body training – the energetic human being); 23 × 31 cm; SGB. Commander's Office Order No. 98, June 8, 1939; DIN A 4; HKW, KL Buchenwald, sygn. 2, str. 39. Gauze package; 20 × 2.5 cm; SGB. Bandage; 21 × 18 × 3 cm; SGB. Foot powder; bottle; 6 × 1.3 cm; SGB. Set of bandages; 8 × 3 × 5 cm; SGB. Commander's Office Order No. 122, Oct. 12, 1939; DIN A 4; HKW, KL Buchenwald, sygn. 2, str. 102. 8 soup plates, SS casino, 1938-1941; ∅ 23 cm; SGB. Coffee pot, SS casino, 1941; 20 × 28 cm; SGB. 5 coffee cups, SS casino, 1941; SGB. Wine bottle, SS casino, 1945; 8 × 28 cm, SGB. Fragments of a soup pot, SS Casino, 1941; SGB. Soup plate, SS casino, 1942; ∅ 20 cm; SGB. SS men with beer bottles, ca. 1940; photo; 11.5 × 8 cm; ThHStA, NS 4 Bu 62. Chair, SS casino, ca. 1939; 50 × 70 × 50 cm; SGB. Postcard, SS casino, 1939; 13 × 8 cm; SGB. 6 casino chips, 1939; ∅ 2.7 cm; SGB. Knife from SS casino, 1939; 23.5 cm; SGB. Beer crate, Jenaer Bier; 45 × 35 × 25 cm; SGB.

2/24 SS Buchenwald falcon yard
Deutscher Falkenorden, No. 4, 1937; photo cover page; 21 × 29.5 cm; DB Leipzig. Fritz Sauckel with Italian guest in Buchenwald falcon yard, 1940; photo; 10.8 × 8 cm; SGB. Commander's Office Order No. 124, Oct. 20, 1939; DIN A 4; HKW, KL Buchenwald, sygn. 2, str. 107. Commander's instruction to guards re public visit to falcon yard, June 21, 1941; DIN A 4; ThHStA, NS 4 Bu 33. "SS Falkenhof," brochure published by command headquarters of Weimar-Buchenwald, 1938; 15.2 × 21 cm; SGB. Photo folder of falcon yard, 1941; 8.5 × 6 cm; Stadtmuseum Weimar. Eagle house of the Buchenwald falcon yard, 1941; photo; 24 × 17 cm; SGB. 29 Reich coins, 1935-1942; SGB.

2/25 The family of Commander Koch
Commander Karl Koch and wife, 1938; photo; 14 × 9.5 cm; SGB. Bojasnij, "Villa Koch," 1944; tempera paint; 30 × 40 cm; SGB. Office of camp commander, 1938; photo; 13 × 18 cm; SGB. 2 pages from Koch photo album; reproduction 29.5 × 21 cm; NARA. Personal data form, Karl Koch, Apr. 18, 1943; DIN A 4; BA BDC, file 0 329 B. Information on arrest of Karl Koch, Aug. 25, 1943; DIN A 4; BA BDC, file 0 329 B. Family cradle, 1939; wood; 60 × 41 × 39 cm; SGB.

2/26 SS "clan" and family
Das Schwarze Korps, Aug. 10, 1939, p. 5; 30 × 42 cm; DB Leipzig. Order by Himmler, Oct. 28, 1939; DIN A 4; BA Koblenz NSD 41/21. Commander's Office Order No. 137, Jan. 10, 1940; DIN A 4; HKW, KL Buchenwald, sygn. 3, str. 2. Garrison physician of the Weimar Armed SS re procurement of condoms, May 25, 1943; 21 × 15; ThHStA, KZ Bu 10. Condom package, 1943; 4 cm; SGB. Marriage certificate Petrick, Nov. 13, 1944; DIN A 4; BwA, 45-4-12.

2.2 The Administration of the Camp

Dept. 1: Camp Command
2/27 Structure of camp hierarchy and functions
Structure of camp assignment and functions; diagram.

2/28 Books and stamps of camp command
Incoming mail stamp; replica; SGB. Richard Glücks re obligation to register incoming orders, Feb. 2, 1942; 21 × 15 cm; BwA. Register of incoming radio messages, 1943; daybook; 21 × 31 cm; ThHStA, NS 4 Bu 65. Register of outgoing radio messages, 1943; daybook; 21 × 31 cm; ThHStA, NS 4 Bu 66.

2/29 Adjutant Hackmann
Hermann Hackmann, 1940; passport photo; 4 × 6 cm; BA BDC. CV for marriage license from RuSHA, 1943; DIN A 4; BA BDC, RuSHA file on Hackmann. SS men in Buchenwald, ca. 1939; photo; 13 × 18 cm; ThHStA, NS 4 Bu 62.

2/30 Camp Commander Pister
Hermann Pister, after 1931; photo; 4 × 6 cm; BA BDC. Fürst zu Waldeck to Himmler re Pister's promotion, Mar. 4, 1943; DIN A 4; BA BDC, RuSHA file on Pister. Presentation of First-Class Distinguished Service Cross by Heinrich Himmler, June 21, 1943; DIN A 4; BA BDC, RuSHA file on Pister. Promotion to regiment commander, Oct. 5, 1943; 2 DIN A 4 sheets; BA BDC, RuSHA file on Pister.

2/31 Everyday work at command headquarters
Pister's desk set, carved by inmate Bruno Apitz; wood; 53 × 29 × 40 cm; SGB. Sketchbook of adjutant's office, 1942; reproduction; 21 × 15 cm; NARA. Telephone, SS area; Siemens & Halske, 1929 model; 25 × 15 × 16 cm; SGB.

Command headquarters telephone directory, ca. 1942; DIN A 4; ThHStA, Ministerium für Wirtschaft und Arbeit 3999, Bl. 51, Lesehefter. Request for information on whereabouts of R. Kratochvil; A 5; ThHStA, NS 4 Bu 104. Request for information on whereabouts of Frank; DIN A 4; ThHStA, NS 4 Bu 104, Bl. 569. Commander's repay re Frank; 21 × 15 cm; ThHStA, NS 4 Bu 104, Bl. 568. Hand-written memo: "liegt im Judenrevier" ("presently in Jews' infirmary"); DIN A 7; ThHStA, NS 4 Bu 104, Bl. 200. Lawyer's request; DIN A 4; ThHStA, NS 4 Bu 104, Bl. 201. Request re Barth; DIN A 5; ThHStA, NS 4 Bu 104, Bl. 715. Commander's reply re Barth; A 5; ThHStA, NS 4 Bu 104, Bl. 714. Request re Woll; DIN A 5; ThHStA, NS 4 Bu 104, Bl. 22. Commander's repay re Woll; A 5; ThHStA, NS 4 Bu 104, Bl. 21.

Dept. II: The Political Department: Branch of the Gestapo

2/32 Committal by local detective police and secret police stations

Radio message from Reich Detective Police Office to the detective police stations, Aug. 6, 1937; 16.5 × 11.8 cm; ThHStA, KZ Bu 9, Bl. 129. Franz Plath's certificate of discharge from penitentiary, 1937; 22 × 30.1 cm; BwA, 52-11-122. Preventive custody order for Franz Plath, 1937; 20.9 × 29.7 cm; BwA, 52-11-122. Punitive report on Ernst Frommhold, Sept. 18, 1937; DIN A 4; ThHStA, NS 4 Bu 101, Bl. 5.

2/33 Registration of inmates

Inmate's personal record card; 20.5 × 14.9 cm; BwA 52-11-790. Inspector of the Concentration Camps re classification of concentration camps, after 1940; DIN A 4; ThHStA, NS 4 Bu 31, Bl. 1. Inmates card of SS Department of Economic Administration, 1944; 21 × 15 cm; BwA, 46-1-19. Request re miners among inmates of Buchenwald, Jan. 25, 1945; 19.9 × 13.9 cm; BwA, 46-1-19. Punched card list of the miners among the inmates of Buchenwald, Jan. 25, 1945; DIN A 4; BwA, 46-1-19. Hollerith (card-punching) machine; Dehomag D-11; photo; SGB.

Dept. III E: Labour Service until 1942

2/34 Dept. III E: Labour allocation

One hundred labour allocation slips, 1939; 20.5 × 14.5 cm; BwA. Wilhelm Burböck re duties of labour allocation officer (Preventive Custody Camp Officer "E") at morning roll call, Nov. 27, 1941; DIN A 4; ThHStA, KZ Bu 18/1, Bl. 170. Form: "Allocation of professions in the camp," Apr. 28, 1942; DIN A 4; ThHStA, NS 4 Bu 206. SS Department of Economic Administration to camp commander re inmates working on Sundays, June 3, 1942; DIN A 4; ThHStA, KZ Bu 18/1, Bl. 382. Claim voucher, 1940; DIN A 4; ThHStA, NS 4 Bu 36, Bl. 10.

2/35 Selection

Letter from Concentration Camp Inspector re "sending along of sick inmates," May 23, 1941; DIN A 4; YVA O 51/5, Bl. 11. Memo by labour allocation officer re selection of sick Jewish inmates, Jan. 20, 1945; 14.6 × 10.5 cm; ThHStA, KZ Bu 9, Bl. 19. List of allocation of labour detachments in Buchenwald, Apr. 17, 1942; DIN A 4; BwA.

2/36 Labour Allocation Officer Grimm

Philipp Grimm, 1934; passport photo; 4 × 6 cm; BA BDC. Grimm's office re missing lists on inmate allocation, Apr. 11, 1942; DIN A 4; ThHStA, KZ Bu 18/1, Bl. 67. File memo of radio station re Grimm, Apr. 12, 1942; DIN A 4; ThHStA, KZ Bu 18/1, Bl. 69.

Dept. III Preventive Custody Camp

2/37 Hans Hüttig, second officer in charge of preventive custody camp

Signpost in command headquarters area to inmates' camp, 1940; wood; 193 × 117 × 13 cm; SGB. Hans Hüttig, 1937; passport photo; 4 × 6 cm; BA BDC. Hans Hüttig in the camp, 1938; photo; 13 × 20.7 cm; SGB. Hans Hüttig, 1938; photo; 9 × 13 cm; BA BDC, RuSHA file on Hüttig. Personal data form, 1941; DIN A 4; BA BDC, RuSHA file on Hüttig. Assessment by Camp Commander Karl Koch, June 20, 1938; 2 DIN A 4 sheets; BA BDC, RuSHA file on Hüttig.

2/38 Formation of inmate groups

Pocket daybook of Hermann Hofschulte, officer in charge of the records department, 1945; cardboard; 24.7 × 11 cm; BwA, 46-1-39. Inmates' roll call, 1944; photo; 18 × 13 cm; SGB. List of inmate groups, Sept. 14, 1938; DIN A 4; ThHStA, NS 4 Bu 137, Bl. 368. Preventive custody camp report, Apr. 30, 1940; DIN A 4; ThHStA, NS 4 Bu 143, Bl. 1. Preventive custody camp report (women), Dec. 15, 1944; DIN A 4; ThHStA, NS 4 Bu 143, Bl. 376. Teaching chart for members of SS Totenkopf squadrons in Dachau, ca. 1937; reproduction; 55.5 × 71.5 cm; SGB.

2/39 Activities of Dept. III: Preventive custody camp command

2 daily record books of block officer, 1941; DIN A 4; ThHStA, NS 4 Bu 20. Assignment of SS block officers, Mar. 10, 1945; DIN A 4; ThHStA, KZ Bu 18/1, Bl. 287. Receipt book for electric torches, 1937/38; 41.7 × 17.3 cm; BwA, 5-3-22. Report on the loss of electric torches, Dec. 8, 1937; DIN A 4; ThHStA, NS 4 Bu 102, Bl. 3.

2/40 Joseph Kestel, labour detachment and block officer

Joseph Kestel, ca. 1934; passport photo; 4 × 6 cm; BA BDC. Concentration camp service instruction (camp regulations), 1941; reproduction; 14.5 × 19.2 cm; BwA, 32-31-2. Preventive custody camp order, Oct. 9, 1937; DIN A 4; ThHStA, NS 4 Bu 31, Bl. 20. Block 5, 1943;

photo 18 × 13 cm; SGB. Herbert Weidlich, room sketch, labour administration office, 1980; DIN A 4; BwA, 32/IV-38/1. Ink bottles; 4.5 × 4.5 × 6 cm; SGB. Punitive report submitted by Kestel, Dec. 17, 1941; 20.9 × 20.2 cm; BwA, 57-25.

2/41 Desk

Olympia typewriter; wooden case; 44 × 30 × 43 cm; SGB. Ashtray; shell limestone; ∅ 15 cm; SGB. Heinrich Himmler in Buchenwald, autumn 1938; photo; 24 × 18 cm; NARA. Punitive report of Armed SS "Totenkopf" Division, Oct. 25, 1943; DIN A 4; ThHStA, NS 4 Bu 105, Bl. 21. Application submitted by first preventive custody camp officer for death sentence of an inmate, Oct. 30, 1943; DIN A 4; ThHStA, NS 4 Bu 105, Bl. 22. Punitive report submitted by a capo, 1941; 13 × 10 cm; BwA, 57-63. Punitive report submitted by a capo, Jan. 22, 1943; 14.2 × 10.1 cm; BwA, 57-61.

Dept. IV: Administration

2/42 The activities of Dept. IV: Administration

5 stamps from Buchenwald Concentration Camp administration, 1945; SGB. Corridor of SS administration barrack, Sept. 30, 1937; photo; 17.2 × 12.4 cm; SGB. Memo from camp administration re shipment of textile fibre ration card of deceased Vinzent Glowacki, Apr. 16, 1942; 14.5 × 10.4 cm; BwA, HKW-Film 21. Richard Glücks on regulation prohibiting shipment of clothing articles of inmates who had been shot to death, July 11, 1942; DIN A 4; ThHStA, NS 4 Bu 31, Bl. 15.

2/43 Crematorium

Crematorium, 1942; photo; 18 × 13 cm; SGB. Buchenwald Concentration Camp administration to chief burgomaster of Weimar re cost of shipping urns, Dec. 23, 1937; A 4; ThHStA, NS 4 Bu 31. Camp physician to Buchenwald Concentration Camp administration re collection of gold fillings, Jan. 31, 1944; 21 × 15 cm; ThHStA, KZ Bu 9. Urns found in crematorium attic, 1997, photo; 12 × 9 cm; SGB. Urns; tin; SGB. Urn lid; tin; ∅ 11.5 cm; SGB. Urn lid, clay; ∅ 12 cm; SGB.

Dept. V: The Camp Physician

2/44 Pathology

16 medicine bottles from inmates' infirmary, 1945; glass (and cardboard); SGB. Textbook from collection of SS garrison physician (Baur/Fischer/Lenz, *Menschliche Erblehre and Rassehygiene*, Munich, 1936); 16 × 23 × 5 cm; SGB. Manual (Mrugowsky, J., *Untersuchung and Beurteilung von Wasser and Brunnen an Ort and Stelle*, Berlin, 1942) from collection of camp physician; 15 × 21 cm; SGB. Textbook on special anatomical pathology from collection of SS garrison physician; SGB. Dissertation Erich Wagner; DIN A 5; SGB. Report on activities of Pathology Department, Sept. 15, 1943; DIN A 4; ThHStA, KZ Bu 9, Bl. 100.

2/45 Activities of Dept. V: Camp physician

SS Department of Economic Administration re economising on vaccinations, June 21, 1944; DIN A 4; BwA, 55-19. Letter re infectious diseases; DIN A 5; ThHStA, NS 4 Bu 48, Bl. 7. SS garrison physician to chief of Office D III re experiment series in Buchenwald Concentration Camp, Jan. 8, 1944; DIN A 5; ThHStA, KZ BU 5/6, Bl. 366. SS garrison physician to command headquarters re sterilisation of inmates, Oct. 12, 1939; DIN A 4; ThHStA, NS 4 Bu 45, Bl. 1. Report to officer in charge of preventive custody camp re suicide of an inmate, Jan. 18, 1938; DIN A 5; ThHStA, NS 4 Bu 101, Bl. 8. SS camp physician to officer in charge of preventive custody camp re self-mutilation of an inmate, Nov. 19, 1937; DIN A 5; ThHStA; NS 4 Bu 101, Bl. 42. Hanns Eisele; passport photo; 4 × 6 cm; SGB.

2/46 T4 The adviser Mennecke

Hotel "Elephant" 1994; photo; 13 × 8 cm; SGB. Friedrich Mennecke; passport photo; 4 × 6 cm; SGB.

3. The Everyday Reality of Crime

3.1 Life in the Barracks, 1937-1942

3/1 Committal

30 tags for personal belongings; metal; ∅ 4 cm; SGB. Inmate's coat; 120 × 45 cm; SGB. Inmate's jacket "Bible researcher," 21 × 29.5 cm; SGB. Black triangle; replica; SGB. Preventive custody camp report, Sept. 16, 1938; DIN A 4; ThHStA, NS 4 Bu 142. Bohumir Hendrych; portrait photo; 6 × 8 cm; BwA, 52-11 758. Inmate's identification tag No.14; cardboard; 8.5 × 15 cm; BwA, 52-11-758. Buchenwald Concentration Camp postcard; 15 × 10.5 cm; BwA, 52-11-758. List of Czech inmates, 1943; DIN A 4; ThHStA, NS 4 Bu 188. List of names of Dutch hostages, July 21-22, 1940; DIN A 4; ThHStA, NS 4 Bu 1. Red triangle "P," fabric; 6.5 × 7.1 cm; SGB. Inmate's personal record card: Ernst Chowaniec; DIN A 5; BwA, HKW-Film 5. Cross; metal; 1.5 × 3 cm; SGB. Inmate's number 15912; textile; 8.5 × 6 cm; SGB. Inmate's number 27824; fabric; 11 × 6.2 cm; SGB.

3/2 Life in the barracks

Dutch-style clogs, 1940; wood and leather; 33.5 × 12.5 8 cm; SGB. Leather shoes with wooden soles; 31 × 10.5 × 9.5 cm; SGB. Drinking vessel; aluminium; 8 × 10 cm; SGB. Spoon; aluminium; 17.5 cm; SGB. Dish; aluminium; ∅ 23 cm; SGB. Bowl; aluminium; 22.5 × 6 cm; SGB. Bread scales; wood; 33 × 33 × 15cm; SGB. Money administration file card of David Schuster, 1938; 15 × 21 cm; SGB. Money collection list, Feb. 11, 1941; 21 × 14.8 cm; ThHStA, NS 4 Bu 269, Vol. 8. Registration of donation to Block 46,

Aug. 22, 1941; 20.8 × 15 cm; ThHStA, NS 4 Bu 269, Vol. 8. Cigarette box; wood; 9 × 10 cm; SGB. Cigarette holder; wood; 9 cm; SGB. Amulet (motif: sailor's grave); bone; 3 × 3.5 cm; SGB. Amulet; bone; 3.6 × 2.7 cm; SGB. Amulet; horn; 2.5 × 4 cm; SGB. Ring; bone; 2.5 × 1.2 cm; SGB. Knife; bone; 18.5 × 2 cm; SGB.

3/3 Life in the barracks
Henri Pieck, "In the Barrack," 1943/45; charcoal drawing, reproduction; 52 × 43 cm; SGB.

3/4 Life in the barracks
Clock on Watchtower 1, 1994; photo; 13 × 9 cm; SGB. Permission to hand out watches to inmates employed in crematorium, Apr. 29, 1942; 13.8 × 10.4 cm; BwA, 56-2-31/I. Pathology physician to SS officer in charge of general records department re distribution of watches, July 19, 1942; DIN A 5; BwA, 56-2-31/I. Pathology physician to SS officer in charge of general records department re distribution of watches, Dec. 27, 1943; DIN A 5; BwA, 56-2-31/I. Pocket watch housing; 3.5 × 3.5 cm; SGB. Wristwatch; 2 × 2.5 cm; SGB. Capo Hans Neumeister to Schobert, officer in charge of preventive custody camp, May 24, 1943; 15 × 10.5 cm; BwA, 56-2-31/II. Daily record book of officer in charge of preventive custody camp, Nov. 22, 1940; DIN A 4; ThHStA, NS 4 Bu 20, Bl. 27. Cigarette case with initials A.V., 1940; wood; 9.5 × 10.5 × 1.5 cm; SGB. Cigarette case of Hans Neumeister, 1944; wood; 7.5 x.11 cm; loan from Gitta Günther.

3/5 Roll call
Inmates' roll call, ca. 1940; photo; 24 × 18 cm; NARA. Block marker on muster ground, 1994; photo; 13 × 9 cm; SGB. List, evening roll call, May 28, 1943; DIN A 4; ThHStA, NS 4 Bu 147, Bl. 5. Song book, handwritten; 10 × 13.5 cm; SGB. Inmate's music band, 1940; photo; 17 × 12 cm; SGB. 3 gate passes, Nov. 18, 1944; 6.5 × 7 cm; SGB. Leather shoes with wooden soles; 30.5 × 10.5 × 8.5 cm; SGB. Dutch-style clogs; wood; 33.5 × 12.5 × 9 cm; SGB. Leather shoes; 29 × 9.5 × 6 cm; SGB. Inmate's cap; textile; ∅ 42 cm; SGB.

3/6 Working day
List of labour detachments, 1943; 29.5 × 20.5 cm; ThHStA, NS 4 Bu 188. 4 sheets of guidelines for capos; 10 × 14 cm; BwA, 51-1-8. Capo ID, No. 394; 10 × 7 cm; SGB. Wood bearers, 1937; photo; 24 × 18 cm; SGB. Accident report on Horst Jonas, Dec. 26, 1938; DIN A 4; ThHStA, KZ Bu 12, Bl. 114. Interrogation minutes, Feb. 3, 1939; DIN A 4; BwA, HKW-Film 4. Kurt Dittmar, "Capos;" coloured pencil sketch; sketch book "Wir and die anderen;" 15 × 21 cm; BwA, 9-96-3. Stone carts, 1961; photo; 18 × 13 cm; SGB. Return march from quarry, ca. 1943; photo; 32 × 22 cm; SGB. Report of quarry capo, Jan. 29, 1941; DIN A 4; BwA, 57-136. Sewage plant capo to SS labour allocation officer re request for labourers, June 29, 1940; 20.5 × 16.2

cm; BwA, 56-2-31/I. Fritz Bodmer, copy of Buchenwald Song; 14 × 21 cm; SGB. Inmate's bread sack; textile; 33 × 20 cm; SGB. Inmate's bread sack; plastic; 40 × 30 cm; SGB. Inmate's infirmary ID; 10.5 × 7.5 cm; BwA, 30/I-0/4. Inmate's ID as electrician; 9.3 × 6.2 cm; SGB. Inmate's ID as wood yard worker; 8 × 6 cm; SGB.

3/7 Workshops
Ernst Grube; portrait photo; 5 × 8 cm; SGB. Letter from Kurt Weigel to mother of Herbert Strobel, May 5, 1939; 2 sheets, lined; 14.8 × 20.9 cm; BwA, 52-11-112. Herbert Strobel, 1939; passport photo; 4 × 6 cm; SGB. Stool and locker, 1994; photo; 13 × 9 cm; SGB. Stool, inmates' carpentry shop; wood; 50 × 50 × 30 cm; SGB.

3/8 Labour detachments of Jewish inmates
Henri Pieck; "Jews Pulling a Wagon (in the century of the motor)", charcoal drawing, reproduction; 41 × 28 cm; SGB. Accident report, May 31, 1939; 20.9 × 14 cm; ThHStA, KZ Bu 12, Bl. 137. Accident report, July 2, 1939; 20.9 × 14 cm; ThHStA, KZ Bu 12, Bl. 143. Punitive report of the inmate Schreiber, May 19, 1942; DIN A 4; BwA, 57-146. Sign: "Durchgang verboten" (no passage), tin; 29.9 × 20 cm; SGB.

3/9 Camp jargon
Karl Schulz, "Heads of the Rubbish Bin Eagles", 1943; coloured pencil drawing; 27.3 × 19.4 cm; SGB. Boris Taslitzky, "Little Gypsy," 1944; pencil drawing, reproduction; 10 × 13 cm; SGB. 4 death reports, 1945; 10.5 × 4.5 cm; SGB.

3/10 "Free time"
Book acquisition list, Jan. 12, 1938; DIN A 4; ThHStA, NS 4 Bu 43, Bl. 1a. 2 reading cards from camp library; cardboard; 7 × 13 cm; SBG. Number card 7188 (Ernst Wiechert); DIN A 6; ThHStA, KZ Bu number file. Ernst Wiechert; portrait photo; 4 × 6 cm; SGB: Wilhelm Jensen, *Unter heißerer Sonne*, Ullstein Publishing Co., no date; book from camp library; 8°; SGB. Hans Krieg, *Menschen, die ich in der Wildnis traf*, Stuttgart, no date; book from camp library; 8°; SGB. Al. Carthill, *Verlorene Herrschaft. Wie England Indien aufgab*, Berlin – Grunewald 1924; book from camp library; 8°; SGB. Heinrich Spiero (ed.) *Wilhelm Raabe und sein Lebenskreis*, Berlin – Grunewald 1931; book from camp library; 8°; SGB. Georg Wilhelm Friedrich Hegel, *System der Philosophie. Erster Teil. Die Logik*, Stuttgart, 1929; book from camp library; 8°; SGB. Table for chess contest, 1940; 2 sheets; 29.5 × 21 cm; BwA, 9-93-7. 36 chess figures 1938/39; wood, inmate's handwork; 6.5 × 2 cm; SGB. 10 handmade domino cards, cardboard; 5 × 7 cm; 4.5 × 2 cm; SGB. 10 playing cards; cardboard; 5 × 7 cm; SGB. Regulations for contents of letters; DIN A 4; ThHStA, NS 4 Bu 31, Bl. 19. Inmate's letter, Karl Schulz, July 9, 1944; 15 × 21 cm; SGB. Record of incoming and outgoing mail of Simon Katzburg; 14.7 × 9.3

cm; SGB. Inmate's letter, Oskar Brill, Apr. 2, 1939; 29.5 × 20 cm; BwA, 52-11-59. Short letter with 25 words, written by a Bible researcher, 21.5 × 15 cm; ThHStA, NS 4 Bu 32, Bl. 6. Inmate's postcard, Jan Kubico; 14.5 × 10 cm; BwA, 52-11-181. Guitar of Herbert Thiele; 97 × 33 × 8 cm; SGB. Stage props (pendant, beard, glasses) of Bruno Apitz; SGB.

3/11 Hygienic and sanitary conditions
Water pitcher; aluminium; ∅ 22 × 41 cm; SGB. Cup; aluminium; 8.5 × 6.6 × 6.3 cm; SGB. Commander's Office Order No. 47, May 16, 1938; DIN A 4; BwA, HKW-Film 1. Jura Soyfer; portrait photo; 4 × 6 cm; SGB. Personal belongings card, Jura Soyfer; DIN A 5; BwA, 52-11-200. Jewish cemetery of Vienna to the cemetery administration of Weimar re shipment of urn of Jura Soyfer, Feb. 20, 1939; DIN A 4; Stadtarchiv Weimar, 6-66-78/3. Reply from Weimar municipal cemetery administration, Mar. 2, 1939; DIN A 4; Stadtarchiv Weimar.6-66-78/3. Hatband; leather; found in former latrine; 36 × 4 cm; SGB. Newspaper fragment *Thüringer Gauzeitung*; found in former latrine; 6 × 4 cm; SGB. Death register, Registry Office II; reproduction; DIN A 4; SGB. Death register of inmates' infirmary; July 8, 1939 – Nov. 15, 1939; 37 × 24.5 cm; ThHStA, KZ Bu 5/19, Bl. 93.

3/6 Working day
List of labour detachments, 1943; 29.5 × 20.5 cm; ThHStA, NS 4 Bu 188. 4 sheets of guidelines for capos; 10 × 14 cm; BwA, 51-1-8. Capo ID, No. 394; 10 × 7 cm; SGB. Wood bearers, 1937; photo; 24 × 18 cm; SGB. Accident report on Horst Jonas, Dec. 26, 1938; DIN A 4; ThHStA, KZ Bu 12, Bl. 114. Interrogation minutes, Feb. 3, 1939; DIN A 4; BwA, HKW-Film 4. Kurt Dittmar, "Capos;" coloured pencil sketch; sketch book "Wir and die anderen;" 15 × 21 cm; BwA, 9-96-3. Stone cart, 1961; photo; 18 × 13 cm; SGB. Return march from quarry, ca. 1943; photo; 32 × 22 cm; SGB. Report of quarry capo, Jan. 29, 1941; DIN A 4; BwA, 57-136. Sewage plant capo to SS labour allocation officer re request for labourers, June 29, 1940; 20.5 × 16.2 cm; BwA, 56-2-31/I. Fritz Bodmer, copy of Buchenwald Song; 14 × 21 cm; SGB. Inmate's bread sack; textile; 33 × 20 cm; SGB. Inmate's bread sack; plastic; 40 × 30 cm; SGB. Inmate's infirmary ID; 10.5 × 7.5 cm; BwA, 30/I-0/4. Inmate's ID as electrician; 9.3 × 6.2 cm; SGB. Inmate's ID as wood yard worker; 8 × 6 cm; SGB.

3/7 Workshops
Ernst Grube; portrait photo; 5 × 8 cm; SGB. Letter from Kurt Weigel to mother of Herbert Strobel, May 5, 1939; 2 sheets, lined; 14.8 × 20.9 cm; BwA, 52-11-112. Herbert Strobel, 1939; passport photo; 4 × 6 cm; SGB. Stool and locker, 1994; photo; 13 × 9 cm; SGB. Stool, inmates' joinery shop; wood; 50 × 50 × 30 cm; SGB.

3/8 Labour detachments of Jewish inmates
Henri Pieck; "Jews Pulling a Wagon (in the century of the motor)," charcoal drawing, reproduction; 41 × 28 cm; SGB. Accident report, May 31, 1939; 20.9 × 14 cm; ThHStA, KZ Bu 12, Bl. 137. Accident report, July 2, 1939; 20.9 × 14 cm; ThHStA, KZ Bu 12, Bl. 143. Punitive report of the inmate Schreiber, May 19, 1942; DIN A 4; BwA, 57-146. Sign: "Durchgang verboten" (no passage), tin; 29.9 × 20 cm; SGB.

3/12 The Block
General records department in Barrack 5, 1943; photo; 18 × 13 cm; SGB. List made according to information from Max Mayr; diagram; BwA, o. S. View of barrack camp, 1945; photo; 24 × 18 cm; SGB. Max Mayr; portrait photo; 4 × 6 cm; SGB. Ernst Busse, Camp Senior 1, to Hermann Florstedt, officer in charge of preventive custody camp, re reduction of barrack duty, Mar. 14, 1941; 2 DIN A 4 sheets; ThHStA, NS 4 Bu 102, Bl. 32 and 33. Block daybook of Barrack 39; 23 × 15 cm; SGB. Group picture, 1945; photo; 8.5 × 12.8cm; SGB. Ernst Wille; portrait photo; 7.5 × 9 cm; SGB. ID, barrack duty Block 41; 6.5 × 4.5 cm; BwA, 52-11-202.

3.2 Daily Terror, 1937-1942

Terror against Jewish Inmates
3/13 The special camp following the anti-Jewish pogroms of 1938
Burning synagogue in Frankfurt, Börneplatz, 1938; photo; 12 × 8 cm; Stadtarchiv Frankfurt/ M. Destroyed synagogue in Arnstadt, November 1938; photo 18.2 × 13 cm; Stadtarchiv Arnstadt. Jewish community centre in Große Rosenstrasse in Kassel following destruction on the night of November 7, 1938; photo; 12 × 14.5 cm; Hessisches Hauptstaatsarchiv, Abt./No. 3008/ 117; photo: Carl Ebert, Kassel. Notification of arrest by Gestapo of Leipzig, Nov. 11, 1938; 21 × 15 cm; ThHStA, KZ Bu 4/11, Bl. 1. Minutes of interrogation on accident of Jewish inmate Loeb, Dec. 9, 1938; DIN A 4; ThHStA, KZ Bu 12, Bl. 111. Postcard, Main Station Weimar; 13.8 × 8.8 cm; SGB.

3/14 The special camp following the anti-Jewish pogroms of 1938
Roll call, November 1938; photo; 24 × 18 cm; American Jewish Joint Distribution Committee, New York. Card from special card file, 1938; 21 × 8.5 cm; BwA, 52-11-657. Camp layout according to memory of J. Freund; 23.3 × 16.4 cm; from book: Julius Freund, *O Buchenwald*, Klagenfurt, 1945, p. 29. Klara Kaufmann to Gestapo of Frankfurt a. Main, Dec. 21, 1938; DIN A 4; ThHStA, NS 4 Bu 104, Bl. 50f. Memo by SS Buchenwald camp command re possible whereabouts of Moritz Kaufmann, Dec. 1938; 21 × 8.5 cm; ThHStA, NS 4 Bu 104, Bl. 50f. Ordinance decreeing exclusion of Jews from Ger-

man economy, Nov. 12, 1938; DIN A 4; RGBl. 1938/I, p. 1580. Identity card J, 1939; 10.5 × 15 cm; SGB.

3/15 The Jewish-Polish special camp in 1939/40, following outbreak of war
R. Heydrich to all State Police (Central) Offices re arrest of Jews of Polish nationality, Sept. 7, 1939; 2 DIN A 4 sheets; ThHStA, MdI P 94, Bl. 33. Undressing of committed inmates, 1939; photo; 24 × 18 cm; United States Holocaust Memorial Museum, Washington. Head shearing and disinfection, 1939; photo; 24 × 18 cm; United States Holocaust Memorial, Washington. Report on possessions of deceased Viennese Jew Norbert Wasserberg, Oct. 20, 1939; 21 × 15 cm; BwA, HKW-Film 31, Bl. 1. Certificate of shipment of wristwatch of Aller-Rachmil Orenbruch, Dec. 9, 1939; 21 × 15 cm; BwA, HKW-Film 26, Bl. 4. Report of inmates' infirmary on death of Polish inmate Karl Rudol, Dec. 16, 1939; 21 × 15 cm; BwA, HKW-Film 28, Bl. 2.

3/16 Dutch Jews, 1941
Isolation of Jews from Amsterdam, Feb. 1941; photo; 16.1 × 11.8 cm; RIOD. Arrest of Jewish residents in Amsterdam, Feb. 22, 1941; photo; 15.7 × 10 cm; RIOD. Amsterdam Jews in Mauthausen Concentration Camp, June 1941; photo, 14.8 × 11 cm; *Das Schwarze Korps*, 1941; DB Leipzig.

3/20 Jewish intellectuals and politicians
Ernst Heilmann, before 1933; portrait photo; 7.2 × 10.2 cm; SGB. Paul Morgan; portrait photo; 8.8 × 12 cm; SGB. Paul Morgan: *Promin-Enten-Teich*, Vienna 1934; repro of cover; 12.5 × 19.3 cm; DB Leipzig. Max Ehrlich/Paul Morgan, *Heulen and Zähneklappern. Das Buch der faulen Witze*, Vienna 1927; reproduction of cover; 12.6 × 17.5 cm; DB Leipzig. Paul Morgan during filming of "Menschen hinter Gittern" (p. 132a of *Promin-Enten-Teich*); 12.5 × 18.8 cm; DB Leipzig.

3/21 Jewish intellectuals and politicians
Robert Danneberg; portrait photo; 11.5 × 17.8 cm; DÖW. Heinrich Steinitz, ca. 1910; portrait photo; 8.8 × 13.6 cm; DÖW. Fritz Löhner-Beda; portrait photo; 13.3 × 16.7; Österreichische Nationalbibliothek Wien. Alfred Grünwald/ Emmerich Foldes/Beda (Fritz Löhner) / Paul Abraham: *Die Blume von Hawaii*, Basel, 1932; reproduction of cover; 11.7 × 16.9 cm; DB Leipzig. Franz Lehár/Ludwig Herzer/Fritz Löhner: *Land des Lächelns*, Vienna, 1938; reproduction of cover; 16 × 23 cm; DB Leipzig. Fritz Grünbaum; ca. 1930; portrait photo; 5 × 7.7 cm; SGB.

Terror against Sinti and Romani
3/17 Romani from Burgenland, 1939-1941
Romani from Burgenland in Dachau, summer 1939; photo; 13 × 18; SGB. Erich Wagner, ca. 1940; portrait photo; 7 × 10; SGB. Letter from City of Salzburg to Buchenwald Concentration Camp re shipment of urn of Josef Baumann, July 10, 1940; DIN A 4; Stadtarchiv Weimar, 6-66-78/ 5. Robert Schneeberger, application for financial support of his co-inmate, Mar. 4, 1941; 20.8 × 13.3 cm; BwA, 52-11- 913. Transport list, Mauthausen Concentration Camp, June 28, 1941; 2 DIN A 4 sheets; ThHStA, KZ Bu 8/1, Bl. 342 f.

3/18 The Sinto Otto Schmidt
Money card, Otto Schmidt; DIN A 5; ThHStA, KZ Bu inmates' money card file. Interim report of Epidemic Typhus Experiment Station of Buchenwald Concentration Camp, Nov. 10, 1942; DIN A 4; ThHStA, KZ Bu 62, Bl. 22 . SS garrison physician Hoven to chief of Office D III re artificial infection of inmates with epidemic typhus, Oct. 16, 1942; 20.6 × 14.4 cm; ThHStA, KZ Bu 62, Bl. 17. Otto Schmidt, end of 1930s; police photo; 12.2 × 17.7 cm; SGB. Memo on recognition of interned Otto Schmidt as father, Aug. 27, 1938; DIN A 4; BwA, 52-11-756. Erna Lauenburger, end of 1930s; police photo; 12.2 × 17.7 cm; SGB. "Race appraisal" of daughter of Otto Schmidt, Marie Lauenburger, July 14, 1941; DIN A 4; BwA, 52-11-756. Alex Wedding (Grete Weiskopf), *Ede and Unku*, 8°; school edition 1987.

3/19 The Sinto Stephan Petermann
File card Petermann in the "Racial Research Office," 1939/40; 20.5 × 13.7 cm; BA Koblenz, R 165/50. Number card Petermann; DIN A 6; ThHStA, KZ Bu number card file. Transport list Sonnenstein T4 facility, July 14, 1941; DIN A 4; ThHStA, KZ Bu 9, Bl. 67.

The Punitive System
3/23 Reports and interrogations
Punitive report by Erich Gust, second officer in charge of preventive custody camp, July 1, 1942; 20 × 14.5 cm; BwA, 57-12. Punitive report on inmate's failure to follow marking regulations, Jan. 14, 1941; 13.5 × 10.2 cm; BwA, 57-62. Punitive report on inmate's failure to take off cap, Mar. 26, 1942, 18.7 × 13.6 cm; BwA, 57-19. Punitive report on inmate's warning of fellow inmates, Oct. 12, 1942; 21.1 × 14.7; BwA, 57-13. Punitive order by Camp Commander Karl Koch for collective withholding of food on May 1, Apr. 29, 1938; DIN A 4; BwA, 57-152. Interrogation of Max Urmann by Heinrich Hackmann, SS officer in charge of general records department, Feb. 3, 1939; DIN A 4; BwA, HKW-Film 4.

3/24 Flogging
Flogging stand; replica (1954); wood; 77 × 74 × 64 cm; SGB. Horsewhip (1954); 100 cm; SGB. Form for execution of flogging punishment on Czeslaus Pabisch, Oct. 3, 1940; 2 DIN A 4 sheets; BwA, HKW-Film 4. Czeslaus Pabisch; photo from camp file; 4.5 × 6 cm; BwA, HKW-Film 4.

3/25 "Bunker"
2 handcuffs; steel; SGB. Foot manacle with chain; steel; SGB.

3/26 "Bunker"
2 flogging sticks; 30 × 4 cm, 24 × 1.5 cm; SGB. 7 cell door signs; plywood; 16 × 6 cm, 15 × 6 cm; SGB. Martin Sommer, ca. 1935; portrait photo; 7.2 × 7.7 cm; BA BDC. Otto Neururer, ca. 1935; portrait photo; 7.1 × 10.2 cm; SGB. Rudolf Opitz, before 1933; portrait photo; 12.2 × 20.2 cm; SGB.

3/27 "Tree-hanging"
Karl Schulz, "Tree-Hanging," 1943; pen and ink drawing; 27 × 19.5 cm; SGB. Karl Schulz, "Tree-Hanging", 1945; pen and ink drawing; 20.9 × 27 cm; SGB.

3/28 The transportable gallows
Transportable gallows (fragment), 1942; wood; SGB. Execution of 20 inmates near Poppenhausen, May 11, 1942; 4 photos; 9.6 × 6 cm; ThHStA Meiningen.

3/29 The public execution in Poppenhausen, 1942
Weimar Gestapo to commander of Buchenwald Concentration Camp re execution in Poppenhausen, May 6, 1942; 2 DIN A 4 sheets; ThHStA, NS 4 Bu 105. Transportable gallows in crematorium courtyard, Apr. 1945; photo; 13.9 × 8.7 cm; SGB.

3/22 "Shot to death during attempt to escape"
Robert Winterstein, 1930s; portrait photo; 7.2 × 14.9 cm; DÖW. Number card of R. Winterstein; DIN A 6; ThHStA, KZ Bu number card file. Walter Krämer, 1930s; portrait photo; 7.1 × 9 cm; SGB. Daybook of officer in charge of general records department: "unnatural deaths," Nov. 6, 1941; 10.5 × 15 cm; NARA, Film 1. Hans Kunke, 1930s; portrait photo; 8.2 × 12 cm; DÖW. Document on cremation of Jewish inmate Erich Kohn in crematorium of Weimar Main Cemetery, Sept. 19, 1939; DIN A 4; Stadtarchiv Weimar 6-66-78/8. Johann Blank; portrait photo; 8.1 × 12.9 cm; SGB. Eduard Hinkelmann; portrait photo; 8.2 × 12.8 cm; SGB.

Terror and Forced Labour – The Quarry

3/30 The delinquent company
Labour allocation slip of quarry labour detachment, June 1, 1940; 20.1 × 14.4 cm; BwA, o. S. Report on inmates in delinquent company, Apr. 22, 1942; 10.3 × 13.2 cm; ThHStA, NS 4 Bu 212, Bl. 335. Report on inmates in K Company, June 13, 1942; 14.5 × 10 cm; ThHStA, NS 4 Bu 212, Bl. 247. Report by quarry capo Johann Herzog, Jan. 10, 1941; 14.9 × 21 cm; BwA, 57-137. Report by quarry capo Johann Herzog, Feb. 2, 1941; 14.7 × 20.8 cm; BwA, 57-138. Stone pick; steel; 21 × 3 × 4 cm; SGB.

3/31 Terror against homosexuals
Death report from inmates' infirmary, Mar. 17, 1940; 20.5 × 14.5 cm; BwA, HKW-Film 22. Report of Barrack 33 block senior to depot, Mar. 17, 1940; 20.8 × 14.6 cm; BwA, HKW-Film 22. Shipment of Arthur Hermann's personal belongings to his father, May 23, 1940; DIN A 4; BwA, HKW-Film 22.

3/32 Accidents with quarry dump cars
Dump car; SGB. Roller for construction of paths and roads; SGB. Inmates carrying out excavation work, Sept. 1937; photo; 22.1 × 16.1 cm; American Jewish Joint Distribution Committee, New York. Accident report on B. Watersack, Dec. 9, 1938; DIN A 4; ThHStA, KZ Bu 12, Bl. 109. Accident report on A. Manasse, Dec. 20, 1938; DIN A 4; ThHStA, KZ Bu 12, Bl. 117. Report by officer in charge of general records departments re dump car accident, May 27, 1939; 21 × 15 cm; ThHStA, KZ Bu 12, Bl. 122.

3/33 Accidents with quarry dump cars
Inmates in quarry, Sept. 7, 1937; photo; 16.8 × 11.7; SGB. Statement by two inmates on accident of Franz Josef Engel, Jan. 11, 1939; DIN A 4; ThHStA, KZ Bu 12, Bl. 103. Statement following interrogation of Franz Josef Engel by Rödl, officer in charge of preventive custody camp, on dump car accident, Jan. 12, 1939; DIN A 4; ThHStA, KZ Bu 12, Bl. 104.

3.3 Mass Murder, 1941-1943

The Murder of 8,000 Soviet Prisoners of War

3/34 Found objects
8 police photographs of Soviet prisoners of war, found in 1945 in liberated camp; 5 × 7 cm; SGB. Field postcard, 1942; 14 × 9.5 cm; SGB. Corpse container in crematorium courtyard, Apr. 1945; photo; 13 × 9 cm; SGB. Mess kit with inscription, 1940; aluminium; 18 × 9 × 14 cm; SGB. Cup with inscription; ∅ 7.5; SGB. Button of Red Army uniform, found in northern section of camp, ∅ 2.2 cm; SGB. 9 POW identification tags: a. Stalag (parent camp) VI A (Hemer/Münster military district), b. Stalag 326 VI K (Forellkrug/Münster military district), c. Stalag 311 XI C (Bergen-Belsen/Hanover military district), d. Stalag X D (Wietzendorf/Hamburg military district), e. Stalag IX B (Bad Orb/Kassel military district), f. Stalag II B (Hammerstein/Stettin military district), g. Stalag 367 (Tschenstochau), h. Stalag IV B (Mühlberg/Dresden military district), i. Stalag VI C (Bathorn/military district Münster); a. 5.2 × 2.1 cm; b. and e. 6 × 2 cm; c., d., f., g., h., i. 6 × 4 cm.

3/35 Structures
Arrest, presumably 1941, picture taken by Wehrmacht propaganda company; photo; 18 × 13 cm; BA Koblenz. Transport, Oct. 1941; photo; 18 × 13 cm; Militärarchiv Freiburg. POW camp Stalag XI D (Oerbke/Hanover military district),

autumn 1941; photo; 18 × 13 cm; Niedersächsisches Hauptstaatsarchiv Hannover. Former stable, 1945; photo; 18 × 13 cm; SGB.

3/36 Biographies
Sketch of execution facility in stable, Apr. 21, 1945; 38 × 21 cm; BwA, 50-2-17. Horst Dittrich; portrait photo in SS Uniform; 8 × 13 cm; HKW. Horst Dittrich, 1946; photo U. S. Military Tribunal Dachau; 8 × 13 cm; NARA, Film 10.

3/37 Biographies
Alexander Makeev, March 1938; passport photo; 4.5 × 6 cm; loan from I. E. Makeeva, Grodno. First day as teacher at a school in Voronezh, 1938; photo; 4 × 6 cm; loan from I. E. Makeeva. Student ID, 1938; 14 × 9.5 cm; loan from I. E. Makeeva. Photo taken at harvest during teaching period at rural school, 1939; photo; 11.5 × 9 cm; loan from I. E. Makeeva. Alexander (nickname Schura or Sascha) with two of his six siblings; photo; 9.5 × 7.5 cm; loan from I. E. Makeeva. With his friend Avdeev, 1937; photo; 9 × 5 cm; loan from I. E. Makeeva. Schura; photo; 6 × 10 cm; loan from I. E. Makeeva. Alexander's colleague and later wife Klava, 1940; photo; 8 × 12 cm; loan from I. E. Makeeva. Diploma as elementary school teacher, 1939; 20 × 29.5 cm; loan from I. E. Makeeva. Alexander Makeev's balalaika; wood; 64 × 15 × 21 cm; SGB. Letters to parents and siblings; bundle of letters, 17 × 20.5 cm; loan from I. E. Makeeva.

The Deportation and Extermination of the Jews
3/38 Deportation to Auschwitz
Punitive report on inmate's spreading of rumours about transport of Jewish inmates away from Buchenwald, Jan. 8, 1942; 18.3 × 15 cm; BwA 57-34. Adjutant Hans Schmidt to the camp command departments re deportation of Jewish inmates to Auschwitz, Oct. 14, 1942; 20.3 × 14.8 cm; ThHStA, NS 4 Bu 133, Bl. 2. Bureau D to commanders of Buchenwald and Auschwitz Concentration Camps re deportation of Jewish inmates, Oct. 12, 1942; 21 × 15 cm; ThHStA, NS 4 Bu 31, Bl. 26.

The Selection and Murder of Persons Deemed "unworthy of life"
3/39 Found objects
Waldemar Hoven, SS garrison physician, to director of pathology, May 7, 1942; 20.9 × 14.5 cm; ThHStA, KZ Bu 9, Bl. 88. Shrunken human skull, Buchenwald, Apr. 1945; photo; 18 × 24 cm; Jacques Rancy, France. Tanned human skin, Buchenwald, Apr. 1945; photo; 18 × 24; Jacques Rancy, France. Shrunken human skull from Buchenwald Memorial Collection, 1990; photo; 18 × 18 cm; SGB. Enno Lolling, chief of Office D III, to SS garrison physician Gerhard Schiedlausky re shipment of tattooed skin, Apr. 17, 1944; DIN A 4; ThHStA, KZ Bu 9,

Bl. 41. Instruments from Buchenwald pathology station; steel; SGB.

3/40 Killing operation 14 f 13
SS Camp Physician Hoven to officer in charge of preventive custody camp under special file reference number 14 f 13, July 26, 1941; 20.9 × 14.6 cm; ThHStA, KZ Bu 5/16, Bl. 698. SS Camp Physician Hoven to Bernburg Sanatorium "re disabled Jews", Feb. 2, 1942; 20.5 × 14.5 cm; ThHStA, KZ Bu 9, Bl. 45. Garages of Bernburg killing facility; photo; 18 × 13; SGB. Page of Sonnenstein transport list, July 14, 1941; DIN A 4; ThHStA, KZ Bu 9, Bl. 68. SS Camp Physician Hoven to officer in charge of preventive custody camp re Martin Gauger (special file reference number 14 f 13), July 23, 1941; 20.3 × 14.9 cm; ThHStA, KZ Bu 15/1, Bl. 15. SS Camp Physician Hoven to Dr. Joachim Gauger, July 27, 1941; DIN A 4; ThHStA, KZ Bu 9, Bl. 44.

3/41 Biographies
Martin Gauger; portrait photo; 12 × 18 cm; SGB. Faybusch Itzkewitsch, mid 1930s; portrait photo; 6 × 7.5 cm; BwA, 52-11-914. Torn-out fragment of newspaper, 1937; 10.5 × 5 cm; BwA, 52-11-914. Torn-out fragment of newspaper, 1937; 10.5 × 14 cm; BwA, 52-11-914. Passport photo during custody, 1939; 4 × 6 cm; BwA, 52-11-914. Portrait photo; 5.5 × 8 cm; BwA, 52-11-914. Documentary evidence of forced confiscation of gold ring from personal belongings of Faybusch Itzkewitsch, Apr. 4, 1939; 20.6 × 14.5 cm; BwA, 52-11-914. Final letter from Buchenwald, June 29, 1941; 29.8 × 21 cm; BwA, 52-11-914. Foreigner's temporary ID, 1939; 9.8 × 15.5 cm; BwA, 52-11-914.

3/42 Biographies
Syringe; SGB. Waldemar Hoven during trial in Nuremberg, 1946; 12 × 16.5 cm; YVA, 132 BO 3.

Józef Szajina: Roll Call
Room installation, 1995
Fibreboard, slag, card file photos from inmate card file of Auschwitz Concentration Camp

3.4 Survival Strategies and Resistance

The Self-Preservation of the Individual
3/43 Self-preservation
3 dominoes; wood; 4 × 2 cm; SGB. Playing figure, castle; 1 cm; SGB. 3 calendars; aluminium; 3 × 6 cm, 3 × 6 cm, 3 × 3.5 cm; SGB. Box; aluminium; 7 × 8 × 2.5 cm; SGB. Eyeglass; 9.5 × 4 cm; SGB. Glasses case; aluminium; 13 × 8 × 1 cm; SGB. 6 cigarette lighters; metal; 3 × 5 × 1.5 cm, 3 × 4.5 × 1 cm, 3 × 5.5 × 1 cm, 3.5 × 6 × 1 cm, 4 × 3 × 1 cm, 4 × 4 × 1 cm; SGB. Match holder; aluminium; 5.5 × 4 × 1.7 cm. 2 pipe bowls; wood; 3.5 × 3 × 2 cm, 4.5 × 3 × 2 cm; SGB. 2 toothbrushes; plastic, aluminium handle; 15 × 2 cm; SGB. Toothbrushes; bone; 51 × 2 cm; SGB. 3 comb fragments; wood; 6.5 × 3 cm,

6.5 × 2 cm, 4.5 × 2.5 cm; SGB. 13 combs; aluminium; 25 × 13 cm; SGB. Comb; aluminium; 7 × 4 cm; SGB. Comb; copper; 9 × 3.5 cm; SGB. Comb; plastic; 7 × 3 cm; SGB. Comb made of ruler; plastic; 8 × 3 cm; SGB. 2 combs, plastic; 10 × 6 cm, 9 × 4 cm; SGB. 3 shaving brushes; 8 × 3 × 5 cm; SGB. Food bowl with inscription; metal; 18 × 8 cm; SGB. Cup; metal; 11 × 8 cm; SGB. 10 spoons; metal/plastic; 22/20 cm; SGB. 2 knives; wood/metal; 2 × 15 cm; SGB. 6 spoons with polished handles; 19 × 6 cm; SGB. (All objects found on camp grounds.) Henri Pieck, "A Break from Work," 1944; charcoal drawing; 22 × 34 cm; SGB. Henri Pieck, "They Had to Live Alongside the Dead," 1944; charcoal drawing; 22 × 34 cm; SGB.

3/44 Resistance for reasons of Christian convictions
Inmate's cap, 1938; Ø 27 cm; SGB. Detention cell book, 1938; DIN A 4; ThHStA; KZ Bu 17, Vol. 6, Bl. 27. Paul Schneider; portrait photo; oval; SGB. File memo from first officer in charge of preventive custody camp, Nov. 24, 1938; 18 × 13 cm; BwA, 52-11-200.

3/45 Resistance by Jewish political inmates
Rudolf Arndt, 1933; portrait photo; 9 × 17 cm; SGB. Rudolf Arndt, 1937; passport photo in custody; 6 × 8 cm; SGB. Labour administration office file card of Rudolf Arndt; 14 × 10 cm; SGB. List of the labour detachment to which the Hamber brothers were assigned, Nov. 5, 1940; DIN A 4; ThHStA, KZ Bu 15, Bl. 44. Money card of Philipp Hamber; DIN A 5; ThHStA, KZ Bu inmates' money card file. Number card Edmund Hamber; DIN A 6; ThHStA, KZ Bu number card file.

3/46 The Last Face
Bruno Apitz, "The Last Face," 1944; oak, clear varnish; height 29 cm; loan from Deutsches Historisches Museum. 3 woodcarving knives by Bruno Apitz; SGB. Bruno Apitz, 1920; portrait photo; 11 × 14 cm; Stiftung Archiv der Künste, Bruno-Apitz-Archiv.

3/47-3/48 Eye-witnesses
Pierre Mania, "In the Wagon," drawing, 1943; print; 18 × 25.3 cm; SGB. Auguste Favier, "In the Little Camp," drawing, 1945; print; 25 × 17.9 cm"; SGB. Auguste Favier, "Arrival of a Transport", drawing, 1945; print; 25 × 17.8 cm; SGB. Auguste Favier "Crematorium", drawing, 1944; print; 18 × 25 cm; SGB. Boris Taslitzky, "Block 51 and the Block of the Human Guinea Pigs", pencil drawing, 1944; print; 19.8 × 13.8 cm; SGB. Boris Taslitzky, "Professor Halbwachs from the Collége de France, During Medical Treatment a Few Days Before his Death", pencil drawing, 1945; print; 12 × 19.8 cm; SGB.

3/49 Eye-witnesses
Alberto Berti, 1992; portrait photo; 14 × 10 cm;

SGB. Personal notes by Alberto Berti; 16 × 11 cm, 15 × 11 cm, 15 × 10 cm; loan from Langenstein/Zwieberge Memorial.

3/50 Illegal practice of faith
Handmade altar, 1943; plaster; 4.5 × 4.5 × 4.5 cm; estate of Maurice Hewitt; loan from Madame Berthin. Prayer book of Maurice Suard; 8.5 × 10 cm; loan from Jacques Suard. 6 handmade crucifixes: leather; 4 × 5.5 cm, SGB; brass; 4.7 × 2.5 cm, SGB; copper; 4 × 2 cm, SGB; wood; 2.6 × 1.7 cm, SGB; metal; 5.5 × 3 cm, SGB; wood; 2.6 × 1.8 cm, SGB. Pendant with figure of Jesus; brass; 2 cm, SGB. Albert Simon, 1945; portrait photo; 9 × 13 cm, SGB.

The Illegal Organisation
3/51 Illegal reception of news
Connection diagram for radio cabinet in entrance building, June 20, 1939; photocopy; 40 × 30 cm; SGB. Short-wave receiver and headphones, reconstructed in 1975 from original parts; 20 × 25 × 20 cm; SGB. Short-wave receiver, 1943; 25 × 20 × 25 cm; SGB. Reinhold Lochmann; passport photo; 3 × 4 cm; SGB. Gwidon Damazyn, after 1945; portrait photo; 4 × 6 cm; SGB. Armin Walther (left) in front of Buchenwald generating set, 1945; photo; 9 × 6 cm; BwA, Material Körner, KZ Bu 1/8. Order by Dresden chief of police for arrest of Armin Walther for carrying out illegal activities for the SPD, Mar. 14, 1936; 21 × 15 cm; BwA, Material Körner, KZ Bu 1/8. Armin Walther; portrait photo; 11 × 15.5 cm; SGB. Walther, certificate of exclusion from army, 1938; DIN A 5; BwA, Material Körner, KZ Bu 1/8.

3/52. The International Camp Committee
Diagram: Members of the International Camp Committee and centres of resistance.

3/53 German Communists in inmate functions
Diagram: Inmate administration. Diagram: Outline of functions of camp administration 1942-1945. Minutes of interrogation of Franz Dobermann, political inmate, 1937-1945, by an SED investigation committee, Oct. 13, 1946; DIN A 4; SAPMO, I/2/3/155, Bl. 64.

3/54 Group self-preservation, secret tribunals
Minutes of interrogation of Fritz Männchen, political inmate, 1937-1945, before an SED investigation committee, Oct. 14, 1946; 2 DIN A 4 sheets; SAPMO, I/2/3/155, Bl. 70f. Money card Johannes Bechert; DIN A 5; ThHStA, KZ Bu inmates' money card file. Wool blanket, Buchenwald Concentration Camp; rolled; SGB. Cigarette package, "Orion" brand; 7.5 × 7 cm; SGB.

3/55 Hand grenade production
3 handmade hand grenades; metal, partially rusted; 30 × 6 cm; SGB. Box of guncotton from stocks of underground organisation, 1945;

16 × 10 × 7 cm; SGB. Makeshift lab in cellar of inmates' canteen; photo; 15 × 20.5 cm; SGB. Pawel Lyssenko; portrait photo; 7.5 × 10.5 cm; SGB. Drawing of hand grenades, 1944; photo; 17 × 23 cm; BwA, 30/VIII-31. Tdzislaw Lewandowski, after 1945; portrait photo; 4 × 5 cm; SGB.

3/56 Military resistance organisation
Plan of military underground organisation, 1945; photocopy, with added drawings in colour; 18 × 27 cm; SGB. Otto Roth with his family; photo; 8 × 13 cm; BwA, Material Körner, KZ Bu 1/6. Page 1 of provisional report on military organisation in Buchenwald Concentration Camp, Apr. 1945; DIN A 4; BwA, 32/II-63, Bl. 21.

Solidarity
3/57 Exchanges of identity
Engagement ring of Marcel Leccia; silver; ⌀ 2 cm; SGB. New arrivals list, Buchenwald Concentration Camp, Aug. 17, 1944; DIN A 4; BwA, 31/274. Number card of Henri Peuleve; DIN A 6; ThHStA, KZ Bu number card file. Forest Yeo Thomas, 1943; portrait photo; 7 × 9 cm; SGB. Eugen Kogon and Heinz Baumeister, 1944; photo; 13 × 18 cm; BwA, 52-11-758. 2 slips of paper from Yeo Thomas for Eugen Kogon, 1945; reproduction; 13 × 10 cm, 10 × 16 cm; NARA, Film 5. Auguste Favier, "Robert Benoist," 1944; drawing; 18 × 25 cm; SGB.

3/58-3/59 Help for children
2 children's shoes from Auschwitz; leather; 14 × 6 × 5 cm; SGB. Stefan Zweig in the camp, Apr. 1945; photo; 24 × 20.5 cm; SGB. Liberated children, Apr. 1945; 2 photos; 12 × 9 cm; SGB. Robert Siewert, after 1945; photo; 10 × 8 cm; BwA, 52-11-408. Henryk Sokolak, 1974; portrait photo; 5.5 × 8 cm; SGB. Labour administration office report on adolescents in the transports of Dec. 2 and Dec. 4, 1944; DIN A 4; ThHStA, KZ Bu 12, Bl. 200. Report on overall number of adolescents, Dec. 5, 1944; DIN A 5; ThHStA, KZ Bu 12, Bl. 204. Labour administration office report to labour allocation officer, Dec. 10, 1944; 21 × 15 cm; ThHStA, KZ Bu 12, Bl. 203. Wilhelm Hammann, after 1945; portrait photo; 6 × 8 cm; SGB. Wooden horse; carving; 19 × 21 cm; SGB. Belt of Aron Bulwa, 1994; photo; 9 × 12 cm; Miriam Rouveyre, Paris. Eliezer Buzyn with his family, 1944; photo; 6 × 9 cm; Miriam Rouveyre, Paris. Desider Adolfowitsch Gross; portrait photo; 5 × 8.5 cm; SGB. Gustav Schiller, 1945; photo; 8.5 × 12 cm; Miriam Rouveyre, Paris.

3/60 National support committees
Collection list of the Italian committee "Italian Solidarity," March 1945; 2 sheets, 13.5 × 21 cm; BwA, 31/59. Red Cross Package; 45 × 26 × 10 cm; SGB. Garrison physician Schiedlausky to

Gerhard Maurer, chief of Office D II, re Red Cross packages, Apr. 11, 1944; 2 sheets, 21 × 15 cm; ThHStA, KZ Bu 10, Bl. 165.

4. The Camp During the "Total War," 1942/43 – 1945

4.1 Change in Function and Mass Committal

"Labour Allocation"
4/1 The plenipotentiary for labour allocation, Weimar headquarters
Neuer Illustrierter Beobachter, Mar. 9, 1943; 27.2 × 37.5 cm; SGB. Appointment of Fritz Sauckel as Plenipotentiary for Labour Allocation, Mar. 21, 1942; 20 × 28 cm; RGBl. 1942/I, p. 179. Hitler and Sauckel in the Weimar Hotel "Elephant" in front of a model of the city, early Nov. 1938; photo; 13.6 × 11.9 cm; *Der Führer in Weimar*, 1938, p. 29. Case of the address machine for registration of foreign workers at factory Reichswerke Hermann Göhring (Reimahg) in Kahla, Thuringia, 1944; metal; 38.3 × 11.5 × 6.6 cm; SGB. One hundred workmen's passports; 10.8 × 14.7 cm; SGB.

4/2 The SS Department of Economic Administration (WVHA), 1942, diagram; 5.2 × 8 cm.

4/3 The new SS camp command of Buchenwald Concentration Camp in 1942
Administration departments in Buchenwald Concentration Camp, 1942; diagram. Hermann Pister, 1941; photo; 6.7 × 9.5 cm; BA BDC. Hans Schmidt; photo; 6.7 × 9.5 cm; BA BDC. Albert Schwartz, 1944; photo; 7 × 9.3 cm; SGB. Otto Barnewald, 1934; photo; 6.9 × 9.5 cm; BA BDC. Max Schobert, 1934; photo; 6.9 × 9.5 cm; BA BDC.

4/4 The human being as raw material
Transport order, Schönebeck Sub-Camp, Dec. 16, 1943; 2 DIN A 5 sheets; ThHStA, NS 4 Bu 133, Bl. 236f. Chief camp administration of Krupp AG re compensation of burial and cremation costs, Mar. 1, 1945; DIN A 4; SGB. Transports, Jan. 20, 1945; 14.6 × 10.5 cm; ThHStA, KZ Bu 9, Bl. 19. Roll call report, sub-camps, Oct. 28, 1944; 6.3 × 25.4 cm; ThHStA, NS 4 Bu 210. Claim voucher, Dec. 6, 1944; DIN A 4; ThHStA, NS 4 Bu 229. 37 factory workers' lapel buttons from various plants; metal; ⌀ 2.5-4.0 cm; SGB. 7 tool chips, Gustloff-Werk II; metal; ⌀ 4 cm; SGB. Factory workers' lapel button, Junkers Flugzeug und Motorenwerke AG, Schönebeck plant, ⌀ 4 cm; SGB. Factory workers' lapel buttons, Hugo Schneider AG, 1944; metal; ⌀ 4 cm; SGB. 5 factory workers' lapel buttons, VDM (Vereinigte German Metallwerke AG Hamburg); metal; ⌀ 3.5 cm; SGB. Urn shipment case for urn of Jewish inmate Joszef Sztern, Essen Crematorium, 1944; SGB.

Deportation to Buchenwald, 1942-1945

Ohannes Tapyuli: Untitled
Wall installation, 1995
Wood, cardboard, transparent foil. 44 plates,
each 76 × 76 × 5 cm.

4/5 Deportation from Poland, Czechoslovakia
and the Soviet Union
Forced labour convicts (men and women) at Ko-
vel railway station (Ukraine), 1943/44; 17.5 × 11.5
cm; SGB. Arrest of "partisan suspects" by auxiliary police in Minsk, undated; 15 × 9 cm; SGB.
Hanging of Russian partisans, undated; photo;
15 × 10.8 cm; SGB. Massacre in Czech village of
Lidice, June 10, 1942; SGB. Raid in Warsaw for
recruitment of forced labour convicts, 1942;
SGB. Deportation of Warsaw civilian population, Oct. 1944; 8.5 × 11.7 cm; SGB. Commander
of security police of Ukrainian city of Nikolajev
to Buchenwald Concentration Camp re inmate
transport, Sept. 30, 1943; DIN A 5; ThHStA, NS
4 Bu 133, Bl. 15. Memo from inmates' infirmary
re transports, 1943; DIN A 4; ThHStA, KZ Bu
10, Bl. 396. Red inmate's triangle with "R" (Russian); textile; 6 cm; SGB. Inmate's personal
record card of Alexander Zubman; DIN A 5;
BwA, 52-11-173. Wladimir Mazijenko; photo;
6 × 4 cm; SGB. Food bowl with engraved
number 70 414; aluminium; 14.5 × 9 cm; SGB.
Number card 70414 (Iwan Omeljanow); DIN A
6; ThHStA, KZ Bu number card file. Examination list, inmates' infirmary, Aug. 28, 1944; DIN
A 4; BwA, 59-101/6. Report on incidents during
transport from Majdanek-Lublin Concentration Camp, Aug. 5, 1943; 21 × 15 cm; ThHStA,
NS 4 Bu 133, Bl. 100. 2 food bowls from Majdanek-Lublin Concentration Camp; tin, enamelled; SGB. Communication from Polish inmate to his father, Aug. 1, 1943; 10 × 13.5 cm;
ThHStA, NS 4 Bu 133, Bl. 103. Zbigniew Sim-
borowski, Polish inmate, to his parents, Aug. 1,
1943; 22 × 16 cm; ThHStA, NS 4 Bu 133, Bl. 101.
Translations of letters ordered by SS, 1943; DIN
A 4; ThHStA, NS 4 Bu 133, Bl. 104. Report on
committal of five escaped Polish inmates, Aug.
9, 1943; 21 × 15 cm; ThHStA, NS 4 Bu 133, Bl. 19.
Postcard to Marian Tasimierski from his mother,
May 26, 1944; 14.7 × 10.5 cm; BwA, o. S. Red
Cross package for Tadeusz Miczulis, Polish inmate, 1943-1945; 28 × 10 × 13 cm; SGB. 2 letters
written in Auschwitz and Buchenwald by Alois
Krol, 1943/44; 22.1 × 15.4; BwA, o. S. Food package for Ludwig Kreisel, Czech inmate, 1939-
1945; 35 × 7.3 × 30.5 cm; SGB. Fragment of star;
limestone; 3 × 2 cm; SGB. Comb with Russian
inscription, 1944; plastic; 13.3 × 4 cm; SGB. Lid
with Polish inscription; aluminium; ∅ 4 cm;
SGB. Signet ring with red triangle and "P";
brass; ∅ 2.3 cm; SGB. 13 Polish Groszy coins;
found objects; SGB. Pocket knife, Polish inscription: "Krynica;" 8.3 × 1.8 cm, SGB. Hand-

made metal tag, inscription: "Supimsi," verso:
"86…45 Warschawa;" 3.5 × 1.5 cm; SGB. Zipper
part, Polish manufacturer; 2.4 × 1 cm; SGB.
Aluminium tag with triangle "P" and inmate's
number; 6 × 2 cm; SGB. Name sign, inscription:
KOWALSKI ROMAN KRAKOW WOLA
JUSTOWSKA/P. 30.277 GROSS ROSEN DY-
HERNFURTH; 7 × 2 cm; SGB. 8 handmade
identification tags with inmates' numbers and
engravings "R," "R Kgf.;" 4.2 × 2.6 cm, 5 × 1.3
cm, 4.7 × 1.8 cm, 4.9 × 1.7 cm, 5.9 × 2.5 cm,
5.4 × 1.8 cm, 4.7 × 1.6 cm, 5.2 × 1.9; SGB. Fold-
out icon of St. Nicholas of Myra; brass, 3 parts;
9 × 6.4 cm; SGB. Cup with engraved number
11119; aluminium; 10 × 10.4 cm; SGB. Inmate's
jacket and trousers of Zdének Syrovatka; fabric;
SGB.

4/6 Deportation from France, Italy, Yugoslavia
Execution by shooting of four members of the
Resistance, undated; photo; 15.4 × 7.5 cm;
Zentner, Kurt *Illustrierte Geschichte des Wider-
stands in Deutschland und Europa 1933-1945*,
Munich, 1966, p. 259. Members of the Résistance, undated; photo; 12.3 × 18 cm; ibid.,
p. 260. Wall inscription: "VIVE DE GAULLE
– A MORT HITLER"; undated; photo;
11 × 23.5 cm; ibid., p. 263. Arrest of members of
Italian Resistance, undated; photo; 12.5 × 9 cm;
*Die Okkupationspolitik des deutschen Faschmis-
mus in Jugoslawien, Griechenland, Albanien, Ital-
ien, Ungarn 1941-1945*. Selection of documents
and introduction by Martin Seckendorf, Berlin,
Heidelberg, 1992, Ill. 37. Italian partisans on the
way to their execution in Fondo Toce, Novara
Province, June 1944; photo; 17.5 × 14 cm; Zentner, Kurt, *Illustrierte Geschichte des zweiten
Weltkrieges*, Munich, 1965, p. 398. "Punitive operation" by Wehrmacht units in Yugoslavia, undated; photo; 12.5 × 8 cm; *Die Okkupationspolitik des deutschen Faschmismus*, Ill. 9. Shooting
execution of Yugoslavian hostages in Pancewo
near Belgrade, 1942; photo; 14 × 9.5 cm; *Topographie des Terrors. Gestapo, SS und Reichssicherheitshauptamt auf dem Prinz-Albrecht-Gelände.
Eine Dokumentation.* Reinhard Rürup (ed.),
Berlin, 1987, p. 152, Ill. 160. Inmate's triangle
"F"; textile; 6 cm; SGB. Railroad car bearing inscription "Compiègne-Buchenwald", 1945; photo; 15 × 8 cm; BwA, taken by Georges Angéli. 17
identification tags of Compiègne Camp; metal;
6 × 4 cm; SGB. Report by camp physician on
transport of French inmates, Sept. 18, 1943; DIN
A 4; ThHStA, KZ Bu 9, Bl. 62. Group of French
inmates in Little Camp, 1945; photo; 17.5 × 12.5
cm; BwA, taken by Georges Angéli. Marcel
Bloch, ca. 1910; photo; dimensions; Charlier,
Claude, Marcel Cassault, Perin, 1992, illustration
section. Marcel Bloch with a group of French
inmates, Apr. 16, 1945; photo; 13 × 10 cm; ibid.
Robert Clop, after 1945; photo; 11.5 × 18 cm; in
private ownership of Robert Clop. Julien Cain,

after 1945; photo; 9 × 13 cm; in private ownership of family. Letter from Julien Cain to his wife, May 20, 1944; DIN A 5; in private ownership of Pierre André Meyer. Envelope from Julien Cain to his wife, May 30, 1944; 16 × 17 cm; loan from Pierre André Meyer. "Capet-Quartett," 1927 concert programme; 19 × 22.3 cm; loan from Madame Berthin. Chess game belonging to Maurice Hewitt, inmates' work 1944; 12 × 12 cm; loan from Madame Berthin. Pierre Durand's inmate trousers; 90 cm; loan from Pierre Durand. Pierre Durand's personal inmate record card; 21 × 15 cm; in private ownership. Henry Krasucki, Aug. 1945; photo; 10 × 15 cm; in private ownership of Henry Krasucki. Deportee's ID of Rene' L'Hopital, Nov. 4, 1950; 11.6 × 7.9 cm; in private ownership of Marie-Sabine Perry. Postcard of the Scout movement founded by René L'Hopital in France, undated; DIN A 6; in private ownership of Marie-Sabine Perry. Charles Richet, 1929; photo; 9.5 × 13 cm; in private ownership of Gabriel Richet. Charles Richet's personal inmate record card; 21 × 14.9 cm; in private ownership. Letter from Charles Richet to his wife, June 18, 1944; 30.3 × 20.8 cm; BwA, Mappe Franzosen. 15 French coins; found objects; SGB. Cup with engraved name; aluminium; ∅ 8.3 × 9 cm; SGB. Razor, engraved; aluminium, steel; 14 × 2.2 cm; loan from Floréal Barrier. Number card 14862 (Marcel Guilleux); DIN A 6; ThHStA, KZ Bu number card file. Food bowl, engraved: 78422 NINO A[ntonio] B[urigana]; aluminium; ∅ 19.2 cm; SGB. Commemorative medal of Italy's campaign against Greece, 1941; found object; SGB. Examination list, inmates' infirmary, July 3, 1944; DIN A 4; BwA, 59-101/3. Telephone chip; ∅ 2.4 cm; found object; SGB. Italian coin, 1942; found object; SGB. Serbian canteen, 1939; found object; 19 × 15 × 7 cm; SGB.

4/7 Jews, Sinti and Romani from Auschwitz, 1944

Auschwitz-Birkenau, Barrack Field B. II, 1943/44; photo; 14 × 10; *Memorial Book. The Gypsies at Auschwitz-Birkenau* 2, Munich/London/New York/Paris, 1993, p. 1572 (orig. photo: YVA). Deportation of Sinti and Romani from Remscheid, March 1943; photo; 13.8 × 9.4 cm; Fings, Karola and Sparing, Frank, "*z. Zt. Zigeunerlager." Die Verfolgung der Düsseldorfer Sinti und Roma im Nationalsozialismus*, publ. by Mahn- und Gedenkstätte Düsseldorf, Cologne, 1992, p. 75, Ill. 60. Occupation of Hungary by German Wehrmacht, March 1944; photo; 12.5 × 9 cm; *Die Okkupationspolitik des deutschen Faschmismus*, Ill. 40. Jews rounded up by Hungarian gendarmerie in Koszegszerdahely (Western Hungary), spring 1944; photo; 11.5 × 8.8 cm; *Enzyklopädie des Holocaust. Die Verfolgung und Ermordung der Juden*, Vol. 3, ed. by Eberhard Jäckel, Peter Longerich, Julius Schoeps, Berlin, 1993, p. 1467. Arrival of

Hungarian Jews in Auschwitz, summer 1944; photo; 20 × 16 cm; "*Auschwitz – Verbrechen gegen die Menschheit*," Staatliches Museum Auschwitz-Birkenau, 1991 (photo taken by member of SS, 1944). Selection of Jewish inmates in Auschwitz-Birkenau, 1944; photo; 16.8 × 10 cm; ibid. Radio message from Auschwitz Concentration Camp to commander of Buchenwald Concentration Camp, June 5, 1944; 21 × 15 cm; BwA HKW-Film 12. Radio message from Auschwitz Concentration Camp to commander of Buchenwald Concentration Camp, June 10, 1944; 21 × 15 cm; BwA HKW-Film 12. Transport list, June 6, 1944; 2 DIN A 4 sheets; BwA, Auschwitz film. List of adolescents in transports from Auschwitz, June 1944; 21 × 15 cm; ThHStA, KZ Bu 10, Bl. 47. Jenö (Eugene) Heimler; photo; 13 × 18 cm; Heimler, Eugene, *Bei Nacht und Nebel. Autobiographischer Bericht* 1944/45, Berlin, 1993, p.6. Transport list, Aug. 3, 1944; DIN A 4; BwA, 59-101/4. Auschwitz Concentration Camp report on transport of Karl R. to Buchenwald, Apr. 16, 1944; 14.9 × 10.6 cm; Nordrhein-Westfälisches HStA Düsseldorf, gypsy personal files BR 2034/1169. Transports of Sinti and Romani from Auschwitz, Apr. and Aug. 1944; 20 photos; 5.5 × 8.3 cm; BA Koblenz, item R 165 (Eugenic Research Centre of the Reich Department of Health). File memo by SS garrison physician on ages of Sinti and Romani committed to Buchenwald, Aug. 3, 1944; 21 × 15 cm; ThHStA, KZ Bu 10, Bl. 46. Boris Taslitzky, "Little Gypsy, fourteen years old", pen drawing, 1944; print; 10 × 13.5 cm; SGB. Buchenwald SS garrison physician to SS garrison physician at Auschwitz, Aug. 4, 1944; 20.8 × 19.4; ThHStA, KZ Bu 8, Bl. 20. List drawn up by SS camp physician, Aug. 5, 1944; 2 DIN A 4 sheets; BwA, 59-101/4. Transport of Sinti and Romani to B XI, May 17, 1944; DIN A 4; BwA, 59-101/2. Jewish inmates in Little Camp, Apr. 16, 1945; photo; 17 × 13.4; SGB. Henri Pieck, "Joden" (Jews), charcoal drawing, 1945; print; 45 × 30 cm; SGB. Consignment note for personal belongings from Auschwitz, July 10, 1944; 2 DIN A 4 sheets; BwA, HKW-Film 12. 7 shaving brushes; found objects; SGB. 8 razors; found objects; SGB. 4 watch housings; found objects; SGB. 43 combs; found objects; SGB. Mirror; found object; 6.8 × 8 cm; SGB. 30 remnants of shoe soles; found objects, SGB.

4/8 Inmates from Gestapo prisons and places of detention

2 foreign workers' passports; 10.5 × 15 cm; SGB. Textile badge "Ost;" 7 × 7.5 cm; SGB. Teleprint message re special inmate transport of Soviet forced labour convicts from Leipzig, Feb. 15, 1943; 20 × 19.5 cm; ThHStA, NS 4 Bu 133, Bl. 116. Ivan Borisow, 1945; photo; 11 × 15 cm; in private ownership of Heinz Albertus. Mess kit, engraved (Eszov Aleksej Nikalajevic); ∅ 19 × 13 cm; SGB. Cup, engraved (9.746 W[ictor]

R[jacenko]); ∅ 10.3 × 9.3 cm; SGB. Mess kit, engraved (12...297); ∅ 15 × 8.8 cm; SGB. Stanley Booker, 1944; photo during custody; 11 × 15 cm; in private ownership of S. Booker. Forged ID card, 1944; 19 × 12.5, cm; in private ownership of S. Booker. Depot card, Paris-Fresnes Wehrmacht Prison, July 4, 1944; 21 × 13.5 cm; in private ownership of S. Booker. Number card (Stanley Booker); DIN A 6; ThHStA, KZ Bu number card file. Stanley Booker's personal record card from Oflag Luft III, Oct. 21, 1944; 20.5 × 14.5 cm; in private ownership of S. Booker. Lieutenant Levitt C. Beck, 1943/44; photo; 11 × 14 cm; in private ownership of family, sent by James D. Hastin, Anacortes, U.S.A. Inmate's jacket, 1944; 40 × 75 × 20 cm; SGB. Teleprint message from RSHA to all state police (central) offices re arrest of former MPs from Central Party, Aug. 21, 1944; DIN A 4; Staatsarchiv Bremen, 5.4 *Geheime Staatspolizei, Staatspolizeistelle Bremen.* Otto Gerig, undated; photo; 15.5 × 23.3 cm; *Widerstand und Verfolgung in Köln* 1933-1945, Exhibition catalogue, Historisches Archiv der Stadt Köln, Cologne, 1981, illustration section, Ill. 19. Dr. Kurt Adams; photo; 8.8 × 13.9 cm; Staatsarchiv Hamburg, Pankammer, PL 215/Ad. 6.1. K. Adams' notice of dismissal as director of Volkshochschule Hamburg, June 26, 1933; DIN A 4; Staatsarchiv Hamburg, 361-3 Education Dept., personnel records, A 718, personal file Kurt Adams. Confidential letter from Gestapo to Hamburg Board of Education re death of Kurt Adams, Nov. 2, 1944; DIN A 4; ibid. Notification of death to Mrs. Adams, Nov. 14, 1944; DIN A 5; Bohn, Jörg, *Dr. Kurt Adams. Lehrer und Bürgerschaftsabgeordneter in Hamburg*, Hamburg, 1982, p. 37. Dr. Fritz Behr, 1945; photo; 16.5 × 23 cm; Stadtarchiv Weimar, Nachlässe 544-40, Nachlaß Fritz Behr 1945-1962. Henry Pieck, "A. Kayser," pencil drawing, 1944; 20.2 × 29.4 cm; SGB.

4/9 Deportation from Belgium, the Netherlands, Luxembourg, Denmark and Norway
Transport of Belgian workers to Germany for forced labour, undated; photo; 15.5 × 10 cm; *Die faschistische Okkupationspolitik in Belgien, Luxemburg und den Niederlanden* 1940-1945. Document selection and introduction by Ludwig Nestler, Berlin, 1990, Ill. 16. Breendonk Transit Camp, 1945; photo; 9.5 × 6.8 cm; *De Oorlogsmisdaden. Bedreven onder de besetting van Belgie* 1940-1945. *Het Folteringskamp Breendonk*, Luik, 1949, illustration section. Deportation of Dutch citizens to Germany for labour allocation, ca. 1943; photo; 13 × 20 cm; *Die Welt der Anne Frank* 1929-1945, publ. by Anne-Frank-Stiftung Amsterdam, Amsterdam, 1985, Ill. 184. Oslo factory destroyed by members of the Resistance; 17 × 24 cm; Zentner, Kurt, *Illustrierte Geschichte des Widerstandes in Deutschland und Europa* 1933-1945, Munich, 1966, p. 166. General

strike in Copenhagen, July 1944; photo; 15.5 × 19.2 cm; ibid. Memo from inmates' infirmary re Danish inmates, Nov. 18, 1944; 14.5 × 19 cm; ThHStA, NS 4 Bu 51, Bl. 67. Report to camp physician on contraction of disease in Little Camp, Nov. 24, 1944; DIN A 5; ThHStA, NS 4 Bu 51, Bl. 57. Dr. Svend Aage Schaldemose Nielsen, 1944; photo; 5 × 6 cm; BwA, 52-11-783. Camp Song of Neuengamme Concentration Camp, recorded on paper by Dr. Schaldemose-Nielsen, Oct. 1, 1944; 17.5 × 21 cm; BwA, ibid. Letter from Dr. Schaldemose-Nielsen to his family, Oct. 15, 1944; 9.8 × 13.5 cm; BwA, ibid. Letter from Dr. Schaldemose-Nielsen to his family, Nov. 5, 1945; 13.5 × 19.5 cm; BwA, ibid. Dr. Schaldemose-Nielsen, List of names of the policemen arrested in Odense and Nyborg on Sept. 19, 1944; 8.5 × 26.5 cm; BwA, ibid. Personal belongings ID tag with inscription (86914 S[chaldemose]-N[ielsen]); cardboard; 8 × 6 cm; BwA, ibid. Bowl and spoon belonging to Danish inmate Hendrik Jensen, engraved (J H, 86273, 7.11.44); spoon 18 cm, bowl ∅ 21 cm; SGB. Ivar Thomsen, "Interior View of Block 57," coloured pen drawing, 1945; facsimile; 24 × 18 cm; SGB. Notification of transfer of Danish policemen to a POW camp, Dec. 8, 1944; DIN A 5; ThHStA, NS 4 Bu 133, Bl. 112. Number card 39295 (Peter Daldorf Dahl); DIN A 6; ThHStA, KZ Bu number card file. Number card 39349 (Sverre per Terjesen); DIN A 6; ThHStA, KZ Bu number card file. Inmate's triangle "B"; fabric; 8 × 8 × 6.7 cm; SGB. Labour administration office ascertainment of skilled workers among Belgian inmates, Aug. 10, 1944; DIN A 4; ThHStA, NS 4 Bu 188, Bl. 81. Jean Fonteyne; photo; 9 × 10 cm; in private ownership of Fonteyne family. Jean Fonteyne's inmate's uniform; loan from Fonteyne family. Jean Fonteyne's inmate uniform; DIN A 5; loan from Fonteyne family. Georges de Bleser; photo; 13 × 18 cm; in private ownership of family. Lucien Aphonse Constant Van Beirs; photo; 11 × 16 cm; Rochette, Daniel and Vanhamme, Jean Marcel, *Les belges a Buchenwald dans ses Kommando exterieurs*, Brussels, 1976, illustration section. Vincent Weijand, early 1940s; photo; 8.9 × 14 cm; SGB. Transport list, Apr. 18, 1944; DIN A 4; ThHStA, KZ Bu 8, Bl. 285. Danish 2-crown coin; found object; ∅ 3 cm; SGB. Name plaque with address, Belgian; found object; metal; 4.3 × 1.9 cm; SGB. Belgian 25-centime coin; found object; ∅ 2.5 cm; SGB. Belgian medal; found object; ∅ 3.1 cm; SGB. Note-paper holder with Dutch motif; found object; metal; 5 × 7 cm; SGB.

Buchenwald as a Transit Camp
4/10 Examination and re-assignment of arriving transports
Medical emergency instrument set; 15.4 × 2.3 × 18 cm; SGB. Examination lists, June 20, 1944; 2 DIN A 4 sheets; BwA, 59-101/2. Otto

Kipp, deputy capo of inmates' infirmary, to Herbert Weidlich, deputy capo of labour administration office, June 12, 1944; 15 × 10.5 cm; BwA 59-101/2. Labour administration office list for the SS labour allocation officer re skilled workers in a transport, Jan. 29, 1945; DIN A 4; ThHStA, NS 4 Bu 109, Bl. 3. Labour administration office to inmates' infirmary re examination of inmates for labour allocation, Jan. 22, 1944; 21 × 15 cm; ThHStA, NS 4 Bu 188, Bl. 74.

4/11 "Special building"
Dayroom of camp brothel, autumn 1943; photo; 18 × 13 cm; SGB. Camp physician Schiedlausky to Enno Lolling, chief of Office D II, re an abortion, Dec. 11, 1943; 21 × 15 cm; BwA, 56-8-2.

4/12 Killing by means of injection
Operation room in inmates' infirmary, 1945; photo; 11 × 8.2 cm; SGB. Syringe; glass; 19.3 × 3.3 cm; SGB. Block daybook of inmates' infirmary, Jan. 31, 1945; ThHStA, NS 4 Bu 114, Heft. 32.

4/13 Inmates' infirmary
Ernst Busse, ca. 1932; photo; 5.7 × 8.6 cm; SGB. Batinan, "Ernst Busse in his Office in Inmates' Infirmary," drawing, 1944; copy; 13 × 17.3 cm; SGB. Henri Pieck, "Ernst Busse," oil painting 1944; wooden cassette; 39 × 47.2 cm × 6.5; SGB. Programme of Christmas party at inmates' infirmary, Dec. 24, 1943; 14.7 × 20.9 cm; BwA, Nachlaß Johannes Brumme, 30/I-0/22. Medical orderly uniform of Kurt Leonhard, SGB. 2 medical orderly arm bands; 18.6 × 7.1 cm, 17.5 × 11.5 cm; SGB. Daybook of Johannes Brumme, clerk in inmates' infirmary; 15.7 × 23 cm; BwA, Nachlaß Johannes Brumme, 30/I-1/8. Inmates' infirmary, Barrack 1, 1945; photo; 4 × 2.6 cm; SGB. Inmates' infirmary, 1945; photo; 17.2 × 11 cm; SGB. Official daybook of inmates' infirmary, DIN A 4; ThHStA, KZ Bu 17 Bd. 11. Kidney dish; 30.5 × 5.2 × 16 cm; SGB. Boot of Walter Veigel, inmate pharmacist; 29.5 × 36 × 28 cm; SGB. Walter Veigel, 1943/44; photo; 5.5 × 8.2 cm; BwA, 52-11-735. Leipzig-Thekla Sub-Camp to labour allocation officer Schwartz re return transport of disabled inmates to Buchenwald, July 12, 1943; DIN A 4; ThHStA, KZ Bu 10. Medical record of the inmate Georgij Skotarenko, 1944 (page 2); DIN A 4; ThHStA, KZ Bu 11, Bl. 316. Appendix to medical record of Georgij Skotarenko, 1944 (temperature curve); DIN A 4; ThHStA, KZ Bu 11, Bl. 330. Operation journal, July 16 -Aug. 5, 1940; 21 × 32 cm; ThHStA, KZ Bu 7 Bd. 1.

4/14 Labour administration and camp protection
Inmate's jacket, Otto Schieck, camp protection; SGB. Inmates from Luxembourg in the camp protection detachment, Apr. 14, 1945; photo; 15.2 × 10.6 cm; SGB. Arm band, camp protection detachment; fabric; 18.5 × 7.6 cm; SGB.

Report by labour administration office on arrangement of a transport to a sub-camp, Mar. 18, 1945; 2 DIN A 4 sheets; ThHStA, NS 4 Bu 135, Bl. 42/43.

4/15 The Little Camp
Henri Pieck, "Buchenwald," drawing, 1945; print; 40 × 30 cm; SGB. Henri Pieck, "Hunger and Frost," drawing, 1945; print; 21 × 28.5 cm; SGB. Order re setup of quarantine zones in the concentration camps, July 28, 1942; DIN A 4; ThHStA, KZ Bu 18, Bl. 7. Barracks in Little Camp before arrival of first inmates, autumn 1942; photo; 18 × 13 cm; SGB. Little Camp, Apr. 1945; photo; 18 × 13 cm; SGB. José Fosty, "The Tents," drawing, 1944; copy, 20 × 15 cm; SGB. Handbill from inmates' infirmary re infectious diseases in Little Camp, November 1944; 17 × 11 cm; ThHStA, NS 4 Bu 51, Bl. 57. ID for barrack duty in tent camp, Wolfgang Ballin, Oct. 8, 1944; 10.5 × 7.5 cm; SGB. Block daybook, Block 57, Feb. 28, 1945; 13.5 × 19.5 cm; ThHStA, KZ Bu 17, Bd. 12. Sub-camps of Buchenwald Concentration Camp; diagram.

4.2 The Sub-Camps

Springen Sub-Camp, 1944-1945
4/16 Everyday life in the Springen underground labour detachment
Mitten, patched, Springen Sub-Camp; fabric; SGB. Glove; Springen Sub-Camp; fabric; SGB. Inmate's cap, Springen Sub-Camp; fabric; loan from Kreisheimatmuseum Dermbach. Wooden shoes, Dutch-style, Springen Sub-Camp; SGB. Inmate's number, Springen Sub-Camp; fabric; 11.4 × 4.9 cm; loan from Kreisheimatmuseum Dermbach. Labour administration office report on transfer of individual inmates to sub-camps, Mar. 22, 1945; DIN A 4; ThHStA, NS 4 Bu 135, Bl. 26. Inmates' sleeping compartments, photo taken in 1958; 18.5 × 13 cm; SGB. Bread scales, Springen Sub-Camp; wood; loan from Kreisheimatmuseum Dermbach. Cutting board, Springen Sub-Camp; wood; 14 × 7.2 cm; loan from Kreisheimatmuseum Dermbach. Red Cross package, Czeslaw Ludwiczak, Springen Sub-Camp; 19.5 × 9.5 × 16.8 cm; loan from Kreisheimatmuseum Dermbach. Handmade checkers-morris game, Springen Sub-Camp; cardboard; 24 × 23 cm; loan from Kreisheimatmuseum Dermbach. 7 game pieces; cardboard; 2.1 × 2.1 cm; loan from Kreisheimatmuseum Dermbach.

Inmates in Underground Labour Detachments of the Rocket and Aircraft Industry
4/17 Dora Sub-Camp
Peenemünde experimental station, undated; photo; 18 × 13 cm; Pachaly, Eberhard/Pelny, Kurt, *Konzentrationslager Mittelbau-Dora. Zum antifaschistischen Widerstandskampf im KZ Dora 1933-1945*, Berlin, 1990, illustration section. Entrance to the underground production plant,

1945; photo; 18 × 13 cm; Dokumentationsstelle der Gedenkstätte Mittelbau-Dora, Bildarchiv. Transport order for first inmate transport to Dora, Aug. 27, 1943; DIN A 4; SGB. Carlo Slama, "Underground Blocks," charcoal, 1945; copy; 12.5 × 17.5 cm; Dokumentationsstelle der Gedenkstätte Mittelbau-Dora, Bildarchiv.

4/18 Dora Sub-Camp

Combustion chamber of an A 4 aggregate; 203 × 110 cm; loan from Mittelbau-Dora Concentration Camp Memorial. Robert Bourgeois; photo; 23.9 × 30.4 cm; SGB. Ruins following strike of a Fi 103 ("V1") in London, 1944; photo; 14 × 9 cm; Groehler, Olaf, *Geschichte des Luftkrieges* 1910-1980, Berlin, 1981, p. 450. A4 rocket ("V2") on a transportable ramp, 1944; photo; 8.5 × 21 cm; Bergschicker, Heinz, *Deutsche Chronik* 1933-1945, Berlin, 1981, p. 450.

4/19 Dora Sub-Camp

Request for death certificates and medical treatment slips, Nov. 28, 1943; DIN A 5; SGB. File memo re completion of crematorium in Dora, Mar. 25, 1944; 21 × 15 cm; BwA, 62-01-16. File memo by garrison physician re visit to Dora Sub-Camp, Apr. 11, 1944; 21 × 15 cm; BwA, 62-01-14. Dora Camp crematorium, crematory oven, 1945; photo; 9.5 × 6.9 cm; Dokumentationsstelle der Gedenkstätte Mittelbau-Dora, Bildarchiv. Construction of inmates' infirmary, 1944; photo; 12.5 × 9 cm; Dokumentationsstelle der Gedenkstätte Mittelbau-Dora, Bildarchiv. Inmates' camp, partial view, 1945; photo; 9.3 × 6.8 cm; Dokumentationsstelle der Gedenkstätte Mittelbau-Dora, Bildarchiv. Report from disinfection detachment to camp physician, Aug. 11, 1944; DIN A 4; ThHStA, NS 4 Bu 48, B. 40.

4/20 Dora Sub-Camp

Dora Sub-Camp report on camp strength, Mar. 4, 1943; DIN A 4; BwA, 62-01-13. Invoice from Mittelwerk GmbH to supreme army command, ordnance chief, re delivery of 20 A4 rockets, Mar. 23, 1945; DIN A 4; Bornemann, Manfred, *Geheimprojekt Mittelbau*, Bonn, 1994, p. 228. A4 rocket assembly track in Tunnel B, 1945; photo; 18 × 13 cm; Dokumentationsstelle der Gedenkstätte Mittelbau-Dora, Bildarchiv. Underground machine hall of North Works, 1945; photo; 18 × 13 cm; ibid. Fi 103 ("V1") in final assembly stage, 1945; photo; 18 × 13 cm; ibid. Hermann Rols, ca. 1940; photo; 10.3 × 15.2 cm; in private ownership. 5 bonus coupons; 6 × 4.8 cm, 10 × 7.5 cm; SGB. Special direction regulation on dealings with inmates, June 22, 1944; DIN A 4; Dokumentationsstelle der Gedenkstätte Mittelbau-Dora, Bildarchiv. Leon Delarbre, "Execution," charcoal drawing, 1945; photo; 15 × 11.6 cm; ibid. Detention cell building ("Bunker"), 1945; photo; 9.3 × 6 cm; ibid.

4/21 Ellrich Sub-Camp

Ellrich Camp, partial view 1944; photo; 11.7 × 7.6 cm; Bornemann, Manfred, *Chronik des Lagers Ellrich* 1944/45, Nordhausen, 1992, p. 105. Transport List B 11, May 11, 1944; DIN A 4; BwA, 59-110/1. Sign: "Mützen ab", (Caps Off), Ellrich Sub-Camp; cardboard; 50.5 × 16.2 cm; loan from Deutsches Historisches Museum Berlin. 2 tin bowls, Ellrich Sub-Camp; ∅ 21.5 cm, ∅ 22.5 cm; loan from Deutsches Historisches Museum Berlin. Fixture for an illuminated barrack number, Ellrich Sub-Camp; iron; 15.5 × 16 × 12.4 cm; loan from Deutsches Historisches Museum Berlin. Sign: "Rauchen verboten," (Smoking Prohibited) Ellrich Sub-Camp; wood; 73.5 × 15 cm; loan from Deutsches Historisches Museum Berlin. Sign: "DEFENSE DE FUMER," Ellrich Sub-Camp; cardboard; 50.5 × 16.2 cm; loan from Deutsches Historisches Museum Berlin.

Jewish Inmates in Sub-Camps, 1944-1945

4/22 "Schwalbe V" Sub-Camp

Garrison physician's record of medical orderly personnel employed in sub-camp with Jewish inmates, Jan. 31, 1945; DIN A 4; ThHStA, KZ Bu 10, Bl. 24. Destroyed industrial facilities of Brabag Zeitz, March 1945; photo; 48 × 22.5 cm; H.G. Carls engineering firm, Würzburg. Transport list of Hungarian-Jewish inmates, Berga/Elster Sub-Camp, Dec. 13, 1945; DIN A 4; BwA, 50-110/4. Berga/Elster Sub-Camp, 1945; photo; 12.3 × 7.8 cm; Bard, Mitchel G., *Forgotten Victims*, Westview Press, Boulder/San Francisco/Oxford, 1994, p. 95. Rock drill, Berga/Elster Sub-Camp, Tunnel 10; 70 cm; SGB.

4/23 "Wille" Sub-Camp

Miguel (Michael) Rozenek with his brother Jurek and their rescuer Arno Bach, 1945; photo; 12.5 × 6.7; BwA, 62-54-6. Garrison physician to commander of Buchenwald Concentration Camp re selection of inmates, Jan. 31, 1945; 2 DIN A 5 sheets; ThHStA, NS 4 Bu 54. Rough sketch of Tröglitz Camp, Aug. 8, 1944; 6.6 × 14.5 cm; ThHStA, NS 4 Bu 54, Bl. 149. Rough sketch of Gleina Camp, Aug. 8, 1944; 16.6 × 11.8 cm; ThHStA, NS 4 Bu 54, Bl. 153. Weekly report of the "Wille" Sub-Camp inmates' infirmary department, June 25, 1944; 2 DIN A 4 sheets; ThHStA, NS 4 Bu 54, Bl. 172. Memo from inmates' infirmary department re transport to Buchenwald, June 19, 1944; 11.9 × 17.8 cm; ThHStA, NS 4 Bu 54, Bl. 175. Garrison physician to district administrator of Zeitz district re cremation of deceased inmates from Tröglitz-Gleina Sub-Camp, July 20, 1944; DIN A 5; ThHStA, NS 4 Bu 54, Bl. 161. Monthly report from inmates' infirmary department to camp physician of Buchenwald Concentration Camp, Sept. 22, 1944; DIN A 4; ThHStA, NS 4 Bu 54, Bl. 145. Entrance to former Rehmsdorf barrack camp, 1957; photo; 18.8 × 7.7 cm; BwA, 62-54-6. Barrack in former Rehmsdorf inmates' camp, 1957; photo; 16 × 11.8 cm; ibid.

4/24 S III/Ohrdruf Sub-Camp

Transport list of Hungarian Jews to S III, Nov. 24, 1944; DIN A 4; BwA, 59-110/3. Notification by officer in charge of administration at Buchenwald Concentration Camp to camp commander re transport of 500 inmates to S III, Jan. 6, 1945; DIN A 5; ThHStA, NS 4 Bu 133, Bl. 11. Secret project S III, Oct. 1945; photo; 54.5 × 11.5 cm; SGB. Map of tunnel system, Oct. 1945; DIN A 4; SGB. Twist drill shank, Tunnel S III; steel; 24 cm; SGB. Oil lamp, fragment, Tunnel S III; iron; Ø 7.2 cm × 20 cm; SGB. Handmade drinking vessel, Tunnel S III; metal; Ø 10.5 cm × 5.5 cm; SGB. Entrance to Tunnel 7, Oct. 1945; photo; 15 × 9.2 cm; SGB. Tunnel 16, Oct. 1945; photo; 9 × 14 cm; SGB. Concrete mixing facility in front of Tunnels 16 and 17, Oct. 1945; photo; 14 × 9.5 cm; SGB. Track system and equipment in front of Tunnels 3 and 4, Oct. 1945; photo; 14.8 × 9.2 cm; SGB. List of deceased inmates of S III Sub-Camp on Feb. 19/20, 1945; DIN A 4; ThHStA, KZ Bu 5, Bd. 16, Bl. 191. Report by Weimar Armed SS garrison physician on physical condition of inmates in S III Sub-Camp, Mar. 31, 1945; DIN A 4; ThHStA, KZ Bu 9, Bl. 72. S III Sub-Camp, Apr. 1945; photo; 10.8 × 8.3 cm; SGB. Corpse barrack in north camp, Apr. 1945; photo; 16.7 × 7.5 cm; SGB. Burial of inmates after liberation, Apr. 1945; photo; 15 × 11 cm; SGB.

Buchenwald Inmates in SS Construction Brigades, 1944-1945

4/25 SS Construction brigades

Radio message from Office D II re transfer of inmates from Buchenwald Concentration Camp to Cologne, Sept. 29, 1942; 20.2 × 14.5 cm; ThHStA, NS4 Bu 133, Bl. 197. Richard Glücks to Buchenwald Concentration Camp command re increase in number of inmates for SS Construction Brigade III, Nov. 6, 1942; 20.3 × 19.7 cm; ThHStA, NS 4 Bu 133, Bl. 173. Inmates of SS Construction Brigade III clearing rubble in Cologne, Oct. 23, 1943; photo; 12.5 × 17.5 cm; Historisches Archiv der Stadt Köln, Nachlaß Peter Fischer F 400/17. Inmates loading a child's coffin, 1943/44; photo; 12.5 × 17.5 cm; BA Koblenz, Fotoarchiv, Nr. 72/40/88. Inmates with defused bomb, Kalkum Bomb Disposal Squad, 1943/44; photo; 13 × 9.2 cm; private photo of Norbert Krüger, Essen. Report on fatalities and injuries during excavation of blind shells, July 26, 1943; DIN A 4; BwA 62-41-3. Report on two inmates "shot during the attempt to escape," July 26, 1943; DIN A 4; BwA 62-41-3. Accident report, Feb. 16, 1944; 18.8 × 14.7 cm; SGB. Report re transfer of remainder of SS Construction Brigade I to SS Construction Bri-

gade III, Feb. 24, 1943; 19.2 × 27 cm; BwA 62-41-3. Officer in charge of SS Construction Brigade III to commander of Buchenwald Concentration Camp re inmate exchange, Mar. 30, 1943; DIN A 5; BwA 62-41-4. List of names of deceased inmates of SS Construction Brigade V, Oct. 9, 1944; DIN A 4; ThHStA, NS 4 Bu 133, Bl. 185.

Women's Sub-Camps – Female Inmates in the Armament Industry, 1944-1945

4/26 Destination: sub-camp

Suzanne Pic, 1944; photo; 10.2 × 15.2 cm; private photo of Suzanne Orts. Female inmate's jacket, loan from Suzanne Orts. Transport list Ravensbrück to Leipzig, July 20, 1944; 2 DIN A 4 sheets; BwA, HKW-Film 10. Bead cross with wire eyelet; 5 × 4 cm; loan from Suzanne Orts. Belt; straw, embroidered; 65 × 1.5 cm; loan from Suzanne Orts. Address book; straw, cover embroidered with the initials S.P.; paper insert; 5.5 × 4.2 cm; loan from Suzanne Orts. Women during inmate count in Auschwitz-Birkenau; photo; 19.5 × 12 cm; Isaacson, Judith Magyar, *Befreiung in Leipzig*, Witzenhausen, 1991, p. 100. Radio message from Auschwitz SS camp physician to camp physician at Buchenwald, Oct. 10, 1944; DIN A 4; ThHStA, KZ Bu 8, Bl. 7. Transport list of female inmates, Auschwitz to Taucha Sub-Camp, Oct. 11, 1944; DIN A 4; BwA, HKW-Film 10. Record of inmate numbers of 300 women from Ravensbrück, Sept. 16, 1944; DIN A 4; BwA, HKW-Film 15. Violette Lecoq, "Selection," drawing, 1944; copy; 31 × 22.5 cm; SGB.

4/27 Destination: Hugo-Schneider-AG (Hasag) Leipzig

Aerial photograph, Hasag Leipzig, Apr. 10, 1945; 25 × 25 cm; H.G. Carls engineering firm, Würzburg. 8.8 cm high-explosive shell L 4.5, 40 × 8.8 cm; loan from Militärhistorisches Museum der Bundeswehr Dresden. Anti-tank rocket launcher, head, wing shaft; loan from Militärhistorisches Museum der Bundeswehr Dresden. Letter to commanders of Ravensbrück and Buchenwald Concentration Camp, Aug. 17, 1944; DIN A 4; ThHStA, KZ Bu 10, Bl. 173. 7 factory workers' label buttons, Hasag AG, Tschenstochau, 1944; found objects; metal; 4 × 4 cm, 5 × 4.5 × 4.5 (triangular), 4.2 × 4.6 (hexagonal); SGB. List of Jewish mothers with children in Hasag-Leipzig Labour Detachment, Aug. 14, 1944; DIN A 4; BwA, Auschwitz film. Letter from SS labour detachment A.T.G. Leipzig-Schönau, Sept. 24, 1944; 21 × 15 cm; ThHStA, NS 4 Bu 233, Bl. 6. Letter from Political Department of Buchenwald Concentration Camp re deportation of female inmates from Hasag-Leipzig to Auschwitz, Oct. 14, 1944; 21 × 15 cm; BwA. Auschwitz film. Red triangle, "P," fabric; 11 × 9 × 9 cm; loan from Danuta Brzosko-Medryk.

Bonus coupon, Hasag Sub-Camp; 6 × 4.8 cm; loan from Danuta Brzosko-Medryk. Fragment of a food bowl, Hasag logo; china; SGB. Food card, Hasag-Leipzig Sub-Camp; 26.5 × 4.5 cm; loan from Danuta Brzosko-Medryk.

4/28 The will to survive

Monthly medical report and report on strength of Hasag-Taucha, Jan. 1945; DIN A 4; ThHStA, NS 4 Bu 54, Bl. 5. 3 recipes written on receipts, 14.5 × 21 cm; loan from Suzanne Orts. Handmade belt; plastic, wire; 74 × 2.6 cm; loan from Suzanne Orts. Handmade brooch; plastic, wire; 4 × 1.5 cm; loan from Suzanne Orts. Handmade case; plastic, wire; 6.5 × 5.5 cm; loan from Suzanne Orts. Poetry book; paper, cover woven from paper and thread; 12 × 17.2 cm; loan from Suzanne Orts. List of 8 escapees, Hasag-Leipzig Sub-Camp; 15 × 21 cm; SGB. France Audoul, "The Forbidden Prayers", drawing, undated; copy; 21 × 21 cm; SGB. 2 postcards, 1945; 15 × 10 cm; loan from Danuta Brzosko-Medryk. Handmade dictionary, 2 sheets; 7.5 × 10.5 cm; loan from Danuta Brzosko-Medryk.

4/29 SS Camp Commander Wolfgang Plaul

Wolfgang Plaul; photo; 12.5 × 18 cm; SGB. Employment and dismissal of forewomen, Ravensbrück, Sept. 1, 1944; DIN A 4; ThHStA, NS 4 Bu 99, Bl. 163. Guard instruction for Mühlhausen SS detachment; DIN A 4; ThHStA, NS 4 Bu 255, Bl. 11. Document accompanying transfer of a forewoman, Nov. 1, 1944; 21 × 15 cm; ThHStA, NS 4 Bu 99, Bl. 403. Weimar SS garrison physician to commander of Buchenwald Concentration Camp re inspection of forewomen, Sept. 5, 1944; DIN A 4; ThHStA, NS 4 Bu 99, Bl. 159. Letter with envelope: "Aufseherin Frau Erika Wilms," (Forewoman Mrs. Erika Wilms) Apr. 10, 1945; 21 × 15 cm; ThHStA, NS 4 Bu 61, Bl. 2.

4.3 Committal for Execution – Prominent Inmates, 1943-1945

Executions

4/30 Executions

Form for execution records, 1945; 21 × 15 cm; BwA, 36-4. Crematorium cellar, 1945; photo; 5.9 × 8.6 cm; SGB.

4/31 August 1944: Ernst Thälmann is killed

Congress of executive committee of the Communist International in Moscow, 1926; photo; 11 × 7 cm; *Ernst Thälmann. Eine Biographie*, ed. by Institut für Marxismus-Leninismus beim Zentralkomitee der SED, Berlin, 1980, p. 305. Memo from Heinrich Himmler, Reich Leader of the SS, re meeting with Adolf Hitler in the "Wolfsschanze," Aug. 14, 1944; copy; SGB. Sketch of the hearing of Marian Zgoda, Munich municipal court, 1948; copy; SGB.

Prominent Inmates

4/32 French politicians

Falcon lodge at the SS falcon yard, 1945; photo; 11 × 8 cm; SGB. Édouard Daladier, ca. 1938; photo; 4 × 6 cm; BwA, Mappe Franzosen. Maurice Gamelin, ca. 1938; photo; 4 × 6 cm; BwA, Mappe Franzosen. Paul Reynaud, ca. 1938; photo; 4 × 6 cm; BwA, Mappe Franzosen. Léon Blum; photo; 4 × 6 cm; Fondation nationale des Sciences politiques, Fonds Léon Blum. Léon Blum in Buchenwald, autumn 1944; photo; 15 × 10 cm; BwA, Mappe Franzosen. Memo from Léon Blum in Buchenwald, 1944/45; copy; 13.7 × 19.9 cm; SGB. Georges Mandel in Buchenwald, 1944; photo; 15 × 11 cm; Archives Nationales, Paris.

4/33 Isolation barrack, 1944

Rudolf Breitscheid with Léon Blum in Paris, ca. 1933; photo; 6.7 × 9.5 cm; Ziebura, Gilbert, *Léon Blum. Theorie und Praxis einer sozialistischen Politik*, Vol. 1, Berlin, 1963. Rudolf Breitscheid in custody, 1943/44; photo; 6.3 × 8.6 cm; SGB. Letter from R. Breitscheid to Sonia Schellong, Buchenwald, Oct. 24, 1943; DIN A 4; Archiv der sozialen Demokratie der Friedrich-Ebert-Stiftung, Bonn. Princess Mafalda of Hesse, ca. 1930; photo; 8.2 × 9.6 cm; SGB. Daughters of the Italian king in San Rossore, 1931; photo; 11.2 × 9.9 cm; Hessen, Heinrich Prinz von, *Der kristallene Lüster*, Munich/Zurich, 1994, illustration section.

4/34 "Kinship inmates" in the isolation barrack, Feb.-Apr. 1945

Sketch by Markwart Graf Schenk von Stauffenberg Jr., 1945; copy; 10 × 5 cm, SGB. Alexander von Stauffenberg after liberation, 1945; photo; 9 × 8 cm; Hassell, Fey von, *Niemals sich beugen: Erinnerungen einer Sondergefangenen der SS*, Munich/Zurich, 1991, illustration section. Markwart and Otto-Philipp von Stauffenberg after liberation, 1945; photo; 9 × 7.8 cm; ibid. Internees' petition initiated by Fey von Hassell after liberation in Niederndorf, Tyrol, Apr. 29, 1945; copy; 2 sheets, 10 × 14.3 cm; ibid.

4/35 Reich Department of Security inmates in Buchenwald, Feb.-Apr. 1945

Cell tract in SS barrack, 1945; sketch based on S. Payne-Best, *The Venlo Incident*, London/New York, 1955. Dietrich Bonhoeffer in Berlin-Tegel Prison, 1944; photo; 9 × 14 cm; SGB. Friedrich von Rabenau; photo; 4.5 × 6.5 cm; SGB. Ludwig Gehre; photo; 4.5 × 6.5 cm; SGB. Hermann Pünder; photo; 4 × 5 cm; SGB. Josef Müller; photo; 4 × 6 cm; SGB.

4.4 Medical Experiments, 1942-1945

4/36 Medical experiments

Special pass for transport of infectious material, 1944; 18 × 9.5 cm (open); SGB. Vaccine packaging from production of Armed SS "Serum Institute" in Block 50, 1944; 12.8 × 10.6 × 1.7 cm; SGB. Instructions for use of epidemic typhus vaccine, 1944; 14.7 × 10.5 cm; SGB. "Serum Institute" Block 50, 1945; photo; 18 × 13 cm; SGB. 6 chemical vials and 2 test tubes, Block 50; SGB. 3 specimen holders, engraved numbers, Block 50; 7.5 × 2.5 cm; SGB. Albert Demnitz, Behringwerke Marburg, to Camp Physician Hoven, Feb. 2, 1943; DIN A 4; ThHStA; KZ Bu 62, Bl. 27. SS Garrison Physician Schiedlausky to chief of Office D III, Jan. 8, 1944; 21 × 15 cm; BwA, 50-3-5.

4.5 The Armament Plant at the Camp – The 1944 Bomb Attack

The Armament Plant at the Camp

4/37 Experimental arms production
Workshop buildings, 1944; photo; 18 × 13 cm; SGB. 34 carbine 98k components; SGB.

4/38 Construction phase of Gustloff-Werk II
Letter from Pohl to Himmler re provisional construction of gun factory in Buchenwald, July 11, 1942; 2 DIN A 4 sheets; Bundesarchiv Berlin, Bestand Persönlicher Stab Reichsführer SS, Film 3601, Bl. 849 f. Heinrich Himmler to Gauleiter Fritz Sauckel re expectations in connection with collaboration with Gustloff-Werke, July 7, 1942; DIN A 4; BwA, 56-5-18.

4/39 Construction phase of Gustloff-Werk II
Gerhard Maurer, chief of Office D II, to Buchenwald Concentration Camp command re deployment of inmates for Weimar Gustloff-Werke, July 28, 1942; 21 × 20 cm; BwA, 56-5-4. Accident report, Mar. 17, 1943; 20 × 7.5 cm; BwA, 57-1-7. Punitive report of 17 inmates re desertion of workplace and damage of a cable trench, Apr. 9, 1943; 12 × 19.5 cm; BwA, 57-53. Gustloff-Werk II, Gate 1, 1943; photo; 18 × 13 cm; SGB. Gustloff-Werk II, south-western section of enclosure, Apr. 12, 1944; photo; 18 × 13 cm; SGB. Passage connecting shop floors, 1943; photo; 13 × 18 cm; SGB. Shop floor, 1943; photo; 18 × 13 cm; SGB. Assembly of machine tools on a shop floor, 1943; photo; 18 × 13 cm; SGB.

4/40
Instructions for use of the high-precision lathe Model DD 15/18; 23 × 30 cm; SGB.

4/41 Inmate forced labour and production
High-speed high-precision lathe DD 15; 190 × 120 × 90 cm; SGB. 15 rifle barrel blanks; iron, rusted; 90 cm; SGB. Bolt housing with barrel of automatic rifle G 43, fragment; 81 cm; SGB. Albert Speer to Heinrich Himmler re SS arms production in Buchenwald, Mar. 25, 1943; 2 DIN A 4 sheets; Bundesarchiv Berlin, Bestand Persönlicher Stab Reichsführer SS, Film 3601, Bl. 862 f. Barrel alignment, Hall 10, 1943/44; photo; 23.1 × 17.1 cm; SGB. Siding track, 1943/44; photo; 18 × 13; SGB. Report by a works engineer re sabotage by inmates, Mar. 21, 1944; 2

DIN A 5 sheets, ThHStA, NS 4 Bu, vorl. 271, Bl. 302 and reverse side. 5 tool chips, Gustloff-Werk II, 1944; metal, enamelled; ∅ 4 cm; SGB. 5 shop floor tags, Gustloff-Werk II, 1944; metal, enamelled; ∅ 3.4 cm; SGB. 3 bonus coupons, 1944; 10.5 × 7.7 cm; SGB. Punitive report of 3 inmates (Yugoslavian, French and Greek), June 23, 1944; 19 × 14 cm; BwA, 57-59.

The 1944 Bomb Attack

4/42 The bomb attack
Flight routes of the 8th American Air Fleet over Germany, Aug. 24, 1944; card from Stanley Booker, British military airman, Buchenwald inmate; 45 × 33 cm; BwA, 52-11-753. Aerial photograph of Buchenwald, Aug. 24, 1944, 4:00 p.m.; photo; 21 × 18 cm; BwA, ibid. Analysis of aerial photograph by member of American force, Aug. 1944; repro; 18 × 13 cm; SGB. Molten glass; SGB. 4 melted inmates' mess kits; SGB. 3 pieces of molten metal; SGB.

4/43 The bomb attack
Report on inmates killed, missing, injured (inpatient and outpatient treatment) during bomb attack, Nov. 16, 1944; DIN A 5; ThHStA, NS 4 Bu 53, Bl. 9. Report on number of cremated corpses of inmates killed during bomb attack, Aug. 30, 1944; 14 × 9.5 cm; ThHStA, NS 4 Bu 53, Bl. 8. Report by Block Senior Karl Müller on death of missing inmates from his block, Sept. 22, 1944; 14.5 × 10.5 cm; ThHStA, NS 4 Bu 53, Bl. 7. Destruction caused by air attack; photo series, 16 photos; 8.3 × 5.3 cm, 7.2 × 5.5 cm, 8.3 × 5.8 cm; SGB. Inmates engaged in clearance work at Gustloff-Werk II; photo; 18 × 13 cm; SGB. Pieces of melted cable; SGB. Cracked pieces of concrete; SGB.

5. Death and Survival, 1944/45

5.1 Mass Death

Extermination Transports to Auschwitz

5/1 Extermination transports to Auschwitz: Jews
Cinema building, 1945; photo; 18 × 13 cm; SGB. Circular re transport of disabled Jewish inmates to Auschwitz-Birkenau extermination camp, Aug. 25, 1944; DIN A 4; ThHStA, KZ Bu 9, Bl. 28. Documentary evidence of arrangement of transport of sick and weak persons to Bergen-Belsen, Jan. 20, 1945; DIN A 6; ThHStA, KZ Bu 9, Bl. 19. Star of David; found object; metal; SGB.

5/2 Extermination transports to Auschwitz: Sinti and Romani
Bruno Z., photo; 5.6 × 8.3 cm; BA Koblenz, Bestand R 165, Kartei Rassenhygienische und kriminalbiologische Forschungsstelle des Reichsgesundheitsamtes, Nr. L 138. Albert W., photo; 5.6 × 8.3 cm; BA Koblenz, ibid., Nr. 135. Egon P., photo; 5.6 × 8.3 cm; BA Koblenz, ibid., Nr. L 257. Pair of children's shoes, Auschwitz; SGB.

Evacuation Transports from Auschwitz and Groß Rosen

5/3 Transports from disbanded extermination centres and ghettos in Poland
Quarterly report by SS Garrison Physician Schiedlausky re medical service, Mar. 31, 1945; 2 DIN A 4 sheets; ThHStA, KZ Bu 10, Bl. 2 and reverse side. Name tag, arm band (inscription: Jozef Szternberg, KL 20253, geb. 6.VI.1925 in Bensburg); found object; metal; 4.3 × 2.4 cm; SGB. Name tag, arm band (inscription: Max Nowytarger, 20169, geb. 5.IX.1923, in Sosnowitz); found object; metal, leather; 7.7 × 3.1 cm; SGB.

5/4 Transports from disbanded extermination centres and ghettos in Poland
16 inmate numbers, yellow number stripe; found objects; fabric; SGB. Boris Taslitzky, "Hungarian Leaving the Shower," drawing, 1945; print; 10.6 × 12.3 cm; SGB.

Place of Death: Little Camp

5/5 Place of death: Little Camp
SS Garrison Physician Schiedlausky to Camp Commander Pister re removal of corpses, Jan. 26, 1945; DIN A 5; ThHStA, KZ Bu 10, Bl. 22. Auguste Favier, "Wooden Barrack in Little Camp," drawing, 1943; print; 25.1 × 18.1 cm; SGB. French Army identification tag (inscription: 1903, Officier, Herz, Villy. verso: Seine 6 B, 2104); found object; metal; 5.9 × 4.8 cm; SGB. French Army identification tag (inscription: Anker, Pierre, 1926. verso: Versailles 5115); found object; metal; 5.8 × 4.9 cm; SGB.

5/6 Place of death: Little Camp
Boris Taslitzky, "Maurice Halbwachs Waiting to Have his Bandages Changed," drawing, 1945; print; 13.5 × 21.3 cm; SGB. Report on changes in inmate strength, Mar. 16, 1945; DIN A 4; BwA, 59-109.

5/7 Found objects from excavations in area of the Little Camp

5/8-5/9 Death certificates
16 reports on changes in inmate strength, Feb./Mar. 1945; BwA, 59-109.

5.2 The End

The Final Days

5/10 Evacuation
Telegraphic message from Camp Commander Pister re evacuation of camp, Apr. 6, 1945; copy; DIN A 5; BwA, 48-27. Roll call list, morning roll call of Apr. 10, 1945; DIN A 4; BwA, 46-1-37. Inmates who died during an evacuation transport, Apr. 1945; photo; 15 × 14 cm; SGB. Box packed by Max Göhrmann in preparation for possible evacuation, 1945; 33 × 9 × 24.5 cm; SGB.

5/11-5/12 Self-preservation
Transmitter; reconstruction with original parts; 55 × 15 × 25 cm; SGB. Field glass, Adolf Scholze; 13.5 × 7 × 22 cm; SGB. Adolf Scholze with fire brigade of camp fire department in front of depot, 1945; photo; 13 × 9 cm; SGB. *Thüringer Gauzeitung*, Apr. 6/7, 1945; 51.5 × 24.5; BwA. André Marie; photo; 5.5 × 6.5 cm; SGB. Eugen Kogon, after 1945; photo; 5.5 × 6.5 cm; SGB. Copy of list of 46 inmates ordered to report to gate on Apr. 6, 1945; DIN A 4; BwA, 75-0-2. Diary of Maurice Eyben, 1945; DIN A 5; loan from M. Eyben. Pencil of M. Suard; 13 cm; SGB. Maurice Eyben; photo; dimensions; source. Letter from Maurice Suard to his family, Apr. 10, 1945; 2 DIN A 5 sheets; BwA, Mappe Franzosen. Maurice Suard, Apr. 18, 1945; photo; 5.5 × 6.5 cm; SGB.

Liberation

5/13 Liberation from within
Floréal Barrier; photo; 5.5 × 6.5 cm; SGB. Inmate's number; fabric; 8.8 × 3.3 cm; loan from F. Barrier. Inmate's triangle; fabric; side length: 5.5 cm; loan from F. Barrier. Walter Bartel, after 1945; photo; 5.5 × 6.5 cm; SGB. Henri Manhès, after 1945; photo; 5.5 × 6.5 cm; SGB. Josef Frank, after 1945; photo; 5.5 × 6.5 cm; SGB. Domenico Ciufoli, after 1945; photo; 5.5 × 6.5 cm; SGB. Banner of the French "Brigade d'Action Libératrice" in Buchenwald Camp, 1945; fabric; 59 × 49 cm; SGB. Group of French "Brigade d'Action Libératrice," after Apr. 11, 1945; photo; 18 × 13 cm; SGB. Marcel Paul, after 1945; photo; 5.5 × 6.5 cm; SGB.

5/14 Liberation from within and without
Thomas Geve, "Liberation", drawing, 1945; copy; 18 × 13 cm; SGB. Appeal by camp leadership, read out at freedom roll call, Apr. 12, 1945; DIN A 4; BwA, 77-2-31.

5/15 Camp senior of liberated camp
Authorisation of Hans Eiden as camp commander by an American officer, Apr. 11, 1945; 10.5 × 11.5 cm; BwA, 52-11-541. Hans Eiden in custody, 1940; photo; 5.5 × 6.5 cm; SGB. First report by camp senior, Apr. 11, 1945; DIN A 5; ThHStA, KZ Bu 47, Bl. 96. Second report by camp senior, Apr. 11, 1945; DIN A 5, ThHStA, ibid., Bl. 97.

5/16 Arrival of U.S. Army
S III (Ohrdruf) Sub-Camp upon arrival of American troops, early Apr. 1945; photo; 12 × 9 cm; SGB. General Eisenhower in Ohrdruf (S III Sub-Camp), early Apr. 1945; photo; 10 × 12 cm; SGB. Armed Americans in front of camp gate, after Apr. 11, 1945; photo; 9 × 12 cm; NARA. GIs in front of gate ("Recht oder Unrecht – mein Vaterland"), after Apr. 11, 1945; photo; 13 × 9 cm; BwA, Jacques Rancy. Red Cross vehicle in from of camp gate, Apr. 1945; photo; 10 × 7.5 cm; BwA, ibid. Crematorium courtyard, Apr. 1945; photo; 13 × 9 cm; SGB. Three GIs in crematorium courtyard, in front of heap

of corpses, betw. Apr. 11 and 15, 1945; photo; 13 × 9 cm; BwA, Jacques Rancy. Crematory ovens with remains of burning process, Apr. 16, 1945; photo; 11 × 10 cm; NARA. Undernourished inmate on transport cart, Apr. 16, 1945; photo; 9 × 12 cm; NARA. Leon Bass, after 1943; photo; 5.5 × 5.6 cm; SGB. Little Camp, betw. Apr. 11 and 15, 1945; photo; 6 × 7 cm; BwA, Jacques Rancy. GIs in Little Camp, Apr. 1945; photo; 9 × 12 cm; NARA. Wool blanket, U.S. Army, 1945; loan from J. Suard. Cooking pot, 1945; metal; loan from J. Suard.

5/17 The Little Camp after liberation
Inmates with blankets in Little Camp, after Apr. 11, 1945; photo; 10 × 14 cm; SGB. Six inmates in Little Camp, after Apr. 11, 1945; photo; 10 × 14 cm; SGB. Sleeping compartments in Little Camp, after Apr. 11, 1945; photo; 10 × 14 cm; SGB. Inmates in sleeping compartments in Little Camp, Apr. 16, 1945; photo; 10 × 14 cm; NARA. Dying inmate in Little Camp, Apr. 16, 1945; photo; 10 × 14 cm; NARA. Former inmates in barracks of Little Camp, Apr. 1945; photo; 13 × 19 cm; SGB.

5/18 First aid
5 bottles for blood plasma and nutritive solutions, U.S. Medical Corps, 1945; found objects; ⌀ 6.8 cm × 17.3 cm; ⌀ 8.4 cm × 16.7 cm; ⌀ 7.6 × 22.7 cm; ⌀ 10.9 × 19.6 cm; SGB. Change of bandages, after Apr. 11, 1945; photo; 9 × 11 cm; YVA, picture archive, No. 2307. American soldiers transporting inmate to hospital, after Apr. 11, 1945; photo; 11 × 8 cm; YVA, picture archive, No. 5302. Former inmates transporting sick person, Apr. 16, 1945; photo; 11 × 8 cm NARA. Buried inmates in mass grave, Apr. 1945; photo; 8 × 11 cm; YVA, picture archive, No. 2643/2. Dying persons in infirmary barrack, Apr. 16, 1945; photo; 11 × 8 cm; NARA. In the infirmary barrack, Apr. 16, 1945; photo; 8 × 11 cm; NARA. List of doctors and nurses who worked for medical service in camp, Apr. 19, 1945; DIN A 4; ThHStA, NS 4 Bu 58b, Bl. 104. Permanent pass, Apr. 19, 1945; 11 × 6.5 cm; BwA, Mappe Franzosen. Joseph Anselme Brau, after 1945; photo; 5.5 × 6.5 cm; BwA, Mappe Franzosen.

5/19 Organisation of everyday life in the camp
Former inmate at latrine, betw. Apr. 11 and 15, 1945; photo; 6 × 8 cm; BwA, Jacques Rancy. Former inmate in front of Little Camp barrack with food bowl, Apr. 14, 1945; photo; 9 × 6 cm; United States Holocaust Memorial Museum, Washington. Instruction for experiment to determine bacteriological contamination, May 1945; 11.2 × 18.7 cm; BwA, 77-3-11. Camp committee instructions on cleanliness of camp, Apr. 20, 1945; DIN A 4; BwA, 77-3-5. Camp committee bulletins, Apr. 14, 1945; DIN A 4; ThHStA, KZ Bu 47, Bl. 117. Former inmates engaged in

food preparation, after Apr. 11, 1945; photo; 12 × 10 cm; SGB. Ladle; found object; metal, rusty; 64 × 15 × 17 cm; SGB. Former inmates in front of barrack in Little Camp, after Apr. 11, 1945; photo; 8 × 6 cm; SGB. Camp committee secretariat to U.S. camp commander, Apr. 23, 1945; DIN A 5; ThHStA, KZ Bu 47, Bl. 50. Clothing committee to international camp committee, Apr. 15, 1945; DIN A 4; ThHStA, KZ Bu 47, Bl. 52.

5/20 Tours of Buchenwald Concentration Camp
Citizens of Weimar in camp, Apr. 16, 1945; photo; 7.5 × 8 cm; NARA. Women from Weimar in camp, Apr. 16, 1945; photo; 9.4 × 10.2 cm; NARA. Citizens of Weimar viewing crematorium courtyard, Apr. 16, 1945; photo; 11 × 8 cm; NARA. Demonstration of tree-hanging with dummy (from front), after Apr. 11, 1945; photo; 5 × 7 cm; SGB. Demonstration of tree-hanging with dummy (from side), after Apr. 11, 1945; photo; 5 × 7 cm; SGB. Model of flogging stand with dummy, after Apr. 11, 1945; photo; 5 × 7 cm; SGB. Text of flogging stand model, after Apr. 11, 1945; photo; 5 × 7 cm; SGB. Demonstration of killing methods in crematorium cellar, Apr. 14, 1945; photo; 9 × 12 cm; NARA. Diary of Adolf Scholze; 11 × 3 × 17 cm; SGB. Apr. 16, 1945; photo; dimensions; source. Handbill issued by information department of International Camp Committee, after Apr. 11, 1945; DIN A 5; BwA, 32/II-63, Bl. 9.

5/21 Recovery
Map of infirmary zone after Apr. 11, 1945, drawing by Wolfgang Schulz, 1945; 19.5 × 14.7 cm, BwA, 77-3-11. Instructions for treating epidemic typhus, Wolfgang Schulz' hand-written notes, June 1945; 11.7 × 14.9 cm; BwA, 77-3-11. Number of sick persons, May 16, 1945; DIN A 4; ThHStA, NS 4 Bu 58b, Bl. 45. Former inmates with blankets in Little Camp, after Apr. 11, 1945; photo; 12 × 9 cm; YVA, picture archive, No. 2500/35. Former inmate with artificial leg, sitting in Little Camp, after Apr. 11, 1945; photo; 6.5 × 9 cm; YVA, picture archive, No. 2500/37. Undernourished former inmates with bandages, betw. Apr. 11 and 15, 1945; photo; 17 × 19.2 cm; BwA, Jacques Rancy. Undernourished former inmate, seated, after Apr. 11, 1945; photo; 6.5 × 9 cm; SGB. Four former inmates in Little Camp, betw. Apr. 11 and 15, 1945; photo; 7.5 × 9 cm; BwA, Jacques Rancy. Van Beirs, Belgian state attorney, in Little Camp, April 1945; photo; 19.2 × 17 cm, BwA, Mappe Belgier. Lucien van Beirs after his return home, May 1945; photo; 9 × 10 cm; BwA, Mappe Belgier.

5/22 The new order
Order by American commander to surrender weapons, Apr. 20, 1945; 13.9 × 9.4 cm; BwA, 76-7-14. Camp regulations, after Apr. 11, 1945; DIN A 4; BwA, 32/II-63. Handbill, Apr. 1945; DIN A

4; ThHStA, KZ Bu 47, Bl. 128. Barrack with slogans ("Hitler muß sterben…" [Hitler must die …]), Apr. 1945 photo; 18 × 13 cm; SGB. Camp committee secretariat to inspection office, Apr. 20, 1945; DIN A 5; ThHStA, KZ Bu 45, Bl. 39. Inspection office to camp committee, Apr. 20, 1945; DIN A 5; BwA, 77-4-5. 2 former Buchenwald foremen, after Apr. 11, 1945 photo; 15 × 15 cm; Lee Miller Archives, 54-21. U.S. soldier interrogating member of the SS, after Apr. 11, 1945; photo; 15 × 15 cm; Lee Miller Archives, 54-14. Turning over of former inmates to Counter Intelligence Corps (CIC), Apr. 27, 1945; DIN A 4; BwA, 77-4-5, Bl. 34.

5/23 Reorganisation of Buchenwald Communists
Party Control Commission to secretariat of Buchenwald collective of party activists, Apr. 27, 1945; 2 DIN A 4 sheets; BwA, 71-2-21. Welcoming of representatives of KPdSU in appeal made by the Buchenwald collective of party activists, Apr. 16, 1945; DIN A 4; ThHStA, KZ Bu 50, Bl. 217. German political inmates' barrack, after Apr. 11, 1945; photo; 18 × 13 cm; SGB. Block 40, after Apr. 11, 1945; photo; 18 × 13 cm; SGB.

5/24 Reports
Camp committee secretariat to information department, Apr. 20, 1945; DIN A 5; ThHStA, KZ Bu 47, Bl. 136. Three inmates writing in crematorium courtyard, after Apr. 11, 1945; photo; 13 × 9 cm; YVA, picture archive, No. 947/2. Information plaque for visitors, Apr./May 1945; photo; 13 × 9 cm; SGB. Inauguration of loudspeaker service of information committee, Apr. 12, 1945; DIN A 4; BwA, 32/II-38. Photo lab of camp committee information service, after Apr. 11, 1945; photo; 12.9 × 8.8 cm; SGB. Secretariat of Communist Party, Buchenwald Section, to the Czech, Soviet, Polish and French Sections of the KP, Apr. 21, 1945; DIN A 4; ThHStA, KZ Bu 47, Bl. 135. Otto Geithner to Karl Reimann, Apr. 24, 1945; DIN A 5; BwA, Nachlaß Johannes Brumme, 30/I-2/1.

5/25 Camp newspapers
Rotaprint printing press, contemporary; 40 × 30 × 45 cm; SGB. *La France Libre*, newspaper for liberated Frenchmen in the camp, Apr. 19, 1945; DIN A 4; BwA, 77-2-34. *Nas glass*, newspaper for the Yugoslavian Committee in Buchenwald, May 10, 1945; DIN A 4; BwA, 77-2-83 and 89. *TRN. Der Dorn*, newspaper for Czech youth, Apr./May 1945; DIN A 4; BwA, 31/545. Joel Sayre, war correspondent of the CIC Press Camp, to commander of American military administration in Weimar, Apr. 20, 1945; DIN A 4; ThHStA, KZ Bu 47, Bl. 34. *mundo obrero*, newspaper for the Spanish Communists in Buchenwald, May 1, 1945; 2 DIN A 4 sheets; BwA, 77-2-22. *MLADE KLB* 45, newspaper for liberated Czechs in Buchenwald, May 8, 1945; DIN A 4;

BwA, 77-2-23. *TRN*, poems commemorating May 1, 1945 (Czech); BwA, 31/545.

5/26 The manifesto of the Democratic Socialists
Hermann Louis Brill, after 1945; photo; 5.5 × 6.5 cm; SGB. Hermann Brill to the Thüringen Komitee in Buchenwald, May 1, 1945; DIN A 5; BwA, 32/II-68-75. Ernst Thape, after 1945; photo; 5.5 × 6.5 cm; SGB. Manifesto of the Democratic Socialists of the former Buchenwald Concentration Camp, Apr. 13, 1945; 2 DIN A 4 sheets; BwA, 32/II-68-16. Benedikt Kautsky, after 1945; photo; 5.5 × 6.5 cm; SGB. Emergency education policy measures, illegal People's Front Committee, 1944; DIN A 4; BwA, Nachlaß Johannes Brumme, 30/I-1/6.

Publicity and Legacy
5/27 Promises
Operational plan for memorial service on Apr. 19, 1945; DIN A 4; BwA, 77-2-21. Muster ground, Apr. 19, 1945; photo; 18 × 13 cm; SGB. Address held by U.S. commander at memorial service, Apr. 19, 1945; DIN A 5; ThHStA, KZ Bu 50, Bl. 281. Address and "Oath of Buchenwald" by former inmates at memorial service, Apr. 19, 1945; DIN A 4; BwA NZ 488. Obelisk made for memorial service, Apr. 19, 1945; photo; 7 × 5 cm; SGB, photo by Eberhard Leitner. March to memorial service, Apr. 19, 1945; photo; 12 × 9 cm; SGB. May 1st demonstration, May 1, 1945; photo; 9 × 12 cm; SGB.

5/28 International publicity
Coke bottle; found object; 17.5 × 5.5 × 7 cm; SGB. Human ashes, Apr. 14, 1945; photo; 18 × 13 cm; NARA. Demonstration of hanging for American soldiers, after Apr. 11, 1945; photo; 8.8 × 12.9 cm; SGB. GIs in Buchenwald, after Apr. 11, 1945; photo; 18 × 13 cm; SGB. GI in sleeping compartment in Little Camp, after Apr. 11, 1945; photo; 6 × 8 cm; SGB. Members of American Congress in crematorium courtyard at Buchenwald, Apr. 24, 1945; photo; 18 × 13 cm; NARA. Members of American Congress in Buchenwald crematorium, Apr. 24, 1945; photo; 18 × 13 cm; NARA. Allied War Crime Commission visits Buchenwald, here entering Little Camp, Apr. 26, 1945; photo; 18 × 13 cm; NARA. Allied War Crime Commission visits Little Camp, Apr. 26, 1945; photo; 18 × 13 cm; NARA. Methodist bishop of New York and president of the Christian churches of the USA examining tattoos on dried human skin, Apr. 27, 1945; photo; 18 × 13 cm; NARA.

5/29 Commemoration
Procession for burial of dead at Bismarck Tower, after Apr. 11, 1945; photo; 15 × 18 cm; Lee Miller Archives, 51-10. Burial of 16 Buchenwald inmates in Lehnstedt, May 6, 1945; 9 photos; 9 × 9 cm; ThHStA, KZ Bu 46, Bl. 10. Shavuot celebration in cinema, May 1945; photo; 19 × 12 cm;

NARA. Funeral service with three military clergymen (Jewish, Protestant, Catholic), June 20, 1945; photo; 18 × 13 cm; NARA. Burial of 1286 urns at Bismarck Tower, June 20, 1945; photo; 18 × 13 cm; NARA. Civilians at funeral service at Bismarck Tower, June 20, 1945; photo; 18 × 13 cm; NARA.

5/30 The end of the war
Newspaper of the Allied Supreme Command, May 7, 1945; 21.1 × 30.9 cm; BwA, 76-7-7. Belgians in front of Block 42, after Apr. 11, 1945; photo; 19 × 21 cm; SGB. Address by Henri Glineurs, member of Belgian national committee, Apr. 18, 1945; DIN A 4; BwA, 77-1-9. Jacques Grippa, head and correspondent of Belgian national committee, to German committee in Buchenwald following his return home, May 25, 1945; 2 DIN A 5 sheets; BwA, 77-4-42. Arrival of former French Buchenwald inmates in Le Bourget, France, Apr. 18, 1945; photo; 12 × 9 cm; SGB. Former French Buchenwald inmates in Le Bourget, following their return, Apr. 18, 1945; photo; 12 × 9 cm; SGB. Reception of former Buchenwald inmates by Charles de Gaulle at the Elysée Palace, Apr. 19, 1945; photo; 12 × 9 cm; SGB. May 1st demonstration in Paris, 1945; photo; 9 × 13 cm; SGB.

5/31 Buchenwald and the surrounding region
Weimar anti-Nazi committee to the Thüringen Komitee, May 9, 1945; DIN A 5; BwA, 77-4-5, Bl. 160. In front of the camp gate, betw. Apr. 11 and 15, 1945; photo; 13 × 10 cm; BwA, Jacques Rancy. Liberated inmates in front of camp gate, betw. Apr. 11 and 15, 1945; photo; 11 × 15 cm; BwA, Jacques Rancy. Falcon yard, after Apr. 11, 1945; photo; 12 × 9 cm; SGB. Pass from Buchenwald to Leutsch, Apr. 22, 1945; DIN A 5; ThHStA, KZ Bu 45, Bl. 92. Pass, Apr. 26, 1945; 10.9 × 6.8 cm; BwA, 77-4-41. Blank pass, May 1945; 15 × 9 cm; BwA, 77-4-41.

The Dissolution of the Camp
5/32 Departure
Children's transport list from Buchenwald to France, June 5, 1945, (excerpt); DIN A 4; BwA, 52-6-10. Children's transport from Buchenwald, June 8, 1945; photo; 19 × 21 cm; SGB. Children's transport from Buchenwald to France, June 7 or 8, 1945; photo; 9 × 12 cm; NARA. List of children who arrived on German convoy, June 8, 1945 (excerpt); DIN A 4; BwA, 52-6-10.

Jüdische Rundschau report on Buchenwald Kibbutz, No.15/16, 1947 (excerpt); copy; DIN A 4; SGB. Survivors of Buchenwald on way to Palestine, July 15, 1945; photo; 11.2 × 12.3 cm; SGB. Adolescents in Little Camp, after Apr. 11, 1945; photo; 13.4 × 14.3 cm; Bourke-White, Margaret, *Deutschland, April* 1945, Munich, 1979. Group diary of Buchenwald Kibbutz, 1945; copy; BwA.

5/33 The road to a post-war society
Former Czech inmates digging earth downhill from depot, May 1, 1945; photo; 9 × 6 cm; SGB. Former Soviet Buchenwald inmates before return to Soviet Union, in barrack in Erfurt, 1945; photo; 9.5 × 6.7 cm; SGB. Austrians in Buchenwald, after Apr. 11, 1945; photo; 4 × 3 cm; SGB. Belgians, after Apr. 11, 1945; photo; 4 × 3 cm; SGB. Departure, 1945; photo; 4 × 3 cm; SGB. Departure, Jehovah's Witnesses, after Apr. 11, 1945; photo; 4 × 3 cm; SGB. Departure, after Apr. 11, 1945; photo; 4 × 3 cm; SGB. Association of Natives of Ruhr, 1945; photo; 4 × 3 cm; SGB. Association of Natives of Saar, after Apr. 11, 1945; photo; 4 × 3 cm; SGB. May 1 in Buchenwald, 1945; photo; 4 × 3 cm; SGB. Camp fence, after Apr. 11, 1945; photo; 4 × 3 cm; SGB. Departure at camp fence, after Apr. 11, 1945; photo; 4 × 3 cm; SGB. Standardised Red Cross postcard for informing family members, May 1945; DIN A 6; BwA, 77-3-11. 2 bonus coupons, 1945; reprint; 10.6 × 7.7 cm; SGB. Richard Grosskopf, head of Buchenwald inspection office, to Werner Hilpert, fiduciary for confiscated assets, June 28, 1945; DIN A 4; ThHStA, Ministerium für Wirtschaft und Arbeit 3999, Bl. 21. Werner Hilpert, after 1945; photo; 5.5 × 6.5 cm; SGB. File memo on investigation of whereabouts of former Polish inmates in Institut Weiss, a girls' school in Weimar; DIN A 4; ThHStA, KZ Bu 24, Bl. 227. Military Government of Germany, questionnaire for concentration camp inmates, 1945; DIN A 4; ThHStA, KZ Bu 24, Bl. 221. Suitcase belonging to the former inmate Ottomar Rothmann, 1945; 60 × 20 × 40 cm; SGB.

6. "We, the resurrected …"

6/1 Life after survival
Image/text collage

6/2 The criminal prosecution of the aggressors
Image/text collage

Biographical Sketches in the Permanent Exhibition: Inmates

The brief biographies form an essential element of the permanent exhibition on the history of Buchenwald Concentration Camp. Biographical sketches and portraits lend faces and names to the accounts of the events as well as to the exhibition objects – those belonging to the Buchenwald Collection and those placed at our disposal by others. The biographical sketches are based on the biographical collection in the Buchenwald Archives, supplemented extensively by research carried out in France and Belgium. Of the inmates commemorated in the exhibition, there were several cases in which only very few facts could be determined. These persons have nonetheless been included.

Dr. Kurt Adams (1889-1944)
Born Dec. 15, 1889 in Hamburg; 1908-1913 studied German, French, History; 1913-1929 teacher in Hamburg, strong involvement with educational reforms and the Social Democratic youth organisation "Kinderfreunde"; 1928 SPD Reichstag election candidate; 1929-1933 director of Hamburg Volkshochschule; 1933 dismissal from school system, worked in a coffee shop to earn the family's living; August 1944 arrested in Greiz within framework of Operation "Gitter", committed to Buchenwald Concentration Camp Little Camp; died Oct. 7, 1944 in Buchenwald. (Catalogue 4.8)

Pierre René Joseph Anker (1906-1945)
Born Aug. 4, 1906 in Paris; lived in Strasbourg, soldier in the 620th French regiment, prisoner of war in Trier; December 1944 arrested by Gestapo for possession of firearms and interception of foreign broadcasting stations; until January 1945 Altenkirchen Prison, deportation to Buchenwald; died Mar. 23, 1945 in Little Camp. (Catalogue 5.5)

Bruno Apitz (1900-1979)
Born Apr. 8, 1900 in Leipzig; 1919 assistant in a bookshop, first publications of short stories and stories; 1926 acting lessons, later actor; 1927 joined KPD; 1930-33 member of the Bund proletarisch-revolutionärer Schriftsteller Deutschlands (association of proletarian-revolutionary writers of Germany) and chairman of Leipzig branch; 1933 arrested, three months in Colditz and Sachsenburg Concentration Camps; 1934 arrested again; 1935-1937 Waldheim penitentiary; 1937-1945 Buchenwald Concentration Camp; 1938 sculpture detachment; 1942 pathology detachment; 1945 following liberation author of radio plays, writer; 1958 novel Nackt unter Wölfen; 1961 honorary citizen of the City of Weimar; 1963 screen adaptation of the novel Nackt unter Wölfen; 1965 married Marlis Kieckhäfer, one daughter; died Apr. 7, 1979 in Berlin. (Catalogue 3.36)

Rudolf [Rudi] Arndt (1909-1940)
Born Apr. 26, 1909 in Berlin as son of a civil servant of Jewish heritage and religion; 1925 member of the Jewish youth group "Schwarzer Haufen"; 1927 joined the Rote Jungfront (Red Youth Front); 1931 concluded apprenticeship as typesetter; 1931 arrest and sentence to 1½ years of fortress detention, served sentence in the Groß-Strehlitz Fortress; 1932-1933 member of central committee of KJVD; 1933 resistance activities in Ruhr District and Berlin; 1933 arrest, 3 years confinement in Brandenburg-Goerden Penitentiary; 1937-1938 Sachsenhausen and Dachau Concentration Camps; 1938 committed to Buchenwald as "Political Jew"; 1938-1939 medical orderly; block senior in Barrack 22; May 3, 1940, following denunciation by criminal inmates, shot to death in quarry "while attempting to escape." (Catalogue 3.45)

Louis Audibert (1874-1955)
Born May 4, 1874 in Bordeaux; general, teacher at military academy in Saumur; 1914-1918 service in World War I, assistant chief of staff under Marshal Foch; mid 1943 affiliation with Resistance movement Forces Francaises de l'Intérieur (FFI), director of FFI West; March 1944 arrest, confinement in Rennes and Compiègne, deportation to Buchenwald Concentration Camp; 1944-1945 inmate in Buchenwald, wife died in Ravensbrück Concentration Camp, son deported to Germany, daughter interned; 1945/46 member of national assembly in which constitution was passed, foundation of a group of MPs for the protection of the material and moral interests of former members of the Resistance; 1946 member of national committee of F.N.D.I.R.P.; died Sept. 19, 1955 in Gorges. (Catalogue 4.6)

Floréal Barrier (born 1922)
Born Jan. 3, 1922 in Trélazé, France; typographer, member of the French Resistance; 1943 arrest, Buchenwald; 1945 member of Camp Protection detachment and French Liberation Brigade; member of board of directors of the International Committee Buchenwald, Dora and Sub-Camps. (Catalogue 5.13)

Walter Bartel (1904-1992)
Born Sept. 15, 1904 in Fürstenberg/Havel to a working class family, commercial apprenticeship in Berlin; 1920 KJVD; 1923 joined KPD; 1929 began 3-year study and novitiate at International Lenin School in Moscow; 1932 return to Germany; 1933 arrest, sentence, 27 months in Brandenburg-Görden Penitentiary; 1936 emigration to Czechoslovakia, there expulsion from

KPD; 1939 arrest, Buchenwald Concentration Camp, carpentry and labour records detachments, member of illegal KPD leadership; from 1943 member of illegal International Camp Committee; 1945 examination and readmission to KPD, department head in Berlin ministry of education; 1946 personal adviser to SED chairman Wilhelm Pieck; 1950 party examination; 1953 dismissal from function, party examination, professor of history in Leipzig; 1957 doctorate, then director of Institut für Zeitgeschichte Berlin; 1970 vice president of International Committee Buchenwald-Dora; 1981 Co-president of the International Committee Buchenwald, Dora and Sub-Camps; died Jan. 16, 1992 in Berlin. (Catalogue 5.13)

Levitt C. Beck (1920-1944)

Born Jan. 2, 1920 in Houston, Texas; 1942 completed pilot's training, U.S. Army; June 1944 shot down over France, betrayed to Gestapo; 1944 Buchenwald Concentration Camp, contraction of rheumatic fever, for that reason remained in tent camp at Buchenwald Concentration Camp; died Nov. 29, 1944 in Buchenwald. (Catalogue 4.8)

Fritz Behr (1881-1974)

Born Feb. 2, 1881 in Leipzig; from 1908 employment as teacher in Weimar; March 1919 joined SPD; 1925-1933 member of municipal council; 1933 dismissal from teaching position; September 1939 temporary confinement; 1943/44 labourer at Weimar freight depot; August 1944 arrest, Buchenwald Concentration Camp; April 1945 co-signer of democratic Socialists' Buchenwald Manifesto; May 1945 – October 1945 burgomaster of City of Weimar; 1945-1948 head of department for secondary schools at Thuringian ministry of education, resignation, member of board of directors of German Shakespeare Society in Weimar, died Oct. 4, 1974 in Weimar. (Catalogue 4.8)

Alberto Berti (born 1921)

Born Nov. 8, 1921 in Pirano, Italy; partisan; 1943 arrest; 1944-1945 Buchenwald Concentration Camp and Langenstein-Zwieberge Sub-Camp; 1945 return to Italy after liberation by Americans, co-founder of Regional Institute for the History of the Liberation Movement in Friuli-Venezia Giulia; 1954 manager and economics expert for industrial development of Northern Italy. (Catalogue 3.48)

Marcel Bloch, later Dassault (1892-1986)

Born Jan. 22, 1892 in Paris; 1912 earned degree as electrical engineer and began study of aviation; 1918 construction of his first airplane in collaboration with partners; 1930 first triple-engine airplane (MB 70); 1936 nationalisation of his company; October 1940 arrested by Vichy regime; March 1944 confinement in various prisons, investigated by Vichy regime "as one of those guilty of the defeat of France"; July 1944 turned over to Gestapo; 1944/45 Buchenwald Concentration Camp, turned down offer by representatives of German Air Force to direct an airplane factory; 1945 re-foundation of his plant as "Dassault-Aviation"; 1945-1986 designer of modern combat aircraft, e.g. Mirage interceptor plane; died Apr. 17, 1986 in Neuilly. (Catalogue 4.6)

Léon Blum (1872-1950)

Born Apr. 9, 1872 in Paris; journalist; 1901 publication of "Neue Gespräche mit Eckermann;" 1919 chairman of parliamentary group of SFIO, the leading Socialist party in France, member of Chamber of Deputies; 1936/37 premier minister of "popular front government" consisting of Socialists and Radical Socialists and tolerated by the Communists; 1940 arrested by Vichy regime; 1942 charged at trial of Riom "as one of those guilty of the defeat of France" along with Georges Mandel, Édouard Daladier, Paul Reynaud and Maurice Gamelin, Gestapo detention; 1943 transport to Buchenwald, interned in falcon lodge with Georges Mandel, accompanied by Jeanne Levylier, his secretary, counselled by Jehovah's Witness Joachim Escher; 1944 marriage to Jeanne Levylier in Buchenwald; 1945 transported to Flossenbürg and Dachau Concentration Camps along with other special inmates; 1946-1947 premier minister and foreign minister of transitional Socialist government, representative of France at U.N.; died Mar. 30, 1950 near Versailles. (Catalogue 4.32)

Dietrich Bonhoeffer (1906-1945)

Born Feb. 4, 1906 in Breslau as son of a professor of psychiatry; 1923-1927 studied theology in Tübingen and Berlin; 1928 curacy in Barcelona; 1930 year of study in New York; 1931 lecturer at University of Berlin and student chaplain at Technische Hochschule Berlin; 1933 pastor in foreign service in London; 1935 director of seminary of Confessional Church in Finkenwalde, Pomerania; 1936 forbidden to teach; 1940 forbidden to speak in public and obligation to register with the police; 1941 forbidden to publish; 1942 met with Bishop of Chichester as representative of German resistance; 1943 confinement in Berlin-Tegel and in Gestapo prison in Prinz-Albrecht-Strasse, Berlin, Feb. 7-Apr. 3, 1945 internment in SS Detention in Buchenwald; Apr. 9, 1945 court martial and execution at Flossenbürg Concentration Camp along with Ludwig Gehre, Hans Oster, Karl Sack, Wilhelm Canaris and Theodor Strünck. (Catalogue 4.35)

Stanley Booker (born 1922)

Born Apr. 25, 1922 in Gillingham, Kent; pilot's training, navigation officer; early June 1944 airplane shot down during attack on railway junction south-west of Paris, helped by local Resistance group, arrest in Paris, Fresnes Prison, interrogations and investigations of identity; August 1944 Buchenwald Concentration Camp along with 167 other Allied pilots; October 1944 air force POW camp – Stalag Luft III – in Sagan; early 1945 evacuation to Luckenwalde near Berlin, liberation by Red Army; May 1945 return to Great Britain. (Catalogue 4.8)

Ivan Alekseevic Borisow (born 1926)

Born Mar. 3, 1926 in Radcino in Brjansk region; 1943 conscripted to Germany, worked in mine near Dortmund, escape, arrest and committal to Herne Penitentiary, contraction of enteric fever, Dortmund Prison, detention camp; 1944 second escape attempt, Gestapo prison in Münster; 1944-1945 Buchenwald Concentration Camp, Little Camp, able to evade transport to Dora by lying about age, following quarantine period transferred to Main Camp, worked on railroad construction, in Gustloff-Werk II; after liberation in May 1945 Ohrdruf Assembly Camp for Displaced Persons; June 1945 conscription to Red Army; 1945-1950 military service. (Catalogue 4.8)

Robert Bourgeois (1910-1944)

Born Apr. 19, 1910 in Besançon; from 1938 priest and teacher at Grand Seminaire in Besancon, after 1940 joined Résistance; October 1943 arrested, prison in Besançon, transport to Compiègne; January 1944 deportation to Buchenwald, Block 62 (Little Camp); March 1944 Dora Sub-Camps; Apr. 8, 1944 transported with other sick inmates to Bergen-Belsen, where he died. (Catalogue 4.18)

Joseph Anselme Brau (1891-1975)

Born Apr. 26, 1891 in Trébons; studied medicine, military service, electro-radiologist, member of – French Resistance; 1943 arrested, Buchenwald Concentration Camp, secret support of inmates and solidarity work (Comité clandestin medical); after liberation appointed chief physician of camp on Apr. 12, 1945, organised return of French inmates to France; 1946-1962 member of National Committee of F.N.D.I.R.P.; died May 11, 1975. (Catalogue 5.18)

Rudolf Breitscheid (1874-1944)

Born Nov. 2, 1874 in Cologne as son of a bookseller; 1884-1889 studied economics in Munich and Marburg; 1898 doctorate, journalist; 1908 co-founder of "Demokratische Vereinigung" (Democratic Association); 1912 joined SPD; 1917 joined USPD, publisher of the weekly newspaper Der Sozialist; 1918/19 Prussian Minister of Interior; 1920 member of Reichstag; 1922 change to SPD, SPD foreign policy spokesman; 1926-1930 member of German League of Nations commission; 1928-1933 chairman of SPD Reichstag group; 1933 emigration via Switzerland to France,

friendship with Léon Blum and advocate of popular front politics; 1940 efforts to obtain visa for Switzerland or exit permit to U.S.; 1941 arrested, turned over to Gestapo by Vichy regime, confinement in Gestapo prison in Prinz-Albrecht-Strasse, Berlin; 1942 internment in Sachsenhausen Concentration Camp in one of four special buildings, accompanied by wife Tony; 1943 internment in isolation barrack of Buchenwald Concentration Camp; died Aug. 24, 1944 during Allied air attack. (Catalogue 4.33)

Hermann Louis Brill (1895-1959)

Born Feb. 9, 1895 in Gräfenroda, Thuringia as son of a Social Democratic master tailor; attended college of education in Gotha; 1920 SPD, ministerial official in Weimar; 1921 department head in Thuringian ministry of education; 1920-1933 member of Thuringian Landtag; 1932/33 member of Reichstag; after 1933 leading role in Social Democratic resistance group "Neu Beginnen"; from 1935/36 co-initiator of "Deutsche Volksfront" (German People's Front); 1938 arrested, sentenced to 12 years penitentiary, confinement in Brandenburg-Görden; 1943-1945 Buchenwald Concentration Camp, collaborated with Werner Hilpert, Ernst Thape and Walter Wolf to form People's Front Committee in camp; 1945 president of administrative district of Thuringia in charge of formation of Thuringian state government; 1946 secretary of state in Hesse; 1948 member of constitutional convention in Herrenchiemsee; 1949-1953 SPD member of Bundestag, professor of constitutional law; died June 22, 1959 in Wiesbaden. (Catalogue 5.26)

Danuta Brzosko-Medryk (born 1921)

Born Aug. 4, 1921 in Pultusk, Poland; member of Girl Scouts and served in Armija Krajowa (Home Army); 1940 first arrest on charges of illegal school-leaving examination; 1942 second arrest, Pawiak Prison, Warsaw; 1943 deported to Majdanek Concentration Camp; April 1944 Ravensbrück Concentration Camp; from June 1944 Hasag Leipzig Sub-Camp; Apr. 14, 1945 liberated from evacuation march by Soviet troops; then studied medicine, doctorate in medicine, dentist and writer; Sept. 1, 1989 Aachen Peace Prize; since 1996 female inmates' representative of International Committee Buchenwald, Dora and Sub-Camps. (Catalogue 4.27)

Ernst Busse (1897-1952)

Born Nov. 24, 1897 in Solingen as son of a grinder; apprenticeship as grinder, worked as harvester during WWI; 1919 joined KPD, odd jobs; 1925 labour union functionary in Mönchengladbach, KPD-municipal councillor in Viersen; 1931 district head of Rote Gewerkschaftsopposition (RGO; Red Labour Union Opposition) in Cologne; 1932 KPD member of Reichstag; 1933 worked underground as illegal district head of RGO in Erfurt, arrested; 1934 sentenced to 3 years confinement on charges of "high treason" and "new formation of parties", solitary confinement in Kassel Penitentiary; 1936 Gestapo detention in Cologne, after serving sentence preventive custody in Lichtenburg Concentration Camp; 1937 Buchenwald Concentration Camp, block senior; 1939 Camp Senior II; 1940 Camp Senior I; 1942 capo in inmates' infirmary, one of three heads of illegal KPD organisation in camp; 1945 after liberation director of Labour Office in Thuringia, deputy minister-president and minister of interior; 1946 party examination of his role as capo in Buchenwald, exoneration; 1947 transfer to Berlin as vice president of Administration of Agriculture and Forestry in Soviet occupied zone; 1949 chairman of central association of agricultural cooperatives in Soviet occupied zone / German Democratic Republic; 1950 arrested by Soviet secret service, sentenced to life imprisonment as "war criminal" due to activities as inmate functionary in Buchenwald; died Aug. 31, 1952 in gulag camp in Vorkuta. (Catalogue 4.13)

Julien Cain (1887-1974)
Born May 10, 1887 in Montmorency; 1911 historian and teacher in Toulon; 1914-1918 combatant in WWI, serious injury; 1919 head of documentation department of foreign ministry; 1927 chief of cabinet of presidents of national assembly; 1930 administrator general of national library; 1940 relieved of post by Vichy regime on account of Jewish heritage; February 1941 arrested on suspicion of collaboration with exile government in London, imprisoned in Paris; 1941-1944 Romainville Camp; 1944 deportation to Buchenwald (Operation "Meerschaum"), Little Camp, sock-darning detachment; 1946-1964 director general of libraries of France; 1952-1958 member of Academy of Fine Arts; from 1958 chairman of French UNESCO Commission, chairman of commission on history of deportation, French historians' committee on the history of World War II; died Oct. 9, 1974 in Paris. (Catalogue 4.6)

Domenico Ciufoli (born 1898)
Born July 3, 1898 in Italy; member of / functionary in Italian Communist party; 1939 confinement in various French penitentiaries; 1943 Compiègne; 1944 deportation to Buchenwald; 1945 member of illegal International Camp Committee; following liberation member of central committee of Italian Communist party; 1948-1953 member of Italian parliament. (Catalogue 5.13)

Robert Clop (born 1924)
Born Apr. 16, 1924 in Nimes; from 1942 member of the Résistance; 1943 arrest, Lyon Military Prison, Compiègne Camp; 1944-1945 Buchen-

wald Concentration Camp, forced labour in Gustloff-Werk in Weimar, where he published hand-written illegal monthly magazine "Les concentres GLORIA" (six copies per month); after 1945 military service for French forces in Germany, return to France, oral surgeon, member of various Gaullist parties, vice president of F.N.D.I.R.P., co-president of Association Buchenwald-Dora. (Catalogue 4.6)

Gwidon Damazyn (1908-1972)
Born Oct. 21, 1908 in Bydgoszcz, Poland; telecommunications engineer, politically independent, radio amateur; 1939/40 partisan, arrested, committal to Pawiak Prison in Warsaw; 1941-1945 Buchenwald Concentration Camp, electricians' detachment, worked in Transformator II, built altogether four receivers; after war worked as electrical engineer; late 1972 died. (Catalogue 3.51)

Dr. Robert Danneberg (1885-1942)
Born July 23, 1885 in Vienna; studied law, doctorate, member of Social Democratic party of Austria; from 1923 president of Landtag of Vienna and deputy chairman of Social Democratic municipal councillors of Vienna; 1932 municipal councillor for finance; 1938 arrested after occupation of Austria, Dachau Concentration Camp, Buchenwald Concentration Camp (latrine detachment, etc.); October 1942 Auschwitz Concentration Camp; Dec. 12, 1942 killed in Auschwitz. (Catalogue 3.21)

Georges de Bleser (born 1911)
Born Nov. 5, 1911 in Brussels; policeman, member of police resistance organisation "Milice patriotique" and "Front de l'Indépendance"; 1942 arrested, solitary confinement in Breendonk until 1943; deportation to Buchenwald (construction detachment and Gustloff-Werk); May 1945 return to Belgium, executive police service. (Catalogue 4.9)

Pierre Durand (born 1923)
Born Aug. 30, 1923 in Muhlhouse; following occupation of France member of the Résistance; January 1944 arrested during execution of assignment for Résistance, interrogations and solitary confinement, committal to Compiègne Camp; May 1944 deportation to Buchenwald, interpreter and liaison between French and German Communists in camp, member of illegal military group of French inmates; Apr. 19, 1945 speaker of Oath of the Inmates of Buchenwald in French; after 1945 journalist and historian; since 1982 president of International Committee Buchenwald, Dora and Sub-Camps. (Catalogue 4.6)

Hans Eiden (1901-1950)
Nov. 24, 1901 born in Trier as son of a railroad worker; lathe operator for German railroad;

1929 joined KPD; 1933 three months preventive custody; 1936 renewed arrest, 3-year penitentiary sentence on charges of "preparations for high treason"; 1939 preventive custody, Wittlich Penal Prison; September 1939 Buchenwald Concentration Camp, barrack room duty in Block 28; from 1940 member of inmates' clothing depot detachment; 1942 special detachment of delinquent company; 1943 Camp Senior II; 1944/45 Camp Senior; Apr. 11, 1945 appointed "camp commander", member of KPD party leadership; May 1945 return to Trier; October 1945 appointment as "municipal advisor" by decree of French military administration; 1947 chairman of VVN in Trier, KPD member of first Landtag of Rheinland-Pfalz; died Dec. 6, 1950. (Catalogue 5.15)

Maurice Eyben (born 1922)

Born Jan. 22, 1922 in Lüttich; office worker, member of reconnaissance unit "Service Zéro" of Belgian Resistance; January 1944 arrested, interrogations and confinement in Lüttich, Cologne and Waldheim; early March 1945 transported to Buchenwald within Operation "Nacht-und-Nebel," labour in quarry; May 8, 1945 return to Belgium. (Catalogue 5.12)

Jean Fonteyne (1899-1974)

Born May 3, 1899 in Ledeberg, Belgium; 1916/17 volunteer in WWI; 1919/20 study of law; 1922 marriage (4 children); 1927 founder of "Révue générale des assurances et responsabilités" for defence of rights of socially disadvantaged and victims of justice system; ca. 1930 joined Belgian Communist party; 1933-1941 provided accommodation to persecuted foreign antifascists; 1941 went underground, member of Résistance movement "Front de l'Indépendance", member of military unit of "Armée belge des partisans", arrested, Breendonk Transit Camp; May 1944 deportation to Buchenwald, co-founder of Belgian support committee whose members were a Catholic, a Liberal, a Communist and a Social Democrat; April 1945 return to Belgium; 1946-1949 Senator; died June 22, 1974. (Catalogue 4.9)

Josef Frank (1909-1952)

Born Feb. 15, 1909 in Plumlov, Prostejov District, Czechoslovakia; 1926 member of Communist party, central secretary of federation of privately employed; 1939 arrested by Gestapo, taken to Buchenwald, labour administration detachment; 1945 member of central committee and politburo of Czech Communist party; 1948 deputy secretary general of central committee of Czech Communist party, member of national assembly; 1951 arrested and charged in Slansky trial of collaboration with SS in Buchenwald; Dec. 3, 1952 execution; 1963 rehabilitated. (Catalogue 5.13)

Dr. Gotthard Martin Gauger (1905-1941)

Born Aug. 4, 1905 in Elberfeld to a pastor's family, fourth of eight children; studied jurisprudence and economics at universities of Tübingen, Berlin, Breslau and Bonn and at the London School of Economics, employment at various courts; 1934 refused to take oath of allegiance to Hitler for reasons of conscience, dismissed from civil service, doctorate in law at University of Münster; January 1935 legal adviser to Confessional Church of Berlin; 1938 turned down offer of professorship at Christian College in Madras (India) in order to continue working for Confessional Church; April 1940 army call-up orders; May 1940 escape to Netherlands, arrested after occupation of Netherlands, injured during arrest by shot in leg; June 1941 Buchenwald Concentration Camp, selected under file number "14 f 13;" July 1941 killed in extermination facility Sonnenstein near Pirna; July 23, 1941 official date of death. (Catalogue 3.41)

Ludwig Gehre (1895-1945)

1914-1918 combatant in WWI; 1920 participation in Kapp coup; from mid 1930s service in military intelligence department under Admiral Canaris, member of staff of Hans Oster and Hans von Dohnanyi; 1937 liaison between Colonel Wilhelm Staehle and Carl Friedrich Goerdeler; 1943 liaison between staff of Central German army group and Berlin group during first attempt to assassinate Hitler by Henning von Tresckow, close contact to Stauffenberg and other conspirators; 1944 under SD observance, went underground in Berlin, arrested and then escaped from confinement; end of 1944 shot his wife to death during renewed arrest and tried to commit suicide, loss of one eye, confinement in Gestapo prison in Prinz-Albrecht-Strasse, Berlin; Feb. 7- Apr. 3, 1945 Buchenwald; Apr. 9, 1945 execution in Flossenbürg Concentration Camp. (Catalogue 4.35)

Otto Gerig (1885-1944)

June 9, 1885 born in Rosenberg, Baden; commercial clerk; 1921 full-time employment with Deutschnationaler Handlungsgehilfen-Verband (DHV; German association of commercial clerks); 1921-1933 Centre Party member of Reichstag; 1933 unemployed, later employed by Ford AG in Cologne; August 1944 arrested during Operation "Gitter," confinement in Cologne fair halls, Buchenwald Concentration Camp; end of September 1944 last sign of life to family; died Oct. 3, 1944 in camp. (Catalogue 4.8)

Max Göhrmann (1882-1965)

Born Nov. 2, 1882 ; 1929 joined KPD; 1937 arrested; 1939 committed to Buchenwald as political inmate (Block 38), work in bookbinding detachment; after 1945 pensioner in Magdeburg; died Feb. 9, 1965. (Catalogue 5.10)]

Ernst Grube (1890-1945)

Born Jan. 22, 1890 in Neundorf, Anhalt as son of a miner; 1896-1904 Volksschule; 1904-1908 apprenticeship as carpenter followed by journeying; 1908 joined German woodworkers' association and SPD; from beg. of 1914 worked as carpenter in Werdau car factory; 1915/16 military service as member of infantry; 1917 co-founder of USPD in Werdau; 1918 chairman of workers' council in Werdau and co-founder of local branch of Spartacus association; 1919 involved in formation of local branches of KPD in and around Zwickau-Werdau; 1920 leadership of Zwickau workers' militia during Kapp coup; 1922-1924 KPD member of municipal council in Zwickau; 1924-1930 political secretary of KPD in districts of Erzgebirge-Vogtland, Magdeburg-Anhalt and Wasserkante; 1924 and 1930-1933 member of Reichstag; 1929 member of central committee of KPD, secretary for sports work; February 1933 arrested, Sonnenburg and Lichtenburg Concentration Camps; July 1937 committal to Buchenwald Concentration Camp, capo of inmates' carpentry shop; 1939 release and forced labour as carpenter in Warsaw; 1941 returned to Berlin, under Gestapo surveillance, contact to Resistance group around Robert Uhrig; 1942 several months in confinement; August 1944 renewed arrest (Operation "Gitter"), committal to Sachsenhausen Concentration Camp; April 1945 Bergen-Belsen Concentration Camp; died Apr. 14, 1945 of epidemic typhus. (Catalogue 3.7)

Fritz Grünbaum (1880-1941)

Born Apr. 7, 1880 in Brünn; lawyer; 1907 began work in Viennese cabaret "Hölle" as compère, developed double compèring with F. Farkas, cabaret artist and revue author, wrote film scripts and opera libretti; 1938 arrested after occupation of Austria, Dachau Concentration Camp, Buchenwald (worked in latrine detachment, among others); 1940 taken to Dachau as sick person; died Jan. 18, 1941 in Dachau. (Catalogue 3.21)

Elisabeth Rachel Grünebaum (born 1923)

Born Dec. 9, 1923 in Sighet, Transylvania; May 19, 1944 deportation to Auschwitz; July 1944 taken to Gelsenkirchen Sub-Camp with 2,000 Hungarian-Jewish women, later Krupp (Essen); March 1945 to Bergen-Belsen, liberated there on Apr. 15, 1945, returned to Timisoara; 1947 emigration to Palestine, in the army after foundation of State of Israel; 1953 emigration to Germany. (Catalogue 4.26)

Maurice Halbwachs (1877-1945)

Born Mar. 11, 1877 in Reims; teacher, studied law, sociology, mathematics; 1909 dissertation in political economics; 1913 publication of thesis on working class and its living standards, taught at universities of Caen and Strasbourg; 1925 at Sorbonne in Paris, publication of chief work (Memory and its Social Conditions), member of Académie des Sciences morales et politiques and of the Institut international de statistique, worked at International Labour Office, Geneva; 1938 president of Institut francais de Sociologie, vice president of Société de Psychologie, professor at Collège de France; July 1944 arrested by Gestapo along with sons and friends in the Résistance, deportation to Buchenwald with youngest son Pierre; Aug. 20, 1944 arrival at Buchenwald Concentration Camp, according to examination by camp physician classified on Aug. 28 as invalid and not transportable (tent camp, Blocks 61, 64, 31, 55); died Mar. 15, 1945 in the Little Camp. (Catalogue 5.6)

Edmund Hamber (1893-1940)

Born July 25, 1893 in Vienna; employee of Viennese film company "Ciba", Social Democrat; 1938 arrested in Vienna after occupation of Austria, Dachau Concentration Camp, Buchenwald Concentration Camp, transport convoy; Nov. 28, 1940 Edmund Hamber died on allegedly "voluntary death" at a time when his brother's murderer, SS Block Officer Abraham, was on duty in camp. (Catalogue 3.45)

Ernst Heilmann (1881-1940)

Born Apr. 13, 1881 in Berlin; studied law and political science; 1898 joined SPD; 1903-1907 member of parliament responsible for submitting parliamentary reports; 1909-1917 chief editor of Erzgebirgische Volksstimme, Chemnitz; 1919 SPD municipal councillor in Berlin-Charlottenburg; 1919 member of Prussian Landtag; 1921-1933 chairman of SPD parliamentary group; 1928-1933 member of Reichstag, staunch Nazi opponent, rejected alliances with Communists; June 1933 arrested, Columbiahaus Concentration Camp, Police Headquarters Alexanderplatz, Plötzensee Penitentiary, Oranienburg, Papenburg, Esterwegen, Dachau and Buchenwald Concentration Camps ("political Jew"); Apr. 3, 1940 killed in detention cell building, presumably by means of injection. (Catalogue 3.20)

Jenö (Eugene) Heimler (1922-1990)

Born Mar. 27, 1922 in Szombathely, Western Hungary; 1944 Szombathely ghetto, deportation to Auschwitz, wife, father and sister killed, taken to Buchenwald with 2,500 Hungarian-Jewish inmates; until beg. of August 1944 in Little Camp; September 1944 rubble clearance work in the Tröglitz Sub-Camp; December 1944 Berga/Elster Sub-Camp; April 1945 escaped from evacuation march in direction of Czechoslovakia; after 1945 professor for Human Social Functioning in Great Britain, the U.S. and Canada; died Dec. 4, 1990 in London. (Catalogue 4.7)

Johann Herzog (born 1902)
Born Mar. 1, 1902 in Sandhausen as son of a mason; Volksschule, learned masonry; 1919 apprentices' final examination, as unemployed person joined French Foreign Legion, aside from brief interruption served 15 years in Algeria, Morocco and Indochina; 1935 arrested upon return to Germany; 1939 Buchenwald Concentration Camp; 1941/42 capo in quarry, known to have committed numerous acts of maltreatment, according to inmates' testimony drove members of dump car detachment to the point of collapse with clubs; 1942 released, worked in Heidelberg; 1945-1947 constable in Baden-Baden; 1947 arrested by French authorities; 1948 released; 1949 renewed arrest and sentence to 12 years penitentiary; further whereabouts unknown. (Catalogue 3.30)

Maurice Hewitt (1884-1971)
Born Oct. 6, 1884 in Asnières, musician; until 1914 member of ensemble "Instruments anciens"; 1918-1930 member of "Capet Quartet", known above all for interpretations of Beethoven string quartets; 1930-1943 concerts with his own quartet; 1943 arrested on grounds of activities for Résistance (channelling Allied paratroopers to Spain), confinement in Fresnes and Compiègne; 1944 deportation to Buchenwald (Operation "Meerschaum"), darning detachment, illegally founded quartet in camp with Polish inmates and played for fellow prisoners on violin procured by inmates from depot; after 1945 teacher at Parisian academy of music and founder of his own chamber orchestra; died Nov. 7, 1971 in Créteil. (Catalogue 4.6)

Werner Hilpert (1897-1957)
Born Jan. 17, 1897 in Leipzig; until 1933 active in Centre Party in Saxony; 1939-1945 Buchenwald Concentration Camp, member of illegal People's Front Committee; May/June 1945 fiduciary for assets confiscated from Nazis; beg. of July 1945 left Thuringia with Americans; after 1945 co-founder of CDU in Hesse, Minister of Economics and Deputy Minister-President of first Land government of Hesse, later Minister of Finances, director of German Railway; died Feb. 24, 1957. (Catalogue 5.33)

Faybusch Itzkewitsch (1891-1941)
Born Aug. 15, 1891 in Lipsk, shoemaker; 1914-1918 conscripted to Russian army; taken prisoner of war by Germans; after 1918 as stateless Jew in Germany, founded workshop for special footwear in Ehmen near Wolfsburg; 1923 began life companionship with a non-Jewish woman, son born; November 1935 Nuremberg laws criminalise interracial life companionships; 1937 a neighbour reports life companionship to authorities; 1938 condemned by regional court of Hildesheim on grounds of "racial disgrace"; November

1938 Buchenwald Concentration Camp, delinquent company, selection under file no. "14 f 13;" July 1941 killed in Sonnenstein Sanatorium near Pirna; July 27, 1941 official date of death. (Catalogue 3.41)

Nicolai Kalcin
Russian inmate; after Apr. 11, 1945 member of Russian Committee in Buchenwald, member of repatriation commission, Soviet secret service; since 1950 whereabouts unknown. (Catalogue 5.13)

Benedikt Kautsky (1894-1960)
Born Nov. 1, 1894 in Stuttgart, son of Social Democratic politician Karl Kautsky; 1921 economic adviser at Chamber of Labourers in Vienna; 1923-1934 editor of Arbeit and Wirtschaft, publications on history, sociology, economics and classical literature; 1938 arrested, Dachau Concentration Camp; September 1938 Buchenwald Concentration Camp ("Political Jew"); 1942 Auschwitz Concentration Camp; 1945 transport to Buchenwald, co-signer of manifesto of the democratic Socialists; 1955 deputy director general of largest Austrian bank institute; 1957 collaboration on party platform of Social Democratic Party of Austria; Apr. 1, 1960 died. (Catalogue 5.26)

Albert Kayser (1898-1944)
Born Nov. 28, 1898 in Stettin; labourer and trade union official in Berlin, initially member of USPD, from 1921 of KPD; 1932 member of Reichstag; 1933 in "preventive custody"; 1935 sentenced to death by 1st Senate of the People's Court on grounds of "high treason"; following international protests commutation of sentence to life imprisonment; 1936-1943 Brandenburg-Goerden Penitentiary; 1943 taken to Buchenwald; died Oct. 18, 1944 of epidemic typhus. (Catalogue 4.8)

Eugen Kogon (1903-1987)
Feb. 2, 1903 born in Munich; studied political economics and sociology; 1927-1932 editor of Catholic weekly magazine, adviser to central commission of Christian trade unions in Vienna; 1938 Dachau Concentration Camp; 1939-1945 Buchenwald Concentration Camp; from 1943 secretary in Block 50 (Hygiene Institute of Armed SS), was smuggled out of camp on Apr. 8, 1945 with forged letter in crate of vaccines; 1945 worked for Psychological Warfare Division of U.S. Army; 1946 co-editor of "Frankfurter Hefte;" from 1947 involvement in European movement, professorship in political science, publicist; died Dec. 24, 1987. (Catalogue 5.11)

Rolf Kralovitz (born 1925)
Born June 15, 1925 in Leipzig as son of a Hungarian; 1939 gravedigger at municipal cemetery in Leipzig, ghettoisation in a "Jew House" along with mother and sister; 1941 barber's assistant in

Jewish community centre; 1943 arrested, mother and sister transported to Ravensbrück Women's Concentration Camp where both were killed, committal to Buchenwald Concentration Camp, Block 22, Construction Detachment I, barber; 1945 return to Leipzig, cabaret artist; 1946 film actor in Munich; 1949 emigration to U.S., employment with stockbrokers' firm in New York; 1952 marriage; 1953 return to Munich, actor; 1960 executive producer at Westdeutscher Rundfunk; 1976 loss of eyesight and early retirement.

Walter Krämer (1892-1941)

Born June 21, 1892 in Siegen; apprenticeship as locksmith; 1911-1918 volunteer in Navy; 1919 member of USPD, after 1921 of KPD, professional party functionary; 1926 sentenced to prison for several years; 1928 amnestied, secretary of KPD in sub-districts of Krefeld, Siegen and Wuppertal; 1932 KPD member of Prussian Landtag; 1933 arrested; 1934-1937 Lichtenburg Concentration Camp; 1937 Buchenwald Concentration Camp, capo of inmates' infirmary, one of leading members of illegal Communist organisation in camp; Nov. 6, 1941 killed in Goslar Sub-Camp by member of SS named Blank. (Catalogue 3.22)

Henry Krasucki (born 1924)

Born Sept. 2, 1924 in Wolomin (Poland), emigration to France; after occupation of France participation in Résistance struggle, leader of Parisian organisation of Communist youth; March 1943 arrested by French police, interrogations and solitary confinement in police prison in Paris, turned over to Gestapo, Fresnes Military Prison; June 1943 deportation to Auschwitz Concentration Camp on grounds of Jewish heritage, forced labour in Jawischowitz Sub-Camp, establishment of resistance group; January 1945 deportation to Buchenwald, construction supervision labour detachment, member of illegal French resistance organisation in camp; April 1945 return to France; 1956-1962 member of central committee of French Communist party; 1964-1994 member of politburo of French Communist party; 1960-1982 secretary of trade union Confédération Générale du Travail (CGT); 1982-1992 chairman of CGT. (Catalogue 4.6)

Georg Krausz (1894-1973)

Born Mar. 2, 1894 in Humené, Slovakia as son of a professor; university studies; after 1918 publicist and editor of various German labourer's newspapers in Bratislava (Pressburg) and Prague; 1922-1933 foreign policy editor of KPD official party organ Rote Fahne; 1933-1936 illegal work in Berlin; 1936 sentenced on grounds of "high treason", penitentiary; 1941 Buchenwald Concentration Camp ("Political Jew"); 1945 head of department of agitation and propaganda (Agitprop) of Buchenwald collective of party activ-

ists; after 1945 renewed arrest by Soviet occupation army as Jew and alleged American spy, confinement in Special Camp No. 2 in Buchenwald and in Torgau Penitentiary; 1948 release, SED press department; from 1950 editor at Neues Deutschland; 1973 died. (Catalogue 5.23)

Hans Kunke (1906-1940)

Born Dec. 12, 1906 in Biala; 1934 member of central committee of Revolutionary Socialist Youth of Austria; 1938 taken to Buchenwald Concentration Camp on transport from Dachau; 1940 transferred to quarry along with all other Jewish members of his sock-darning labour detachment; Oct. 31, 1940, in act of desperation brought about by severe abuse, ran through guard chain and was shot to death. (Catalogue 3.22)

René-Michel L'Hopital (1885-1960)

Born Dec. 8, 1885 in Paris; artillery colonel; 1914-1918 participation in WWI as officer, injured, wartime adjutant of Marshal Foch; 1920 member of French delegation to peace negotiations in Versailles; 1919-1929 peacetime adjutant to Marshal Foch, then withdrew from military service; 1929-1936 founder and leader of scout movement in France; 1938-1940 mobilisation for army; April 1940 Deputy Chief of Staff of 1st Army, withdrew from military service following armistice; August 1940 founded resistance organisation "Armee volontaire"; 1941 two months' confinement; January 1942 renewed arrest ("Nacht-und-Nebel-Erlass"); 1942-1944 Fresnes Military Prison, subsequent confinement in Hinzert, Wittlich, Trier and Sachsenhausen Concentration Camps; 1944/45 Buchenwald Concentration Camp; 1945 testimony in Nuremberg Trial, after 1945 Secretary of State in Ministry of Defence, chairman of Alliance Atlantique des Anciens Combattants; Oct. 21, 1960 died in Suresnes. (Catalogue 4.6)

Kurt Leonhard (1903-1980)

Born Nov. 16, 1903 in Leipzig; miner; 1930 member of KPD; 1934-1937 Waldheim Penitentiary; 1937-1945 political inmate in Buchenwald, initially quarry and Construction Labour Detachment III, barrack room duty Block 30, Block Senior in Block 42, delinquent company; until 1943 medical orderly in inmates' infirmary, then medical orderly in Kassel Sub-Camp. (Catalogue 4.13)

Reinhold Lochmann (born 1914)

Born Feb. 5, 1914 in Dresden; 1928 joined KJVD, later KPD; 1928-1932 apprenticeship as mechanic and member of workers' radio association; 1933 first arrest and committal to Hohnstein Concentration Camp; 1933 release; 1935 renewed arrest and sentenced to 4 years penitentiary; 1935-1937 Zwickau Penitentiary; 1937/38 Aschendorfer Moor Concentration Camp; 1938-

1945 Buchenwald Concentration Camp, electricians' labour detachment, radio workshop; 1945 marriage, 2 children; 1949-1974 officer of German people's police; member of Buchenwald camp study group. (Catalogue 3.51)

Dr. Fritz Löhner, pen name Beda (1883-1942)

Born June 24, 1883 in Wildenschwerdt; freelance writer of operettas, pop songs ("Ausgerechnet Bananen", "Was machst Du mit dem Knie lieber Hans …"), chansons, great success as librettist for Franz Léhar and Paul Abraham, vice president of Austrian writers' association, member of Jewish academic association "Kadimah"; 1938 arrested, Dachau, then Buchenwald Concentration Camp (latrine detachment, among others), author of Buchenwald Song; October 1942 Auschwitz Concentration Camp; Dec. 4, 1942 killed in Auschwitz. (Catalogue 3.21)

Pavel Lyssenko [known in camp as Alex Mironow] (born 1919)

Born Feb. 28, 1919 in Prokopjevsk, Kemerovo Province; 1940 completed training at artillery school of Tomsk; 1940-1941 field grade officer in Kuibichev; 1941 taken prisoner of war by Germans near Poltava, escaped from camp in Adabash; 1943 deportation to Germany to POW Camp 326; 1943-1945 Buchenwald Concentration Camp, excavation detachment, Gustloff-Werk II, inmates' canteen; 1945 evacuated two days before liberation, escaped, met Red Army near Chemnitz, return to Siberia; 1950 completed study of medicine; 1950-1972 lecturer at medical university in Sysran. (Catalogue 3.55)

Princess Mafalda of Hesse (1902-1944)

Born Nov. 19, 1902 in Rome as daughter of Italian king Victor Emanuel III; 1925 marriage to Prince Philip of Hesse, nephew of William II., domicile in Rome, 4 children; 1933 Minister-President of Prussia Hermann Göring appointed Philip of Hesse as Senior President of Province of Hesse-Nassau, moved to Kassel; 1938/39 Philip acted as liaison between Hitler and Mussolini; 1943 after Italy's armistice with Allies, Mafalda arrested in Rome by the Gestapo, transported to Berlin-Wannsee, then to Buchenwald, accommodation in isolation barrack, religious guidance by Jehovah's Witness Maria Ruhnau; Aug. 24, 1944 grave injury during bomb attack; Aug. 28, 1944 death as result of loss of blood following improperly executed amputation of left arm by SS physician. (Catalogue 4.33)

Alexander Makeev (1920-1942)

Born Nov. 21, 1920 in Obwal; 1937 school diploma; 1937-1939 studied education in Voronezh, graduated as elementary school teacher; 1939-1941 teacher, final teaching position in Grodno; 1941 conscription into Red Army, taken as prisoner of war, ultimately in Stalag X D (Wietzendorf, Hamburg military district); Oct. 18, 1941 committal to Buchenwald; died Jan. 3, 1942. (Catalogue 3.37)

Louis-Georges Rothschild, later Mandel (1885-1944)

Born June 5, 1885 in Alsace to Jewish businessman's family; journalist; 1917 chief of cabinet under Clemenceau; 1934-1940 various ministerial positions: Postmaster General, colonial minister under Édouard Daladier and minister of interior in the final French government of Paul Reynaud; 1942 charged in trial of Riom along with Léon Blum, Edouard Daladier, Paul Reynaud, Maurice Gamelin and others, sentenced to life imprisonment, deportation to Sachsenhausen Concentration Camp; 1943 transport to Buchenwald, internment in falcon lodge with Jeanne and Léon Blum; 1944 turned over to French militia for death of Philippe Henriot, information minister of Vichy regime, transported to Paris to Gestapo headquarters; July 7, 1944 killed by French militia while travelling in automobile. (Catalogue 4.32)

Henri Manhès [called Frédéric] (1889-1959)

Born June 9, 1889 in France; journalist; 1933 officer in French Legion of Honour; 1936 combatant in Spanish Civil War in "International Brigades"; 1940 participation in establishment of "Free French Army"; 1941 member of Comité National Francais; 1943 arrested, death sentence; 1943/44 Compiègne; 1944/45 Buchenwald, founded illegal committee for French interests and led French liberation brigade along with Marcel Paul; 1946 honorary president of federation of members of Résistance; died June 25, 1959. (Catalogue 5.13)

André Marie (1897-1972)

Born Dec. 3, 1897 in Honfleur, France; lawyer; 1924 member of French chamber of deputies; 1933 secretary of state, member of French Résistance; 1943 arrested, deported to Buchenwald; 1947 minister of justice; 1948 premier minister; 1951 minister of education; until 1962 member of parliament; died June 12, 1972. (Catalogue 5.11)

Max Mayr (1896-1985)

Jan. 3, 1896 born in Kempten, Allgäu as son of a master weaver; apprenticeship as locksmith and latheman, soldier in WWI; after 1918 worked for German railway, joined USPD, change to KPD, active involvement in metal workers' association, joined youth group Internationaler Jugendbund (IJB); 1926 member of ISK; 1931 unemployed; 1932-1933 editorial work for ISK newspaper Der Funken; 1933-1936 resistance work in Kassel; 1936 arrested; 1936-1938 Kassel-Wehlheiden Penitentiary; 1938-1945 Buchenwald Concentration Camp; 1939 camp administration department; 1941-1945 commanders' secretary: daily records of block inhabitants, blocks, patients in inmates' infirmary and composition of labour detachments; after 1945 head of department of reparation at government headquarters in Kassel, SPD member of municipal council, member of working group of persecuted Social Democrats (AVS); Sept. 15, 1985 died. (Catalogue 3.12)

Vladimir Mazijenko (1927-1993)

Born Jan. 24, 1927 in Zaporozhye, Ukraine; school pupil; 1942 arrested in Zaporozhye, confinement in Dnepropetrovsk and Igren Camp; September 1943 deportation to Buchenwald Concentration Camp, detachment Gustloff-Werk II; beg. of 1944 admission to Children's Block 8; April/June 1945 after liberation worked in Buchenwald as nurse in military hospital; June 1945 returned to USSR, worked as geologist; 1993 died in Vassilyevka, Ukraine. (Catalogue 4.5)

Paul Morgan (1886-1938)

Born Oct. 1, 1886 in Vienna as son of the lawyer Morgenstern; 1911 name changed to Morgan, worked as actor, cabaret artist, feuilletonist, well-known satirist in Berlin of Weimar Republic; 1933 return to Austria; 1938 arrested after occupation of Austria, Dachau, then Buchenwald Concentration Camp ("Political Jew"); died Dec. 10, 1938 as result of maltreatment. (Catalogue 3.20)

Josef Müller (1898-1979)

Born Mar. 27, 1898 in Steinwiesen; lawyer; before 1933 active in Bavarian People's Party (BVP) and Centre Party; confidante of Bavarian Minister-President Heinrich Held; 1933 arrested, released, then advisor to archbishop of Munich; 1939 active in military intelligence department of Wehrmacht supreme command, as representative of resistance group around Colonel Beck and Admiral Canaris attempted to make contact with British government by way of Vatican; 1943 arrested on charges of high treason; trial, acquittal by Volksgerichtshof (People's Court); 1944 custody in Gestapo prison in Prinz-Albrecht-Strasse, Berlin; 1945 special RSHA inmate in Buchenwald, Flossenbürg, Dachau Concentration Camps; liberation in South Tyrol, cofounder of CSU, its chairman until 1949; 1947-1949 Bavarian Deputy Minister-President; 1947-1952 Bavarian Minister of Justice; until 1962 member of Bavarian Landtag; Sept. 12, 1979 died in Munich. (Catalogue 4/35)

Otto Neururer (1882-1940)

Born Mar. 25, 1882 in Piller, South Tyrol; 1903-1907 studied Catholic theology at Brixen Seminary; from 1914 employment as priest; 1938 refused to conduct wedding of fanatic NSDAP member with woman from his congregation, arrested by Gestapo; 1939 Dachau Concentration Camp, delinquent company; September 1939 Buchenwald Concentration Camp, delinquent company; May 1940 detention cell building on account of spiritual charge of fellow inmates, hung from his ankles by Martin Sommer until his death on May 30, 1940; 1996 beatified by John Paul II.. (Catalogue 3.26)

Rudolf Opitz (1908-1939)

Born Feb. 19, 1908 in Leipzig; photo lab technician; 1923 member of KJVD; 1931 joined KPD; 1933-1935 resistance work; 1937 sentenced to two years penitentiary for "preparations for high treason;" 1938 Buchenwald Concentration Camp, worked in photo department, took photos illegally, confined in detention cell building following discovery during routine control; killed there on Aug. 7, 1939. (Catalogue 3.26)

Suzanne Orts, née Pic (born 1927)

Born Apr. 12, 1927 in Sète, Southern France; 1943 affiliation with Résistance as member of Gaullist group; May 1944 arrested in Perpignan; June 1944 deportation with stops in: Perpignan, Romainville, Neue Bremm (Saarbrücken), Ravensbrück, Leipzig; July 1944 inmate in Hasag women's external camp in Leipzig-Schönefeld; April 1945 evacuation march, encountered Soviet soldiers in Cavertiz near Oschatz; May 1945 fled to Paris. (Catalogue 4.26)

Marcel Paul (1900-1982)

July 12, 1900 registered as foundling in birth register in Paris; 1915 youth organisation of Socialist party, active military service, apprenticeship as electrician; 1923 joined French Communist party, secretary general of electricians' union, municipal councillor in Paris; 1940 taken prisoner of war, escaped, active in Résistance; 1941 arrested and sentenced to 4 years confinement; 1944 deportation to Auschwitz, then Buchenwald, coordination of French resistance in camp; 1945/46 member of parliament, minister of energy in first three post-war governments, member of central committee of French Communist party, chairman of energy industry union, founded Buchenwald-Dora Association and F.N.D.I.R.P., president of International Buchenwald Committee; died Nov. 11, 1982. (Catalogue 5.13)

Hermann Pünder (1888-1976)

Born Apr. 1, 1888 in Trier; lawyer; 1926-1932 Secretary of State and Chief of Reich Chancellery as Centre Party member; 1932 president of administrative district of Münster; 1933 dismissed from civil service; 1944 special inmate in various concentration camps, fellow prisoner of Dietrich Bonhoeffer in SS Detention at Buchenwald Concentration Camp; 1945 liberation, cofounder of CSU; 1945-1948 chief burgomaster of Cologne; 1948 director-in-chief of administrative board of Vereinigtes Wirtschaftsgebiet (united economic area); 1949-1957 member of Bundestag; 1952-1957 vice-president of senior board of European Coal and Steel Company; died Oct. 3, 1976 in Fulda. (Catalogue 4/35)

Friedrich von Rabenau (1884-1945)

Retired artillery general; 1932-1934 town major of Breslau, gave lectures on military history at university; 1934-1936 selective service inspector in Münster, affiliation with Count of Galen; 1936 commissioned by Chief of Staff Ludwig Beck to set up military archives; 1941 refusal to suppress files on German crimes in Poland; 1937-1940 work on two-volume biography of Colonel General Seeckt, published 1938/1940, began studies at department of Protestant theology at University of Berlin; 1941 prohibited from using military archives for thesis on military religious welfare; 1942 dismissed from post as director of military archives; 1943 discharged from army; 1944 permit to preach, friendship with Beck and Carl Friedrich Goerdeler, contacts with Generals Brauchitsch and Guderian; 1944 arrested; Feb. 24 – Apr. 3, 1945 internment in SS Detention in Buchenwald; killed between Apr. 9 and Apr. 14, 1945 in Flossenbürg Concentration Camp. (Catalogue 4.35)

Charles Richet (1882-1966)

Born Dec. 11, 1882 in Paris; doctor; 1940 elected to Académie de medicine Paris; following occupation joined Résistance, leader of resistance group "Stephane Renault" and the group's medical service "Ceux de la Liberation;" 1943 betrayal and arrest, Fresnes Military Prison, Compiègne Camp; January 1944 deportation to Buchenwald Concentration Camp (Operation "Meerschaum"), camp physician in Little Camp; 1945 testified in Nuremberg Trial; 1945-1956 professor of medicine at university and director of all hospitals in Paris, studied physical consequences of deportation, founded "Ligue pour la neutralité de la médecine en temps de guerre"; died July 17, 1966 in Paris. (Catalogue 4.6)

Herman Rols (born 1917)

Born Dec. 13, 1917 in Labastide sur l'Hers; 1938-1940 soldier, participated in action in Alsace; August 1940 demobilisation; March 1943 arrested for refusal to carry out forced labour in Germany, Poitiers Prison, Compiègne Camp; September 1943 deportation to Buchenwald; January 1944 Dora Sub-Camp, accommodation in tunnels of Kohnstein, forced labour in rocket assembly, tibia fracture as result of accident, inmates' infirmary; following recovery office work in bomb disposal detachment near Osnabrück; May/June 1945 stay in Sweden, contracted typhus, returned to France; after 1945 commercial representative. (Catalogue 4.20)

Otto Roth (1905-1969)

Born Mar. 20, 1905 in Frankfurt/Main; 1919 joined SAJ and labour union, apprenticeship as electro-mechanic; 1930 member of KPD; 1939 arrested and committed to Buchenwald Concentration Camp; 1939-1945 Buchenwald Concentration Camp, quarry, electricians' detachment, one of leaders of military resistance organisation; beg. 1945 involvement in VVN in Frankfurt/Main; May 9, 1969 died. (Catalogue 3.56)

Michael Rozenek (born 1914)

Born Apr. 10, 1914 in Dzialoszyce, Poland; beg. of 1940 family deported to Lodz Ghetto, he himself spared from deportation through receipt of certificate of employment, death of eldest brother, wife of same and youngest sister; August 1944 deportation to Auschwitz, parents and another sister killed there, forced labour in Czechowice Sub-Camp; January 1945 deported along with brother to Buchenwald, Little Camp, Rehmsdorf Sub-Camp, transport and rubble clearance work; from February 1945 camp laundry; April 1945 evacuation transport in direction of Czechoslovakia, escaped with brother to Erz Mountains, hidden by farmer's family; May 1945 liberation; July 1945 returned to Poland; 1952 emigration to Argentina on account of anti-Semitic tendencies in Poland. (Catalogue 4.23)

Dr. Svend Aaage Schaldemose-Nielsen (1900-1944)

Born May 16, 1900 in Frederiksbord; studied law, doctorate in law, chief of police in Odense; September 1944 taken into custody with altogether 2,000 Danish policemen, Neuengamme Concentration Camp; October 1944 Buchenwald Concentration Camp, accommodation in Barrack 57 (Little Camp), contracted scarlet fever; died Nov. 26, 1944 in Buchenwald. (Catalogue 4.9)

Otto Schmidt (1918-1942)

Born Feb. 15, 1918 in Luckenwalde; labourer; 1938 committed to Buchenwald Concentration Camp as Sinto within framework of June operation, daughter born during period of confinement; 1942 artificially infected with epidemic typhus pathogens and, as "control person", not given treatment; Nov. 20, 1942 killed by means of injection following conclusion of experiment. (Catalogue 3.18)

Paul Schneider (1897-1939)

Born Aug. 29, 1897 in Pferdsfeld, Hunsrück as son of a pastor; 1915-1918 voluntary active service; 1919-1922 studied theology in Giessen, Marburg, Tübingen and Koblenz; 1922 practical training in industry, Ruhr district; 1923 Protestant seminary in Soest; 1923-1926 assistant preacher in Berlin, Rotthausen, Essen, etc.; 1926-1937 pastor in Hochelheim and Dickenschied, supported Confessional church; 1926 married pastor's daughter Margarete Dietrich, six children; from 1934 several arrests; 1937 disobeyed order to leave Rhine province, renewed arrest, preventive custody, committal to Buchenwald Concentration Camp; 1938 beginning of confinement in "Bunker" and subjection to torture; July 18, 1939 tortured to death in infirmary during treatment by SS physician Dr. Ding. (Catalogue 3.44)

Adolf [Adi] Scholze (1913-1983)

Born Mar. 1, 1913 in Bohemia; member of Czech Social Democratic party (SPC); 1939-1945 in Buchenwald, member of camp fire brigade, from 1943 member of illegal organisation of KPD and of illegal military organisation (IMO); 1945/46 local / municipal administration of Czechoslovakia; 1946 People's Police in Soviet occupied zone, member of SED, from 1951 cultural and labour director in construction industry; died Feb. 1, 1983. (Catalogue 5.11)

Robert Siewert (1887-1973)

Born Dec. 30, 1887 in Schwersens, Posen; bricklayer's apprenticeship; 1906-1919 SPD; 1915-1918 active duty on Eastern front; 1918-1919 Spartacus association/KPD, member of soldiers' council; 1920-1929 member of Saxon Landtag; 1929 expelled from KPD due to affiliation with Communist party opposition (KPO); 1933 organisational director of illegal KPO Reich leadership; 1935-1938 Luckau Penitentiary; 1938-1945 Buchenwald Concentration Camp, capo of Construction Labour Detachment I; 1945 first vice president of provincial administration, minister of interior in Saxony-Anhalt; 1950 removal from office; 1950-1967 executive employee in construction ministry; died Nov. 2, 1973. (Catalogue 3.59)

Albert Charles Simon (born 1925)

Born June 23, 1925 in La Flèche/Sarthe, France; began training as architect, Catholic; 1943 arrested by Gestapo on account of activities for resistance organisation Forces Françaises Combattantes; 1944/45 Buchenwald Concentration Camp, quarry, Gustloff-Werke II and wood yard detachments; May 1945 returned to France, worked as sales representative. (Catalogue 3.50)

Henryk Sokolak (born 1921)

1940-1945 in Buchenwald Concentration Camp as Polish political inmate; from November 1941 director of school for Poles, later nurse in inmates' infirmary; after 1945 ambassador of People's Republic of Poland. (Catalogue 3.59)

Jura Soyfer (1912-1939)

Born Dec. 8, 1912 in Charkov as son of a Jewish businessman, emigrated with his parents to Vienna, associated with Socialist schoolmates; 1930 studied history and German; early 1930s published poems in Arbeiter-Zeitung, Vienna, Socialist; 1934 novel fragment "So starb eine Partei"; after February Revolt of 1934 author in Viennese cabaret milieu; March 1938 arrested during attempt to cross Swiss border illegally; June 1938 Dachau Concentration Camp, author of "Dachau Song"; September 1938 Buchenwald Concentration Camp, corpse bearer, author of satirical plays performed in camp; Feb. 16, 1939 died of enteric fever in Buchenwald. (Catalogue 3.11)

Dr. Heinrich Steinitz (1879-1942)

Aug. 30, 1879 born in Bielitz; studied law in Vienna, doctorate, worked as judge and lawyer; 1915 active service; 1916-1918 taken prisoner of war by Russians, member of Social Democratic party of Austria; 1933 founding member of "Vereinigung sozialistischer Schriftsteller" (association of Socialist writers), wrote poems, plays and political treatises; after 1934 lawyer in various trials of members of Republican Defence Corps; 1938 arrested, Dachau Concentration Camp, Buchenwald Concentration Camp, joinery, sock-darning and latrine detachments; October 1942 Auschwitz Concentration Camp, killed a few days after arrival. (Catalogue 3.21)

Maurice Suard (1897-1965)

Born Jan. 4, 1897 in Angers, France, pharmacologist and professor in department of medicine in Angers, member of resistance group Notre Dame de Castille; 1943 arrested, taken to Buchenwald via Compiègne, production of vaccine in epidemic typhus experimental station; after war founded Fédération des Pharmaciens de France; 1953 member of Conseil Supérieur de la Santé; died Nov. 13, 1965. (Catalogue 5.12)

Ernst Thälmann (1886-1944)

Born Apr. 16, 1886 in Hamburg; 1900 worked in parents' shipping company; 1902 dockyard and shipping worker in New York among other places; 1903 joined SPD; 1915 conscription to army; 1918 desertion, joined USPD; 1920 changed to KPD; 1922/23 leader of left-wing opposition in KPD; 1924-1933 member of Reichstag; 1925 national chairman of Roter Frontkämpferbund (Communist veterans' association) and chairman of KPD, party turned to Stalinism; 1925 and 1932 KPD Reich-presidential candidate; 1933-1944 confinement in Berlin, Hanover and Bautzen; killed Aug. 18, 1944 in Buchenwald. (Catalogue 4.31)

Ernst Thape (1892-1985)

Born May 29, 1892 in Klein Aga, Thuringia, apprenticeship as locksmith, member of SPD and until 1932 editor of Magdeburger Volksstimme; 1933/34 several arrests; 1939 Buchenwald Concentration Camp; 1944 member of illegal People's Front Committee; 1945 minister of popular education in Saxony-Anhalt, chairman of SPD; 1946 member of provincial commission for realisation of land reform, vice president of province of Saxony; 1948 left Soviet occupied zone; 1949-1957 press and public relations officer of Lower Saxon state chancellery; died July 25, 1985. (Catalogue 5.26)

Fritz Thyssen (1873-1951)
Born Nov. 9, 1873 in Mülheim/Ruhr; 1898 joined father's business; 1923 provided financial support to NSDAP; 1926-1933 chairman of board of directors of Vereinigte Stahlwerke AG, member of "Stahlhelm" and DNVP; 1930 within Reich association of German industry vehement commitment to establishment of "national government" under Adolf Hitler; 1931 member of executive committee of DNVP, joined NSDAP; 1932 decisive participation in establishment of contacts between Germany's heavy industry and Adolf Hitler; 1933 member of Reichstag, councillor of state in Prussia, active in committee for racial hygiene and racial policies; 1938 differences with the NS regime over persecution of Jews; 1939 emigration to Switzerland following German-Soviet nonaggression pact; 1940 detailed interviews in Monte Carlo, arrested in France; 1941 publication of book "I Paid Hitler" on basis of interviews; end of 1944 confinement in isolation barrack in Buchenwald; 1948 classified as less incriminated person by denazification tribunal; died Feb. 8, 1951 in Buenos Aires. (Catalogue 4.33)

Lucien Aphonse Constant Van Beirs (1900-1970)
Born Aug. 25, 1900 in Schaerbeck; studied law, lawyer, royal prosecutor; 1941-1943 repeatedly arrested as hostage; 1943 arrested during attempt to cross Spanish border, deported to Buchenwald via Compiègne, wood-yard and load-bearers' detachments, Ohrdruf Sub-Camp, April 1945 return to Belgium, active in judicial service; from 1965 president of court of appeal; died Aug. 2, 1970. (Catalogue 4.9)

Walter Veigel (1908-1980)
Born Nov. 1, 1908 in Großgartsch, Württemberg as son of a moulder; training as commercial clerk; 1925 occasional labour; 1928 moved to Duisburg, assembly worker; 1931 joined KPD; 1932 ran his own repair shop for radios and bicycles, sentenced to 1 month's confinement for holding unregistered assemblies; 1933 worked for KPD underground, arrested; 1934 commercial representative for bicycle spare parts, renewed arrest, sentenced to 4 years' confinement on charges of high treason; 1938-1945 after serving sentence committed to Buchenwald Concentration Camp, director of inmates' pharmacy; 1943 Duisburg Sub-Camp; 1943-1945 food storehouse detachment; 1945 after liberation marriage in Weimar, senior clerk in chemicals department of state office of economy in Thuringia; 1947 head of wood industry section of ministry of economy in Thuringia; 1949 head

of state contract bureau of Thuringia; 1952 commercial attaché in "Diplomatic Mission of the German Democratic Republic" in Prague; 1953 commercial councillor in GDR embassy in Bucharest; 1955 in charge of commercial policy in foreign trade enterprise DIA Chemie; 1958 department of commercial policy in GDR embassy in Moscow; 1967 commercial attaché in Belgrade; 1970 vice-consul in GDR Consulate General in Zagreb; 1973 retired; Oct. 13, 1986 died in Berlin. (Catalogue 4.13)

Armin Walther (1896-1969)
Born Sept. 27, 1896 in Radebeul; 1911-1914 apprenticeship as electrician; 1911 joined SAJ and labour union; 1916-1918 soldier in WWI; 1920 married, one daughter; 1920 joined SPD; 1920-1929 member of works council in Gröpa; 1925-1932 member of workers' radio association; 1929 full-time cashier for metalworkers' association in Riesa; 1933 preventive custody in Hohnstein Concentration Camp, released; 1936 arrested, Zwickau Penitentiary; 1938-1945 Buchenwald Concentration Camp, electricians' detachment, in charge of construction and repair of broadcasting, transmitter, teletype and signal units, capo of radio shop; 1945-1949 director of Riesa electricity works; 1949-1961 various positions in energy industry; died Oct. 14, 1969. (Catalogue 3.51)

Vincent Weijand (1921-1945)
Born Oct. 31, 1921 in Bergen, Noord-Holland; after completion of secondary school studied classical literature and philosophy, poet; summer of 1944 arrested for refusing to betray friends who had gone underground, deported to Bergen-Belsen and Buchenwald; died Feb. 21, 1945 in Barrack 45 of Buchenwald Concentration Camp. (Catalogue 4.9)

Ernst Wiechert (1887-1950)
May 18, 1887 born near Sensburg, East Prussia as son of a forester; active service in WWI, secondary school teacher; 1933 freelance author; 1938 arrested for openly criticising regime, committed to Buchenwald Concentration Camp; 1939 released, secretly wrote novel "Der Totenwald"; 1948 emigration to Switzerland; died Aug. 24, 1950 in Uerikon. (Catalogue 3.10)

Ernst Wille (1894-1944)
Born Apr. 20, 1894; commercial clerk; 1913 joined SPD, chairman of local branch in Groß-Ottersleben near Magdeburg; 1924 co-founder of republican defence organisation "Reichsbanner Schwarz-Rot-Gold;" 1933 several arrests; September 1939 to April 1943 Buchenwald Concentration Camp, Block 39, barrack room duty; December 1943 to May 1944 Neuengamme Concentration Camp; killed May 27, 1944 in Neuengamme. (Catalogue 3.12)

The biographical sketches of the members of the SS are based on the personnel files in the Bundesarchiv (formerly the BDC) and on the interrogation records of various legal proceedings. As the biographies of Camp Commanders Karl Koch and Hermann Pister were discussed in detail in the main text of this publication, they were not included below.

Otto Barnewald (1896-1973)

Born Jan. 10, 1896 in Leipzig as son of a machinist; 1910-1913 employment with court bailiff and commercial apprenticeship; 1913 joined Imperial army, active service; 1919 discharged from army; 1919-1922 temporary labourer; 1922-1928 commercial clerk; 1928-1933 unemployed; 1929 joined NSDAP and SA; 1931 joined SS and acted as treasurer there; 1933 worked for Nationalzeitung (newspaper) in Essen; 1934-1938 various administrative activities in SS Disposal Troops (e.g. head cashier of SS District West); 1938-1940 officer in charge of administration at Mauthausen Concentration Camp; 1940-1942 same position at Neuengamme Concentration Camp; 1942-1945 same position at Buchenwald Concentration Camp, last rank SS Sturmbannführer; May 1945 arrested by US-military authorities; 1947 sentenced to death at Buchenwald Trial in Dachau; 1948 sentence changed to life imprisonment; 1950 sentence changed to 18 years' imprisonment; 1954 released from imprisonment; died 1973. (Catalogue 4/3)

Erwin Ding, after Sept. 15, 1944 Schuler (1912-1945)

Born Sept. 19, 1912 in Bitterfeld; 1916 became orphan, adopted by businessman's family Ding (Königsberg, later Leipzig); 1932-1937 studied medicine at University of Leipzig; 1932 joined NS students' association (acted as NS university leader), SA and NSDAP; 1934/35 volunteer in Reichswehr for 7 months; 1936 joined SS; from May 1936 active for SD; 1937 special scholarship from University of Leipzig, doctorate in child psychology; September 1937 joined SS-Totenkopf Squadron, SS medical officers' school; 1938/39 camp physician Buchenwald Concentration Camp; 1939/40 adjutant to chief physician of SS "Totenkopf" Division; 1940/41 SS medical academy in Graz; 1941-1945 head of department of epidemic typhus and virus research at Hygiene Institute of Armed SS in Berlin, Buchenwald branch (Blocks 46 and 50), responsible for killing of at least 150 persons, final rank SS Sturmbannführer; Aug. 14, 1945 committed suicide in confinement. (Catalogue 4/36)

Hanns Eisele (1912-1967)

Born Mar. 13, 1912 in Donaueschingen as son of a church painter; 1931-1933 studied medicine in Freiburg; 1933-1935 temporary employment as organist and private tutor; 1935-1938 studied medicine in Freiburg, medical assistant; 1939 assistant physician; 1940 chief physician of Sigmaringen Hospital; 1940 conscription to Armed SS; 1941 troop and camp physician in Buchenwald, experimental operations and murder of inmates by means of injection, camp physician in Natzweiler Concentration Camp; 1942 SS Division "Das Reich"; 1945 camp physician in Dachau Concentration Camp; 1945 arrested by Allies, sentenced to death during Dachau Trial against members of SS active at Dachau Concentration Camp; 1946 sentence changed to life imprisonment; 1947 sentenced to death at Buchenwald Trial held in Dachau; 1948 sentence changed to life imprisonment; 1950 sentence changed to 10 years imprisonment; 1952 released from imprisonment; 1953 doctor in Munich; 1958 preliminary legal proceedings in Munich, escaped to Egypt, opened medical practice in Cairo; died May 3, 1967 in Cairo. (Catalogue 2/45)

Hellmuth Gommlich (1891-1945)

Born July 11, 1891 in Dresden as son of a bank clerk, secondary school until 7th year; 1908-1913 vocational training as helmsman and radio operator; 1913 voluntary enlistment in Navy; 1914-1920 active service, voluntary mine-locating service, dismissed due to personnel reduction (first lieutenant); 1920-1924 trained as police superintendent in Bremen, police service; 1924-1926 head of security department of North German Lloyd Bremerhaven; 1926-1930 detective inspector at state criminal inspection department in Weimar; 1931 clandestine membership in NSDAP; 1930-1934 police councillor in Zella-Mehlis, member of SS and SD; 1934-1935 chief investigator of proceedings in preparation for expropriation of Jewish arms company Simson (Suhl), deputy head of police department at Thuringian ministry of interior; 1935 special promotion to senior executive officer as reward for assiduity in Simson Co. expropriation case, chief of police department; 1936 representative of Thuringian ministry of interior as well as special commissioner to Himmler regarding establishment of Concentration Camp in Thuringia, chose Ettersberg as location, took charge of all formalities for 3 years, promoted to SS Obersturmführer in SD, resided in Weimar; 1938-1939 deputy district administrator in Meiningen; 1939-1945 district administrator in Meiningen, SS Sturmbannführer, from 1940 also spa director of Thuringian State Spa; Apr. 3, 1945 committed suicide. (Catalogue 2/1)

Philipp Grimm (born 1909)

Born Apr. 1, 1909 in Zwiesel, Bavaria as Philipp Billenstein; 1910 death of mother; 1920 adopted by uncle Philipp Grimm; 1923 and 1924 joined the two right-wing radical youth organisations Völkischer Jungsturm (Wunsiedel branch) and Nationaler Verband Jung-Bayern (Bayreuth branch) resp.; 1927 apprentice's final examination as baker and confectioner; 1928 practical trainee in paper factory in Nuremberg; 1930 joined NSDAP; 1931 completed commercial apprenticeship, automobile salesman; 1932 took over parents' "Weinstube Grimm" in Bayreuth; 1933 joined SS, married; 1936 full-time employment in SS administration; 1939 vocational training at SS school of administration in Berlin; 1940 treasurer and deputy chief of administration of SS Totenkopf Regiment, inmate allocation officer Buchenwald Concentration Camp; from 1941 officer in charge of labour allocation; 1942 officer in charge of labour allocation at Sachsenhausen Concentration Camp; 1943 Office D II of WVHA, member of command staff at Plaszow Concentration Camp, Kraków; 1944 labour allocation officer at Neuengamme Concentration Camp, took in foster child; 1945 arrested by Allies; 1947 sentenced to death at Buchenwald Trial in Dachau; 1948 sentence changed to life imprisonment; 1950 sentence changed to 15 years' imprisonment; early 1950s released from imprisonment. (Catalogue 2/36)

Hermann Hackmann (born 1913)

Born Nov. 11, 1913 in Osnabrück as son of a construction foreman; 1930 left school with intermediate level certificate; 1933 apprentice's examination as mason, joined SS; 1934 joined guard unit of Esterwegen Concentration Camp; 1937 report officer at Buchenwald Concentration Camp; 1939 adjutant to Camp Commander Karl Koch in Buchenwald Concentration Camp, involved in embezzlement of funds and killing of inmates; 1941 member of concentration camp inspection staff (Oranienburg), officer in charge of preventive custody camp at Lublin Concentration Camp (Majdanek); 1942 transferred to SS Division " Prinz Eugen"; 1943 married, arrested and confined in SS detention cell building in Buchenwald; 1944 brought before SS special court with Karl Koch for "continued theft" of Reich property, double death sentence and committal to SS / police detention camp in Dachau; 1945 arrested by Allies; 1947 sentenced to death in Buchenwald Trial in Dachau; 1948 sentence changed to life imprisonment; 1950 sentence changed to 25 years' imprisonment; 1955 released from imprisonment, representative of furniture company in Uslar (Lower Saxony); 1975 brought before court in Majdanek Trial in Düsseldorf; 1981 sentenced to 10 years' imprisonment. (Catalogue 2/29)

Waldemar Hoven (1903-1948)

Born Feb. 10, 1903 in Freiburg/Br., attended secondary school; 1919/20 agricultural work in Sweden; 1921-1925 in USA, worked temporarily as extra in Hollywood; 1925-1930 worked at parents' estate and sanatorium; 1929 married, 4 children (1 illegitimate); 1930-1933 casual labourer in Paris; November 1933 joined SS; 1934/35 secondary school-leaving certificate; 1935 began study of medicine at University of Freiburg in order to work in parents' sanatorium; October 1939 provisional medical examination before conscription; Oct. 1939 – Sept. 1943 camp and troop physician in Buchenwald, involved in medical experiments, killing of sick persons, selection for extermination; July 1943 doctorate in medicine with dissertation written to a large extent by inmates; autumn 1943 arrested by SS within framework of proceedings against former Camp Commander Koch on charges of corruption; March 1945 SS proceedings suspended, released, renewed employment in Buchenwald; 1947 sentenced to death by US Military Tribunal I in Nuremberg; June 2, 1948 executed in Landsberg/Lech. (Catalogue 3/42)

Hans Hüttig (born 1894)

Born Apr. 5, 1894 in Dresden; 1900-1908 attended elementary school; 1911 rejected by Imperial army; 1913 broke off apprenticeship as pharmacist, salesman in parents' photo shop; 1914 commercial representative in German East-African colonies, vice-sergeant in German East Africa Corps; 1920 released from British POW camp, casual labour; 1924 joined "Stahlhelm"; 1926 opened photo shop; 1930 bankruptcy; 1931 manager of aerial photography service in Meissen; 1932 joined SS and NSDAP; 1933 member of SS guard troop of Sachsenburg Concentration Camp; 1937 leader of guard troop of Lichtenburg Concentration Camp; 1938 adjutant at Buchenwald Concentration Camp; 1939 second officer in charge of Buchenwald preventive custody camp; 1939 command staff of Flossenbürg Concentration Camp (Oberpfalz); 1940 commander in chief of Sachsenhausen Concentration Camp (Oranienburg); 1941 commander of guards battalion of concentration and labour camps in Norway; 1942 commander of Natzweiler Concentration Camp (Alsace); 1944 commander of 's Hertogenbosch Concentration Camp (Netherlands); after the war sentenced to death by French court, released after 11 years' imprisonment; pensioner in Wachenheim/Weinstrasse. (Catalogue 2/37)

Josef Kestel (1904-1948)

Born Oct. 29, 1904 in Kronach, Upper Franconia, attended elementary and vocational school, casual labour; 1919-1928 labourer in shoe factory; 1928-1933 construction worker; 1933 joined NSDAP and SS, joined guard troop of Dachau Concentration Camp; 1937 block officer in

Dachau Concentration Camp, married, 3 children; 1940-1945 block and labour detachment officer in Buchenwald Concentration Camp; 1945 arrested by Allies; 1947 sentenced to death in Buchenwald Trial in Dachau; Nov. 19, 1948 execution. (Catalogue 2/40)

Wolfgang Plaul (born 1909)

Born Apr. 5, 1909 in Freiburg; 1931 joined NSDAP and SS; 1933-1936 SS Unterführer at Sachsenburg and Sachsenhausen Concentration Camps; 1939 labour detachment officer and preventive custody camp commander in Wewelsburg, second officer in charge of Buchenwald preventive custody camp; from end of 1944 camp commander of Hasag-Leipzig Women's Sub-Camp. (Catalogue 4/29)

Dr. Gerhard Schiedlausky (1906-1947)

Born Jan. 14, 1906 in Berlin; 1939 conscription to Armed SS; until 1943 worked as SS doctor in Mauthausen, Flossenbürg, Ravensbrück and Natzweiler Concentration Camps; 1943-1945 chief camp physician and garrison physician of Armed SS of Weimar-Buchenwald; April 1945 escaped with command staff; May 1945 arrested by US military authorities; 1945-1946 imprisonment in Ludwigsburg, Augsburg and Dachau, turned over to British military jurisdiction, defendant at Ravensbrück Trial in Hamburg; 1947 sentenced to death; May 3, 1947 executed in Hameln. (Catalogue 4/3)

Hans Schmidt (1899-1951)

Born Dec. 25, 1899 in Höxter/Weser; 1917-1918 active service in WWI; 1919 volunteer corps; 1919-1920 Reichswehr, commercial apprenticeship, worked as commercial clerk in Belgium, Holland and elsewhere; 1932 member of NSDAP and General SS; 1940 changed to Armed SS; 1940-1941 SS Special Camp Hinzert; 1941-1945 Buchenwald Concentration Camp; from 1942 adjutant to camp commander and court officer; April 1945 escape; May 1945 arrested by US military authorities; 1947 sentenced to death at Buchenwald Trial in Dachau; 1951 executed. (Catalogue 4/3)

Max Schobert (1904-1948)

Born Dec. 25, 1904 in Würzburg as son of an office porter; 1919 metalworker in engine works; 1925-1927 mechanical engineering school in Würzburg; 1927-1934 alternately unemployed, employed as machinist; 1932 member of NSDAP and General SS; 1934 changed to SS Totenkopf Squadrons; 1934-1938 Dachau Concentration Camp (block officer, depot detachment officer); 1938-1940 Flossenbürg Concentration Camp (barrack construction detachment officer); 1940-1945 Buchenwald Concentration Camp, initially second officer in charge of preventive custody camp; 1942 appointed first officer in charge of preventive custody camp; April 1945 escape to Austria; May 1945 arrested by US military au-

thorities; 1947 sentenced to death by American military tribunal in Buchenwald Trial in Dachau; 1948 executed. (Catalogue 4/3)

Albert Schwartz (born 1905)

Born Apr. 11, 1905 in Schwarzenau, West Prussia as son of an estate owner, attended trade school in Danzig, member of right-wing radical youth organisation Großdeutscher Jugendbund; 1925 employment with municipal savings bank, Danzig, attended university-level trade school in Danzig and specialised savings bank school in Hanover; 1930 member of NSDAP and SA; 1931 joined General SS, treasurer of SS regiment; 1938 completion of vocational training as savings bank inspector; 1939 conscription to police reserve of Danzig; 1939-1942 in charge of administration of prison camps under chief police commissioner of Danzig; November 1941 admitted to Armed SS; 1942 adjutant to commander of Stutthof Concentration Camp; 1942-1945 labour allocation officer at Buchenwald Concentration Camp; May 1945 taken prisoner by US military authorities in Austria; 1947 sentenced to death at Buchenwald Trial in Dachau; 1948 sentence changed to life imprisonment; 1950 sentence changed to 10 years' imprisonment; early 1950s released from imprisonment, subsequently worked in industry. (Catalogue 4/3)

Martin Sommer (1915-1988)

Feb. 8, 1915 born in Schkölen, Weißenfels District as son of a farmer; elementary school, assisted at parents' inn; 1931 joined NSDAP and SA; 1933 member of SS; 1934 joined Totenkopf Squadrons, SS "Sonderkommando Sachsen", where his battalion commander was the later Camp Commander Karl Koch; 1935 Sachsenburg Concentration Camp; 1937 Buchenwald; 1938-1943 detention cell building warder, notorious torturer and murderer, known for cruel physical abuse; 1943 front service with Armed SS, arrested in connection with proceedings against Karl Koch for corruption but not sentenced; March 1945 SS delinquent unit ("front probation"), injured, stay in military hospital; 1945-1947 in American internment; 1950 arrested; 1958 sentenced at Bayreuth to 25 times life imprisonment; 1971 exempted from imprisonment until death; 1988 stay in Rummelsburger Anstalten nursing home. (Catalogue 3/26)

Erich Wagner (1912-1959)

Born Sept. 15, 1912 in Komotau; studied medicine; 1939 camp physician at Buchenwald Concentration Camp; 1940 doctorate with help of inmates ("On the Issue of Tattooing"); 1941 transferred, final rank SS Sturmbannführer; 1945 taken prisoner by Americans; 1948 escaped, lived under false name in Bavaria for 6 years; 1957 worked in wife's medical practice in Lahr, Black Forest; 1958 arrested, Mar. 22, 1959 committed suicide during detention pending trial. (Catalogue 3/17)

German-English / English-German glossary of terms and abbreviation

Aktion: (mass arrest) operation

Armed SS: *Waffen-SS*, SS formation established after the outbreak of war as part of the Wehrmacht (see below). In the second half of the war, the concentration camp guard units were part of the Armed SS.

BA: *Bundesarchiv*, (see below)

BDC: Berlin Document Centre

Bl.: *Blatt*; sheet

Brigadeführer (SS): SS rank corresponding to brigadier general

Bundesarchiv: Federal (German) Archives

Bundestag: Federal German Parliament since 1949

BwA: *Buchenwald Archiv*, Buchenwald Archives, Weimar

camp senior: highest inmate function within the camp

CDU: *Christlich-Demokratische Union*; Christian Democratic Union (political party)

CSU: *Christlich-Soziale Union*; Christian Social Union (political party in Bavaria)

DAW: *Deutsche Ausrüstungswerke*; German Armament Works, an arms factory with a branch in Buchenwald

DB: *Deutsche Bücherei*; German National Library

Department of Economic Administration (SS): *Wirtschaftsverwaltungshauptamt* (SS), the department of the SS administration concerned with the economic activities of the organisation in general as well as the concentration camps in particular

Department of Economic Management / Construction (SS): *Hauptamt Haushalt/Bauten* (SS), the predecessor of the Dept. of Economic Administration (see above), which did not, however, include Concentration Camp Inspection. The latter was an independent authority until the creation of the Dept. of Econ. Adm.

depot: *Effektenkammer*; storage building for inmates' personal belongings

DESt: *Deutsche Erd- und Steinwerke GmbH*

DIN A 4, 5, 6, 7, etc.: German industrial norms for paper sizes: DIN A 4 – 30 × 21 cm; A 5 – 21 × 15 cm; A 6 – 15 × 10.5 cm; A 7 – 10.5 × 7.5 cm

DNVP: *Deutschnationale Volkspartei*; German National People's Party

DÖW: *Dokumentationsarchiv des Österreichischen Widerstandes*; Documentation Archives of the Austrian Resistance, Vienna

DVP: *Deutsche Volkspartei*; German / Democratic People's Party

F.N.D.I.R.P.: *Fédération Nationale des Déportés et Internés Résistants et Patriotes*, (French national association of deportees, internees, members of the Resistance and patriots), Paris

Führer: leader, refers here to Hitler

Gauleiter: regional Nazi party leader

Gautag: regional Nazi party convention

GDR: German Democratic Republic

GmbH: *Gesellschaft mit beschränkter Haftung*; limited liability company

Gruppenführer (SS): SS rank corresponding to major general

Gustloff-Werk II: arms factory located on the grounds of Buchenwald Concentration Camp

Hauptscharführer (SS): SS rank corresponding to sergeant major

Hauptsturmführer (SS): SS rank corresponding to captain

HKW: German abbr. for *Archivum Glownej Komisji Badania Zbrodni przeciwko Narodowi Polskiemu*; Main Commission for Investigation of Crimes Against the Polish People

Hollerith: machine for data administration by means of card-punching

HStA: *Hauptstaatsarchiv*; Main State Archives

International Camp Committee: *Internationales Lagerkomitee*; international committee of Communists within the camp

ISK: *Internationaler Sozialistischer Kampfbund*; International Socialist Combat Alliance

KJVD: *Kommunistischer Jugendverband Deutschland*; German Communist Youth Association

K.L. or KL: *Konzentrationslager*; concentration camp

K. Z. or KZ: *Konzentrationslager*; concentration camp

K.L. Bu: *Konzentrationslager Buchenwald*; Buchenwald Concentration Camp

KGL: *Kriegsgefangenenlager*; prisoner-of-war camp

KPD: *Kommunistische Partei Deutschlands*; German Communist Party

KPD (*Opposition*): splinter group of the KPD (see above)

KPdSU: German abbr. for Communist Party of the Soviet Union

labour discipline inmate: *Arbeitserziehungshäftling*; committed to concentration camp temporarily for repeated violations of rules at workplace

Land: state; one of the territorial and political units forming the country of Germany

Landtag: German Land (state-level) parliament

Little Camp: *Kleines Lager*; special zone of Buchenwald inmates' camp originally set up in 1943 as quarantine and labour allocation camp, characterised by rampant overcrowding, disease and death

main camp: *Hauptlager*; main zone of Buchenwald inmates' camp, as opposed to the Little Camp (see above)

MdI: *Ministerium des Innern*; Ministry of the Interior

M.d.R.: *Mitglied des Deutschen Reichstags*; member of the German Reichstag (see below)

Mittelschule: school leading to General Certificate of Education Ordinary Level

NARA: National Archives and Record Administration, Washington

NS: *nationalsozialistisch*; National Socialist, Nazi

NSDAP: *Nationalsozialistische Deutsche Arbeiterpartei*; National Socialist (Nazi) German Workers' Party

o. S.: *ohne Signatur*; no classification number

Oberführer (SS): SS rank, no direct correspondence to an army rank: between brigadier and colonel

Obergruppenführer (SS): SS rank corresponding to lieutenant general

Oberscharführer (SS): SS rank corresponding to Amer. sergeant 1st class

Obersturmbannführer (SS): SS rank corresponding to lieutenant colonel

Obersturmführer (SS): SS rank corresponding to first lieutenant

Oflag: *Offizierslager*; POW camp for officers

parent camp: *Stammlager*; Buchenwald Concentration Camp as the centre of a complex comprising sub-camps and external labour detachments

Reich: The official designation of the (all-)German state until 1945. The NS state conceived of itself as the "*Third Reich*" (following the Holy Roman Empire of the German Nation and the German Empire of 1870/71-1918). After the annexation of Austria and other "German" territories, the designation *Großdeutsches* (Pan-Germanic) *Reich* was used increasingly.

Reich Department of Security: *Reichssicherheitshauptamt*; Reich authority formed in 1939 and comprising the Secret State Police, the Detective Police and the Security Police

Reich Leader, Reich Leader of the SS: supreme commander of the SS

Reichsstatthalter: leading Reich government official on state level

Reichstag: parliament of the Reich (see above)

Reichswehr: German army until 1936

RGBl.: *Reichsgesetzblatt*; Reich statute roll

RIOD: *Rijksinstituut voor Oorlogsdocumentatie,*; National Institute of War Documentation, Amsterdam

RSHA: *Reichssicherheitshauptamt*; Reich Department of Security (see above)

RuSHA: *Rasse und Siedlungshauptamt* (SS); SS Department of Race and Settlement

SA: *Sturmabteilungen*; Storm Troops, paramilitary organisation of the NSDAP

Sanitätsdienstgrad (SS): SS rank of medical orderly officer

SAJ: *Sozialistische Arbeiterjugend*; Socialist Labour Youth

SAPMO: *Stiftung Archiv der Parteien und Massenorganisationen der DDR im Bundesarchiv*; Foundation Archives of the Parties and Mass Organisations of the German Democratic Republic in the Federal German Archives, Berlin

Scharführer (SS): sergeant

SD: *Sicherheitsdienst*; Security Service, the secret service of the SS

security detention inmate: *Sicherungsverwahrter*; inmate kept in custody for security reasons following completion of prison sentence

SED: *Sozialistische Einheitspartei Deutschlands*; Socialist Unity Party of Germany (German Democratic Republic)

SGB: *Sammlung Gedenkstätte Buchenwald*; Buchenwald Memorial Collection

SPD: *Sozialdemokratische Partei Deutschlands*; Social Democratic Party of Germany

SS: *Schutzstaffel*; a paramilitary unit of the NSDAP (see above) which originally emerged from Hitler's body guard

Stalag: *Stammlager*; parent camp (see above)

"*Stahlhelm*": politically powerful veterans' association

Standartenführer (SS): SS rank corresponding to colonel

Sturmbannführer (SS): SS rank corresponding to major

SV: *Sicherungsverwahrter*; security detention inmate (see above)

ThHStA: *Thüringisches Hauptstaatsarchiv Weimar* (see above)

Thüringisches Hauptstaatsarchiv Weimar: Thuringian Main State Archives, Weimar

Trutzgau: military defence district

UfA: *Universum-Film AG*; German film company

Unterführer (SS): SS rank corresponding to sergeant

Unterscharführer (SS): SS rank corresponding to corporal

USHMM: United States Holocaust Memorial Museum, Washington

USPD: *Unabhängige Sozialdemokratische Partei Deutschlands*; Independent Social-Democratic Party of Germany

Volksschule: German school comprising lower and upper divisions of elementary school

VVN: *Vereinigung der Verfolgten des Naziregimes*; association of victims of Nazi persecution

Wehrmacht: the German armed forces during the Nazi period

WVHA: *Wirtschaftsverwaltungshauptamt* (SS); Department of Economic Administration (SS) (see above)

YVA: Yad Vashem. Martyrs' and Heroes' Remembrance Authority, Archives, Jerusalem

Index of names

Index of Places

Index of Subjects

Acknowledgements of Support for the Exhibition

On behalf of all the many persons who supported the preparations and installation of the exhibition, let us begin by expressing our gratitude to Dr. Werner Brans, Staatssekretär a.D. With prudence and objectiveness, while at the same time deeply moved by the history of Buchenwald, he returned from his retirement to serve as acting director of the memorial in the spring of 1994. In an atmosphere characterised to a considerable extent by political hysteria, he created the conditions for the productive development of the memorial. Without the support of the director of the Thüringisches Hauptstaatsarchiv, Dr. Wahl, and the responsible department head, Dr. Post, both of whom treated the exhibition as their own and provided unbureaucratic assistance in the best sense of the word, the exhibition could not have been realised in this form. The director of the Museum für Ur- und Frühgeschichte, Dr. habil. Sigrid Dušzek, placed craftsmen from her institution at our disposal for the exhibition installation, allowing its punctual completion. This gesture stands for the fact that the history of Buchenwald Concentration Camp can become a person's concern even if the topic has no evident connection to that person; what is more, it helped us through a period charged with political irrationalities. Of very great significance were the contributions made from the heart by many former inmates, who saw this extension of the remembrance of Buchenwald as an acknowledgement of their fates, something they hardly expected at this late date. Let Robert Büchler, Dr. Danuta Brzosko-Medryk, Rolf Kralovitz and Józef Szajna be mentioned here on behalf of all of them. We are obliged to Dr. Pierre Durand, the chairman of the International Committee of Buchenwald, Dora and Sub-Camps as well as the chairman of the concentration camp inmates' advisory board, Floréal Barrier, for their constructive collaboration – and for turning scepticism into confidence. With the support of the federal government, the Free State of Thuringia spent more on the preparations for and installation of this exhibition, as well as the entire new conception of the Buchenwald Memorial, than any German state in the past, thus creating the fundamental prerequisites for careful and professional work. We are deeply indebted to the Thuringian Ministry of Science, Research and Culture for having appointed a historians' commission – in other words, not a political one – in 1991 in order to draw up the guidelines for the new conception. Under the chairmanship of Prof. Dr. Jäckel, a board of trustees emerged from this commission – a group of persons without whose strong and active commitment the scientific standard of the exhibition and the work of the memorial in general would be inconceivable. Equally worthy of mention is the fact that the craftsmen, technicians, designers and architects involved in the construction and installation of the exhibition turned night into day, and did so with conviction. Nobody was counting the hours anymore, and despite the pressure, the working atmosphere remained calm and concentrated, always borne by the knowledge of who the customer was. On behalf of all these persons, let us mention by name Uwe Kleineberg, Stefan Lewinson, Axel Pohl, Ohannes Tapyuli and Peter Wentzler.

American Jewish Joint Distribution Committee, New York
Hans Andersen, Oster Ulslev
Georges Angéli, Vouneuil a Vienne
Archiv der Akademie der Künste, Berlin
Archiv der Fédération Nationale des Déportés et Internés Résistants et Patriotes, Paris
Archiv der Gedenkstätte Auschwitz, Oświęcim
Archiv des Collège de France, Paris
Archiv des United States Holocaust Memorial Museum, Washington
Archiv für Kunst und Geschichte, Berlin
Archives Nationales, Paris
Archivum Głownej Komisji Badania Zbrodni przeciwko Narodowi Polskiemu, Warschau
Association Française Buchenwald-Dora et Commandos, Paris
Edgar Bamberger, Heidelberg
Floréal Barrier, Saint-Cyr sur Loire
Alberto Berti, S. Donato Milanese

Bibliothèque de l'Université de Caen, Caen
Bibliothèque Municipale, Bayonne
Bibliothèque Municipale, La Ferté-Sous-Jouarre
Georges de Bleser, Brussels
Dr. Heinz Boberach, Koblenz
Evelin Bock, Weimar
Stanley Booker, Bracknell
Dr. Werner Brans, Wetzlar
Dominique Brau, Seignosse
Charles Brusselaire, Merksem
Dr. Danuta Brzosko-Medryk, Warsaw
Robert J. Büchler, Givat Haviva
Bundesarchiv, Berlin-Lichterfelde
Bundesarchiv, Koblenz
Buchenwald-Archiv, Brussels
Emil Carlebach, Frankfurt am Main
Claude Carlier, Perrin
Lucien Chapelain, Bondy
Lothar Czoßek, Rehmsdorf
Jean Daladier, Paris

319

Deutsche Bücherei, Leipzig
Deutsches Historisches Museum, Berlin
Dokumentationsarchiv des Österreichischen
   Widerstandes, Vienna
Dr. Klaus Drobisch, Berlin
Dr. Pierre Durand, Paris
Prof. Dr. Rainer Eisfeld, Osnabrück
Maurice Eyben, Liège
Karola Fings, Cologne
Willy Fogel, Paris
Michelle Lemaire-Fonteyne, Hantes-Wiheries
Gedenkstätte Langenstein-Zwieberge
Familie Henri Glineur, Roux
Familie von Jacques Grippa, Brussels
Franka Günther, Weimar
Gitta Günther, Weimar
Dr. Karl-Heinz Hänel, Erfurt
James D. Hastin, Anacortes
Max Heilbronn, Paris
Hentrich-Verlag, Berlin
Prof. Dr. Ulrich Herbert, Freiburg
Marcelle Heurtaux, Chantilly
Y. Hewitt-Berthin, Garches
Historisches Archiv der Stadt Köln
Prof. Dr. Eberhard Jäckel, Stuttgart
Karin Johannes, Weimar
Michael Kloft, Hamburg
Dr. Cornelia Klose, Nordhausen
Prof. Dr. Eberhard Kolb, Cologne
Rolf Kralovitz, Cologne
Henri Krasucki, Paris
Kreisheimatmuseum Dermbach
Norbert Krüger, Essen
Gabriele Krynitzki, Weimar
Kultur- und Dokumentationszentrum Deutscher
   Sinti und Roma, Heidelberg
KZ Gedenkstätte Dora-Mittelbau, Nordhausen
Landeshauptarchiv, Magdeburg
Rolf Lange, Gaberndorf
Lee Miller Archive, Chiddingly, East Sussex,
   England
Leo Baeck Institut, New York
Dr. Rolf Lettmann, Erfurt
Yaacov Lozowick, Jerusalem
Luftbilddatenbank Ingenieurbüro H. G. Carls,
   Würzburg
Mairie de Riom, Riom Cedex
Iraida Efimovna Makeeva, Grodno
Claude Mandel, Paris
Mel Mermelstein, Huntington Beach
Prof. Dr. Manfred Messerschmidt, Freiburg
Pierre-André Meyer, Paris
Militärhistorisches Museum der Bundeswehr,
   Dresden

Ministère des anciens combattants et victimes
   de guerre, Bureau des Archives, Caen
Moreshet Archives, Givat Haviva
Dr. Renate Müller-Krumbach, Weimar
Musée de la Résistance et de la Déportation,
   Besançon
National Archives, Washington
Dr. Walter Naasner, Koblenz
Prof. Dr. Lutz Niethammer, Jena
Nordrhein-Westfälisches Hauptstaatsarchiv,
   Düsseldorf
Krystyna Oleksy, Oświęcim
Suzanne Orts, Perpignan
Österreichische Nationalbibliothek, Vienna
Památnik Terezin, Terezin
Gaston Papeloux, Paris
Marie-Sabine Perry, Blois
Dr. Bernhard Post, Weimar
Jacques Rancy, Paris
Frank Reuter, Heidelberg
Prof. Gabriel Richet, Paris
Olivier Richet, Neuilly sur Seine
Rijksinstituut voor Oorlogsdocumentatie,
   Amsterdam
Herman Rols, Laroque d'Olmes
Lucia Rombaut, Antwerpen
Carmen Rosenkranz, Weimar
Dr. Wilhelm Rösing, Frankfurt am Main
Ottomar Rothmann, Weimar
Miriam Rouveyre, Paris
Naomi Tereza Salmon, Jerusalem, Weimar
Willi Schmidt, Frankfurt am Main
Albert Simon, Montpellier
Tochter von Eugène Soudan, Brussels
Stadtarchiv, Frankfurt am Main
Stadtarchiv, Nuremberg
Stadtachiv, Weimar
Stadtmuseum, Weimar
Jacques Suard, Nantes
Józef Szajna, Warsaw
Ohannes Tapyuli, Braunschweig
Boris Taslitzky, Paris
Thüringisches Hauptstaatsarchiv, Weimar
Thüringisches Staatsarchiv, Meiningen
Topographie des Terrors, Berlin
Marc van Beirs, Girez-Doiceau
Verlag Walter de Gruyter GmbH & Co., Berlin
Dr. Volker Wahl, Weimar
Prof. Dr. Wolfgang Wippermann, Berlin
Yad Vashem, Martyrs' and Heros' Remem-
   brance Authority, Jerusalem
Bengt von zur Mühlen, Chronos-Film GmbH,
   Kleinmachnow
Dr. Michael Zimmermann, Essen